THE JUSTICE OF CONSTANTINE

LAW AND SOCIETY IN THE ANCIENT WORLD

The study of law in ancient societies has a distinguished tradition in both Anglo-American and continental scholarship. Many of our fundamental ideas about ancient society were built on research into legal sources. These traditions continue to provide a foundation for newer approaches to law and society. More recent scholarship draws on a range of methodologies to analyze legal practices, including critical legal studies, sociology of law, economics, and literary criticism.

This series, distinguished by its emphasis on interdisciplinary approaches to law and society, seeks out innovative approaches to ancient legal studies that bring new perspectives to legal topics as well as to broader questions concerning the impact of law on commercial, political, and cultural practices in the ancient world.

The Justice of Constantine

Law, Communication, and Control

John Noël Dillon

THE UNIVERSITY OF MICHIGAN PRESS
ANN ARBOR

Published in the United States of America by
The University of Michigan Press
Manufactured in the United States of America
♾ Printed on acid-free paper

2015 2014 2013 2012 4 3 2 1

A CIP catalog record for this book is available from the British Library.

Library of Congress Cataloging-in-Publication Data

Dillon, John Noel.
The justice of Constantine : law, communication, and control / John Noel Dillon.
p. cm. — (Law and society in the ancient world)
Includes bibliographical references and index.
ISBN 978-0-472-11829-8 (cloth : alk. paper) — ISBN 978-0-472-02838-2 (e-book)
1. Roman law—Sources. 2. Roman law—History. 3. Roman law—History—Sources. 4. Constantine I, Emperor of Rome, d. 337. 5. Rome—History—Constantine I, the Great, 306–337. 6. Rome—History—Constantine I, the Great, 306–337—Sources. 7. Justice, Administration of (Roman law)—History. I. Title.
KJA395.D 2012
340.5'4—dc23 2012005025

I DEDICATE THIS BOOK TO MY GRANDPARENTS:

JOHN AND MARGARET DILLON

AND

ROBERT AND MARGUERITE CARTIER

Preface

The present book is the revision, largely accomplished in Heidelberg, Germany, of my doctoral dissertation, "The Legislation of Constantine the Great: Justice, Administration, and Reform," which I submitted at Yale University in October 2008. I was blessed to call the Yale Department of Classics my academic home, and I am profoundly grateful to Yale University for supporting my graduate education. I owe special thanks to John Matthews, my dissertation advisor, who brought me to the world of Late Antiquity. The choice of the subject of this book resulted from the coincidence of my interest in Roman law and government, his expertise in the vibrant field of Late Antiquity, and the irresistible draw of Constantine himself. I realized only later, when well into the project, that the 1,700-year jubilee of Constantine's elevation to emperor was imminent.

I am grateful to all my friends at Yale, Heidelberg, and beyond, who have helped me reach this point. It is my honor to thank the Fulbright Program of the United States Department of State for sponsoring my first year of research, at Ludwig-Maximilians-Universität Munich, from 2005 to 2006. I am indebted to Jens Uwe-Krause at the Historisches Seminar, who supported my Fulbright application, encouraged my work, and acted as my *Ersatzdoktorvater* during my stay; and to Alfons Bürge and his colleagues at the Leopold-Wenger-Institut für Rechtsgeschichte, who took me in as one of their own. Munich still holds a special place in my heart. I am moreover grateful to the Mrs. Gales Whiting Foundation for the generous funding I received while finishing my dissertation, 2007–2008.

It is humbling to think of all those who have helped me complete this book. First of all, I thank the readers of my dissertation: Bill Metcalf, Michael Peachin, and Anders Winroth. I owe a special debt to Claudia Kreuzsaler. I further thank fellow Yale students Felix Racine and Tristan

Taylor, whose advice and insights, and even patience, bore me up as I struggled to write a μέγα βιβλίον that was not a μέγα κακόν.

Heidelberg was an ideal place for revising the work and preparing it for publication. I am grateful to the Heidelberger Akademie der Wissenschaften, which sponsored my current research project on the Roman Republic in the WIN-Kolleg "Raumordnung, Norm und Recht in historischen Kulturen Europas und Asiens" and enabled me to live and work in Heidelberg. I moreover wish to express my gratitude to Kai Trampedach and Christian Witschel, under whose auspices I worked as a postdoc in the outstanding Seminar für Alte Geschichte und Epigraphik in Heidelberg. I am happy to acknowledge the debt of gratitude I owe Ted Lendon, whose comments and criticism of my work we often discussed at the Heidelberg Mensa. Johannes Wienand, Harold Drake, and Noel Lenski each read the manuscript; their comments and criticism have been very valuable. I am particularly grateful to Alexandra Eppinger, who generously helped check and chase stray references in Heidelberg. Ellen Baurlee and Mary Hashman at the University of Michigan Press have been wonderful guides through the publication of my first book. Yii-Jan Lin has done more than her fair share of reading, discussing, and commenting both on the dissertation and on its revision; I owe it to her if I have become a smarter reader and a better scholar. Finally, and above all, I thank my friend and colleague, Sebastian Schmidt-Hofner, who patiently read and commented on the entire text and gladly discussed with me the most diverse historical questions. His thoughts and advice have been invaluable.

To my parents, John and Mary Ellen Dillon, I owe everything.

Contents

Abbreviations

AARC	*Atti dell'Accademia Romanistica Costantiniana.* Perugia.
AE	*L'Année Épigraphique*
ANRW	*Aufstieg und Niedergang der römischen Welt*
Barnes, *CE*	Barnes, T. D. *Constantine and Eusebius.* Cambridge, MA, 1981.
Barnes, *NE*	Barnes, T. D. *The New Empire of Diocletian and Constantine.* Cambridge, MA, 1982.
Berger	Berger, A. *Encyclopedic Dictionary of Roman Law.* Philadelphia, 1953.
Bruns, *Fontes*^{7}	Bruns, C. G. *Fontes Iuris Romani Antiqui.* 7th ed. Edited by O. Gradenwitz. Tübingen, 1909.
CAH XII^{2}	Bowman, A. K., P. Garnsey, and Av. Cameron, eds. *The Cambridge Ancient History, Vol. XII: The Crisis of Empire, A.D. 193–337.* 2nd ed. Cambridge, 2005.
CAH XIII	Cameron, Av., and P. Garnsey, eds. *The Cambridge Ancient History, Vol. XIII: The Late Empire, A.D. 337–425.* Cambridge, 1998.
CIL	Corpus Inscriptionum Latinarum
CJ	Codex Justinianus: Krüger, P., ed. *Corpus Iuris Civilis,* Vol. 2: *Codex Iustinianus.* 11th ed. Berlin, 1954.
Coll.	Mosaicarum et Romanarum Legum Collatio
Cons.	Consultatio Veteris Cuiusdam Iurisconsulti
Corcoran, *ET*^{2}	Corcoran, S. *The Empire of the Tetrarchs: Imperial Pronouncements and Government, AD 284–324.* Revised paperback ed. Oxford, 2000.

CTh.	Codex Theodosianus: Mommsen, T., and P. Meyer, eds. *Theodosiani libri XVI cum constitutionibus sirmondianis et leges novellae ad Theodosianum pertinentes.* Berlin, 1905.
De Marini Avonzo, "Giustizia I"	De Marini Avonzo, F. "La giustizia nelle province agli inizi del Basso Impero." In *Synteleia Arangio Ruiz,* vol. 2 (Naples, 1964), 1037–62. [= "La giustizia nelle province agli inizi del Basso Impero. I. Principi generali del processo in un editto di Costantino," *Studi Urbinati* 31 (1962–63), 291–328]
De Marini Avonzo, "Giustizia II"	De Marini Avonzo, F. "La giustizia nelle province agli inizi del Basso Impero. II. L'organizzazione giudiziaria di Costantino," *Studi Urbinati* 34 (1965–66), 171–229.
Dig.	Digest: Mommsen, T. and P. Krüger, eds. *Corpus Iuris Civilis, Vol. I: Institutiones, Digesta.* 16th ed. Berlin, 1954.
FIRA^2	Riccobono, S., J. Baviera, C. Ferrini, J. Furlani, and V. Arangio-Riuz, eds. *Fontes iuris Romani anteiustiniani.* 2nd ed. Florence, 1968–69.
FV	Fragmenta Vaticana: Mommsen, T., ed. "Fragmenta quae dicuntur Vaticana." In P. Krüger, Th. Mommsen, G. studemund, *Collectio librorum iuris anteiustinian;* vol. III (Berlin, 1878), 1–106.
Gothofredus	*Codex Theodosianus cum perpetuis commentariis Iacobi Gothofredi.* Edited by Antonius Maurillius. Leipzig, 1736–45.
ILS	Dessau, H. *Inscriptiones Latinae Selectae.* Berlin, 1892–1916.
Jones, *LRE*	Jones, A. H. M. *The Later Roman Empire, 284–602: A Social, Economic and Administrative Survey.* Oxford, 1964.
Kaser-Hackl	Kaser, M. *Das römische Zivilprozessrecht.* 2nd ed. Edited by K. Hackl. Munich, 1996.
Krüger	*Codex Theodosianus, Fasciculus I, Liber I–VI.* Berlin, 1923. *Fasciculus II, Liber VII–VIII.* Berlin, 1926.
Lewis and Short	Lewis, C. T., and C. Short. *A Latin Dictionary Founded on Andrew's Edition of Freund's Latin Dictionary.* Oxford, 1879.

Millar, *ERW*[2]	Millar, F. *The Emperor in the Roman World: 31 BC–AD 337*. 2nd ed. Ithaca, 1992.
Mommsen	Mommsen, T., ed. *Theodosiani libri XVI [...], Vol. 1.2: Textus cum apparatu*. Berlin, 1905.
Mommsen, *Proleg.*	Mommsen, T. *Theodosiani libri XVI[...]. Vol. 1.1.: Prolegomena*. Berlin, 1905.
Mommsen, *StrR.*	Mommsen, T. *Römisches Strafrecht*. Leipzig, 1899.
Nov.	Novellae (Iustiniani)
NT	Novellae Theodosiani II
NV	Novellae Valentiniani III
OLD	Glare, P., ed. *Oxford Latin Dictionary*. Oxford, 1982.
Pharr	Pharr, C., trans. *The Theodosian Code*. Princeton, 1952.
PLRE I	Jones, A. H. M., J. R. Martindale, and J. Morris, eds. *The Prosopography of the Later Roman Empire*. Vol. 1, *A.D. 260–395*. Cambridge, 1971.
PS.	Pauli Sententiae: Krüger, P., ed. "Pauli libri quinque sententiarum." In P. Krüger, Th. Mommsen, and G. Studemund, *Collectio librorum iuris anteiustiani*. Vol. II (Berlin, 1878), 39–137.
Seeck, *Regesten*	Seeck, O. *Regesten der Kaiser und Päpste für die Jahre 311 bis 476 n. Chr. Vorarbeit zu einer Prosopographie der christlichen Kaiserzeit*. Stuttgart, 1919.
Silli	Silli, P. *Testi Constantiniani nelle fonti letterarie*. Materiali per una Palingenesia delle Costituzioni Tardo-Imperiali, 3. Milan, 1987.
St. / Scr.	*Studi / Scritti in onore di*

References to Mommsen, Krüger, or Gothofredus, *ad loc.*, are to their respective editions of the Codex Theodosianus.

Abbreviations are otherwise those of *L'Année Philologique*.

Introduction

The present book treats several related subjects concerning the administration of the Roman Empire under Constantine the Great: the record of his legislation in the Codex Theodosianus; its formal characteristics and novel features; the transition from Diocletian to Constantine as reflected in imperial legislation; the administration of justice under Constantine and its public face; the control and punishment of imperial officials; means of controlling the imperial bureaucracy; reform of the appellate system; and, in all this, the efforts of Constantine to augment his authority and power.

The popularity of Constantine as a subject of scholarly inquiry requires no lengthy justification. In a thousand years of Roman history and among as many famous persons, Constantine belongs to those few who tower over distinguished peers. He might justly be ranked among the founders of Rome: Romulus, Brutus, Augustus; and yet the city founded by Constantine, Constantinople, would succeed Rome and survive the collapse of the Western Roman Empire a thousand years. The inaugurator of Late Antiquity, Constantine shaped the separate fates of old and new Rome. Even after 1,700 years, the hand of Constantine can still be detected in the fabric of the Western world. The son of an emperor and, so it is alleged, a stablewench, Constantine possessed good fortune and genius in equal abundance. He was as successful as he was daring, and his continued success perhaps inspired, and certainly confirmed, his decision to convert to a religion that would shape the subsequent history of Rome, Europe, and the world.

The consequences of the actions of Constantine may be important and clear enough; the nature of the man himself, his motives and ends, however, remain contested. The very ambiguity of Constantine seems to demand explanation, even if scholarly work has more frequently resulted in greater controversy than consensus. Rival interpretations of Constantine have been advanced virtually since his death, May 22, 337. As we now find ourselves in the midst of a series of 1,700-year jubilees—his accession was celebrated in 2006; the anniversary of the Battle of the Milvian Bridge looms ahead—the time has seemed especially apt to reconsider the history and legacy of the ever-controversial first Christian emperor.

A footnote the length of this page would not suffice to list all the biographies written on Constantine or the studies dedicated to his conversion. Recent years have seen several works that, by contrast, address the reign of Constantine with new approaches and questions. The 1,700th anniversary of Constantine's accession to power was felicitously celebrated at an international colloquium and an imposing exhibition in his erstwhile capital, Trier,[1] and by the publication of an outstanding, if not divine, *Companion.*[2] The long-awaited second edition of *CAH* XII, which concludes with the reign of Constantine, appeared the year before.[3]

The Christianity of Constantine, however, remains the foremost concern of Constantinian scholarship, historical and legal, and no doubt will continue to do so. Interpretation of Constantine has itself undergone several conversions. Jacob Burckhardt, who denied the sincerity of the conversion in a famous and deservedly notorious early work, has the distinction of kindling the modern debate.[4] Burckhardt saw in Constantine a masterful politician who confessed Christianity, not from conviction, but from an insatiable will to power and self-preservation. Burckhardt's thesis brought the Christianity of Constantine to the forefront of late antique studies, if at first in the form of refutations; in the aftermath, the fact that it was at all feasible to deny the Christianity of Constantine inspired scholars to approach the subject with greater subtlety and criticism.[5] The eloquent lecture by Norman Baynes is perhaps the most famous piece of scholarship from this

---

1. A. Demandt and J. Engemann, eds., *Konstantin der Grosse. Geschichte—Archäologie—Rezeption. Internationales Kolloquium vom 10.–15. Oktober 2005* (Trier, 2006); A. Demandt and J. Engemann, eds., *Konstantin der Grosse. Ausstellungskatalog. Begleitband zur gleichnamigen Ausstellung in Trier, 2007* (Mainz, 2007).

2. N. E. Lenski, ed., *The Cambridge Companion to the Age of Constantine* (Cambridge, 2006). I allude to the article by A. D. Nock, "The Emperor's Divine *Comes*," *JRS* 37 (1947), 102–16.

3. A. K. P. Bowman, P. Garnsey, and Av. Cameron, eds., *The Cambridge Ancient History, Vol. XII: The Crisis of Empire, A.D. 193–337,* 2nd ed., (Cambridge, 2005).

4. J. Burckhardt, *Die Zeit Constantins des Großen,* 2nd ed. (Leipzig, 1898). English translation: *The Age of Constantine the Great,* trans. M. Hadas (Berkeley, 1983).

5. See the fascinating study of Burckhardt by T. Heinze, *Konstantin der Große und das konstantinische Zeitalter in den Urteilen und Wegen der deutsch-italienischen Forschungsdiskussion* (Munich, 2005), 73–91. Heinze also devotes chapters to Theodor Mommsen and Otto Seeck.

time.[6] Baynes accepted the genuineness of the conversion of Constantine and attributed inconsistencies in his actions to the exigencies of politics. This has been the view held, speaking very generally, in subsequent accounts of Constantine, which it is not the purpose of the present book to rehearse at length.[7]

Study of the written testimony of Constantine further enriched our knowledge. In two studies published almost simultaneously, Hermann Dörries and Heinz Kraft sought to let Constantine confess his faith in his own words, in a *Selbstzeugnis* compiled from the many documents penned by the emperor that have survived the centuries.[8] While not without their weaknesses, these treatments draw a compelling picture of Constantine as the first Christian emperor from the battered mosaic of his written testimony: the result allows for unshakeable belief, shallow theology, and the inconsistencies and contradictions that make Constantine all too human.

The authoritative work by Timothy Barnes, *Constantine and Eusebius,* and its technical companion, *The New Empire of Diocletian and Constantine,* have been the first books to consult on the events of the reign of Constantine since their publication. The Constantine of Barnes, in fact, strongly resembles the Constantine of Baynes: he is "neither a saint nor a tyrant" but sees his foremost task as the conversion of the Roman Empire to Christianity.[9] Since the appearance of *Constantine and Eusebius,* however, it has been precisely the priority of Christianity under Constantine that has been challenged. Among ancient historians, movement away from an explicitly Christianizing Constantine was signaled already by Averil Cameron in her critical review of the "totally Christian Constantine" of Barnes.[10] Thomas

---

6. N. H. Baynes, *Constantine the Great and the Christian Church (The Raleigh Lecture on History 1929),* 2nd ed. (i.e., repr. of 1st ed.), pref. by H. Chadwick (London, 1972).

7. Significant treatments prior to Barnes, *CE,* include A. Piganiol, *L'empereur Constantin* (Paris, 1932); A. Alföldi, *The Conversion of Constantine and Pagan Rome,* 1st ed. (Oxford, 1948), 2nd ed. (Oxford, 1969); A. H. M. Jones, *Constantine and the Conversion of Europe,* 1st ed. (London, 1948); 2nd ed. (New York, 1962); J. Vogt, *Constantin der Große und sein Jahrhundert,* 1st ed. (Munich, 1949), 2nd ed. (Munich, 1960); R. MacMullen, *Constantine* (New York, 1969).

8. H. Dörries, *Das Selbstzeugnis Kaiser Konstantins* (Göttingen, 1954); H. Kraft, *Kaiser Konstantins religiöse Entwicklung* (Tübingen, 1955). See the critical review of Dörries by Jones, *English Historical Review* 71 (1956), 136–37, and of both by H. U. Instinsky, *Gnomon* 30 (1958), 125–33. For more recent syntheses in German, J. Bleicken, *Constantin der Große und die Christen* (Munich, 1992); B. Bleckmann, *Konstantine der Große* (Reinbek, 1996); M. Clauss, *Konstantin der Grosse und seine Zeit,* 3rd ed. (Munich, 2007) (1st ed. 1996); and H. Brandt, *Konstantin der Grosse. Der erste christliche Kaiser. Eine Biographie* (Munich, 2006).

9. Barnes, *CE,* 275 (citing *Oratio ad sanctos* 11.1). On Baynes: Barnes, *CE,* 405 n. 21.

10. Av. Cameron, "Constantinus Christianus," review of T. D. Barnes, *Constantine and Eusebius* and *The New Empire of Diocletian and Constantine, JRS* 73 (1983), 184–90.

Grünewald more broadly sought to illustrate the official propaganda of Constantine by using a variety of sources: panegyric, coins, and, above all, inscriptions.[11] Although Grünewald's focus lies foremost on the dynastic preoccupations of the emperor, he also assesses Constantine's religious message, in particular the message behind the words *instinctu divinitatis* on the Arch of Constantine. In contrast to Barnes, Grünewald finds Constantine rather less overtly Christian and rather more tolerant of paganism.[12]

Roman legal historians now long have been reluctant to stress the Christianity of Constantine in interpreting his legislation. This wariness owes much to the excesses of Romanistic scholarship of the early twentieth century. As Christian influence was once taken for granted by legal historians, so from around the middle of the twentieth century, following the lead of Jean Gaudemet, proof came to be demanded before any such assumption was permitted to stand. Romanist scholarship on the legislation of Constantine will be discussed in chapter 3. It suffices to say at this point that the trends among Roman historians and Romanists converge in the important monograph by Judith Evans-Grubbs, *Law and Family in Late Antiquity: The Emperor Constantine's Marriage Legislation,*[13] which made the family legislation of Constantine a subject for the social history of the fourth century.

Qualification of Constantine's Christian fervor continued in *Constantine and the Bishops* by Harold Drake: Drake illustrates how Constantine strove to attain broad religious consensus and general tolerance.[14] The coercion and hostility to paganism that ultimately dominate the later fourth century were unintended consequences, after Constantinian consensus collapsed.[15] The latest, nonbiographical study of Constantine, *The Roman Revolution of Constantine* by Raymond Van Dam, is framed as a response to Sir Ronald Syme, whose influence (so Van Dam) is responsible for the prominence of Constantine's Christianity in modern histories.[16] Van Dam rightly deprecates endless speculation on the depth of Constantine's religiosity; he turns his attention instead to the anonymous petitioners of the cities Hispellum and Orcistus, who received rescripts from Constantine that are pre-

11. T. Grünewald, *Constantinus Maximus Augustus: Herrschaftspropaganda in der zeitgenössischen Überlieferung* (Stuttgart, 1990).

12. Grünewald, *Herrschaftspropaganda*, 78–86, with a discussion of previous scholarship.

13. J. Evans-Grubbs, *Law and Family in Late Antiquity: The Emperor Constantine's Marriage Legislation* (Oxford, 1995).

14. H. A. Drake, *Constantine and the Bishops: The Politics of Intolerance* (Baltimore, 2000), e.g., 305–8, 408, 419–20.

15. See also the critical review by T. D. Barnes, *Phoenix* 54 (2000), 381–83.

16. R. Van Dam, *The Roman Revolution of Constantine* (Cambridge, 2007), 3–6.

served in inscriptions.[17] I have not been able to incorporate the many new surveys and other studies that have since appeared.[18]

The present book is an essentially secular study. The project began as a study of Roman law under Constantine, largely inspired by the questions of the decline of jurisprudence and the rise of vulgar law (i.e., popular law) in Late Antiquity. Constantine had no small part in these phenomena, however one assesses them, but the more fundamental question, how the administration of justice functioned under Constantine, soon took precedence. The reason for this change of inquiry lies in the constitutions of Constantine themselves. The edicts and official letters of Constantine bear witness to an intensely personal effort to enforce legitimate procedure and crush administrative abuse and corruption. The means with which Constantine attempted to achieve these ends, the processes of legislation and communication themselves, proved to rank among the most important innovations of Constantine's reign.

The present book aspires to be, in a quiet way, an interdisciplinary study that unites recent advances in the understanding of government and imperial self-representation in English-language scholarship, and technical work on legal history and late antique legislation by scholars predominantly in Germany, France, and Italy. The laws of Constantine are accordingly examined in two ways: both as legal documents that shaped the administration of the empire and as carefully composed communication between the emperor and his subjects and officials. One of the greatest legacies of Constantine is his utilization of the communicative potential of legislation to court the favor of his subjects and to control the representatives of the imperial government. Constantine effects significant change in administration and law and simultaneously asserts the supremacy of the emperor over a rapidly swelling bureaucracy.

This study is, in a sense, a case study of the Roman administration under Constantine. It follows important work on the nature of the government of the Roman Empire that has appeared in the last twenty years. The starting point of any study of the imperial administration remains *The Em-*

17. Van Dam, *Roman Revolution of Constantine,* 23–34, on reference to pagan ceremony in the rescript to Hispellum (ILS 705, ll. 46–47: *contagiose superstitionis*); 150–220, on the religious apprehensions of the people of Orcistus.

18. These include K. M. Girardet, *Der Kaiser und Sein Gott. Das Christentum im Denken und in der Religionspolitik Konstantins des Großen* (Berlin, 2010); F. Carlà and M. G. Castello, *Questioni: tardoantiche. Storia e mito della "svolta constantiniana"* (Rome, 2010); R. Van Dam, *Remembering Constantine at the Milvian Bridge* (Cambridge, 2011); and J. Bardill, *Constantine, Divine Emperor of the Christian Golden Age* (Cambridge, 2011).

peror in the Roman World, by Fergus Millar. Millar showed that the Roman emperors, including Constantine, were essentially passive partners in a continuous exchange of information and support for patronage and power. An incessant stream of petitions and requests from throughout the empire reached the emperor: in the civil administration of the empire, the Roman emperors needed only to react to the information that reached them; they could do as much as they were willing to do. The fundamental nature of the relationship between the Roman emperor and his empire remained the same in Constantine's day; the means of communication and command had not changed, and the emperor was as ever the focus of his subjects, perhaps more so, but the nature of the administration itself had changed and the distance between the emperor and his subjects had grown in tandem with the size of the imperial bureaucracy.

Constantine confronted these difficulties with characteristic aggressiveness. To bridge the widening space between himself and his subjects, Constantine subordinated the burgeoning administration of the Roman Empire to ever stricter and ever more involved control. He redefined the public persona of the Roman emperor. The monolithic tetrarchic character gives way to an impassioned and righteous emperor, who seems to have almost as little in common with Diocletian as he does with his own stony-faced son. Constantine shows himself ever concerned for his subjects and wary of the officials who rule them; he would bequeath both these significant innovations in persona to his successors. The greater legislative initiative shown, for example, by Valentinian might be considered in this light.[19] The legislation of Constantine must be analyzed both for its legal and administrative significance and for its rhetorical formulation as an expression of the imperial will and as a projection of the imperial persona. Constantine transformed a passive government typical of the High Empire into a relatively proactive, popularizing autocracy that would persist long after his reign. Constantine sought to bind his subjects to him, to create an intimate dynamic that enabled him to speak to their concerns while strengthening his power over the imperial bureaucracy and his own absolute authority.

The central chapters of this book bear on questions of government raised in part by Peter Brown in *Power and Persuasion in Late Antiquity: Towards a Christian Empire* and by Ted Lendon in *Empire of Honour: The Art*

---

19. See the conclusion of S. Schmidt-Hofner, *Reagieren und Gestalten. Der Regierungsstil des spätrömischen Kaisers am Beispiel der Gesetzgebung Valentinians I.* (Munich, 2008).

of Government in the Roman World.[20] Brown explored how shared culture and education, *paideia,* might commend provincial governors to the urban elite among the governed, smooth relations between them, and mitigate conflict. Lendon established the power of honor in governing the Roman Empire: both honor imparted on favorites and officials by the emperor, and the rival honor of provincial governors and the distinguished provincial elite. This book has, by contrast, much to say about government but fairly little to say about the urban elite and their traditional ties to the court: it explores instead how Constantine sought allies both above and below the provincial elite and their ordinary governors. Constantine appealed to the anonymous crowd for loyalty and aid; he also introduced a number of eminent officials, men who stood closest to himself in power and loyalty, to assist in the task of controlling ordinary governors and administrators, and to whom poor provincials might turn when wronged. This book has much in common with Clifford Ando's *Imperial Ideology and Provincial Loyalty in the Roman Empire.*[21] Ando asks why the subjects of Rome remained loyal to the emperors; this study asks how Constantine sought to inspire such loyalty. It stands as a kind of case study in contrast to the systematic treatment by Ando. Although widely divergent in approach—Ando draws on the theories of Weber, Foucault, and Habermas, while the present study began with a philological study of the texts of the constitutions—both works envision a Roman Empire governed more or less successfully by law and imperial charisma.

This book is divided into eight chapters. The first three chapters treat technical aspects of the legislation of Constantine but also serve to introduce Roman law and administration in Late Antiquity. Chapter 1, "The Sources and the Codex Theodosianus," is dedicated foremost to the Codex Theodosianus, the primary source for the constitutions of Constantine. Since the laws of Constantine survive almost exclusively in this work of the fifth century, it is necessary to understand why and how they were collected. The constitutions of Constantine in fact add to our general understanding of the Codex Theodosianus and provide important evidence for the sources from which the Theodosian compilers assembled their text. The kinds of laws that are preserved in the Codex Theodosianus are also

20. P. Brown, *Power and Persuasion in Late Antiquity: Towards a Christian Empire* (Madison, 1992); J. E. Lendon, *Empire of Honour: The Art of Government in the Roman World* (Oxford, 1997).

21. C. Ando, *Imperial Ideology and Provincial Loyalty in the Roman Empire* (Berkeley, 1999).

discussed in chapter 1, as well as the question whether obsolete laws were also collected. The decision of Theodosius II to collect all laws from the time of Constantine is considered anew; and finally, with respect to the earliest laws preserved in the Codex Theodosianus, an explanation is sought for the fact that the record of Constantine's legislation begins in 312, not upon his elevation in 306.

Chapter 2, "Formal Characteristics of the Legislation of Constantine," treats precisely what its title advertises. Traditional forms of Roman legislation—edicts, letters, orations or rather letters to the Senate, and private rescripts—are illustrated by examples from the legislation of Constantine itself. Special attention is given to the means by which various legislative texts were disseminated and published. One trait of late antique legislation is the frequent use of circular letters disseminated downward through the imperial hierarchy as official correspondence. These letters were addressed to imperial officials and were published upon receipt; they might thus be recorded by interested private parties. Imperial edicts, however, are addressed explicitly to a large audience. Constantine appears to have favored a mixed form of edict, in which he addresses his audience, often the population of the empire, directly with epistolary forms. This kind of edict, which here has been dubbed the "epistolary edict," appears to fall into desuetude after the reign of Constantine.

The vexed question of the transition from the legislation of the tetrarchs to that of Constantine is the subject of chapter 3, "Changes in Legislation from Diocletian to Constantine." The chapter begins with a brief discussion of the respective classicism of Diocletian and Constantine: that is to say, how conservative the legislation of both emperors was with respect to the classical law of the High Empire and the city of Rome. The discussion turns next to the questions of the Latin style and the legal forms preferred under each emperor. It has been contested for nearly a century whether the legislation of Constantine genuinely differs from that of Diocletian or whether its appearance has merely been distorted by an accident of transmission. Recent Anglo-American scholarship tends to reject the idea of a large distinction. The opposite view is taken here, with certain reservations: in terms of the legal forms favored under each regime, Diocletian and Constantine were largely similar. In terms of Latin style, however, the enactments of these emperors differ in important ways. The private rescripts and official letters of each are contrasted in two sections; a final section treats tetrarchic antecedents of the baroque Latin of Constantine and the significance of this style as an instrument of communication. The chapter concludes with a brief reflection on the distinct ways in which the tetrarchs and Constantine portray their relationship to their patron deities in general edicts, which is resumed in the next chapter.

Chapter 4, "The Propagation of Justice," considers several edicts issued by Constantine primarily after the conquest of the East in 324. The chapter begins with reflections on edicts generally as instruments of communication between Constantine and his subjects. These texts are studied both as evidence of administrative innovation and as documents of the manner in which Constantine appealed to the populace and presented himself and the ideals of justice cultivated under his regime. The discussion turns first to an edict issued shortly after the defeat of Licinius, who is styled as a tyrant and whose laws are abrogated. The pretensions of Constantine as a just ruler are discussed with reference also to the aftermath of the defeat of Maxentius.

Soon after the conquest of the East and shortly before the Council of Nicaea, Constantine issued an edict to the inhabitants of the empire that is the subject of the next section. This universal edict, CTh. 9.1.4, merits close attention for several reasons: First, it attests the fundamental suspicion that Constantine harbored against officials in the imperial bureaucracy. Constantine ostensibly construes his relationship to his administrators as one of a paternal trust, yet he accepts no responsibility for wrongdoing on their part; he himself is the victim of deception. Constantine instead takes the side of his provincial subjects against the imperial bureaucracy, and he encourages his subjects to approach his person to denounce the corrupt among his officials. The punishment of imperial officials becomes an act of personal vengeance, just as the act of disobedience becomes a personal insult to the emperor. Constantine concludes this remarkable edict with a prayer: here religion and Constantine's conception of divine favor make their appearance in this study. Constantine predicates his salvation on the success of his administration and moreover proclaims this publicly. The use of prayer in the constitutions of Constantine may interest scholars of the religious history of the fourth century.

Further means with which the provincial population might assist the emperor in controlling the administration occupy the middle part of chapter 4: these means include the creation of a chain of redress through the officials closest to Constantine in the civil administration, the praetorian prefects and imperial *comites*. The chapter concludes with a discussion of other special delegates or agents, whom the emperor dispatched to obtain information about the governance of his empire.

Chapter 5, "Constantine and the Provincials" is dedicated to the reforms introduced by Constantine in the attempt to improve the experience of provincial justice, general access to law, and justice generally to the benefit of his subjects. First, two fragments of an edict issued in 331, CTh. 1.16.6–7, are examined at length. The first fragment raises the subject of trial procedure under Constantine. Constantine insists that provincial governors adhere to the procedures of Roman law. Far more remarkably, however, Constantine authorizes the record and submission of public acclamations as a means of assessing the conduct of provincial governors. This innovation both reflects and encouraged the prominence of public acclamations in Late Antiquity. In the second fragment of the edict of 331, Constantine violently denounces bureaucratic corruption and the collection of illicit fees for legal transactions, *sportulae.* An excursus on the semipublic institution of *episcopalis audientia,* which Constantine introduced as an alternative to the cumbersome provincial justice system, concludes the chapter. Constantine attempted to use bishops as instruments of justice by authorizing them to resolve legal disputes, even if only one party to a dispute demanded it. Imperial administrators were to see that the ruling of the bishop was enforced.

Chapter 6, "Constantine and the Imperial Bureaucracy," is a survey of official correspondence in which Constantine addresses corruption and administrative abuse. It constitutes a kind of potpourri of punishment. This chapter serves as a counterpart to the preceding chapter, in that it attempts to reconcile the administrative correspondence of Constantine with his public pronouncements, to show how Constantine implemented the declared aims of his administration. If a majority of such letters to officials were inspired by inquiries from the officials themselves, it is plausible that the orders of Constantine were also executed. A range of incidents attested in correspondence between Constantine and various imperial officials is evaluated to this end. Since there is, however, no evidence of the execution of Constantine's orders, nothing more than plausibility is claimed. These constitutions to imperial officials, however, do offer insight into the way in which Constantine presented himself to the imperial bureaucracy and how he sought by various means to manipulate and compel its loyalty and obedience.

Further means of cultivating official loyalty and obedience are the subject of chapter 7, "Control and Consultation: *Breves, Relationes, Consultationes.*" The three items of the title are discussed in order. These forms of correspondence between provincial administrators and the emperor were fostered in part because Constantine generally privileged documentary records of transactions as guarantors of transparency. By encouraging correspondence and inquiries from the provincial administration, Constantine created a stream of information from the provinces by which imperial administrators could be subjected to greater control, but their authority in the provinces strengthened by the responses of Constantine himself. Steady communication between the court and provinces helped to empower provincial administrators before overpowerful private citizens; the resultant dependency of imperial administrators augmented the authority of the emperor. The procedure of the *consultatio,* whereby a provincial governor wrote to the emperor for legal advice before delivering a ruling—the administrative equivalent of the system of petition and response by private rescript—is treated at length. Constantine instituted and maintained strict procedural rules in order that the process was not misused by provincial governors, that responses to *consultationes* remained an effective expression of imperial authority, and that the appellate system was not undermined.

Appeal under Constantine is treated in the final chapter, "*Appellatio.*" The appellate system is emblematic of the innovations of Constantine in law, administration, and imperial control. A successful appellate system not only should improve the administration of justice to the benefit of the provincial population, but also depends directly on the integrity of imperial administrators. The system of appeal as reconstituted by Constantine required extensive documentation, which should furnish a sound basis upon which the emperor might exercise his authority. The extant constitutions of Constantine attest his efforts to enforce new procedural rules in a variety of situations. The subject of appeal thus unites the separate threads of this book: provincial justice, administrative control, and imperial authority. After a brief discussion of the traditional form of appeal under the Roman Empire, the chapter treats the constituent parts of Constantinian "appeal by consultation" (*appellatio more consultationis*), which closely resembles the procedure of *consultatio* elaborated in the preceding chapter. The final sections of chapter 8 are dedicated to difficulties encountered in implementing this system of appeal; the chapter itself concludes with the paragraphs on appeal contained in an extensive general edict issued in 331, by which date the reform of the appellate system appears to have been complete.

A conclusion recapitulates the findings of this book.

1

The Sources and the Codex Theodosianus

The Sources of the Legislation of Constantine

Constantine was remembered as a prolific legislator even in antiquity, whether one celebrated or reviled him.[1] A study of the legislation of Constantine presumes the survival of a substantial amount of that legislation some 1,700 years after the reign of its author. Much of the legal and administrative work of Constantine would be lost today were it not for the work of the fifth-century compilers of the Codex Theodosianus. The decision of Emperor Theodosius II to begin his great collection of imperial law with Constantine blessed posterity with the most extensive record of his constitutions.

That record is the subject of the present chapter. The sources of the constitutions of Constantine may be divided into two disproportionate groups: these are the Codex Theodosianus on the one hand and all other evidence on the other, from sources of widely varying character and value. Owing to the limited extent of this second group, it will briefly be surveyed first; the rest of this chapter will be dedicated to the Codex Theodosianus. Since the Codex Theodosianus surpasses all other sources in range and depth for the

1. Eutrop. 10.8.1: *Multas leges rogavit, quasdam ex bono et aequo, plerasque superfluas, nonnullas severas.* Julian the Apostate *apud* Amm. Marc. 21.10.8: *Tunc et memoriam Constantini ut novatoris turbatorisque priscarum legum et moris antiquitus recepti vexavit;* on which, see J. Szidat, *Historischer Kommentar zu Ammianus Marcellinus Buch XX–XXI. Teil III: Die Konfrontation* (Stuttgart, 1996), 110–13. Cf. also Nazarius, *Pan. Lat.* X 38: *novae leges regendis moribus et frangendis vitiis constitutae. veterum calumniosae ambages recisae captandae simplicitatis laqueos perdiderunt.*

legislation of Constantine, some consideration of its composition is indispensable. The methods of selection applied in the composition of the Codex Theodosianus determined not only the extent of the legislation preserved but also the type of constitutions represented. Over the course of this chapter, attention will also be drawn to some of the formal idiosyncrasies of the Constantinian legislation, which may be documented both in the Codex Theodosianus and in other sources.

Sources outside the Codex Theodosianus

The number of Constantinian constitutions known from sources other than the Codex Theodosianus is vanishingly small. First is a collection of eighteen constitutions appended to Mommsen's edition of the Codex Theodosianus, the *collectio Sirmondiana,* which preserves two Constantinian constitutions. The Sirmondians derive from an early medieval collection of eighteen constitutions; the collection takes its name from its first editor, Jacques Sirmond, who published it in 1631. It is thought that the original collection was assembled before the introduction of the Codex Theodosianus itself in 438.[2] The first and fourth of the Sirmondian constitutions (Sirm. 1 and 4) are complete copies of two letters sent by Constantine to praetorian prefects.[3] Sirm. 1 in particular has been discussed extensively among legal historians. Its radical provision granting hearings before a bishop even over the objections of one party—"*inter nolentes*"—has led scholars to impugn the authenticity variously of the passage, the constitution, or the entire collection.[4]

The second legal collection preserved independently of the Codex Theodosianus is the so-called *Fragmenta Vaticana.* This very extensive collection of classical jurisprudence and imperial law appears to have been composed in the Western Empire before the defeat of Licinius in 324.[5] Only

---

2. On the Sirmondians, see M. Vessey, "The Origin of the Collectio Sirmondiana: A New Look at the Evidence," in *The Theodosian Code,* ed. J. D. Harries and I. Wood (Ithaca, 1993), 178–99; A. J. B. Sirks, *The Theodosian Code: A Study* (Friedrichsdorf, 2007), 247–63; O. Huck, "Encore à propos des Sirmondiennes . . . Arguments présentés à l'appui de la thèse de l'authenticité en réponse à une mise en cause récente," *AntTard* 11 (2003), 181–96.

3. CTh. 16.9.1 and 16.8.5 correspond to parts of Sirm. 4.

4. Sirks, *Study,* 251–55, on Sirmondian 1 with recent literature. In defense of the authenticity of Sirm. 1, O. Huck, "À propos de CTh 1, 27, 1 et CSirm 1. Sur deux textes controversés relatifs à l'episcopalis audientia constantinienne," *ZRG* 120 (2003), 78–105; Huck, "Encore."

5. D. Liebs, "Recht und Rechtsliteratur," in *Restauration und Erneuerung: Die lateinische Literatur von 284 bis 374,* ed. R. Herzog (Munich, 1989), 64–65.

part of it survives as a palimpsest, but even this is sufficient to preserve no fewer than eleven Constantinian constitutions. Still greater importance attaches to the evidence of the *Fragmenta Vaticana* because it also includes private rescripts, which were not collected in the Codex Theodosianus, and unabridged letters or edicts.[6]

A handful of inscriptions also attest Constantinian constitutions, but reattribution to other emperors in recent years has diminished their number. Among these, the famous Brigetio Tablet was authored by Licinius, and it is now believed that the well-known *Edictum de Accusationibus*, of which fragments attributed to Constantine appear as CTh. 9.5.1 and CJ 9.8.3, was issued by Galerius.[7] Two famous inscriptions attest correspondence between Constantine and individual cities. A dossier of texts has survived that documents the elevation of the town Orcistus in Asia Minor to the rank of a city. The texts include a letter to a vicar, an imperial *adnotatio*, and a rescript to the town council of the city.[8] A letter addressed to the Italian town Hispellum (mod. Spello) is also extant, in which Constantine notably grants permission for the construction of a temple to his family provided it not be "contaminated by superstition."[9] A fragment of a letter to the proconsul of Africa has been found;[10] and, finally, an inscription in Rome records a letter sent to the Senate in 337 in praise of one of its members, Proculus.[11]

While many papyri, including court records of proceedings, attest the legal and administrative culture of Egypt under Constantine, papyri finds

---

6. Rescripts: FV 32–34, 274, possibly 287, and 290–91 (the last three very fragmentary); cf. appendix C, "Private Rescripts of Constantine," in Corcoran, *ET*², 301–2. Letters and edicts: FV 35, 248–49, and 273.

7. Brigetio Tablet: *FIRA*², vol. 1, no. 93 = *AE* 1937.232. Corcoran, *ET*², 145ff. *Edictum de Accusationibus: FIRA*², vol. 1, no. 94; S. Corcoran, "Galerius' Jigsaw Puzzle: The Caesariani Dossier," *AntTard* 15 (2007), 221–50.

8. *FIRA*², vol. 1, no. 95; D. Feissel, "L'*adnotatio* de Constantin sur le droit de cité d'Orcistus en Phrygie," *AntTard* 7 (1999), 255–67; F. Jacques, "Les moulins d'Orcistus. Rhétorique et géographie au IVe s.," in *Institutions, société et vie politique dans l'empire romain*, ed. M. Christol et al. (Rome, 1992), 431–46; most recently, Van Dam, *The Roman Revolution of Constantine*, 150–220.

9. ILS 705 (= CIL 11.5265); J. Gascou, "Le rescrit d'Hispellum," *MEFRA* 79 (1967), 609–59; R. Andreotti, "Contributo alla discussione del rescritto costantiniano di Hispellum," in *Atti del I Convegno di Studi Umbri, Gubbio, 26–31 maggio 1963* (Perugia, 1964), 249–90; Van Dam, *Roman Revolution of Constantine*, 23–34.

10. R. Cagnat, A. Merlin, and L. Chatelain, *Inscriptions Latines d'Afrique (Tripolitaine, Tunisie, Maroc)* (Paris, 1923) no. 269 (= *AE* 1919.30); E. Schallmayer et al., eds., *Der römische Weihebezirk von Osterburken I* (Stuttgart, 1990), no. 747 (pp. 577–79); Corcoran, *ET*², 353.

11. CIL 6.40776 = *AE* 1934.158; cf. *PLRE* I, Proculus 11.

of imperial constitutions are very rare: the only specimen is P.Col. VII 175, which cites a rescript of Constantine issued to the decurion Agrippinus.[12]

Several literary sources contain letters sent by Constantine or allude to legislation. While these sources are not legislative texts, they often provide useful *comparanda* for the interpretation of official enactments. The *Panegyrici Latini* delivered before Constantine are witnesses to his early reign and occasionally refer to legislation.[13] The Church Fathers have preserved several letters of Constantine's that pertain to the Donatist and Arian controversies. Most important among these are the documents collected by Eusebius of Caesarea, which include edicts issued to the provincials of the East after the defeat of Licinius. The appendices of Optatus preserve original letters and other documents pertaining to the Donatist controversy; and both Athanasius and Augustine also cite letters.[14]

Finally, two legal works of the fourth century, the spurious Sentences of Paul and the Opinions of Ulpian, are useful witnesses of the state of Roman law in the Constantinian age and facilitate the interpretation of numerous constitutions.[15]

The Codex Theodosianus

The vast majority of the constitutions of Constantine owe their survival to the Codex Theodosianus. In its present state, the Codex Theodosianus con-

---

12. Cf. SB XVI 12692; C. J. Kraemer and N. Lewis, "A Referee's Hearing on Ownership," *TAPhA* 68 (1937), 357–87.

13. *Pan. Lat.* VII (a. 307), VI (a. 310), V (VIII, a. 311/12), XII (IX, a. 313), IV (X, a. 321); C. Castello, "Il pensiero politico-religioso di Costantino alla luce dei panegirici," *AARC* 1 (1975), 47–117; C. E. V. Nixon, "Latin Panegyric in the Tetrarchic and Constantinian Period," in *History and Historiography in Late Antiquity,* ed. B. Croke and A. M. Emmett (Sydney, 1983), 88–99; generally, C. Ronning, *Herrscherpanegyrik unter Trajan und Konstantin. Studien zur symbolischen Kommunikation in der römischen Kaiserzeit* (Tübingen, 2007).

14. For literary sources: P. Silli, *Testi costantiniani nelle fonti letterarie,* Materiali per una palingenesi delle costituzioni tardo-imperiali 3 (Milan, 1987); V. Keil, *Quellensammlung zur Religionspolitik Konstantins des Großen,* 2nd ed. (Darmstadt, 1995). See in general, K. M. Girardet, *Kaisergericht und Bischofsgericht, Studien zu den Anfängen des Donatistenstreits (313–315) und zum Prozeß des Athanasius von Alexandrien* (328–346) (Bonn, 1975).

15. Pseudo-Paul: D. Liebs, "Römische Jurisprudenz in Africa," *ZRG* 106 (1989), 230–47; D. Liebs, "Römische Provinzialjurisprudenz," *ANRW* II.15 (1976), 315–19; D. Liebs, "Die pseudopaulinischen Sentenzen II. Versuch einer neuen Palingenesie," *ZRG* 113 (1996), 132–242; D. Liebs, *Römischen Jurisprudenz in Africa mit Studien zu den pseudopaulinischen Sentenzen,* 2nd ed. (Berlin, 2005). Pseudo-Ulpian: Liebs, "Römische Provinzialjurisprudenz," 332–38; D. Liebs, "Ulpiani Opinionum libri VI," *TR* 41 (1973), 279–310.

tains approximately 389 fragments of Constantinian origin; these in turn represent approximately 336 individual constitutions.[16] Since the most recent authority counts 2,777 extant fragments derived from 2,307 original constitutions in the entire Codex Theodosianus, the 389 fragments of Constantinian legislation would represent roughly 14 percent of those extant. It is estimated that the Codex Theodosianus once consisted of circa 3,250 fragments of late antique constitutions, but the work has not come down to us in its entirety.[17] In particular, the first six books of the Codex Theodosianus have suffered in transmission. The constitutions lost in these books are supplied in part by the Codex Justinianus, but the integrity of fragments restored from the latter compilation is often uncertain. The editors of the Codex Justinianus enjoyed far greater powers to edit and alter texts selected for inclusion.[18]

To understand the range of Constantinian constitutions preserved in the Codex Theodosianus, it is imperative to consider how the Codex Theodosianus was compiled. The project began almost a century after the death of Constantine. In 429, Emperor Theodosius II ordered a commission of nine men to prepare a collection of all general imperial constitutions from the time of Constantine to his own day.[19] This collection, with which the Codex Theodosianus as we have it should be identified, was intended as a preliminary collection for a much more ambitious legal compilation. The latter compilation, sometimes called the *codex magisterium vitae* by Roman legal historians, anticipates the efforts of Justinian to codify Roman law.

---

16. My calculations are based on Mommsen, *Proleg.*, ccix–ccxxiv, and include only texts in the Codex Theodosianus and Justinianus. Using Seeck's *Regesten*, 159–84, D. Liebs, "Konstantin als Gesetzgeber," in *Konstantin der Grosse. Geschichte—Archäologie—Rezeption. Internationales Kolloquium vom 10.–15. Oktober 2005*, ed. A. Demandt & J. Engemann (Trier 2006), 98, counts 361 constitutions, which, however, include Constantine's rescripts and some other texts. J. Gaudemet, "Les Constitutions constantiniennes du Code Théodosien," *AARC* 5 (1983), 139, adopted, with few exceptions, Seeck's proposals for combining fragments and arrived at a count of 276 constitutions. The proposals of Seeck must always be used cautiously. See the devastating critique of Mommsen, "Das theodosische Gesetzbuch," *ZRG* 21 (1900), 179–85 (= *Juristische Schriften*, vol. 2, 397–401), and the critical review by W. E. Voß of the new edition of O. Seeck, "Die Zeitfolge der Gesetze Constantins," ed. M. Sargenti, *ZRG* 106 (1989), 632–45.

17. Sirks, *Study*, 84–85.

18. Gaudemet, "Constitutions constantiniennes," 154–56, appends a list of constitutions in the CJ excluded from Mommsen's edition of the CTh. These were incorporated in the partial edition of Krüger. Cf. n. 59 below on the *Breviarium*.

19. CTh. 1.1.5 = *Gesta Senatus* 4; cf. CTh. 1.1.6. pr. On motives behind the project, D. Nörr, "Zu den geistigen und sozialen Grundlagen der spätantiken Kodifikationsbewegung (Anon., de rebus bellicis XXI)," *ZRG* 80 (1963), 109–40; J. F. Matthews, *Laying Down the Law: A Study of the Theodosian Code* (New Haven, 2000), 10–30; Sirks, *Study*, 36–53.

Theodosius II planned to combine the constitutions of the emperors with the works of the classical Roman jurists in a work that would unite all Roman law within its pages. Obsolete laws would be removed; contradictions would be eliminated. This, the project of 429, was never realized. The undertaking was begun anew in 435, but in the constitution that proclaims the revision of the work, CTh. 1.1.6, Theodosius omits mention of the grand *codex magisterium vitae*.[20] Thus, after nearly a decade of work, the collection of imperial law since Constantine was completed. This work was named after Emperor Theodosius II and promulgated in the East on 15 February 438; it was received in the West on 25 December.[21]

It is generally acknowledged that the constitutions preserved in the Codex Theodosianus do not represent the total number of constitutions issued in Constantine's name. The grounds for this inference and the extent of the material excluded from the Codex Theodosianus remain, however, subjects of scholarly debate. It is unclear where the compilers of the Codex Theodosianus found the legislation that was edited and arranged for their compilation. Many have asked whether the compilers drew upon provincial archives, even overseas, or skimmed an imperial archive housed in Constantinople to recover imperial legislation since the reign of Constantine. The validity of the constitutions preserved in the Codex Theodosianus has also been disputed: does the Codex Theodosianus exclude obsolete laws or contain only laws that were valid in 438? The answers to both these questions affect our estimation of the extent of late antique legislation.

As regards the former question—what was the immediate source of the constitutions in the Codex Theodosianus?—A. J. B. Sirks has argued in several publications that the Theodosian compilers drew foremost on archives located in Constantinople.[22] Sirks challenges the argument once advanced by Seeck that the compilers turned to the provinces for want of adequate archives at home. Seeck posited that a large number of the texts included in the Codex Theodosianus derived from provincial copies. He extrapolated

---

20. On the delay before the completion of the Codex Theodosianus, see below, n. 64.

21. Promulgation: NT 1, reproduced also by Mommsen, *Proleg.*, x. Arrival in the West: *Gesta Senatus*. Only the author of the *Chronica Gallica* (a. 452) records the publication of the Code in the fifteenth regnal year of Theodosius II: *Theodosianus liber omnium legum legitimorum principum in unum conlatarum hoc primum anno editus* (Mommsen, ed., *Chron. Min.* I, 660): Mommsen, *Proleg.*, x–xi. Sirks argues that the Codex Theodosianus was never ratified in the West (Sirks, *Study*, 206–23); there is indeed no evidence of formal ratification, but in light of the fact that the Codex Theodosianus was used in the West as if it had been ratified, the ratification either has not been transmitted to us or was considered irrelevant.

22. See Sirks, *Study*, 117–58, with bibliography; on central archives, 130–35.

from the surviving record of the receipt or publication of constitutions (usually *accepta* or *proposita* in their subscriptions) that many more, indeed most, of the constitutions in the Codex Theodosianus had been found by the compilers in the provincial archives of the original recipients.[23] Seeck's position, however, rests upon a series of assumptions, not least that the appointees of Theodosius will have traversed the empire in search of copies of old imperial legislation; by exposing these flaws, Sirks has undermined much of Seeck's argument.[24] Sirks concludes instead that approximately 90 percent of the texts in the Codex Theodosianus were recovered from the central imperial archives of Constantinople.[25]

While this conclusion must be nearer the truth, it seems unwise to presume that the collection of imperial constitutions could be accomplished merely by "perusing the archives of Constantinople." We know nothing of such archives, much less their completeness. Sirks believes that the emperors kept archives with them when they traveled, until they could be deposited in Rome or Constantinople.[26] He has in mind here documents produced en route, but what of records already extant? As Sirks notes, the purpose of copybooks, of which such archives will have consisted, was "to enable the sender to know what and to whom he wrote"; we might further assume that the emperors brought their archives with them on their travels, and to this end Sirks considers it plausible that the archives were of manageable size and easy to consult.[27] Still numerous accidents could and did interrupt the regular deposition of imperial documents. To cite one macabre example, after the Battle of Adrianople, not even the corpse of the emperor Valens was recovered: what then of his archives? Not a single constitution of Valens from the year 378 survives.[28] It is likely that the better, more regular record of constitutions of the late fourth and early fifth century owes more to the fact that the emperors seldom strayed from their capitals than to any inherent efficiency posited in late antique archival practice.[29]

---

23. Seeck, *Regesten* 2–11; summarized by Sirks, *Study*, 118–20.

24. See Sirks, *Study*, 120–30 for refutation of Seeck.

25. Ibid., 152.

26. Ibid., 131–32.

27. Ibid., 132 with n. 332.

28. Mommsen, *Proleg.*, ccliv.

29. Sirks, *Study*, 157, speculates that western copybooks will have been transported from Rome or Ravenna to Constantinople, but this is highly unlikely. The western court will surely have needed its own archives in the meanwhile. Will copies really have been made to send to Constantinople, as Sirks suggests?

With respect to Constantine, it is very likely that the Theodosian compilers made use of intermediate collections. The first laws of Constantine to record their place of publication come precisely from the capitals of Italy and Africa.[30] Carthage and Rome together account for two-thirds of such constitutions before 324, and Rome alone accounts for half. From 325, Rome and Carthage each represent almost half of such constitutions. Constantinople claims about one-sixth for the period 325–337, or a full third after 331. Carthage meanwhile represents about two-fifths of such constitutions from the same period. The number of constitutions that ultimately derive from publication in the western capitals must be even larger: of 336 individual Constantinian constitutions in the Codex Theodosianus, 125 or 37 percent record a *proposita, accepta, lecta,* etc., but only 89 of this total record the place associated with these marks.

It is striking that the constitutions of Constantine comprise circa 40 percent of all constitutions in the Codex Theodosianus that bear publication marks in their *subscriptiones* (a total of 318). Not only do a significant number of the constitutions of Constantine derive from copies originally taken down far from Constantinople, but the numerous records of *proposita, accepta, lecta* and other publication notices in them, which cannot derive from central archival copies, very strongly suggest that the Theodosian commissioners acquired most of these laws at second hand.

Two formal peculiarities of the constitutions of Constantine also suggest that the Theodosian compilers drew upon an intermediate collection or collections. First, most addressees of imperial constitutions whose office is not recorded fall under the reign of Constantine.[31] Copies recovered from the imperial archives should have contained this information. Second, many constitutions issued under Constantine give both the *nomen* and *cognomen* of the addressees, whereas most constitutions in the Codex Theodosianus record only the *nomen.* The magistrates so addressed are active primarily in Rome, Italy, and Africa. Only a handful of further examples can be found after the reign of Constantine. Sirks rightly dismisses this

30. E.g., Rome: CTh. 10.10.2 (Dec. 312; *Corcoran, ET*^{2}, 188); 10.10.1 and 13.10.1 (Jan. 313); Carthage: CTh. 1.12.1, 1.12.3, 8.10.1, 10.15.1, 11.1.2, 11.7.1 (*dat.* Nov. 313, *acc.* Mar. 314). On these constitutions, which all belong to the same law, see Seeck, *Regesten,* 78–79; Barnes, *NE,* 170. Corcoran, *ET*^{2}, 304, prefers the date 314/315 with R. Delmaire, "Étude sur les souscriptions de quelques lois du Code Théodosien: les lois reçues à Regium," in Christol et al., *Institutions,* 319–20. On the western provenance of Constantinian constitutions, Gaudemet, "Constitutions constantiniennes," 144–54; Gaudemet, "Constitutions constantiniennes destinées à l'Afrique," in Christol et al., *Institutions,* 329–34.

31. Mommsen, "Das theodosische Gesetzbuch," 396 (= *Juristische Schriften,* vol. 2, 179).

naming convention as evidence that the compilers collected the letters of the addressees from provincial archives, but the suggestion that the discrepancy reflects a change of procedure in entering the constitutions into the imperial copybooks fails to explain the erratic occurrence of *cognomina* in constitutions both of Constantine and of later emperors.[32] It would be absurd to assume that the editors of the Codex Theodosianus took pains to include the *cognomen* of primarily Constantinian officials; rather, they must have found this convention of nomenclature in an intermediate source, from which they largely copied the constitutions affected.[33]

It should excite little surprise that only an imperfect record of the constitutions of Constantine was available to the compilers of the Codex Theodosianus in the imperial archives of Constantinople. A full century had elapsed between the death of Constantine and the completion of the Codex Theodosianus. It is likely that many constitutions had fallen victim to neglect and to the disruption of the imperial court by the time that Theodosius II ordered them to be collected. We do not know whether or how the constitutions of Constantine had been archived even in his own day. If they were, it remains doubtful whether such an archive might have survived the movements of the imperial court and the succession of new emperors. The resources of the archives of Constantinople, whatever their state in the fifth century, were incomplete and unsatisfactory for the reign of Constantine, and one or more extant collections, probably of Italian or African origin, filled this gap.

The constitutions recovered by the commissioners of Theodosius were further reduced by a process of selection and editing. The editing of the constitutions consisted generally in the removal of the prefaces, epilogues, and formalia inessential to their legal content.[34] The criteria of selection were stricter: these determined which of Constantine's constitutions extant in the fifth century would survive to the next and beyond.

The criteria of selection in the Codex Theodosianus bring us to the second question posed above: were obsolete laws also included in the Codex Theodosianus? The prevailing view, from Seeck to Matthews, had been that the compilers of the Codex Theodosianus included every constitution they recovered that satisfied the broader requirements established by the emperor (on which, see below).[35] Sirks has contested this view in several pub-

32. Sirks, *Study*, 122.

33. Matthews, *Laying Down the Law*, 219–21, with a list of the examples on p. 220.

34. Cf. the case study ibid., 121–67; Matthews summarizes material generally omitted, 160–64.

35. Ibid., 64–65.

lications and contends that the compilers of the Codex Theodosianus excluded legislation that was no longer in force.[36] Sirks bases his argument largely on the instructions given to the compilers. The project as planned in 429 foresaw the completion of a collection of all general laws, both valid and obsolete, from the time of Constantine. It is explicitly stated that this preliminary effort should include obsolete laws.[37] This collection was to serve as part of the sources for the *codex magisterium vitae,* from which then all ambiguity and contradiction, and all defunct law, should be removed. Sirks argues that the Codex Theodosianus is the collection of imperial constitutions planned in 429 and revived in 435, but the compilers will have excised all discrepancies and all obsolete laws, as planned originally for the final *codex magisterium vitae.*[38] Sirks supports his view by interpretation of the phrase *vis sanctionis,* which appears in the renewal of the codification project in 435. The full sentence is as follows: *circumcisis ex quaque constitutione ad vim sanctionis non pertinentibus solum ius relinquatur.*[39] This appears to restate the editing principles described in the constitution of 429, and indeed there too Theodosius speaks of removing matters that are not *rei sanciendae adiuncta.*[40] Sirks does not dispute the meaning of the phrase in CTh. 1.1.5, but asks what *vis sanctionis* in CTh. 1.1.6 should mean. According to Sirks, "*Vis* means 'force, power' and may refer to the obligatoriness of a rule or legal act." He cites CTh. 10.8.1: . . . *integro statu . . . hoc verbo ea vis continebitur, quam antea scribebamus.* The word *vis* here however means neither "force" as Sirks defines it nor "force" as in the validity of a law; it means "meaning" or "significance,"[41] specifically what Constantine means by *integro statu*: "In this phrase shall be contained the (same) meaning of which We wrote previously." Sirks further cites NT 1.5,

36. Most recently, Sirks, *Study,* 158–67; cf. Sirks, "Observations sur le Code Théodosien," *SGron* 2 (1985), 21; "From the Theodosian to the Justinian Code," *AARC* 6 (1986), 265; "The Sources of the Code," in Harries and Wood, *The Theodosian Code,* 57; contra Matthews, *Laying Down the Law,* 65; B. Albanese, "Sul programma legislativo esposto nel 429 da Teodosio II," *APal* 38 (1985), 251–69 (= *Estudios de derecho romano en honore de Alvaro D'Ors,* vol. 1 [Pamplona, 1987], 123–40).

37. CTh. 1.1.5 = Gesta Senatus 4: *scholasticae intentioni tribuitur nosse etiam illa, quae mandata silentio in desuetudinem abierunt.*

38. Sirks, *Study,* 159–60.

39. CTh. 1.1.6 pr. "With everything that does not pertain to the *vis sanctionis* removed from each constitution, only (substantive) law shall remain."

40. Matthews, *Laying Down the Law,* 65; CTh. 1.1.5: *post haec, ut constitutionum ipsa etiam verba, quae ad rem pertinent, reserventur, praetermissis illis, quae sanciendae rei non ex ipsa necessitate adiuncta sunt.*

41. See *OLD* s.v. *vis* 18; Lewis and Short, s.v. *vis* IIB; cf. also *LSJ* s.v. δύναμις III for the Greek equivalent.

in which it is stated that a constitution from the Western Empire cannot have *vis legis* unless it is confirmed in the East. This phrase means "the force of a law," that is, binding, legal force, but *vis* here has nothing to do with the abstract validity of the law, the quality we describe as "being in force," but rather with its efficacy.[42] Sirks has confused modern and ancient idiom and made an English expression ("in force") into a Latin one. The *vis* in *vis sanctionis* is not the validity of a constitution but its force insofar as what it does. Properly speaking, a constitution does not have "force of law" but "the force" or "effect of a law."

The force of a law in this sense derives not from its abstract validity, whether it is in force or not, but from its content. Several similar uses of *vis* paired with a genitive illustrate this meaning. The emperors often command that no one violate the *vis* of a law. The validity of a law cannot be violated; its purport can.[43] *Vis* expresses in one word what a given law does, what it effects, and the efficacy of a law consists in its substantive parts. Hence, Valentinian and Valens command Seneca, *vim illius legis aspicito eique pareto,* "you shall observe the *vis* of that law and obey it" (CTh. 8.15.4). Seneca might observe whether a law is in force or not, but he clearly cannot obey anything other than the tenor of that law. This use of *vis* is closely related to another, whereby something exercises the *vis* of something else, accomplishing the same thing. For instance, the last wishes of Manichaeans do not have *vis testamentorum,* "the force of a (legal) will," according to CTh. 16.5.18.1.

Sirks's claim that his reading of *vis sanctionis* is more natural (particularly, more natural than Matthews's) is not justified. We might have been spared such extensive discussion of this phrase, however, had it not been put to debate torn from its context. As noted above, the full sentence in CTh. 1.1.6 reads, *circumcisis ex quaque constitutione ad vim sanctionis non pertinentibus solum ius relinquatur.* We read that the compilers are to remove what does not pertain to *vis sanctionis* (whatever the phrase means) from each constitution (*ex quaque constitutione*); the conclusion that all obsolete constitutions have been removed from the Codex Theodosianus simply does not follow. That something has been removed from individual constitutions does not mean that whole constitutions have been removed

42. See *OLD* s.v. *vis* 13a.

43. E.g., CTh.8.11.3: *ceterum si quis iudicum vim decretorum nostrorum violaverit;* CTh. 8.5.46: *etiamsi post contra vim legis aliquam indepti sint dignitatem.*

from the Codex Theodosianus. There are no grounds for the argument that the compilers of the Codex Theodosianus were instructed in 435 to exclude obsolete constitutions.

An analysis of the entire Codex Theodosianus for obsolete and contradicting legislation would, as Sirks observes,[44] settle the question once and for all, although it was apparent enough to the editors of the text.[45] Even recently, the presence of contradictions and obsolete legislation has been confirmed. Book 16 in particular contains several obsolete constitutions.[46] This redundancy has been attributed to the subject matter, church strife and Arianism,[47] but if one accepts that the compilers received no instructions to omit obsolete legislation, these findings are unremarkable. Sirks himself argues that "there were no superfluous rules present" in the titles concerning the corpora charged with the food supply of Rome and Constantinople.[48] This may be, but the present work shall proceed on the premise that all extant laws were included by the compilers of the Codex Theodosianus, provided that they satisfied the general conditions for inclusion. We now turn to these.

The compilers of the Codex Theodosianus received instructions to collect, not all imperial constitutions, but all *leges generales*. In the constitution of 429 in which Theodosius initiated the project, *leges generales* or "general laws" are described as "all constitutions resting on the strength of edicts or imperial generality."[49] In the revision of the project of 435, the emperor elaborates, calling general laws "all edictal and general constitutions or those ordered [*sic*] to be published in certain provinces or places."[50] We shall discuss what these constitutions were below, turning first to constitutions not included in the Codex.

The number of constitutions the compilers could include was limited from the beginning of the project. In no circumstances did the commis-

44. Sirks, *Study*, 166–67.

45. Mommsen, *Proleg.*, xxix; P. Krüger, *Geschichte der Quellen und der Literatur des römischen Rechts*, 2nd ed. (Munich, 1912), 326 with n. 10.

46. T. Honoré, *Law in the Crisis of Empire, 379–455 A.D.: The Theodosian Dynasty and Its Quaestors* (Oxford, 1998), 142–49.

47. In which Sirks, *Study*, 116 and 166, concurs with Honoré.

48. Ibid., 116, referring to his work *Food for Rome: The Legal Structure of the Transportation and Processing of Supplies for the Imperial Distributions in Rome and Constantinople* (Amsterdam, 1991).

49. CTh. 1.1.5: *cunctas . . . constitutiones . . . edictorum viribus aut sacra generalitate subnixas.*

50. CTh. 1.1.6 pr: *omnes edictales generalesque constitutiones vel in certis provinciis seu locis valere aut proponi iussae.*

sioners admit imperial constitutions *ad privatos*.[51] The Codex Theodosianus pretended to the status of general law; by omitting constitutions affecting individuals, the commissioners of Theodosius tacitly observed the separation of such constitutions from public legislation, as enshrined in the Twelve Tables (*privilegia ne irroganto*). Imperial constitutions that conferred individual privileges were excluded; with them—much more significantly for the legal history of the Later Roman Empire—private rescripts. The latter were responses given in the name of the emperor or emperors in response to the requests for legal advice submitted by private citizens. Private rescripts seldom created new law, but rather clarified existing law as it pertained to the case described by the petitioners. Rescripts were decisive so long as the information presented in the petition was found to be consistent with the facts by the judge.[52] Under Diocletian private rescripts appear to have become so significant a source of law that they were systematically collected and still survive in great numbers.[53] By the time of Theodosius, however, it had become clear that the imperial government could not check the issue of private rescripts that flouted the law or prevent their use as precedents in unrelated cases. Strict limitations came to be imposed, and in 398 Arcadius outlawed altogether the use of rescripts in cases for which they had not been issued.[54]

Military and financial records and other miscellaneous documents kept in official archives were also omitted from the Codex Theodosianus. Unlike imperial constitutions, these documents remained in force and could still be cited in court.[55] Unlike private rescripts, the content of such documents will have had little to do with imperial law.

The Codex Theodosianus was to consist of "general laws." General laws (*leges generales*) could be of many formal types, which it is useful to review. The term itself might be translated as "[laws] of general application" or "en-

---

51. Mommsen, *Proleg.*, xxix: "Sed hoc religiose videntur observasse, ut excluderent constitutiones omnes emissas ad homines privatos"; Mommsen, *Proleg.*, cliii: "Constitutiones imperatorum, quae quidem legis vicem obtineant, excludunt emissas ad privatos." Cf. Krüger, *Quellen*², 326; Matthews, *Laying Down the Law*, 66.

52. Kaser-Hackl, §67.III, pp. 450–51: "Legt eine Partei dem Richter das von ihr erwirkte Reskript mit dem Gutachten des Kaisers vor, dann sieht man den Richter als an die darin enthaltene Rechtsansicht gebunden an, sofern der zu entscheidende Fall mit dem im Reskript begutachteten übereinstimmt."

53. See below, chapter 2, p. 58.

54. CTh. 1.2.11.

55. NT 1.6: *exceptis his, quae habentur apud militum sancta principia vel de titulis publicis expensarum aliarumque rerum quae in regestis diversorum officiorum relata sunt.*

tactments . . . *to be obeyed in all relevant circumstances.*"[56] Foremost among *leges generales,* and most easily identifiable, were edicts and letters to the Senate. Valentinian III had established their status as general, their *generalitas,* and the Theodosian commissioners will have observed this definition insofar as it was not superseded by the constitutions of Theodosius himself.[57] Theodosius does not mention letters to the Senate in CTh. 1.1.5–6; they were unambiguously *generalis.*

Most imperial constitutions, however, were letters to imperial officials, the *generalitas* of which it was left to the Theodosian compilers to determine.[58] In assessing *generalitas,* the compilers initially followed a law of Valentinian III (CJ 1.14.2–3), issued in 426. This constitution had been included in the Codex Theodosianus but was omitted from the Visigothic *Breviarium.*[59] It is for this reason we are constrained to use the excerpts of it preserved in the Codex Justinianus. In light of the certain inclusion of Valentinian's law in the Codex Theodosianus, it is natural to assume it will have influenced the designation of general constitutions at least as conceived in the initial plans of 429.[60]

Valentinian denied *generalitas* to constitutions sent in response to the *relationes* or *suggestiones* of governors and to all privileges granted by imperial constitution to specific corpora, legates, provinces, cities, or town councils.[61] The exclusion of constitutions that conferred specific privileges is not

---

56. Matthews, *Laying Down the Law,* 65 and 70. The italics are his.

57. CJ 1.14.3: *Leges ut generales ab omnibus aequabiliter in posterum observentur, quae vel missa ad venerabilem coetum oratione conduntur vel inserto edicti vocabulo nuncupantur.*

58. As Mommsen, *Proleg.,* xxix, elegantly puts it, "omnino ex rescriptis ad magistratus datis quaenam essent generalia, necessario pendebat a compositorum arbitrio."

59. On the *Breviarium:* Matthews, *Laying Down the Law,* 85–120; J. Gaudemet, *Le Bréviaire d'Alaric et les Épitomés* (Milan, 1965).

60. G. G. Archi, "Nuove prospettive nello studio del Codice Teodosiano," in *Istituzioni giuridiche e realtà politiche nel tardo impero (III–V sec. d.C.). Atti di un incontro tra storici e giuristi, Firenze, 2–4 maggio 1974,* ed. G. G. Archi (Milan, 1976), 285–302; Archi, *Teodosio II e la sua codificazione* (Naples, 1976), 27–31; Matthews, *Laying Down the Law,* 65–67.

61. CJ 1.14.2: *Quae ex relationibus vel suggestionibus iudicantium per consultationem in commune florentissimorum sacri nostri palatii procerum auditorium introducto negotio statuimus vel quibuslibet corporibus aut legatis aut provinciae vel civitati vel curiae donavimus, nec generalia iura sint, sed leges fiant his dumtaxat negotiis atque personis, pro quibus fuerint promulgata, nec ab aliquo retractentur.* Valentinian reiterates the point in CJ 1.14.3: *interlocutionibus, quas in uno negotio iudicantes protulimus vel postea proferemus, non in commune praeiudicantibus, nec his, quae specialiter quibusdam concessa sunt civitatibus vel provinciis vel corporibus, ad generalitatis observantiam pertinentibus.* The expression *in commune* appears in both constitutions, but in CJ 1.14.2 it refers only to a discussion in the consistory among the members; in CJ 1.14.3 *in commune* is used to indicate general legislation. The sentences are not contradictory.

surprising. This accords well with Arcadius's restriction on the use of rescripts. The exclusion of letters to magistrates, however, is contradicted by the Codex Theodosianus itself, in which an overwhelming majority of constitutions consists precisely of responses to the *relationes, suggestiones,* and *consultationes* of imperial administrators.[62]

To learn why these constitutions came to be included, the modifications of the criteria of *generalitas* introduced by Theodosius must be studied. Valentinian had acknowledged as *leges generales* both imperial constitutions explicitly labeled edicts and constitutions published throughout the empire in the edicts of governors; additionally, any constitution that referred to itself as *generalis* was regarded as equivalent to an edict.[63] Theodosius's order to collect *leges edictales generalesque* takes the first and third of these criteria of Valentinian as given. Valentinian had stipulated straightforward internal, textual criteria: if a constitution contained the words *edictum* or *generalis,* the Theodosian commission could confidently include it in the Codex Theodosianus. It was perhaps anticipated that these rules would have simplified the collecting of constitutions for the final codex. Failing those words, however, according to the second criterion of Valentinian, the commissioners would have required evidence of the publication of a given constitution throughout the empire (*per omnes populos divulgari*). This last point must have caused considerable difficulty. In essence, the compilers would have needed an explicit reference to publication throughout the empire, such as the formulaic publication orders found in the post-Theodosian Novels. Many early constitutions, however, survived in fragmentary form and recorded only that they were published in a specific place, if they recorded where or when they had been published at all. This was especially common of the Constantinian legislation, which yet figured so prominently in the conception of the codification project.

The Theodosian commission may have been able to infer (much as modern scholars do) whether such a constitution had been promulgated generally from references to *omnes* or *universi provinciales* or *omnes iu-*

62. Sirks, *Study,* 86, puts this figure at ca. 94 percent.

63. CJ 1.14.3: (pr.) *Nam satis est edicti eas* [sc. *leges*] *nuncupatione censeri vel per omnes populos iudicum programmate divulgari . . .* (1.) *Sed et si generalis lex vocata est vel ad omnes iussa est pertinere, vim obtineat edicti.* Valentinian adds one further criterion, which I translate because of its torturous grammar (even by late antique standards): *satis est . . . vel expressius* [sc. *in eis constitutionibus*] *contineri, quod principes censuerunt ea, quae in certis negotiis statuta sunt, similium quoque causarum fata componere.* "It is sufficient (i.e., for constitutions to be considered "general") . . . that it is quite manifestly contained (in those constitutions) that the emperors deem that what has been established in those specific issues also decides the fate of similar cases."

dices, rectores, etc., in the inscriptions of the laws, but such references appear inconsistently. If a law contained neither the words *edictum* or *generalis* nor explicit reference to general publication, the commissioners would have been compelled to omit it from the Codex. The criteria of Valentinian, rigorously applied, would have led to the exclusion of numerous general constitutions and potentially even edicts that had reached the compilers only in intermediary collections derived from the copies of local magistrates. This appears to have been the dilemma that Theodosius addressed in the revision of the codification project of 435. Theodosius permitted the compilers to include, alongside the acknowledged forms of *leges generales,* also *constitutiones in certis provinciis seu locis valere aut proponi iussae.*[64]

Why Constantine?

The compilers of the Codex Theodosianus were ordered to collect all constitutions from the time of Constantine to their own day. Since Constantine was the first Christian emperor, and Theodosius II a man of notable religious conviction, many scholars have imputed Theodosius's design to religious motivations: Theodosius will have intended the Codex Theodosianus as a Christian code of law for a Christian empire.[65]

Closer scrutiny reveals secular considerations. First, it is not unreasonable to wonder whether Theodosius saw any need to collect the legislation of emperors before Constantine. The declared models of the Codex Theodosianus, the Codex Gregorianus and the Codex Hermogenianus, had been created under Diocletian, but subsequent editions of these works incorporated legislation of the second tetrarchy, including that of Constantine. The Codex Gregorianus contained private rescripts from the emperor Hadrian to the year 291; a small number of constitutions from the years 295 and 302 were later added.[66] The Hermogenianus contained rescripts of Diocletian

64. Archi, "Nuove prospettive," 308–13; Archi, *Teodosio II,* 32–37; Matthews, *Laying Down the Law,* 70; Sirks, *Study,* 191–92 and 198–200 on the revision of 435.

65. W. Turpin, "The Law Codes and Late Roman Law," *RIDA*[3] 32 (1985), 339–53, who cites (344 n. 11) Gibbon (ed. Bury, vol. 4, 453): "The third [sc. code], which is still extant, was digested in sixteen books by the order of the younger Theodosius, to consecrate the laws of the Christian princes from Constantine to his own reign." Cf. Sirks, *Study,* 47–49.

66. On the latest constitution attributed to the Codex Gregorianus (Coll. 15.3), see D. Liebs, *Die Jurisprudenz im spätantiken Italien, 260–620 n. Chr.* (Berlin 1987), 37 n. 9; on the Codex Gregorianus, pp. 134–37; Krüger, *Quellen*[2], 317; Liebs, "Recht und Rechtsliteratur," 60–61 (where Liebs appears to support the date 297 for Coll. 15.3).

from the years 293 and 294, but its author appears to have reedited the collection at least twice before the fall of Licinius, adding texts both from the second tetrarchy and from the early reign of Constantine.[67] For instance, constitutions found in the Codex Justinianus with the inscription *Impp. Constantinus et Licinius AA.* must come from the Codex Hermogenianus. Theodosius's compilers erased the name of Licinius in the inscriptions of all laws passed during his and Constantine's joint rule.[68] It is hardly surprising that Theodosius had little incentive to collect further specimens of the legislation of the successors to Diocletian and Maximian, wedged as they were between two giants, while the legislation of Constantine had only begun to be collected.

Finally, it must be remembered that Theodosius's original ambition was not to produce the Codex Theodosianus that has survived but a grand code that would have contained the works of the pagan jurists and the constitutions of pagan and Christian emperors alike. The intended sources of the project were the Codex Gregorianus, the Codex Hermogenianus, Theodosius's own codification of imperial constitutions from Constantine on, and the writings of the (pagan) jurists.[69] Had the ambitious plan succeeded, the collection we call the Codex Theodosianus might well have been known merely as the Codex Antiochius,[70] for it was the final, grand code, the *codex magisterium vitae,* that was intended to bear the emperor's name. The latter project was never realized, but when one considers its scope, it is absurd to assert that Theodosius intended to exclude the pagan emperors by beginning with the legislation of Constantine. Besides the works of pagan jurists, a very substantial part of this codex would have consisted of the constitutions of pagan emperors and even the rescripts of the great persecutor himself, Diocletian. Christian piety certainly did not prevent Theodosius from including the legislation of Julian the Apostate (apostasy being a much graver sin than mere paganism).[71] That the Codex Theodosianus began

67. Contra, Turpin, "Law Codes," 343: "The later years of the First Tetrarchy, and the confused decade which followed, are almost entirely ignored by the legal collections."

68. Krüger, *Quellen*², 320; cf. Mommsen, *Proleg.*, clx. On the legislation of Licinius, see Corcoran, *ET*², 274–92; S. Corcoran, "Hidden from History: The Legislation of Licinius," in Harries and Wood, *The Theodosian Code,* 97–119. Licinius was left standing in consular dates, usually stripped of his abbreviated imperial title *A.* (i.e., *Augustus*). On the editions of the Codex Hermogenianus: Liebs, *Jurisprudenz im spätantiken Italien,* 141.

69. CTh. 1.1.5, lines 14–17: *ex his autem tribus codicibus, et per singulos titulos cohaerentibus prudentium tractatibus et responsis . . . noster erit alius . . . nostro nomine nuncupatus.*

70. Matthews, *Laying Down the Law,* 72, 75–76, and 81–82, on Antiochus Chuzon, "the guiding genius of the project."

71. Cf. the constitutions in the title dedicated to apostates: CTh. 16.7.

with the legislation of the first Christian emperor may indeed have flattered Theodosius's sentimentality, but the state of the tradition made the choice obvious and practical.[72]

Laws before 312

The constitutions of Constantine preserved in the Codex Theodosianus all were enacted after Constantine's victory over Maxentius at the Milvian Bridge, 28 October 312, and thus also after Constantine's conversion to Christianity. The earliest constitutions attributed to Constantine, according to their received dates, were issued at the end of 312 or in early 313. CTh. 11.29.1 is recorded to have been issued on 27 December 312 and posted in Rome on 6 February 313.[73] CTh. 10.10.1 and 13.10.1, both excerpts from the same edict, were posted in Rome on 18 January 313; the date of issue is not recorded. The emendations of modern scholars have produced yet earlier dates. CTh. 13.10.2 (recorded date: 1 June 313) was long identified as the earliest constitution in the Codex Theodosianus. It was in fact issued by Maximinus Daia, 1 June 312.[74] The oldest constitution in the Codex Theodosianus securely attributed to Constantine is CTh. 10.10.2, supposedly issued and posted in Rome in the Forum of Trajan on the same day;[75] its date has been emended to 1 December 312.[76] The earliest known constitution of Constantine in any source is FV 32 (29 August 312), a private rescript; it is the only Constantinian constitution that antedates the Battle of the Milvian Bridge.[77]

Many regard the victory of Constantine over Maxentius as the date at which the Theodosian compilers began their collection of *cunctae constitutiones.* The date is convenient: it not only coincides with the conquest of Italy and the elevation of Constantine to senior Augustus but also must fall after his conversion to Christianity. Christian writers spoke of the vision of

72. Mommsen, *Proleg.*, xxix, too notes that the Codex Gregorianus and Hermogenianus and the Codex Theodosianus were "non recte continua," i.e., Theodosius did not choose Constantine because his laws began where the extant collections ended. Mommsen, however, resorts to tenuous constitutional argument to justify Theodosius's decision to begin with Constantine. On the contrary, the materials available to Theodosius were *continua* enough.

73. Modern scholars have emended these dates to 314 and 315, respectively. See Corcoran, ET^2, 305.

74. Corcoran, ET^2, 151.

75. Impossibly, according to Mommsen, *Proleg.*, clv. The *subscriptio* must be corrupt, one date having dropped out.

76. Corcoran, ET^2, 188–89.

77. Corcoran, ET^2, 272 and 301.

Constantine as if it had occurred immediately before the Battle of the Milvian Bridge, not earlier,[78] and one might think such a date would have appealed to the religious preoccupations of Theodosius. On the face of it, the commissioners of Theodosius appear to have collected all constitutions after the victory of Constantine, his conversion, or both.

The instructions of Theodosius reproduced in the first title of the Codex Theodosianus (CTh. 1.1.5–6), however, mention neither the defeat of Maxentius nor the conversion of Constantine. In the programs of both 429 and 435, Theodosius orders his commissioners to collect all constitutions (429: *cunctas;* 435: *omnes*) that satisfy the criteria of *generalitas.* Theodosius stipulates no event or date at which the compilers of the Codex Theodosianus should begin. The commission could not have made so significant an editorial decision as to begin after the victory at the Milvian Bridge without the consent of the emperor. The supplementary instructions of 435 show how cautiously the commissioners approached their editorial tasks.[79] If Theodosius gave no explicit instructions from what date to collect Constantine's constitutions, other reasons for the late onset of the record of Constantine's legislation should be considered, before an unwritten understanding between Theodosius and his commissioners is assumed.

Perhaps the simplest explanation why the commissioners reproduce no constitutions prior to 312 is that they found none, yet it is incredible that Constantine could have issued no constitutions until 312. Constantine possessed legislative authority, or at the very least the means to legislate, from the time he was first proclaimed emperor at in 306.[80] The *comitatus* of Constantius was at his disposal; with it, the entire apparatus necessary for the production of laws. What was lacking at York could be got at Trier, Constantius's former residence, which Constantine entered soon thereafter.[81] With the important exceptions of Italy and Africa, Constantine ruled unchallenged in the West. After the official Augustus of the West, Severus, was captured and killed in 307, Constantine received the title of Augustus from Maximian, who had emerged from retirement. Galerius meanwhile contin-

78. Lact., *DMP* 44.5–6; Eus., *VC* 1.28–29. The anonymous panegyrist of 310 (*Pan. Lat.* VI 21.4) speaks of a vision of Apollo accompanied by Victory.

79. Matthews, *Laying Down the Law,* 64.

80. The opinion that Constantine titled himself as Augustus from 306 seems mistaken. Although Lactantius, *DMP* 24.8.–25.1 suggests that *Constantinus Augustus* sent his *laureata imago* to Galerius, the title *Augustus* appears on no contemporary inscription or coin: J. Wienand, "Der Kaiser als Sieger. Untersuchungen zur militärischen Repräsentation Constantins I.," PhD diss., Konstanz, 2010, 73–74.

81. Barnes, *NE,* 68.

ued to regard Constantine as Caesar and elevated Licinius to Augustus ahead of him in 308. Constantine was grudgingly recognized as Augustus in the East only in 310, after Maximinus Daia usurped the title.[82] The balance for these years is nonetheless bleak: no constitutions survive from the entire period between the elevation of Constantine on 25 July 306, and the invasion of Italy in 312, before or after Constantine was acknowledged as Augustus in the rest of the empire.[83]

When Constantine entered Rome after the defeat of Maxentius, the Senate conferred on him the title of Maximus Augustus. Constantine thereby became the highest-ranking Augustus of the empire—an affront to Maximinus Daia, who had become Caesar legitimately in 305 and Augustus in 310, and Licinius.[84] Otto Seeck saw in the conferral of the rank of senior Augustus the constitutional foundation on the strength of which Constantine at last dared to issue laws. According to Seeck, until the Senate recognized Constantine as Maximus Augustus in 312, he issued only private rescripts; public legislation under the tetrarchic system was the preserve of the senior Augustus, a rule that appears to have functioned under Diocletian.[85] While Constantine was Caesar, he will have remained beholden to Galerius, just as Maximian had once deferred to Diocletian. This deference of Constantine would account for the six years of delay before the record of his legislation begins. Licinius, in contrast, did not hold himself to this tetrarchic rule. Unlike Constantine, who required Galerius's support until Maxentius was eliminated, Licinius had no need to recognize the superiority of Constantine by granting him an exclusive right to legislate.[86]

Seeck's hypothesis, however, rests upon a number of assumptions that undermine its credibility, most notably that one can still speak of a tetrarchic system at all after 310, when Galerius, Maximinus Daia, Licinius, and Constantine all were *Augusti,* while Maxentius claimed the same title without, Maximian with, interruption. The confusion after 310 moreover af-

---

82. See Barnes, *CE,* 28–33; T. Grünewald, *Constantinus Maximus Augustus: Herrschaftspropaganda in der zeitgenössischen Überlieferung* (Stuttgart, 1990), 57 with n. 277.

83. For the history of the years 306–12, see Grünewald, *Herrschaftspropaganda,* 13–61; summarized, p. 173–74.

84. On the politics, see Wienand, "Der Kaiser als Sieger," 156–61.

85. Corcoran, *ET*², 266–74. There are no certain examples of edicts or letters from the coemperors of Diocletian. Only after his abdication do they appear, in the much more volatile second tetrarchy.

86. O. Seeck, "Die Zeitfolge der Gesetze Constantins," *ZRG* 10 (1889), 47–48; J. Gaudemet, "Constantin, restaurateur de l'ordre," in *St. Solazzi* (Naples, 1948), 653.

fects only the latter part of the period from which no laws of Constantine survive. In 307, Constantine regarded, not Galerius, but Maximian as senior Augustus: it was the latter who ceremonially elevated Constantine to Augustus. From the time that Maximian emerged from retirement until the conference of Carnuntum in 308, it would have been to him that Constantine paid respect as senior Augustus, if to anyone.

The conference of Carnuntum temporarily settled the status of the four mutually acknowledged members of the imperial college, Galerius, Licinius, Maximinus Daia, and Constantine. Maximian retired once more;[87] Maxentius was acknowledged by none. Among his peers, Constantine was Caesar; in his own territories, he continued to usurp the title Augustus.[88] If the hypothesis of Seeck holds for any period, it would be for that after the conference of Carnuntum, after Maximian again retired. But the order established in Carnuntum was of short duration. When Maximinus Daia usurped the title Augustus in 310, Constantine's pretensions could no longer be ignored. Now all were *Augusti,* though the seniority of Galerius seems, at least somewhat, to have persisted. It was in the name of all emperors that Galerius decreed toleration for Christianity by edict in 311, just as Diocletian had once enacted the Great Persecution.[89]

A different explanation for the lacuna in Constantine's legislation may be sought in the discrepancy between the territories controlled by Constantine before 312 and those from which the commissioners of Theodosius recovered his constitutions. The year 429, which saw the conception of the Codex Theodosianus, also witnessed the crossing of the Vandals into Africa. Barbarians and usurpers alike had taken a high toll on the Western Empire. Control of Britain had been lost; the German provinces, and with them much of Gaul, stood under barbarian occupation. The erstwhile residence of Constantine, Trier, had been sacked in the invasion begun on the last day 406. The western emperor Honorius eventually reasserted Roman rule over central and southeastern Gaul. Rome retained nominal control over the kingdoms of the Burgundians and Visigoths, but the territories that had witnessed the rise of Constantine—Britain and northern Gaul—had been irretrievably lost. Conflict continued in Spain as the Vandals

---

87. On the activity of Maximian after 308, see C. E. V. Nixon and B. S. Rodgers, *In Praise of Later Emperors: The* Panegyrici Latini (Berkeley, 1994), 213–14.

88. Cf. Barnes, *CE,* 32.

89. Cf. ibid., 39.

moved southward. The imperial government retained a precarious grasp on parts, or it employed federated barbarians to do so in its name, but fighting continued throughout.[90] The losses to the Western Empire engulfed almost the entire territory ruled by Constantine in the years immediately after his elevation. Only victory over Maxentius in 312 brought Italy and Africa under his sway.

Even if one grants that the compilers of the Codex Theodosianus made use of provincial archives to recover older imperial legislation, they would have found it an impossible task to collect constitutions published or preserved in provincial archives in virtually all of the territory Constantine controlled before 312. That the commissioners of Theodosius proceeded in this way, however, is highly unlikely. The hypothesis of Mommsen, that the Theodosian compilers made use of one or more intermediate collections, probably composed by jurists in Carthage and Rome, must be correct, particularly for the reign of Constantine before 324.[91] The ultimate source of most constitutions in the Codex Theodosianus may have been official archives, but contemporary jurists, not the compilers of Theodosius, will have first collected much of the legislation of Constantine for their own purposes.[92] That such collections appear to derive from the capitals of Italy and Africa, which were controlled by Maxentius until 312, suggests a plausible solution to the mystery of the missing constitutions of the years 306–312. Whatever legislation Constantine may have passed prior to 312 was either not received or not recognized in the territory of Maxentius. Even if it had been, it would have been annulled at the commencement of hostilities or observed in the name of Maxentius.[93] Constantine would have had to reintroduce and authorize any such legislation once he seized Rome, and only after Constantine had gained control over Rome and Carthage

90. For an overview, *CAH* XIII^2, 118–33; A. Demandt, *Die Spätantike. Römische Geschichte von Diocletian bis Justinian, 284–565 n. Chr.*, 2nd ed (Munich, 2007), 175–91; J. Matthews, *Western Aristocracies and Imperial Court A.D. 364–425* (Oxford, 1975), 307–22. See P Heather, *The Fall of the Roman Empire* (London, 2005), 191–250, 262–72, 288–91; idem, *Empires and Barbarians: Migration, Development and the Birth of Europe* (London, 2009), 151–206, esp. 173ff. Cf. E. A. Thompson, *Romans and Barbarians: The Decline of the Western Empire* (Madison, 1982), 15–19.

91. Mommsen, "Das theodosische Gesetzbuch," 169–72/388–91 (= *Juristische Schriften*, vol. 2, 169–72); Matthews, *Laying Down the Law*, 280–89. Contra: Sirks, "Sources of the Code"; Sirks, *Study*, 45–67.

92. On provincial archives, see R. Haensch, "Das Statthalterarchiv," *ZRG* 109 (1992), 209–317, esp. 228–30, 231 n. 58, 233 n. 62.

93. *Pan. Lat.* IV 12 describes the *abolitio memoriae* of Constantine in Rome under Maxentius: *venerandarum imaginum acerba deiectio et divini vultus litura deformis.*

could his laws be published there regularly and recorded by local jurists. If we accept that the compilers of the Codex Theodosianus resorted to intermediary copies of Constantinian legislation made in Rome and Carthage, the omission of all legislation before 312 becomes intelligible. Theodosius II ordered his commissioners to collect all the extant laws of Constantine, but the record of them, they found, began only after 312.

2

Formal Characteristics of the Legislation of Constantine

The Constitutions of Constantine

The extant legislation of Constantine attests all of the forms that late antique legislation might take, including edicts, official letters, "orations" to the Senate, as well as private rescripts; but beyond offering excellent specimens for general acquaintance with the sources of law, the constitutions of Constantine also illustrate the means of their dissemination. Decisions taken at court were transmitted to the administrators and subjects of the empire by a variety of means, and the traces of this process that remain in the extant legislation add to our understanding of its breadth. What survives in the Codex Theodosianus as a copy addressed to one administrator often proves to be part of a chain of correspondence to a much larger circle of persons, and this is true both of edicts and official correspondence. Close analysis of Constantinian edicts further shows that Constantine blurred the traditional distinction between edicts and imperial letters. Constantine dispenses with the impersonal manner of traditional Roman edicts and adopts the direct tone of correspondence, addressing his subjects in his own person. This short-lived epistolary form seems to have been one way in which Constantine advertised his popularizing sympathy for his subjects.

Edicts in the Codex Theodosianus

The power to issue edicts, the *ius edicendi,* was the ancient prerogative of Roman magistrates, appropriated by Augustus in his *maius imperium* and exercised by all emperors after him. Both formal and stylistic characteristics distinguish an edict from other constitutions. The most obvious formal characteristic is the heading or *inscriptio* of an edict: the name of the issuing emperor and his titles are given; these are followed by the word *dicit*; in Greek or Greek translation, by λέγει. An edict was by nature addressed to the public. As the competence of the emperor was universal, the audience of his edicts might, in principle, comprise the whole empire. No addressee is mentioned in the formal heading of an edict itself. Such information is regularly added, however, in legal collections. There we find such headings as *Imp. Constantinus A. ad populum.* Interested jurists, or the compilers of the legal collection in which an edict appears, supply for the reader the party to whom an edict was originally addressed, be it the inhabitants of a city (*ad populum,* i.e., the people of Rome or Constantinople), or the empire at large (e.g., *ad provinciales, ad universos provinciales*). In some cases, the intended addressee of an edict is indicated in the text of the edict itself. The addressee of an edict would also have been mentioned in any intermediate administrative communication dispatched in the process of transmitting an edict from the emperor to his intended audience, before it was published in the appropriate place. Edicts *ad populum* and *ad universos provinciales* predominate under Constantine and his successors, but edicts to other, smaller groups also survive.[1] As we shall see, however, they are often difficult to distinguish from imperial letters.

Imperial edicts were first published at the residence of the emperor. When this coincided with the location of the addressee, no further action needed to be taken. An edict addressed to the population of a capital (*ad populum*), for instance Rome or Constantinople, could be posted in this way. But often the emperor was far away, and his edicts had to be communicated to their addressees with the help of potentially several imperial officials. The involvement of the administration was indispensable when the intended recipients of an imperial edict were *universi provinciales,* the population of the empire. In such cases, the emperor first communicated his edict to high officials throughout the empire. The text of the edict would be appended to a letter to such an official, who was thereby charged with its publication or further dissemination. Predominantly, though not exclusively (see below), the emperor turned first to the highest civil officials of the empire, the praetorian and urban prefects. These men, in turn, dissem-

1. Listed by Mommsen, *Proleg.,* clxiii–clxv.

inated the imperial edict to the provincial governors in their territory in letters of their own.[2]

Contemporary lawyers and the Theodosian compilers understandably preferred the text of an edict to accompanying letters sent to administrators in the course of publication. With few exceptions we encounter excerpts only of edicts proper in the Codex Theodosianus. Nevertheless some constitutions preserve traces of the epistolary dissemination of edicts, and the legislation of Constantine provides us with excellent examples. One such example is CTh. 1.5.1, a letter to the praetorian prefect. Constantine begins with the statement, "We advise all provincials by edict to call upon Your Gravity, if they have been ignored when calling upon their own governors."[3] Constantine thereby notifies his praetorian prefect of the contents of an edict that has recently been issued to all provincials (note the present tense: *monemus*). A copy of the edict itself, with instructions for its dissemination, must have been attached to the original. An attempt has been made to associate this letter with a contemporary edict preserved in the Codex Theodosianus, but it seems that the edict to which Constantine refers here has not been preserved.[4] This would suggest that the compilers of the Codex Theodosianus resorted to the communiqué of the emperor, because they did not possess a copy of the edict itself.

In another example, Constantine forwards an edict to a provincial governor:[5]

CTh. 7.20.1 (a. 324)

IMP. CONSTANTINVS A. FLORIANO PRAESIDI. Veteranis, qui die V nonarum Iuliarum, cum prima per Thraciam victoria universo orbi inuxit, et qui postea

2. See N. van der Wal, "*Edictum* und *lex generalis.* Form und Inhalt der Kaisergesetze im spätrömischen Reich," *RIDA*[3] 28 (1981), 277–313, especially 277–80 and 282–84; T. Kipp, s.v. "Edictum," *RE* 5.2 (1905), 1940–48, especially 1947–48; Mommsen, *Proleg.*, cliii–cliv. Less useful, J. Gaudemet, *La formation du droit séculier et du droit de l'Église aux IVe et Ve siècles* (Paris, 1957), 30–33. The only monograph dedicated to publication remains F. von Schwind, *Zur Frage der Publikation im römischen Recht* (Munich, 1940).

3. CTh. 1.5.1 (a. 325): *Edicto omnes provinciales monemus, ut, si interpellantes proprios praesides contempti fuerint, gravitatem tuam interpellent . . .*

4. See above, 109–10.

5. Mommsen, *Proleg.*, cxcix–cci, for further constitutions sent to *praesides.* The laws of Constantine concerning veterans are summarized by J. Gaudemet, "Privilèges constantiniennes en faveur des militaires et des vétérans," in *St. Sanfilippo,* vol. 2 (Milan, 1982), 179–90 (= *Droit et Société* [1992], 105–16); cf. D. Liebs, "Privilegien und Ständezwang in den Gesetzen Konstantins," *RIDA*[3] 24 (1977), 304–7.

aput Nicomediam nostram missionem meruerunt, certa per edictum indulsimus, quae scribendi tabulis vel encauto et cerussa conscribere detur eis licentia. Edictum autem continens indulgentiam nostram ad devotionem tuam misimus, ut et tua dicatio et cuncti alii recognoscant, quid praestitimus memoratis. PROPOSITA IIII ID. APRIL. LICINIO V ET CRISPO CAESARE CONSS.

EMPEROR CONSTANTINE AUGUSTUS TO FLORIANUS, GOVERNOR. We have granted by edict certain privileges to the veterans who earned their discharge on the third of July, when the victory in Thrace first shone over the whole world, and to those who earned discharge later at Our city Nicomedia. Let them have the freedom to write these privileges down on tablets or with ink or with white lead. We moreover send Your Devotion the edict containing Our liberality, so that Your Sanctity and all others may observe what We have provided to the aforesaid men. POSTED 10 APR. (318[324]) IN THE CONSULSHIP OF LICINIUS, CONSUL FOR THE FIFTH TIME, AND OF CRISPUS CAESAR.[6]

In few words, the emperor describes the occasion of the edict and its contents. The order that the governor publish the edict is delicately oblique: Constantine claims he has sent the governor the text of the edict so that he and *cuncti alii* may learn of its contents. It was of course the responsibility of the governor to see to it that *cuncti alii* were duly informed.

A third example reveals the emperor communicating with the sons of veterans in Italy through the vicar of Italy, with local administrators as intermediaries:

CTh. 7.22.2 (a. 318)[7]

[IMP. CONSTANTINVS] A. AD SEVERVM [VICARIVM ITALIAE]. Veteranorum filios propter privilegia parentibus eorum indulta vacare non patimur, sed programmate per omnes civitates proposito diligenter quaesitos ad alterutrum conpelli iubemus, ut aut decurionatus muneribus obtemperent aut militarent, observaturo devotionis tuae officio . . . Singularum autem civitatum decurionibus intimetur, ut veteranorum filios . . . si militare noluerint vel minus inveniantur idonei, ad curalia vocare non morentur obsequia . . . DAT. III KAL. AVG. AQVILEIA CONSTANTINO A. VII ET CONSTANTIO CAES. CONSS.

[EMPEROR CONSTANTINE] AUGUSTUS TO SEVERUS [VICAR OF ITALY]. We do not allow the sons of veterans to be idle on account of the privileges granted

6. See Corcoran, *ET*², 197–98, on the date.
7. On the date, see Barnes, *NE*, 144, with Seeck, *Regesten*, 65.

to their parents, but rather We order that they be diligently found out by the posting of an edict in all cities and compelled toward one thing or the other, either to fulfill the liturgies of curial status or to serve in the army. The staff of Your Devotion will ensure that . . . Let it be made known to the decurions of each city that . . . they should not hesitate to summon veterans' sons to curial duties if they refuse to serve in the army or are found to be unsuitable . . . GIVEN 30 JULY (326[318]) AT AQUILEIA IN THE CONSULSHIP OF CONSTANTINE AUGUSTUS, CONSUL FOR THE SEVENTH TIME, AND OF CONSTANTIUS CAESAR.

Constantine instructs the vicar of Italy both to publish the edict and to address letters to town councils on a further matter. As the emperor makes clear, the edict affects the sons of veterans in all Italy (*programmate per omnes civitates proposito*), and letters from the vicar must reach the decurions of every city (*Singularum . . . civitatum decurionibus intimetur*). Various ways how this might happen can be imagined. The vicar Severus might send the emperor's edict, accompanied by a letter of his own, to the councilmen of each city directly. Imperial constitutions to cities are not unknown, if uncommon.[8] More probably, and certainly more efficiently, Severus might promulgate the edict by dispatching it to the *correctores* of Italy, who fulfilled the duties of *praesides* in the provinces into which Italy had been divided.[9] The *correctores* will in turn have forwarded the imperial edict and any instructions of the vicar to the cities within their province. This route is attested by the edict FV 35, the *subscriptio* of which records that the praetorian prefect sent it from Aquileia to the *corrector Piceni* at Alba,[10] and by the fully preserved publication order found in Sirm. 4, addressed to the praetorian prefect Felix:

Sirm. 4 (a. 336)

. . . ac volumus, ut excellens sublimitas tua litteris suis per dioecesim sibi creditam commeantibus iudices moneat instantissime huiuscemodi debitam reverentiam custodiri.

---

8. Listed by Mommsen, *Proleg.*, clxiv. CTh. 16.8.3 (*Decurionibus Agrippiniensibus*) is the only straightforward Constantinian example in the Codex Theodosianus; cf. CTh. 11.16.3 (*ad edictum Calchedoniensium et Macedoniensium*) with Mommsen, *ad loc.* See p. 14 above for the constitutions sent to Orcistus and Hispellum.

9. Jones, *LRE*, 45; cf. 106–7; F. Millar, "Italy and the Roman Empire: Augustus to Constantine," *Phoenix* 40 (1986), 310–18.

10. FV 35.7: D. IIII KAL. SEPT. A PRAEFECTO PRAETORIO AD CORRECTOREM PICENI AQVILEIA. ACC. XIIII KAL. OCT. ALBAE CONSTANTINO AVG. III. CONS.

. . . and We wish that Your Excellent Sublimity should, in letters traversing the diocese entrusted to it, advise the governors most insistently that due reverence in matters of this sort is to be observed.

A letter to Ablabius, probably vicar at the time, furnishes another example:[11]

CTh. 11.27.1 (a. 319)

IMP. CONSTANTINVS A. AD ABLAVIVM. Aereis tabulis vel cerussatis aut linteis mappis scribta per omnes civitates Italiae proponatur lex, quae parentum manus a parricidio arceat votumque vertat in melius. Officiumque tuum haec cura perstringat, ut, si quis parens adferat subolem, quam pro paupertate educare non possit, nec in alimentis nec in veste inpertienda tardetur, cum educatio nascentis infantiae moras ferre non possit. Ad quam rem et fiscum nostrum et rem privatam indiscreta iussimus praebere obsequia. DAT. III ID. MAI. NAISSO CONSTANTINO A. IIII ET LICINIO IIII [AA.][12] CONSS.

EMPEROR CONSTANTINE AUGUSTUS TO ABLABIUS. May the law that averts the hands of parents from parricide and changes their wish for the better be posted throughout the cities of Italy, written on bronze tables, or on boards whitened with lead,[13] or on linen cloths. This duty shall bind your staff so that, if any parent should bring[14] his offspring, which he cannot rear on account of his poverty, let there be no hesitation in granting it food and clothing, for the rearing of newborn infancy can bear no delays. We have ordered Our Fiscus and Private Property to show instant obedience concerning this matter. GIVEN 13 MAY (315 [319]) AT NAISSUS IN THE CONSULSHIP OF CONSTANTINE AUGUSTUS, CONSUL FOR THE FOURTH TIME, AND LICINIUS, CONSUL FOR THE FOURTH TIME.[15]

This text reveals the part played by several members of the administration in the promulgation and enforcement of an edict. It also illustrates the use-

11. The letter of Constantine to the vicar of Asia (CTh. 8.15.2, a. 334), in which he writes, *Damus provincialibus facultatem* might also concern a lost edict.

12. The abbreviation AA. (= *Augustis*) that appears in the subscription is a mistake. Constantine is already described as *Augustus* (CONSTANTINO A.), as usual, but the abbreviation A. is otherwise regularly removed from Licinius's name in the Codex Theodosianus. It appears that the Theodosian compilers forgot to strike AA. when they edited the subscription. The original would have read: CONSTANTINO IIII ET LICINIO IIII AA. CONSS.

13. Reference is to the *album;* not "waxed tablets" (Pharr).

14. Pharr: "report."

15. See Corcoran, *ET*², 310; Seeck, *Regesten,* 54 and 179, dates this constitution to 329; cf. Barnes, *NE,* 78.

fulness of the letters to officials that accompanied edicts. The emperor emphasizes the role of the recipient in carrying out the precepts of the edict and informs him that other magistrates whose assistance he might require have also been notified. Ablabius (the correct form of the name) was probably vicar of Italy;[16] like the vicar Severus above, he is charged with publishing the imperial edict throughout Italy.[17] In the accompanying letter, Constantine draws his attention to the new obligations that the edict imposes on him, no doubt reiterating what appeared in the edict itself.[18] Constantine also informs Ablabius that he may expect the cooperation of two other important magistrates, the chief financial officers of the emperor: the praetorian prefect, Ablabius's superior who administered the *fiscus,* and the *magister rei privatae.*[19] Constantine has communicated the edict to them as well and will probably have described their role in its enforcement in the same manner as for Ablabius. One might compare a statement in an edict that Constantine addressed to all *palatini:* "Concerning this matter, We have directed letters to the praetorian prefects and to the urban prefect."[20] Many constitutions from the late fourth and early fifth centuries, for which the compilers of the Codex Theodosianus might find reliable records, explicitly attest the dispatch of letters to several magistrates at the promulgation of an edict.[21] This practice was customary already under Constantine.

Letters to Magistrates

Almost all other constitutions included in the Codex Theodosianus were composed in epistolary form. These include constitutions addressed to the

---

16. Constantine takes it for granted that Ablabius's jurisdiction embraces all Italy, yet Ablabius cannot have been praetorian prefect, because Constantine also treats the *fiscus,* administered by the prefect, as a wholly separate entity. Cf. Corcoran, *ET*², 310.

17. *Per omnes civitates Italiae proponatur lex.* Constantine generously leaves it to discretion of the cities, whether they post the edict in bronze, white lead, or on linen cloth: *Aereis tabulis vel cerussatis aut linteis mappis scripta.* These publication methods seem to be given in descending order of costliness. Cf. the similar list of writing materials above in CTh. 7.20.1.

18. CTh. 11.27.1: *Officiumque tuum haec cura perstringat.*

19. CTh. 11.27.1: *et fiscum nostrum et rem privatam indiscreta iussimus praebere obsequia.*

20. CTh. 6.35.5 (328): *De qua re ad praefectos praetorio et ad praefectum urbis scripta direximus.*

21. E.g., the subscription of CTh. 1.8.1 (a. 415): SCRIPTA EODEM EXEMPLO SAPRICIO MAGISTRO MILITVM, HELIONI MAGISTRO OFFICIORVM ET EVSTATHIO QVAESTORI. Cf. J. Gaudemet, "Un problème de la codification théodosienne: les constitutions géminées," *RIDA*³ 4 (1957), 253–67 (= *Études,* vol. 1 [1979], 301–17).

Senate, anachronistically (as we shall see) called *orationes*; constitutions addressed to corporations, in particular to those obliged to fulfill public duties;[22] and, overwhelmingly, constitutions sent to imperial officials. Most such constitutions take the form of a letter addressed to a single official and concern a single question, very often, it seems, one raised by the official himself. Yet several imperial letters of the Constantinian period seem to have been disseminated to numerous officials simultaneously and differ only in name from edicts. It has been said that the manner in which constitutions were published distinguished them most.[23] This was true, however, only when the emperor published an edict directly. Both imperial letters and edicts might be disseminated throughout the empire through the same administrative channels, and the recipients published both in the same way: the imperial text was posted above (*antelata* or *praelata*) an edict of the official (*edictum* or *programma*).[24]

The path of a constitution from emperor to subject followed the structure of the imperial administration.[25] Constantine introduced several changes to the civil administration that he had inherited from the tetrarchy. He created two new officers, the *magister peditum* and *magister equitum*, to command his field army and perhaps also to supervise the *duces*, who since Diocletian had assumed command of the troops in most military provinces.[26] The military function of the praetorian prefects thereby ceased, probably upon the dissolution of the Praetorian Guard in 312.[27] The praetorian prefects were henceforth the highest-ranking officials of the judiciary and the *fiscus*. The deputies of the praetorian prefects, the vicars, persisted in the supervision of provincial governors, but several appear to have been suspended. Constantine replaced them with *comites provinciarum*, newly created officials dispatched from the court.[28] The *comites provinciarum* appear to have been intended to monitor provincial administrators and report abuses directly to Constantine. They fell into desuetude

22. Especially the *navicularii*, but also various *ordines* throughout the empire: see Mommsen, *Proleg.*, clxiv–clxv.

23. Van der Wal, "*Edictum* und *lex generalis*," 305.

24. Mommsen, *Proleg.*, clvi–clvii, s.v. "*praelatae*."

25. For an overview, Jones, *LRE*, 42–68; A. Demandt, *Die Spätantike: Römische Geschichte von Diocletian bis Justinian, 284–565 n. Chr.*, 2nd ed. (Munich, 2007), 292–303; B. Palme, "Die *Officia* der Statthalter in der Spätantike," *AntTard* 7 (1999), 95–98.

26. Jones, *LRE*, 97–100.

27. Ibid., 100.

28. On vicars: M. T. W. Arnheim, *The Senatorial Aristocracy in the Later Roman Empire* (Oxford, 1972), 63–65; M. T. W. Arnheim, "Vicars in the Later Roman Empire," *Historia* 19 (1970), 593–606; on *comites provinciarum*, Arnheim, *Senatorial Aristocracy*, 70–72.

after Constantine's death, and vicars resumed regular oversight of the dioceses; only the *comes Orientis* remained a fixture of the late antique administration.[29]

The governors of the provinces fell into four groups. Most prestigious were the proconsuls, who governed Africa, Asia, and, since Constantine, Achaia. The proconsuls of Africa and Asia were exempted from the system of dioceses and answered directly to the emperor, bypassing both vicars (or *comites*) and praetorian prefects.[30] *Consulares* ranked beneath the proconsuls but had, or received, senatorial rank.[31] Next came the *correctores*, who still were generally recruited from the Senate; and lastly, equestrian *praesides*.[32]

The following examples of letters to officials are typical:

Lact., *DMP* 48.12 (a. 313)[33]

Ut autem huius sanctionis <et> benivolentiae nostrae forma ad omnium possit pervenire notitiam, prolata programmate tuo haec scripta et ubique proponere et ad omnium scientiam te perferre conveniet, ut huius nostrae benivolentiae [nostrae] sanctio latere non possit.

So that the contents of Our decree and benevolence may come to the attention of all, it will behoove you to post this text, affixed at the beginning of your edict, everywhere and to bring it into the knowledge of all, so that the decree of this Our benevolence cannot be hidden.

FV 249.10[34]

quae (*sc.* lex), ut omnes cognos<cant quae iussimus . . . programma>ti tuo praeferenda est.

That all may learn of what We have ordained, this law is to be attached to the front of your edict.

---

29. Jones, *LRE*, 105; A. Piganiol, *L'Empire Chrétien, 325–395*, 2nd ed., ed. A. Chastagnol (Paris, 1972), 354–55; Arnheim, *Senatorial Aristocracy*, 71–72; Palme, "Die *Officia* der Statthalter," 97 n. 66.

30. On the proconsul of Achaia, see Arnheim, *Senatorial Aristocracy*, 60–63; Palme, "Die *Officia* der Statthalter," 98 n. 70.

31. Arnheim, *Senatorial Aristocracy*, 56–60.

32. Arnheim, *Senatorial Aristocracy*, 52–56; Palme, "Die *Officia* der Statthalter," 98; Jones, *LRE*, 45–46 and 106–7.

33. From the "Edict of Milan," conveyed by letter to the governor of Bithynia by Licinius.

34. From Constantine's famous reform of *donationes:* AD MAXIMVM PRAEFECTVM VRBI: cf. CTh. 8.12.1; Corcoran, *ET*^{2}, 313.

CTh. 11.1.25 (a. 398)

PROPOSITA IN PROGRAMMATE VARI VIRI CLARISSIMI VICARII VRBIS ROMAE.

POSTED IN THE EDICT OF VARUS, *VIR CLARISSIMUS*, VICAR OF THE CITY OF ROME.

Administrative enactments that affected the subjects of the empire or a wide range of administrators were often disseminated directly in letters addressed to high-ranking officials. Constantine writes the following to the *comes* of Africa:

CTh. 12.1.15 (a. 327)

Universis provinciarum rectoribus intimato nostram clementiam statuisse veteranorum filios curialibus muniis innectendos . . .

All provincial governors having been informed[35] that Our Clemency has established that the sons of veterans must be enrolled for curial liturgies . . .

Similar expressions are found in other constitutions: to three different praetorian prefects, Constantine writes: "The provincial governors are to be advised,"[36] "It behooves Your Gravity to send letters to all governors,"[37] and, "Your Shrewdness will advise the competent offices."[38] Sometimes the existence of such letters may be inferred, as when Constantine tells a recipient what *iudices universi* (*vel sim.*) are required to do, as in CTh. 11.1.3 (here, governors must fill out tax registers in their own hand).[39]

The *generalitas* of letters to magistrates has been discussed in chapter 1: such constitutions must have exercised the judgment of the compilers the most. Not every piece of imperial correspondence contained elements of general law, and it was left to the discretion of the editors to determine which constitutions did. The Codex Theodosianus accordingly is not want-

35. CTh. 12.1.15 is an ablative absolute construction governed by *intimato* (governing the dative *universis . . . rectoribus*) that has been excerpted without the foregoing main clause. Pharr interprets *intimato* as a future imperative: "You shall inform . . . "

36. CTh. 11.16.4: *rectores provinciarum monendi sunt.*

37. CTh. 14.8.1: *Ad omnes iudices litteras dare tuam convenit gravitatem.*

38. CTh. 8.1.3: *tua sollertia competentia monebit officia.*

39. Cf. CTh. 1.16.4: *Praesides provinciarum oportet.*

ing in surprising inclusions.[40] We have no proper control for omissions, but, in principle, the compilers were to include every relevant text.

"Epistolary" Edicts

The reign of Constantine is noteworthy for the emergence of a form of constitution that combines the stylistic elements of official letters and edicts. It may be called an epistolary edict. In a traditional Roman edict, the emperor simply speaks, *dicit.* The language of the Roman edict is aloof and impersonal: the emperor may speak about himself as "I" or "We," but he speaks of those who must obey the edict in the third person, as "he" or "they"; orders are similarly impersonal.[41] The emperor does not address his audience directly as "you." This practice stands in marked contrast to both private and the administrative rescripts, in which the emperor addresses the recipient directly. The chief distinction between private and official rescripts in Late Antiquity is that officials are frequently distinguished by such honorific circumlocutions as "Your Sublimity" (*tua sublimitas*) or, particularly common, "Your Gravity" (*tua gravitas*).[42]

Of the edicts of Constantine preserved in the Codex Theodosianus, only one preserves an epistolary address:

> CTh. 5.10.1 (a. 329)[43]
>
> IMP CONSTANTINVS A. ITALIS SVIS. Secundum statuta priorum principum si quis a sanguine infantem quoquo modo legitime comparaverit vel nutriendum putaverit . . . poenae subiiciendis ihis, qui contra hancegem venire tentaverint. DAT. XV KAL. SEPTEMB. SERDICA CONSTANTINO A. VIII ET CONSTANTINO CAES. IV CONSS.

---

40. Mommsen, *Proleg.*, cliii–cliv; J. F. Matthews, *Laying Down the Law: A Study of the Theodosian Code* (New Haven & London, 2000), 66–68; J. D. Harries, "'Sacra generalitas': The Administrative Background to the Theodosian Code," in *Estudios de Historia del Derecho Romano: Homenaje al profesor G. Martínez Díez,* ed. R. P. Bustamonte, vol. 1 (Madrid, 1994), 31–42. Unusual constitutions in the Codex Theodosianus: P. Krüger, *Geschichte der Quellen und der Literatur des römischen Rechts,* 2nd ed. (Munich, 1912), 326; Matthews, *Laying Down the Law,* 69–70.

41. E.g., the interchange of the first-person plural for Constantine and the indefinite third person used for the *populus,* the addressee of this edict: CTh. 11.7.3 (a. 320): *Nemo carcerem . . . expavescat . . . si quis tam alienus ab humano sensu est . . . Qua facultate praebita omnes fore credimus proniores ad solvenda ea, quae ad nostri usus exercitus pro communi salute poscuntur.*

42. Corcoran, *ET*², appendix F, "Abstract Forms of Address," 324–36.

43. 329 according to Corcoran, *ET*², 194; contra Seeck, *Regesten,* 65; cf. Barnes, *NE,* 74 (a. 319?).

EMPEROR CONSTANTINE AUGUSTUS TO HIS ITALIANS, (GREETINGS). According to the statutes of past emperors, if anyone by any means legitimately acquires a newborn infant or thinks to raise one . . . Those who attempt to violate this law are to be subjected to punishment. GIVEN 18 AUG. (329) AT SERDICA IN THE CONSULSHIP OF CONSTANTINE AUGUSTUS, CONSUL FOR THE EIGHTH TIME, AND OF CONSTANTINE CAESAR, CONSUL FOR THE FOURTH TIME.

The text cited is a famous edict concerning *infantes a sanguine*, that is, infants exposed shortly after birth, and rescued and raised by others, whether as free children or, more commonly as it seems, as slaves. The excerpt itself is concerned with the latter case and is famous, or notorious, because it breaks with the legal tradition that a Roman citizen could not be sold into slavery. This edict further contradicts another constitution of Constantine's; how the two should be reconciled is not clear.[44]

At present, the *inscriptio* of this text is more interesting. If the abbreviations are expanded, it reads: *Imp(erator) Constantinus A(ugustus) Italis suis (salutem dicit)*. This is the traditional form of greetings found in Latin letters. To cite a contemporary example, the inscription of a letter sent to the Senate begins: *Imp(erator) Constantinus A(ugustus) consulibus, praetoribus, tribunis plebis, senatui salutem dicit* (CTh. 8.18.1). An identical example appears on an inscription that records a letter sent in the names of Constantine and the Caesars Constantine II, Constans, and Dalmatius (whose name has been erased), to the Senate in praise of Proculus. The greeting reads:[45]

Imp. Caes. Fl. Constantinus [. . .] et / Fl. Cl. Constantinus [. . .] et / Fl. Iul. Constantius et Fl. Iul. / Constans [[et Fl. Iul. Dalmatius]] / nobb. Caess. / consulibus praetoribus tribunis plebis / senatui suo salutem dicunt. Si vos liberique / vestri valetis, bene est; nos exercitusque / nostri valemus.

Emperor Caesar Flavius Constantine [. . .] and Flavius Claudius Constantine [. . .] and Flavius Julius Constantius and Flavius Julius Constans [[and Flavius Julius Dalmatius]], most noble Caesars, to the consuls, praetors, tribunes of the plebs, (and) Senate, greetings. If you and your children are well, it is good; We and Our armies are well.[46]

---

44. FV 34 and CTh. 5.9.1. See D. V. Simon, *Konstantinisches Kaiserrecht. Studien anhand der Reskriptenpraxis und des Schenkungsrechts* (Frankfurt am Main, 1977), 35–45; cf. M. Sargenti, *Il diritto privato nella legislazione di Constantino: Persone e famiglia* (Milan, 1938), 28–41.

45. CIL 6.40776 = *AE* 1934.158. NB: the brackets [. . .] mark my omissions, not defects of the text.

46. Cf. Cicero, *ad fam.* 5.2.1: *Si tu exercitusque valetis, bene est.*

Although CTh. 5.10.1 is the only edict of Constantine's in the Codex Theodosianus that bears an epistolary *inscriptio,* Eusebius preserves local copies of two such edicts among the documents collected for his *Vita Constantini.*[47] Both bear the same epistolary salutation: Νικητὴς Κωνσταντῖνος Μέγιστος Σεβαστὸς ἐπαρχιώταις Παλαιστίνης, which presumably would have appeared in the Latin original as *Victor Constantinus Maximus Augustus provincialibus Palaestinae* (*salutem dicit*). The first of the edicts moreover bears the publication command at the end: Προτεθήτω ἐν τοῖς ἡμετέροις ἀνατολικοῖς μέρεσιν (i.e., *proponatur in nostris partibus Orientis*).[48] Eusebius states that this subscription was written in the emperor's own hand.[49] In the second edict, Constantine addresses the provincials directly in the second person: "I for my part will try to confess my own hopes *to all of you* as clearly as possible."[50] The personal tone of his words is unmistakable.

Constantine published both of these edicts throughout the East late in 324, in the aftermath of the overthrow of Licinius and shortly before the Council of Nicaea. Unlike most documents in Eusebius' *Vita,* these texts are not letters addressed to single officials, bishops, or groups of bishops, but speak to whole populations. The first edict contains numerous legal enactments restoring Christians to the status they enjoyed before the Licinian persecutions. In the second edict, Constantine justifies both his Christian convictions and the destruction of the persecutors; he offers intermittent prayers to God, whom he openly invokes. In terms of substance, the second edict demands general religious toleration, apparently for pagans above all, whose rites and ceremonies (writes Constantine) some overzealous Christians had declared utterly destroyed.[51]

Athanasius preserves another potential epistolary edict in his work *De decretis Nicaeenae synodi,* 39.[52] This edict, which is attested in Greek, Latin, Arabic, and Syriac versions, is addressed Νικητὴς Κωνσταντῖνος Μέγιστος

---

47. Eus., *VC* 2.24–42 and 2.48–60 (= Silli, nos. 16 and 18). Barnes, *CE,* 208–9, and Millar, *ERW*², 222 and 319–20, note the unusual juxtaposition of epistolary and edictal forms.

48. Eus., *VC* 2.42.

49. Eus., *VC* 2.23.3: εἴληπται δ' ἐξ αὐθεντικοῦ τοῦ παρ' ἡμῖν φυλαττομένου βασιλικοῦ νόμου, ᾧ καὶ τῆς αὐτοῦ δεξιᾶς ἔγγραφος ὑποσημείωσις τῆς τῶν λόγων πιστώσεως οἷά τινι σφραγῖδι κατασημαίνει τὴν μαρτυρίαν.

50. Eus., *VC* 2.48.2: ἐγὼ δ' ὡς ἔνι μάλιστα φανερῶς περὶ τῶν κατ' ἐμαυτὸν ἐλπίδων πᾶσιν ὑμῖν ὁμολογῆσαι πειράσομαι. Constantine means a "confession" in the religious sense, in German *Bekenntnis* rather than *Geständnis.* Cf. P. Dräger, *Eusebios. Über das Leben des glückseligen Kaisers Konstantin (De vita Constantini)* (Oberhaid, 2007), *ad loc.:* "Ich aber will versuchen, so gut es möglich ist, Euch allen meine persönlichen Hoffnungen offen zu bekennen."

51. Cf. Barnes, *CE,* 208–212, on the provisions of these edicts.

52. = Silli, no. 42, issued a. 333.

Σεβαστὸς ἐπισκόποις καὶ λαοῖς.[53] The letter begins and ends, as other Constantinian letters to bishops or Christian communities, with an epistolary greeting and a personal, Christian subscription: καὶ ἄλλῃ χειρί· ὁ θεὸς ὑμᾶς διαφυλάξει, ἀδελφοὶ ἀγαπητοί.[54] In the body of the text itself, however, Constantine not once addresses the recipients as "you," as is customary in the two dozen other examples of such texts. Constantine declares that the Arians will henceforth be called Porphyrians, all the writings of Arius are to be burned, and whosoever is found guilty of concealing such writings will suffer capital punishment. Constantine speaks of all these people in the third person. The formal framework of the text is typical of the Christian letters of Constantine, but the text itself recalls an edict in traditional Roman style. On a last note, Hall has argued that the letter addressed to Arius and Alexander (Eus., *VC* 2.64–72) was in fact addressed to the bishops at the Synod at Antioch generally, but this is far from certain.[55]

The full epistolary greeting *salutem dicit/dicunt* in the Codex Theodosianus is most often found in letters addressed to the Roman Senate and to provincial councils. The formula also appears in scattered rescripts addressed to imperial officials. CTh. 11.30.5–6 both are addressed *Idem [sc. Constantinus] A(ugustus) Petronio Proboiano suo salutem.* Here only *dicit* is omitted (which is nothing remarkable). Many more examples may be found where the addressee appears simply in the dative case, with the entire phrase *salutem dicit/dicunt* omitted, though obviously implied.

As jurists copied and compiled imperial laws, the epistolary form of address was most commonly reduced to a standard formula consisting of the name of the emperor or emperors in the nominative case and the name of the recipient in the accusative case following the preposition *ad.* This form could be used in *all* constitutions, as can easily be observed in the Codex Theodosianus. In the edict CTh. 1.1.1, the first constitution of the Codex Theodosianus, we find the inscription *Imp. Constantinus A. ad Lusitanos.* The preposition *ad* also appears in letters to the Senate, which we know would have been addressed with an epistolary formula. For example, in CTh. 6.4.5 we read: *Idem [sc. Constantius] A. ad Senatum.* By far most letters to officials likewise attest this form of inscription.

---

53. "Constantine, victor, greatest Augustus, to the bishops and peoples." Cf. Silli, 155–56. I quote the text in Athanasius because it is unknown which of the Latin versions, if any, is original.

54. "And in another hand: God will preserve you, dear brothers."

55. S. G. Hall, "Some Constantinian Documents in the Vita Constantini," in *Constantine: History, Historiography, and Legend,* ed. S. N. C. Lieu and D. Montserrat (London, 1998), 86–97.

The Codex Theodosianus nonetheless retains the dative case derived from the traditional greeting in several constitutions, such as that to Petronius Probianus cited above. Since no Latin writer would address a letter with *ad* and the name of the recipient in the accusative case, it seems safe to conclude that the *inscriptiones* in the Codex Theodosianus were altered already in intermediary sources or in the process of compilation: they were shortened, as we have seen in the example above in which *salutem* or *salutem dicit* were omitted, or (more commonly) they were rewritten in the shorter form with *ad* and the name of the recipient in the accusative case. The *inscriptio* of CTh.5.10.1, *Imp. Constantinus A. Italis suis,* thus may have been abridged but must otherwise be a faithful record of the original address of the text. The qualification of the Italians with the adjective *suus* is an epistolary mark of familiarity or friendship.[56] Its appearance cannot be ascribed to the error of a compiler. We thus may qualify the edict attested in CTh. 5.10.1 an epistolary edict.

Before the reign Constantine, scattered edicts attest epistolary forms. Corcoran, who discusses the confusion of edictal and epistolary forms during the tetrarchic period, has identified several texts.[57] The earliest is an edict of Marcus Aurelius preserved in a fragmentary inscription, which refers to itself as a letter: "After this letter was read at Athens . . ."[58] Williams, who identifies the text as an edict, regards the reference to "this letter" as mere error.[59] Unfortunately, because the *inscriptio* of the text has not survived, and no *subscriptio* appears, the question of its formal status cannot be answered with greater precision.

The second example noted by Corcoran derives from the preface to the Edict of Maximum Prices. After expatiating at length on the greed of those who manipulate the prices of goods, the tetrarchs declare (lines 84–85): *eorum avaritiae modum statui, provinciales nostri, communis humanitatis ratio persuadet.* Corcoran rightly observes that the phrase *provinciales nostri*

56. Cf. CTh. 11.30.5–6: *Petronio Probiano suo salutem.* Cf. the discussion of the epistolary use of *mi* in E. Dickey, *Latin Forms of Address from Plautus to Apuleius* (Oxford, 2002), 214–24.

57. Corcoran, *ET*², 198–203; Corcoran, "Galerius's Jigsaw Puzzle: The Caesariani Dossier," *AntTard* 15 (2007), 228; cf. M. H. Crawford and J. Reynolds, "The Publication of the Prices Edict: A New Inscription from Aezani," *JRS* 65 (1975), 162; and F. Dölger and J. Karayannopulos, *Byzantinische Urkundenlehre. Erster Abschnitt: Die Kaiserurkunden* (Munich, 1968), 72–73.

58. IG III.62: tab. II ll. 37–38 (= Oliver no. 184): μετὰ τὸ ἀναγνωσθ[ῆναι] / τὴν ἐπιστολὴν ταύτην Ἀθήνησιν . . .

59. W. Williams, "Formal and Historical Aspects of Two New Documents of Marcus Aurelius," *ZPE* 17 (1975), 40–51.

is a direct appeal to the provincials in the vocative case, defining the audience of the Edict.[60] The usage anticipates Constantine's letters to the provincials of Palestine and to *his* (*nostris*) eastern provinces.[61]

In an interesting twist, recently noticed epigraphic evidence has shown that Diocletian's edict was regarded as a letter by one of its recipients. A British team visiting the site of the copy of the Prices Edict at Stratonicea in 2007 found the letters *ESL* inscribed above the preface.[62] The Stratonicea copy of the Prices Edict, one of the most extensive, was inscribed without its formal *inscriptio,* which would have shown the titulature of the emperors and clarified the legal form of the text. The letters *ESL* now found above the inscription of the preface stand for *exemplum sacrarum litterarum,* a standard phrase applied in inscriptions and with some frequency in legal sources, such as the Codex Justinianus, to copies of imperial letters.[63] Whether local authorities at Stratonicea or the governor who circulated the text are responsible for the abbreviation remains unclear. Corcoran cautiously suggests that the designation *sacrae litterae* might also include edicts.[64] Given, however, that the phrase elsewhere is applied exclusively to forms of letters and the word *litterae* itself means "a letter," *sacrae litterae* should not, properly, denote edicts as well as letters. Rather than consider the term less precise than previously thought, we might postulate that the governor or the Stratoniceans themselves distinguished less precisely between the two legal forms. The designation of the Prices Edict as a letter is symptomatic of the erosion of the distinction between these legal forms in the tetrarchic period.

Our last example stems from Constantine's contemporary, Galerius. Galerius implies that his famous edict of toleration is a letter in stating that he will write *another* letter to his governors: "We will indicate to the governors in another letter what they should observe."[65] The phrase "in another letter" (*per aliam epistolam*) seems to be a lapse caused by the use of *alius:* Galerius states he will issue letters to the governors; the contents of these

60. Corcoran, *ET*², 198 and 211.

61. Corcoran, *ET*², 198.

62. See S. Corcoran, "The Heading of Diocletian's Prices Edict at Stratonicea," *ZPE* 166 (2008), 295–302.

63. Ibid., 296–98, collects the evidence.

64. Ibid., 300.

65. *<Per> aliam autem epistolam iudicibus significaturi sumus quid debeant observare.* Crawford and Reynolds, "Publication of Prices Edict," 162, citing Lact., *DMP* 34.5 = Eus., *HE* 8.17.9: δι' ἑτέρας δὲ ἐπιστολῆς . . . δηλώσομεν. On Galerius and the inconsistencies of edicts of this period, see Corcoran, "Galerius' Jigsaw Puzzle," 228.

accompanying letters would have largely repeated the precepts of the edict. Galerius expresses the inherent similarity of the contents of the cover letters to that of the edict with the infelicitous choice of the words *alia epistola.* The text issued to the provincials was clearly an edict and is called so twice by Lactantius, who reproduces the Latin text.[66] Further confirmation in the form of the *inscriptio* and *subscriptio* of the edict is lacking: the copy in Lactantius lacks the *inscriptio* entirely. Eusebius's translation records the names and titles of the emperors but no equivalent to Latin *dicunt;* the epistolary greeting and the inclusion of the name and titles of Licinius that follow in some manuscripts are considered spurious.[67]

The lapse in the edict of Galerius and the general confusion of epistolary and edictal forms is indicative of changes in the practice of publishing imperial constitutions, particularly the use of universal edicts, which increased during the reign of Constantine. The similarity of edicts and administrative letters in preparation and publication in time led to a confusion of their forms. If an edict were directed to *universi provinciales,* it had to be disseminated throughout the empire first by letter to provincial administrators. Such an edict might be sent first to the praetorian prefects, perhaps then to the vicars, from thence to the provincial governors themselves and beyond.[68] The praetorian prefects were certainly the first officials to whom laws affecting the entire empire were sent in the later fourth century and in the fifth. Since the praetorian prefects under Constantine seem not yet to have been fixed regional officials, it is likely that Constantine also addressed such edicts to vicars and to *comites provinciarum,* whom he dispatched throughout the empire in their place.[69]

It is under Constantine that constitutions to officials in epistolary form begin to contain substantive changes to law, especially administrative law.[70] For such constitutions, it was possible to use the same system of dissemination as for edicts: notice of an administrative change affecting the imperial

---

66. Lact., *DMP* 33.11 (*Et iam deficiens edictum misit huiusmodi*) and 35.1 (*Hoc edictum proponitur Nicomediae*).

67. Some MSS of Eus., *HE* 8.17.4, record the greeting καὶ Αὐτοκράτωρ Καῖσαρ Οὐαλέριος Λικιννιανὸς Λικίννιος . . . ἐπαρχιώταις ἰδίοις χαίρειν.

68. D. W. Hobson, "The Impact of Law on Village Life in Roman Egypt," in *Law, Politics and Society in the Ancient Mediterranean World,* ed. B. Halpern and D. W. Hobson (Sheffield, 1993), 195–97, notes that edicts of the prefect of Egypt were very well known even in remote Egyptian villages.

69. On the praetorian prefects, see pp. 108–13.

70. T. Honoré, "Roman Law AD 200–400: From Cosmopolis to Rechtstaat [*sic*]," in *Approaching Late Antiquity: The Transformation from the Early to Late Empire,* ed. S. Swain and M. Edwards (Oxford, 2004), 110 and 117–18.

administration at large might be distributed in nearly identical letters sent by the imperial *scrinia* to officials throughout the empire. Each official published the letter sent to him, just as all might publish copies of imperial edicts. As the means of publication grew similar, edicts and letters grew less distinct.

The epistolary form held a distinct stylistic advantage over the traditional edict. The epistolary edict conveyed the same content as a traditional edict, but it addressed those affected by it directly. CTh. 6.35.1, for instance, is addressed to retired *palatini*:[71]

> CTh. 6.35.1 (a. 314)
>
> IMP. CONSTANTINVS A. PALATINIS BENE MERITIS SVIS SALVTEM. A palatinis tam his, qui obsequiis nostris inculpata officia praebuerunt, quam illis, qui in scriniis nostris, id est memoriae epistularum libellorumque, versati sunt, procul universas calumnias sive nominationes iubemus esse summotas, idque beneficium ad filios eorum atque nepotes ipso ordine sanguinis pervenire atque inmunes eos a cunctis muneribus sordidis et personalibus permanere cum universis mobilibus et mancipiis urbanis, neque iniurias eis ab aliquibus inferri, ita ut, qui haec contempserit, indiscreta dignitate poenas debitas exigatur. DAT. IIII KAL. NOV. TREVIRIS VOLVSIANO ET ANNIANO CONSS.
>
> EMPEROR CONSTANTINE AUGUSTUS TO HIS HONORABLY DISCHARGED PALATINI, GREETINGS. We order all frivolous allegations or rather nominations (for liturgies) to be banished far from the *palatini,* both those who have given blameless service in their duties to Us and those who have served in Our bureaus, that is, of Memory, of Letters, and of Petitions; and (We order) that this privilege shall accrue to their sons and grandsons according to descent by blood and they, with all their moveable property and urban slaves, shall remain immune to sordid and personal liturgies; nor may injustices be inflicted on them by anyone, so that he who disregards these regulations will suffer due punishment without any distinction of rank. GIVEN 29 OCT. (314) AT TRIER IN THE CONSULSHIP OF VOLUSIANUS AND ANNIANUS

It is impossible that Constantine sent a letter to every retired *palatinus* in the empire. This text, too, must be an edict—and it reads as one. The *palatini* are

71. CTh. 6.35.1 encompasses both the *palatini* in the judicial *scrinia* of the court and the financial staff of the *sacrae largitiones* and *res privata;* cf. R. Delmaire, *Largesses Sacrées et* res privata. *L'aerarium impérial et son administration du IVe au VIe siècle* (Rome, 1989), 125–27.

mentioned only in the third person. The regulations that affect them would have applied throughout the territory that Constantine controlled. Yet by singling the *palatini* out as the addressees of his edict, Constantine appears to extend them his personal attention. Use of the familiar *suus* might even convey a kind of paternal affection: Constantine greets *his* former *palatini*. At the same time, the specificity of the address could demonstrate to all readers of the edict precisely to whom its contents pertained.

The epistolary form of edicts attested in the *inscriptio* and greeting appears once more in the Codex Theodosianus in a constitution issued by Valentinian from Milan, CTh. 8.11.2 (a. 365): IDEM (*sc.* VALENTINIANVS ET VALENS) AA. PROVINCIALIBVS SALVTEM DICVNT.[72] The text of the constitution is impersonal; all parties are mentioned in the third person.[73] The Codex Theodosianus contains no later edicts bearing epistolary greetings, but personal appeals and references to "you" appear in two other edicts, one issued by Constantine and one by Constantius.[74] In his edict *ad populum* forbidding haruspices to enter private dwellings (CTh. 9.16.2, a. 319), Constantine exhorts the Romans to practice their religion publicly, choosing imperative forms in the second-person plural: "Those of you, however, who believe this to be to your benefit, go to the public altars and temples and celebrate your customary rites."[75] One consequence of this variation between direct address in the second person and impersonal description in the third is that Constantine separates those who legally practice pagan rituals from the haruspices and their hosts, who face (unspecified) punishment if they disobey.[76] Constantine speaks of the haruspices impersonally but engages his obedient subjects directly. Constantine anticipates a potential misinterpretation of his orders and explains, "For We do not forbid the solemnities of former practice to be conducted in the open light (of day)."[77] The expression *usurpatio praeterita*, translated as "former practice" above, anticipates the obsolescence of pagan religion, as if the

72. The unusual *inscriptio* of this constitution and of CTh. 5.10.1 was noticed by Mommsen, *Proleg.*, p. cliii.

73. CTh. 8.11.2: *nihil quisquam exigat, nihil audeat postulare. Si quis vero honoratorum sponte quid offerre voluerit, id tantum recte dandum iudicamus.*

74. CTh. 9.16.2 (a. 319) and CTh. 7.9.1 (a. 340).

75. CTh. 9.16.2: *Qui vero id vobis existimatis conducere, adite aras publicas adque delubra et consuetudinis vestrae celebrate sollemnia.* There is no reason why Constantine could not have written, *qui vero id sibi existimant conducere, adeant aras publicas,* etc.

76. In CTh. 9.16.1 Constantine specifies that the haruspex should be burned alive, his host deported to an island and his property confiscated.

77. CTh. 9.16.2: *nec enim prohibemus praeteritae usurpationis officia libera luce tractari.*

times have "passed it by," but Constantine's words here are much milder than in a related letter to the praetorian prefect: "Those desirous of indulging their superstition will be able to perform their rite [*sic: ritum*] publicly."[78] Constantine suggests that he views the adherents of the old religion as slaves to their belief, which they "serve" (*servire*), rendered as "indulging" above to convey the reprehensible connotation of the word. That such rites amount to no more than superstition, *superstitio,* is a pointed slight. *Superstitio* amounted to excessive *religio,* an exaggerated attachment and devotion to religious rituals, frequently out of fear, which distinguished the fanatical from the pious. *Superstitio* was often the source of foreign or private—and therefore potentially subversive—practices that threatened the political and religious harmony of the Roman state.[79] Christianity, too, had been viewed as such a contemptible *superstitio.*[80] Constantine now communicates the opposite: it is pagan ritual, not merely the private consultation of diviners, but even public sacrifice in the temples, that the ruler of the Roman world disdains as "superstition."[81]

Constantine's letter to the praetorian prefect is in all probability the accompanying letter to the edict itself, published in Rome some nine months after the issue of the edict in the Balkans.[82] With the reservation that we possess only excerpts of both edict and accompanying letter, their differ-

78. CTh. 9.16.1: *superstitioni enim suae servire cupientes poterunt publice ritum proprium exercere.*

79. D. B. Martin, *Inventing Superstition: From the Hippocratics to the Christians* (Cambridge, 2004), 125–39; M. Stachura, "Kritik der superstitio und Affirmation der Orthodoxie in den Gesetzen des Codex Theodosianus," in *Studies on the Late Roman History,* ed. E. Dabrowa (Kraków, 2007), 33–62.

80. Martin, *Inventing Superstition,* esp. 135–39.

81. Cf. *contagiose superstitionis* in the rescript to Hispellum: ILS 705, l. 46–47 (above, p. 14). Several scholars have argued that *superstitio* is used by Constantine in its traditional sense, without any Christian undertone: R. Van Dam, *The Roman Revolution of Constantine* (Cambridge, 2007), 29–34; C. Ronning, "Pontifex Maximus, charismatischer Herrscher, 'allen gemeinsamer Bischof' oder 'dreizehnter Apostel'? Das römische Herrschaftsverständnis und der christliche Kaiser," in *Konstantin der Große. Kaiser einer Epochenwende,* ed. F. Schuller and H. Wolff (Lindenberg 2007), 139–41. Constantine uses the word *superstitio* with characteristic ambiguity, but it is not necessarily the word that suggests veiled hostility to paganism, but who uses it and about what. It still seems more plausible to the present author that a reader of Constantine's words in Hispellum in the years 333–35 would interpret them as a vague prohibition of pagan sacrifice in the temple of the imperial family—what exactly, no one could, nor can, say. In this sense, A. D. Lee, "Traditional Religions," in *The Cambridge Companion to the Age of Constantine,* ed. N. E. Lenski (Cambridge, 2006), 175–76.

82. Barnes, *NE,* 74 on Constantine's whereabouts; 117–18 on Maximus. Seeck, *Regesten,* 58, corrects the date of CTh. 9.16.1 from 319 to 320, since the praetorian prefect Maximus did not hold office until Sept. 319 (cf. also 68). It is possible that the recorded month is wrong (Mommsen, *ad loc.,* suggests September).

ence in tone is striking—and yet both were published. The *subscriptio* of the letter to the praetorian prefect reveals that it was published in Rome, from where the copy incorporated in the Codex Theodosianus must ultimately derive. The date of both texts, 319, leaves no doubt that the *populus* addressed in the edict must have been the inhabitants of the city of Rome. Constantine addresses pagan religion in widely differing manners in the two texts. Constantine appears tolerant, if indifferent, to traditional Roman religion in the edict addressed to the people. He addresses the people directly and even encourages them to perform their rites in the public temples of the city. In his letter to the praetorian prefect, Constantine communicates his disdain for the traditional religion. This discrepancy seems to suggest the different publicity enjoyed by edicts and official letters. Although we do not know how each text was published, it is probably not far from the mark to assume that the edict was published in a much more prominent place or in several places, and perhaps displayed for a longer time than the letter to the prefect, which might have been posted, for example, in the Forum of Trajan.[83] The edict and letter aptly illustrate the different communicative potential of different legal media. Constantine appears to have utilized the universality of the Roman edict as a tool for speaking directly to the people. The epistolary forms and direct appeals of his edicts demonstrate that questions of self-representation and communication evidently outweighed strict adherence to traditional legal form.

Yet legal form would ultimately prevail, for specimens of epistolary edicts disappear not long after the death of Constantine.[84] This desuetude might be related to the revival of the study of jurisprudence and the changing legal culture of the later fourth and early fifth centuries.[85] As the emperors struggled to set criteria for the applicability of past constitutions, their own constitutions followed traditional formal conventions more rigorously. The emperors begin to identify edicts and other forms of legislation as such explicitly. Valentinian III may have attempted to circumvent precisely the ambiguity between traditional and epistolary edicts in his fa-

---

83. On places of publication in late antiquity, D. Liebs, "Promulgationslokale im spätantiken Rom," in *Satura Roberto Feenstra Oblata,* ed. J. A. Ankum, J. E. Spruit, and F. B. J. Wubbe (Freiburg, 1985), 215–28.

84. Constans still speaks to his subjects as "you" in an edict *ad provinciales* (CTh. 7.9.1).

85. Matthews, *Laying Down the Law,* 21–30; J. H. W. G. Liebeschuetz, *Antioch: City and Imperial Administration in the Later Roman Empire* (Oxford, 1972), 242–55. Cf. the interest of the *Scriptores Historiae Augustae* in the classical jurists: R. Syme, "Fiction about Roman Jurists," *ZRG* 97 (1980), 78–104.

mous letter to the Roman Senate in 426.[86] He requires that constitutions either contain the word *edictum* or (like edicts) have been published throughout the empire. The distinction neatly juxtaposes past and present practice: in Valentinian's day the texts of edicts and *leges generales* refer to themselves as such; the precise nature of the constitutions of past emperors often remained indeterminate.

Yet the epistolary form of the Roman edict did not die out entirely, as two edicts of Marcian demonstrate. The *inscriptio* of CJ 1.12.5 reads *Imp. Marcianus A. ad populum,* but in the excerpt of the edict cited by Justinian Marcian bluntly addresses the people before continuing in the third person typical of edicts:

> CJ 1.12.5 (a. 451)
>
> IMP. MARCIANVS AD POPVLVM. Denuntiamus vobis omnibus, ut in sacrosanctis ecclesiis et in aliis quidem venerabilibus locis . . . abstineatis omni seditione. Nemo conclamationibus utatur . . .
>
> EMPEROR MARCIAN TO THE PEOPLE. We proclaim to all of you that you should abstain from all sedition . . . in the holy churches and other venerable places. Let no man raise an outcry . . .

This usage was apparently no exception, for Marcian also uses the second-person plural to address his subjects in the edict Nov. Marc. 1 (a. 450):

> (pr.) Videtis enim agmina, videtis catervas adeuntium infinitas non solum a finitimis provinciis, verum extremo orbis Romani limite confluentes et adversum suos adversarios conquerentes . . . (3.) His pro commodo vestro et pro nostri imperii humanitate dispositis unusquisque vestrum . . . haec quae dicta sunt observare debebit . . . (8.) Ergo consulite vestris commodis, nostris saluberrimis parete praeceptis.
>
> (pr.) For you see the throngs, you see the numberless crowds not only from the neighboring provinces, but streaming in from the farthest bounds of the Roman world and complaining against their adversaries . . . (3.) Having decreed these things for your benefit and according to the humanity of Our empire, each and every one of you must observe that which has been said . . . (8.) Therefore, take heed of your benefits, obey Our most salubrious precepts.

86. Discussed in chapter 1.

The rhetorical force of his words is obvious. No explanation of this brief revival of the epistolary edict comes to mind as readily as that which probably motivated Constantine himself: preference for advantages of direct and forceful language over the niceties of formal legal tradition.

Letters to the Senate

Letters to the Senate are perhaps the only unambiguous form of general law. These texts are properly designated "letters" foremost because the *oratio in senatu habita* known to the early empire is for our period defunct, if not entirely forgotten.[87] The church historian Socrates (ca. 380–440), for example, makes the surprising claim that Julian the Apostate was the first and only emperor since Julius Caesar to deliver a speech personally in the Senate![88] The claim is false but not incredible: in the fourth and fifth centuries, it was usual to address the Senate as any magistrate, by letter. Even the famous constitution of Valentinian III that contained the Law of Citations, which pedantically calls itself an *oratio* (CTh. 4.1.1: *Atque ideo hac oratione sancimus*), was nonetheless a letter sent to the Senate from Ravenna.[89] Of the two clear Constantinian specimens of such texts, one preserves the epistolary address:[90] IMP. CONSTANTINVS A. CONSVLIBVS, PRAETORIBVS, TRIBVNIS PLEBIS, SENATVI SALVTEM DICIT. The *oratio* was identical to other imperial letters; only its addressee distinguished it.[91] That inevitably someone had to read such letters aloud to the Senate perhaps justified the

---

87. High Empire: R. A. Talbert, *The Senate of Imperial Rome* (Princeton, 1984), 290–97; cf. Millar, *ERW*², 277, 341, and 353–54. Millar compares the salutation of CTh. 8.18.1 (discussed immediately below) to letters to provincial cities, although the formula had been in use at least since the reign of Commodus. Cf. Dölger and Karayannopulos, *Byzantinische Urkundenlehre,* 71; A. Chastagnol, "Constantin et le Sénat," *AARC* 2 (1976), 49–69.

88. Socr., *HE* 3.1.54; cf. Libanius, *Or.* 18.154; M. Radin, s.v. "Oratio," *RE* 18.1 (1939), 869–73, here: 871: "Natürlich war das nur Antiquitätsliebhaberei"; G. C. Hansen, *Sokrates Kirchengeschichte* (Berlin, 1995), 186.

89. Fragments listed by Mommsen, *Proleg.*, p. ccci.

90. CTh. 8.18.1. The other is CTh. 15.14.4. Corcoran, *ET*², 154–55, identifies both as *orationes in senatu habitae.* He accepts, rightly, I believe, the proposal of Seeck to redate CTh. 15.14.4 to 313 and suggests that the constitution may have been delivered by Constantine personally. That can hardly be the case, however, in CTh. 8.18.1, as the epistolary greeting makes clear.

91. Mommsen, *Proleg.*, p. cliv (s.v. "*Constitutiones directae ad senatum*"); Radin, "Oratio," 870, ll. 57ff.; Van der Wal, "*Edictum* und *lex generalis,*" 279–80 and 284–85. The same epistolary forms are used long after the publication of the Codex Theodosianus: NV. 1.3 (a. 450); *Collectio Avellana* 113 (a. 516), which ineptly attributes *tribunicium imperium* to the emperor and mistakenly begins *proconsulibus consulibus.* The senate replies in *Collectio Avellana* 114, which the compilers title a *rescriptum.*

retention or revival of the antique name. The word *oratio* in the Codex Theodosianus is explicitly applied to a constitution sent to the Senate first under Valentinian and Valens, in a constitution that is in fact addressed to the urban prefect.[92] Similarly, it was the urban prefect, Vettius Rufinus, who read Constantine's letter to the Senate in 315: RECITATA APVT VETTIVM RVFINVM PRAEFECTVM VRBI IN SENATV (CTh. 8.18.1).[93] The same procedure of communicating laws to the Senate may lie behind other constitutions addressed to the urban prefect that bear the words *lecta* or *recitata* in their subscriptions.[94] Otherwise, letters to the Senate would appear not to have been made public. They are never accompanied by a publication command, although they were probably recorded in the *acta senatus.*[95] If such letters were first delivered to the urban prefect and read by him in the Senate, he might also have published them at his court. Many copies of such letters could thus owe their survival to this practice.

Private Rescripts

The exclusion of all but *leges generales* fundamentally distinguished the Codex Theodosianus from earlier codifications of imperial law. The two great collections made under Diocletian, the Codex Gregorianus and Codex Hermogenianus, consisted almost entirely of private rescripts.[96] Theodosius adopted the organizational principles of the Diocletianic codices for the Codex Theodosianus; he even intended to incorporate these collections into the grand *codex magisterium vitae* that was meant to unite all valid law; but Theodosius refused to admit private rescripts into his codification of the imperial law of the fourth and early fifth centuries. In consequence, the Codex Theodosianus offers us examples of Constantine's edicts and letters to the Senate, myriad administrative letters, and even rare records of proceedings, but not a single private rescript. Approximately ten

92. CTh. 6.4.21.7 (a. 372): *providendum nos hac oratione censemus.*

93. A similar letter to the urban prefect might explain the curious *subscriptio* of CJ 2.52.6: the letter is addressed *ad Iulianum PV,* but the *subscriptio* reads PP. ROMAE AD SENATVM.

94. Mommsen, *Proleg.*, clv (s.v. *lectae*).

95. Talbert, *Senate of Imperial Rome,* 308–36; A. Chastagnol, *La préfecture urbaine à Rome sous le bas-empire* (Paris, 1960), 241–51.

96. Krüger *Quellen*^{2}, 316–24; Liebs, "Recht und Rechtsliteratur," in *Restauration und Erneuerung: Die lateinische Literatur von 284 bis 374,* ed. R. Herzog (Munich, 1989), 61 and 63; Corcoran, *ET*^{2}, 25–42; S. Connolly, *Lives behind the Laws: The World of the Codex Hermogenianus* (Bloomington, 2010).

private rescripts of Constantine's are preserved in the *Fragmenta Vaticana*, a private collection made sometime in the fourth century; its author indiscriminately cites juristic writings, "general laws," and private rescripts.[97] Whether the incongruous formal sources of the law codes of Diocletian and Theodosius reflect a genuine change in the production of imperial legislation in the time of Constantine is a question that will occupy us in the next chapter.

97. See above, p. 14; G. G. Archi, "Il problema delle fonti del diritto nel sistema romano del IV e V secolo," in *St. Grosso*, vol. 4 (Turin, 1971), 19–22.

3

Changes in Legislation from Diocletian to Constantine

Legal Classicism

The figure of Constantine looms over the legal history of the Later Roman Empire no less than the religious. The reign of Diocletian marked the passing of an age, the reign of Constantine the birth of another. The reign of Constantine marked a rupture not with classical law, for most of it remained in force, nor with classical jurisprudence, which continued to be consulted and, for the first time, officially sanctioned.[1] The break with the past made by the Constantinian chancellery consisted in a retreat from the tenacious defense of classical law and classical jurisprudence made by Diocletian. The breach was effected in part by a new attitude toward the complexity of law. Under Constantine, the law of the *veteres* was indeed venerated, but too often its complexity was perceived as verging on perversity.[2] The spirit that animated the legislation of Constantine preferred to cut the knots of the classical law rather than labor to loosen them.[3]

Diocletian is known to Roman legal history as the last defender of classical Roman law. His private rescripts tell a story of empire-wide confusion, ignorance, and neglect. "What you request is illegal and outra-

1. Constantine confirmed the (spurious) *Sententiae Pauli* (CTh. 1.4.2) and banned the notes of Paul and Ulpian on Papinian (CTh. 1.4.1); F. M. de Robertis, "Un precedente costantiniana alla cosiddetta 'Legge delle Citazioni' del 426 di Teodosio II e Valentiniano III," *SDHI* 64 (1998), 245–52; F. Wieacker, *Textstufen klassischer Juristen* (Göttingen, 1960), 34–44.

2. E.g., CTh. 3.2.1: *Quoniam inter alias captiones praecipue commissoriae legis crescit asperitas;* CJ 6.9.9: *verborum inanium excludimus captiones.*

3. Constantinian innovations in private law are indicated below.

geous," replies Diocletian to one Alexander.[4] Alexander had requested that Diocletian restore to him, by imperial fiat, title to a slave that he had legitimately conveyed to another person. In other words, he asked the emperor to break the law, to issue a rescript *contra ius.* Diocletian begins another rescript with an elementary lesson on the law of property: "An action *in rem* is applicable not against the seller but against the possessor. Therefore your request that the person claiming ownership go to trial not with you, but with the person from whom you purchased the property, is invalid, since you assert that you are in possession."[5] The petitioner, Pancratius, has been sued by someone who claims as his own property that Pancratius has bought from a third party. The emperor reminds Pancratius that he cannot force his adversary to sue the seller, since an *actio in rem* is valid against the possessor of the property, and Pancratius has admitted that he is in possession. Further examples of this sort abound in the rescripts of Diocletian. The word *frustra* alone, with which the emperor often chastises the illegal contentions and requests of his subjects, garners a rich harvest of similar passages.[6]

It has long been held that Diocletian resolved to maintain the purity of Roman law. In a study of the rescripts of Diocletian published in 1923, Taubenschlag argued that the legislation of Diocletian was simultaneously both conservative and progressive.[7] This provocative and somewhat paradoxical conclusion provoked swift response and was rejected by most legal historians. Albertario, in his review of Taubenschlag's work and in subsequent articles, demonstrated that, on the contrary, most innovations discovered in the rescripts of Diocletian were interpolations, the work of the editors of the Codex Justinianus.[8] Diocletian was indeed the defender

4. CJ 3.32.12: *Incivile atque inusitatum est quod postulas.*

5. CJ 3.19.t1: *In rem actio non contra venditorem, sed contra possidentem competit. Frustra itaque desideras non tecum congredi, sed cum auctore tuo dominium vindicantem, cum te possidere contendas.*

6. CJ 2.4.34, 2.6.4 (= 6.19.1), 2.40.4 (= 5.42.3), 2.45.2; 3.28.21; 4.2.5, 4.12.1, 4.16.3, 4.19.8, 4.35.20, 4.38.4 (= FV 293), 4.44.11, 4.46.2 (= FV 22); 5.37.15, 5.37.17, 5.46.3; 6.16.2, 6.22.4; 7.35.6; 8.41.7; 9.51.10; 10.42.6–7; FV 276; Cons. 5.6. M. Amelotti, *Per l'interpretazione della legislazione privatistica di Diocleziano* (Milan, 1960), 63 n. 24, for further specimens and relevant literature.

7. R. Taubenschlag, *Das römische Privatrecht zur Zeit Diokletian's* (Kraków, 1923).

8. E. Albertario, review of Taubenschlag (see above), *Archivio Giuridico* 92 (1924), 104–7. See also E. Albertario, "Le classicisme de Dioclétien," *SDHI* 3 (1937), 115–22 (= "La romanità di Diocleziano," in *Studi di diritto romano,* vol. 5 [Milan, 1937], 195–204), and "Da Diocleziano a Giustiniano," in *Conferenze per il XIV centenario delle Pandette* (Milan, 1931), 391ff. (= *Studi,* vol. 5, 205–53).

of the classical law.[9] This description has since been repeatedly confirmed.[10]

The character of the legislation of Diocletian attracted scholarly interest above all because Roman legal historians were at the time attempting to determine when, or under which emperor, unofficial and even (at least in origin) non-Roman legal traditions and practices began to find their way into the imperial legislation. The groundbreaking work of Ernst Levy, who, perhaps naively, chose the designation "vulgar law" in preference to a term such as *Volksrecht* used by Ludwig Mitteis a generation before, opened a debate on the nature of late antique Roman law that remains unresolved today.[11] Despite the opprobrium surrounding the term "vulgar law," which has led to unfair condemnation of the very scholars most responsible for making late antique Roman law a subject of scholarly inquiry,[12] the concept is a genuine attempt to describe real phenomena: late antique Roman law undergoes considerable change, ultimately emerging in the Roman-barbarian law codes of the West and in the classicizing Justinian *Corpus* of the East. That is not to say that classical Roman law was simply discarded, a point emphasized by none other than Levy;[13] but the pace of change increased, and legal historians invented concepts such as *Volksrecht*, vulgar

9. F. Schulz, *Prinzipien des römischen Rechts* (Munich, 1934), 91, would elevate Diocletian's efforts to a "heroic struggle against peregrine popular law" (i.e., non-Roman, vulgar law). One early scholar to acknowledge juristic quality of the rescripts of Diocletian is F. Hofmann, "Der Verfall der römischen Rechtswissenschaft," in *Kritische Studien im römischen Rechte* (Vienna, 1885), 20–26. Hofmann instead condemned Constantine (p. 23).

10. O. E. Tellegen-Couperus, *Testamentary Succession in the Constitutions of Diocletian* (Zutphen, 1982), 1–4, with relevant literature; cf. D. Johnston, "Epiclassical Law," *CAH* XII^2, 202–7; Amelotti, *Interpretazione*; J. Herrmann, "Diokletians Reskripte zur Landpacht," in *Studien zur antiken Sozialgeschichte. Festschrift Friedrich Vittinghoff* (Cologne, 1980), 453–63 (= *Kleine Schriften zur Rechtsgeschichte* [Munich, 1990], 373–83).

11. L. Mitteis, *Reichsrecht und Volksrecht in den östlichen Provinzen des Römischen Kaiserreichs* (Leipzig, 1891); E. Levy, *West Roman Vulgar Law: The Law of Property* (Philadelphia, 1951); E. Levy, *Weströmisches Vulgarrecht. Obligationenrecht* (Weimar, 1956). See further, G. G. Archi, "Il volgarismo e il diritto postclassico, Inchiesta: Quarta puntata," *Labeo* 7 (1961), 210–17; F. Wieacker, "Vulgarrecht und Vulgarismus. Alte und neue Probleme und Diskussionen," in *St. Biscardi*, vol. 1 (Milan, 1982), 33–51; H. J. Wolff, "Das Vulgarrechtsproblem und die Papyri," *ZRG* 91 (1974), 54–105; D. Simon, "Marginalien zur Vulgarismusdiskussion," in *Festschrift für Franz Wieacker zum 70. Geburtstag*, ed. O. Behrends et al. (Göttingen, 1978), 154–74.

12. E.g., J. Evans-Grubbs, *Law and Family in Late Antiquity: The Emperor Constantine's Marriage Legislation* (Oxford, 1995), 2, 50, and 341; Corcoran, *ET*^{2}, 3; and P. Garnsey and C. Humfress, *The Evolution of the Late Antique World* (Cambridge, 2001), 53–54.

13. Levy, *West Roman Vulgar Law*, 70: "Accordingly, an abrupt break with the past is completely absent."

law, and Christian law[14] to identify the sociocultural currents that informed the new directions taken in the imperial legislation.[15]

What this meant for the study of the legislation of Constantine was that scholars went in search of influences, Eastern or oriental but above all Christian. Contemporary studies of the legislation of Constantine reflected the vicissitudes of the legal historical debate. Christian influence on the legislation of Constantine attracted the attention of Vogt;[16] Ehrhardt elevated the handful of laws that suggest Christian influence to a proper *Religionspolitik.*[17] Edoardo Volterra attributed the drafting of some of the most radical Constantinian constitutions to Christian clerics.[18] Christian influence could be detected everywhere one looked. Similar assessments of this Christian policy of Constantine persist in more recent work.[19]

Among legal historians, at least, qualification and refutation swiftly ensued. The most imposing voice was that of Jean Gaudemet, who asked already in 1950, "What did Constantine know of Christian ethics in 320?"[20] "Little" was his answer, a position he maintained in numerous subsequent studies devoted to Constantine over his long, distinguished career.[21] The most recent monograph in English dedicated to the legislation of Constantine concurs: Judith Evans-Grubbs does not deny the Christianity of Constantine but regards any Christian influence with deep skepticism. Reprising the position of Gaudemet, she asks "what Constantine himself can be expected to have known, particularly in the first half of

---

14. Esp. B. Biondi, *Il diritto romano cristiano,* 3 vols. (Milan, 1952–54).

15. For a sobering example of the danger of revisionist attempts to dismiss vulgar law, see the withering review by R. Vigneron of *Recht und Rhetorik in den Kaisergesetzen der Spätantike,* by W. E. Voß, *ZRG* 102 (1985), 637–44, esp. 639–42, which concern the efforts of Voß to identify classical law "encoded" in highly rhetorical passages.

16. J. Vogt, "Zur Frage des christlichen Einflusses auf die Gesetzgebung Konstantins des Grossen," in *Festschrift für Leopold Wenger,* vol. 2 (Munich, 1945), 118–48.

17. A. Ehrhardt, "Constantin des Grossen Religionspolitik und Gesetzgebung," *ZRG* 72 (1955), 127–90. Reprinted in *Konstantin der Grosse,* ed. H. Kraft (Darmstadt, 1974), 388–456.

18. E. Volterra, "Quelques remarques sur le style des constitutions de Constantin," in *Mélanges Lévy-Bruhl* (Paris, 1959), 325–34, esp. 329ff.

19. E.g., Barnes, *CE,* 49–53.

20. J. Gaudemet, "Droit romain et principes canoniques en matière de mariage au Bas-Empire," *St. Albertario,* vol. 2 (Milan, 1950), 173–96 (= *Études,* vol. 3 [1979], 163–88), 186: "Que connaissait Constantin, en 320, de la morale chrétienne? Sans doute peu de chose, lui qui ne verra jamais dans les querelles religieuses que le trouble à la paix de l'état."

21. E.g., J. Gaudemet, "Les transformations de la vie familiale au Bas-Empire et l'influence du Christianisme," *Romanitas* 5 (1962), 58–85 (= *Études,* vol. 3 [1979], 281–310); J. Gaudemet, "Tendances nouvelles de la legislation familiale au IVe siècle," in *Transformations et conflits au IVe siècle après J.-C.* (Bonn, 1978), 187–207.

his reign before he took over the eastern half of the Empire (where most Christians lived) and participated in the Council of Nicaea."[22] The alternative proposed—that Constantine was reviving the morals of archaic Rome or confirming popular practice or sentiment[23]—rests on concepts more nebulous than even early Christian ethics, for which one may adduce the canons of church councils, the writings of the Patristic Fathers, and (not least) the Bible.

Study of the legislation of Constantine remains beholden to the search for origins and authenticity that preoccupied the participants of the debate on vulgar law. Legal historians formerly distinguished official from unofficial, popular, or vulgar; classical from late; and above all Roman from non-Roman. The pendulum has now swung in the opposite direction: one tries to rehabilitate the legislation of Constantine by discovering its, and implicitly its author's, hidden *Romanitas.* This is hardly necessary: rather than claiming that Diocletian fought a battle to preserve the purity of classical Roman law, one might with good reason conclude that Diocletian was a conservative legislator who applied Roman law as it had been developed in the capital, with little modification. Constantine, by contrast, was less beholden to this legal tradition—one might call his approach "progressive," although the often crude, draconian, and arbitrary innovations of Constantinian legislation are rightly criticized by legal historians who esteem legal sophistication and nuance.[24]

Constantine authored change in numerous areas of the law of the Roman Empire:[25] some of the most significant changes affected family law, which has lent itself well as a subject of sociohistorical study by ancient historians.[26] Other innovations affected the law of persons, slavery, testamen-

---

22. Evans-Grubbs, *Law and Family,* 88; cf. 38–39.

23. Ibid., 338–42.

24. D. Liebs, "Unverhohlene Brutalität in den Gesetzen der ersten christlichen Kaiser," in *Römisches Recht in der europäischen Tradition. Symposion aus Anlass des 75. Geburtstags von Franz Wieacker* (Ebelsbach, 1985), 89–116, esp. 89–92 and 113–14.

25. See the survey by M. Sargenti, "Il diritto privato nella legislazione di Costantino. Problemi e prospettive nella letteratura dell'ultimo trentennio," *AARC* 1 (1975), 229–332.

26. M. Sargenti, *Il diritto privato nella legislazione di Constantino. Persone e famiglia* (Milan, 1938) offers a good survey; less insightful, C. Dupont, *Les constitutions de Constantin et le droit privé au début du IVe siècle: Les personnes* (Lille, 1937). Evans-Grubbs, *Law and Family,* is the latest work to appear; cf. also G. G. Archi, "Contributo alla critica del Codice Teodosiano. Osservazioni su C. Th. 8, 18, 1 e C. T. 8, 18, 2," in *Symbolae iuridicae et historicae Martino David dedicatae,* vol. 1 (Leiden, 1968), 33–44; T. A. J. McGinn, "The Social Policy of Emperor Constantine in Codex Theodosianus 4, 6, 3," *TR* 67 (1999), 57–73.

tary law, the law of sale, and a variety of other areas.[27] In terms of legal substance, then, Constantine was prepared to intervene aggressively, and the range of Constantine's innovative legislation appears all the more remarkable when contrasted with the conservatism of his most significant predecessor. It must be said, however, that these legal innovations, whatever their inspiration or the alleged influences behind them, were as Roman as the emperor who sanctioned them.

Differences in Style and Form

The legal classicism of the constitutions of Diocletian and Constantine has yielded to consideration of the Latin style cultivated by the chancellery of each ruler and of the form of enactment favored under each regime. These questions are closely related and liable to confusion, for it appears that, at least until the age of Constantine, different styles were employed in different legal documents. Eugène Vernay made this observation in a noted article published in 1913.[28] Vernay impugned the classicism of the Latin style cultivated under Diocletian and earlier in a survey of rhetorically colored legislation from the High Empire. The most evident example is the apologetic edict on *aurum coronarium* promulgated by Alexander Severus.[29] Vernay observed that traits of the late antique style were already present in the edicts and even in the rescripts of Diocletian. Vernay's observation on the nature of the extant legal sources themselves would prove his most influential legacy. Vernay argued that the contrast in style commonly alleged between the constitutions of Diocletian and of Constantine is more apparent than real: the extant constitutions of both emperors constitute two incom-

27. Persons and slavery: Sargenti, *Il diritto privato;* testamentary law: e.g., B. Albanese, "L'abolizione postclassica delle forme solenni nei negozi testamentari," in *Sodalitas: Scr. Guarino,* vol. 2 (Naples, 1984), 777–92; sale: M. Sargenti, "La compravendita nel tardo diritto romano. Indirizzi normativi e realtà sociale (Contributo all'interpretazione di Vat.Fr. 35)," in *St. Biscardi,* vol. 2 (Milan, 1982), 341–63; status and corporations: J. Gaudemet, "Constantin et le recrutement des corporations," in *Atti del Congresso internationale di diritto romano e di storia del diritto. Verona, 27–28–29 settembre 1948,* vol. 3 (Milan, 1951), 19–25 (= *Études,* vol. 3 [1979], 445–53); J. Gaudemet, "Constantin et les Curies municipales," *IVRA* 2 (1951), 44–75 (Études, vol. 2 [1979], 97–130); cf. also J. Gaudemet, "La constitution 'ad populum' du 31 Janvier 320," in *Estudos em Homenagem aos Profs. Manuel Paulo Merêa e Guilherme Braga da Cruz* (Coimbra, 1983), 3–22 (= *Droit et Société* [1992], 117–36).

28. E. Vernay, "Note sur le changement de style dans les constitutions impériales de Dioclétien a Constantin," in *Études d'histoire juridique offertes a Paul Frédéric Girard,* vol. 2 (Paris, 1913), 263–74.

29. J. H. Oliver, "On the Edict of Severus Alexander (P. Fayum 20)," *AJPh,* 99 (1978), 474–85.

patible groups. From Diocletian survive private rescripts (preserved in the Codex Justinianus via the Hermogenianus and Gregorianus); from Constantine there survive predominantly official letters addressed most frequently to functionaries of the imperial administration (collected in the Codex Theodosianus). Uncritically compared, these distinct groups offer no sound basis for an assessment of legislative style of Diocletian and Constantine.[30] According to Vernay, two bureaus (*a libellis* and *ab epistulis*) affecting two different styles had been responsible for the composition of imperial pronouncements since the Principate. The *scrinium a libellis* wrote in the dry, juristic style of private rescripts; the *ab epistulis* (*Graecis* and *Latinis*) in the rhetorical style of imperial letters. With respect to *magistri libellorum* and *epistularum* of Diocletian and Constantine, Vernay considered the apparent triumph of the rhetorical style under Constantine to be no more than a product of distortion inherent in the legal sources: the picture would change if our sources permitted a direct comparison of rescripts with rescripts and letters with letters.

Not all of Vernay's arguments have since found favor. The inference that texts similar to the highly elaborate pronouncements of Late Antiquity must also have emanated from the early imperial chancellery—a claim made as if the style of early imperial pronouncements could not be assessed at first hand—has been refuted definitively by Eich and Eich.[31] The observation that private rescripts and imperial letters are incompatible legal genres, however, has been invoked in many studies of late antique legislation. The distinct styles of private rescripts and imperial letters were often neglected in older scholarship, but they are now taken into account in assessments of the forms of legislation typical of late antiquity. The sources suggest that rescripts declined steeply in popularity after Diocletian, while edicts and imperial letters under Constantine and his successors became the favored vehicles for the promulgation of new law.[32] In light of the con-

30. Vernay, "Note," 269.

31. A. Eich and P. Eich, "Thesen zur Genese des Verlautbarungsstils der spätantiken kaiserlichen Zentrale," *Tyche* 19 (2004), 92–93; on Diocletian: Amelotti, *Interpretazione*, 18–32. Volterra, "Quelques remarques," attempted to vindicate Constantine's classicism by attributing some of the most egregiously nonclassical constitutions to Christian clerics (e.g., CTh. 3.16.1, the notoriously misogynistic ban on unilateral divorce).

32. E.g., already Hofmann, "Verfall," 25: "Unter Constantin trat, wie in so vielem Anderen, so auch in der Form der Gesetzgebung eine Aenderung ein: statt der Rescripte bedienten sich die Kaiser immer häufiger 'jener neuen Form der Edicte, die für die eingreifenderen, zum Theil gewaltsamen Veränderungen des Rechts in der That die allein passende war.' Von da an wird die Gesetzgebung immer unrömischer"; cf. Sargenti, *Il diritto privato*, 180; E. Albertario, "Alcune osservazioni sulla legislazione di Costantino," in *Studi di diritto romano*, vol. 5 (Milan, 1937), 257–58.

clusions of Vernay, however, this inference is now generally rejected—although there may be some truth in it. At least from the time of the tetrarchs, general edicts gain unprecedented prominence across the empire, most famously, but not exclusively, in the Edict of Maximum Prices;[33] Constantine himself cultivated the edict particularly as a vehicle for the sweeping legislative change.[34]

An influential article by William Turpin exemplifies the position of recent scholarship regarding the transition in legislative style and form from Diocletian to Constantine or, more broadly put, from the High Empire to Late Antiquity.[35] Turpin takes the inherent bias of the legal sources observed by Vernay still further, reasoning that the legislation of Constantine must in fact have been no different from that of Diocletian, because religious, not legal, reasoning informed the choice of Theodosius II to codify the imperial letters and edicts issued after the accession of Constantine. The Codex Theodosianus commences with the legislation of Constantine "simply because Theodosius II was not interested in collecting the legislation of his pagan predecessors."[36] According to Turpin, any perceived change in style or form from Diocletian to Constantine is the product of the skewed picture created by the failure of Theodosius to collect Diocletianic letters and edicts.[37]

This conclusion is far too schematic. As was argued in chapter 1, it is mistaken to assume that the Christianity of Constantine moved Theodosius to choose his constitutions as the earliest authorities in the Codex Theodosianus. It moreover does not follow that the legislation of Constan-

---

Amelotti, *Interpretazione,* 16, 28–32, and 95, views the choice of private rescripts or *leges generales* as indicative of profoundly distinct legislative attitudes; cf. C. Dupont, "Constantin et les constitutions impériales," in *St. Volterra,* vol. 1 (Milan, 1971), 549–50.

33. See S. Corcoran, "Galerius' Jigsaw Puzzle: The Caesariani Dossier," *AntTard* 15 (2007), 222–23, on the wide publication of edicts under the tetrarchs and Constantine.

34. E.g., the abolishment of the Augustan penalties for celibacy, CTh. 8.16.1, which was part of a larger edict; cf. Evans-Grubbs, *Law and Family,* 103–39; J. Gaudemet, "La constitution 'ad populum.'" Similarly, the incredibly harsh law on *raptus* (CTh. 9.24.1; Evans-Grubbs, 183–202); as well as CTh. 4.12.3 and CTh. 9.9.1, on the *SC Claudianum* and sexual relations with slaves (Evans-Grubbs, 263–316).

35. W. Turpin, "The Law Codes and Late Roman Law," *RIDA*^{3} 32 (1985), 339–53. Cf. L. Wenger, *Die Quellen des römischen Rechts* (Vienna, 1953) 536–41; Corcoran, *ET*^{2}, 3–4. Specifically on Constantine: Evans-Grubbs, *Law and Family,* 50–51. Contra: J. D. Harries, "How to Make a Law-Code," in *Modus Operandi: Essays in Honour of Geoffrey Rickman,* ed. M. Austin, J. D. Harries, and C. Smith (London, 1998), 66–71 and 78. Evans-Grubbs, *Law and Family,* 158–59, accepts a decline in the rescript system already in the late reign of Diocletian, despite her support of Vernay.

36. Turpin, "Law Codes," 339.

37. See chapter 1, esp. 27–29 above on the compilation of the Codex Theodosianus.

tine must have resembled Diocletian's, even if Theodosius had excluded the legislation of Diocletian from the Codex Theodosianus on religious grounds.[38] Direct comparison of the legislation of Constantine and Diocletian would still be necessary. Even an analysis based on the extant sources, despite their deficiencies, is preferable to the assumption of stylistic uniformity a priori. Although the extent of our sources is limited, they exist in sufficient numbers to give at least a general impression of the respective nature of the legislation of Diocletian and Constantine.[39]

Latin Style: Private Rescripts

It is well known that the rescripts of Diocletian are generally, as in legal content, so also in style, classical. The chancellery of Diocletian composed private rescripts in a Latin style consistent with the language of classical jurisprudence, the remains of which are preserved in the Digest. By contrast, even the few rescripts of Constantine that survive betray a tendency toward an ornate language inappropriate in a traditional juristic *responsum*[40] but exemplary of the stylistic virtuosity of the fourth century.[41] Private rescripts once answered petitioners in terse legal language and laid out applicable remedies at law. It was necessary to elaborate these responses in clear terms so that a litigant, and especially a judge, could determine to what circum-

---

38. Turpin, "Law Codes," 353: "If Theodosius' choice of a Constantinian starting date was dictated by religious considerations instead of legal ones, it follows that our surviving evidence does not by itself present an accurate picture of Roman Law." On the contrary, the picture may be accurate, but this must be proven; it does not follow that it must be inaccurate.

39. Cf. Wieacker, *Textstufen klassischer Juristen,* 429 n. 14, on Vernay and Volterra: "Diese Urteile sind nur als relative berechtigt: auch die große Masse der rein juristisch inspirierten Gesetze Konstantins zeigt rhetorische Stilisierung, und auch der Stilwandel von Diokletian zu Konstantin ist nicht einfach mit Vernay allein durch eine Art optische Täuschung (nämlich durch die Überlieferung von Reskripten bis Diokletian, von Erzeugnissen der Kanzlei *ab epistulis* seit Konstantin) zu erklären."

40. This emerges clearly in the careful study by D. V. Simon, *Konstantinisches Kaiserrecht. Studien anhand der Reskriptenpraxis und des Schenkungsrechts* (Frankfurt a. M., 1977), 20–49, an analysis and discussion of extant private rescripts of Constantine, focusing specifically on FV 273–74 and 33–34; cf. Amelotti, *Interpretazione,* 27 and 50. These findings are nothing new: Hofmann, "Verfall," 25, cites Padeletti, *Lehrbuch der römischen Rechtsgeschichte. Deutsche Ausgabe von Holzendorff* (1879), 387: "Schon unter Constantin bemerkt man einen bedeutenden Verfall; von ihm und seinen Nachfolgern erhaltene Rescripte sind sowohl rücksichtlich ihrer Form, als auch ihrem Inhalte viel mangelhafter."

41. In general, H. Zilliacus, *Zur Abundanz der spätgriechischen Gebrauchssprache* (Helsinki, 1967); G. Vidén, *The Roman Chancery Tradition: Studies in the Language of Codex Theodosianus and Cassiodorus' Variae* (Göteborg, 1984); M. Roberts, *The Jeweled Style: Poetry and Poetics in Late Antiquity* (Ithaca, 1989).

stances the rescript of the emperor applied. If a petitioner received a rescript in his favor, it remained for judge to determine whether the facts of the case corresponded to those provided by the petitioner and presumed by the emperor.

The draftsmen in the chancellery of Constantine had higher, literary ambitions. The following is an example of a Constantinian rescript concerning gifts between spouses:

FV 273 (a. 315)

D(OMINVS) CONSTANTINVS ET CAESS. Prisca legum aequitate praeclusa, variis ambagum versutiis exquisita donatio, licet titulum emptionis vel debiti tenorem conprehendere videatur, tamen claris testationibus probata, debet in irritum devocari, si quidem consultissima ratione videatur esse provisum matrimonio constante donationes inter virum et uxorem altrinsecus agitatas nullam firmitatem habere. Nec sibi debent mulieres blandiri, si tamquam venditores vel debitores ad eludendas legum sanctiones mariti earum se falso videantur esse professi. Quare Vettium Rufinum, clarissimum virum praefectum urbi, amicum nostrum, cuius notio est, adire non prohiberis, qui partium allegationibus examinatis petitioni tuae secundum iuris providebit iustitiam. DAT. XIIII KAL. NOV. MEDIOLANO CONSTANTI[n]O ET LICINIO [iiii] CONSS.

LORD CONSTANTINE AND CAESARS. Precluded by the justice of former laws, a donation made through various ruses of dissimulation, though it seem to have the token of a sale or the tenor of a debt, nevertheless, when proven so by clear testimony, ought to be declared void, for it appears to have been established by most expert reasoning that donations reciprocally made between husband and wife while their marriage abides have no validity. Nor should women delude themselves, if their husbands have claimed dishonestly that they are sellers or debtors in order to cheat the sanctions of the laws. Wherefore you are not forbidden to approach Vettius Rufinus, *clarrissimus vir,* urban prefect, Our friend, under whose jurisdiction your case falls, who, having examined the allegations of the parties, will attend to your petition according to the justice of the law. GIVEN 19 OCT. (315) AT MILAN IN THE CONSULSHIP OF CONSTANTINE AND LICINIUS FOR THE FOURTH TIME.

The Latin of this constitution is a model of precious abstraction and decorative *variatio.* The style is indeed so ornate as to be interpretable only with the greatest difficulty.[42] As MacMullen once put it, "Meaning is hidden, like a penny in a sofa."[43] The diction serves first to distribute praise or blame; precise elucidation takes a distant second place. An illegal donation is characterized circuitously with the words *variis ambagum versutiis exquisita donatio.* Not until the clause beginning *si quidem* is it revealed what the insidious *donatio* to which reference is made in fact is: a gift between husband and wife. That such donations are illegal, whatever their nature, is stated by a kind of logical anastrophe in the elaborate opening phrase *prisca legum aequitate praeclusa* (*donatio*).[44] Women should not "flatter" or "delude themselves" if their husbands claim to be sellers or debtors. Even the routine instruction to the petitioner to take his case to the urban prefect smacks of refinement: the litotes *non prohiberis,* the disturbed word order of *secundum iuris providebit iustitiam,* the substitution of the pleonastic expression *secundum iuris iustitiam*—also an etymological pun—for *secundum ius* or a similar expression (e.g., *iure*). If by some chance the final sentence had been lost, the language of this constitution would have led most scholars to conclude that it was not a private rescript at all, but a typically ornate edict or letter to an official.

Gifts between spouses were neither new nor peculiar to the age of Constantine. They occurred with such regularity that it is possible to compare how Diocletian describes such gifts in his own rescripts. The contrast is instructive. Diocletian issued one such rescript to a certain Theodorus. The emperor touches on specious transactions between spouses in conspicuously anemic language, as follows: "If your father did not make a real contract, but under the pretext of a sale made a donation of property to your mother . . ."[45] Another rescript by Diocletian on illegal gifts between spouses, sent to a woman named Materna, reads as follows:

42. Cf. Simon, *Konstantinisches Kaiserrecht,* 35: "Als Ergebnis der Untersuchung von Vat. 273 ist festzuhalten, daß das Reskript zwar unklar aufgebaut ist, auch die simulierte Abrede nicht konkret mitteilt (*titulus emptionis vel debiti*) und zudem die klare und nüchterne Diktion der diokletianischen Reskripte vermissen läßt, daß es aber gleichwohl in der Sache nach klassischem Recht entscheidet."

43. R. MacMullen, "Roman Bureaucratese," in *Changes in the Roman Empire. Essays in the Ordinary* (Princeton, 1990), 75. See this article generally (pp. 67–77 = *Traditio* 18 [1962], 364–78), for a concise survey of the linguistic characteristics of the grand bureaucratic style.

44. Note the hypallage of *prisca,* which properly should modify *legum* (cf. *prisci iuris* in CJ 9.9.27).

45. CJ 5.16.15: *Si non verum contractum pater vester gessit, sed sub specie venditionis donationem possessionis in matrem vestram contulit.*

CJ 5.16.18 (a. 293)

DIOCL. ET MAXIM. AA. ET CC. MATERNAE. A marito in uxorem donatione collata matrimonii tempore nec initio dominium transferri potest nec post, si divortium intercesserit vel prior persona quae liberalitatem accepit rebus humanis fuerit exempta vel ab eo qui donavit fuerit revocata, potest convalescere. SVB. DIE IIII K. IVL. SERDICAE AA. CONSS.

DIOCLETIAN AND MAXIMIAN AUGUSTUS AND THE CAESARS TO MATERNA. Ownership can neither be transferred through a donation made by a husband to his wife during their marriage in the first instance nor revive thereafter, if divorce has occurred or the woman who received his generosity should depart this life first or the donation is revoked by him who made it. SIGNED 28 JUNE (293) AT SERDICA IN THE CONSULSHIP OF THE AUGUSTI.

Again, the Diocletianic text limits itself to plain statement of facts and their legal consequences. The language is terse; if it is at all difficult, the difficulty is due rather to the complexity of the legal concepts delineated therein than to the preciosity of the draftsman's conceits. Comparison of FV 274, a rescript addressed by Constantine to Aurelia Sabina *sive* Gaudiosa, with Diocletianic rescripts on the same subject also collected by the compiler of the *Fragmenta Vaticana* (FV 276–79) further illustrates the wide discrepancy in style between their chancelleries.[46]

While the surviving rescripts of Constantine strive for universal majesty of expression and rhetorical brilliance, the Diocletianic chancellery vents its indignation in moralistic diction chiefly in cases of sexual crimes,[47] a tendency that will be seen below in the famous edict on incestuous mar-

46. Simon, *Konstantinisches Kaiserrecht*, 24–32, citing FV 277–78 with further rescripts from the CJ.

47. Cf. esp. CJ 9.9.20: *Foedissimam earum nequitiam, quae pudorem suum alienis libidinibus prosternunt, non etiam earum, quae per vim stupro comprehensae sunt, inreprehensam voluntatem leges ulciscuntur, quando etiam inviolatae existimationis esse nec nuptiis earum aliis interdici merito placuit;* CJ 9.9.24: *Etsi libidine intemperatae cupiditatis ex actorum lectione exarsisse te cognitum est, tamen cum ancillam comprehendisse et non liberam stuprasse detectum sit, ex huiusmodi sententia gravatam potius opinionem tuam quam infamia adflictam esse manifestum est.* These rescripts, both addressing cases of rape, are the most moralistically colored in this title cited by Vernay, "Note," 296–97. The rest are typical rescripts spiced with single words or phrases that express the moral condemnation of the emperors: e.g., CJ 9.9.23.1–2: *ad . . . ulciscendam turpis lucri cupiditatem . . . censuram cum foedissimo flagitio accepit;* cf. FV 280 (= CJ 3.29.7) for an indignant description of a case of *querella inofficiosi testamenti.*

riages. The rescripts of Diocletian address even inadvertent confessions of wrongdoing with cool moderation.[48]

Latin Style: Administrative Letters

We are not constrained to compare only the private rescripts of Diocletian with the administrative letters, or even with the few extant private rescripts, of Constantine. Several administrative letters issued from the chancellery of Diocletian are extant, most preserved in the Codex Justinianus.[49] These official letters enable us to assess the stylistic tendencies of constitutions intended for internal communication within the provincial administration. The letters of Diocletian consist, on the whole, of colorless instruction. They recall the unaffected style of the rescripts, just as the rescripts of Constantine recall the style of his letters. The fact that even more administrative letters of Diocletian's must lurk unidentified among the private rescripts collected in the Codex Justinianus is a testament to the similarity of their styles. Such official letters of Diocletian are indistinguishable not only because of the abridgement of their *inscriptiones* but because of their pedestrian style as well.

Examples of rhetorical virtuosity in the letters of Diocletian that rival the ornamentation typical of Constantinian constitutions may indeed be found, but such examples more often consist of single rhetorical flourishes than whole paragraphs of purple prose. For instance, in CJ 9.41.8,[50] Diocletian and Maximian instruct the governor Sallustianus that veterans may be tortured under no circumstances, even if they have been discharged from service early. The emperors add that judges should not initiate an inquiry with torture but should resort to it only after they have assessed the arguments of the litigants and other evidence. The emperors describe this evidentiary process with some vividness:

---

48. E.g., CJ 4.7.5: *Promercalem te habuisse uxorem proponis: unde intellegis et confessionem lenocinii preces tuas continere et cautae quantitatis ob turpem causam exactioni locum non esse. Quamvis enim utriusque turpitudo versatur ac soluta quantitate cessat repetitio, tamen ex huiusmodi stipulatione contra bonos mores interposita denegandas esse actiones iuris auctoritate demonstratur.* CJ 10.42.6 is an amusingly terse rebuke sent to a philosopher who requested immunity from liturgies on his property: *Professio et desiderium tuum inter se discrepant. Nam cum philosophum te esse proponas, vinceris avaritiae caecitate et onera quae patrimonio tuo iniunguntur solus recusare conaris. Quod frustra te facere ceterorum exemplo poteris edoceri.* Cf. also CJ 2.12.15.

49. Catalog with discussion compiled by Corcoran, *ET*², 125–42.

50. Letter no. 17 in Corcoran, *ET*², 129.

CJ 9.41.8.2 (undated)

Et si his (*sc.* argumentis) veluti certis indiciis ducti investigandae veritatis gratia ad tormenta putaverint esse veniendum, tunc id demum facere debebunt, si personarum condicio pateretur.[51] Hac enim ratione etiam universi provinciales nostri fructum ingenitae nobis benevolentiae consequentur.

Led by these (proofs) as if by sure marks for tracking down the truth, if they should judge that they must resort to torture, then they at last ought to do so, if the status of the persons permits it. For in this way, even all Our provincials will reap the fruit of Our native benevolence.

The conceit of following *argumenta* like a path to the truth is a pleasant metaphor, and the emphasis laid on the benefit derived by the provincials from the benevolence of their monarchs is a suitably flattering conclusion. The style of the preceding part of the letter, which here has been omitted, is thoroughly unremarkable.

Another moderately colorful example is CJ 1.51.1, a letter sent to one Paulinus, dated 286:[52]

IMPP. DIOCL. ETIANVS ET MAXIM. IANVS AA. PAVLINO. Studiorum labor meretur, ut hi, qui in publicis administrationibus constituti sociari sibi consiliorum participes cupiunt, spe praemiorum atque honorificentia sua provocent eos, quorum prudentiam sibi putant esse necessariam, non metu terribili et necessitate incongrua libertati. D. PRID. ID. IVL. TIBERIADE MAXIMO II ET AQVILINO CONSS.

DIOCLETIAN AND MAXIMIAN AUGUSTUS, TO PAULINUS. The labor of scholarship warrants that those in public office, who desire to join to themselves men to participate in their deliberations, must induce those whose expertise they consider indispensable by the hope of rewards and their own commendation, not by horrible fear and compulsion, which ill suits free men. GIVEN 14 JULY (286) AT TIBERIAS IN THE CONSULSHIP OF MAXIMUS, CONSUL FOR THE SECOND TIME, AND OF AQUILINUS.

Paulinus had perhaps offended his own counsel, whose complaints provoked this reprimand from the emperors.[53] Despite ample opportunity for

51. *Sic* Krüger, *ad loc.* Read *patiatur.*
52. Letter no. 1 in Corcoran, *ET*^{2}, 125.
53. Cf. Corcoran. *ET*^{2}, 242–43.

moralistic extravagance, the emperors express their sentiment in homely platitudes: they appeal to the magistrate's sense of respect for the men on whose knowledge he depends. The description of these counselors as *consiliorum participes* underlines their entitlement to fair treatment as equal parties in the deliberations of the judge. The most remarkable word in the fragment is *honorificentia,* incidentally a favorite of the author of the *Historia Augusta.*[54]

An elevated style, in contrast, is encountered in CJ 2.13.1,[55] a letter addressing the notorious patronage of *potentiores* in legal disputes:[56]

CJ 2.13.1 (a. 293)

IMPP. DIOCLETIANVS ET MAXIMIANVS AA. ET CC. ARISTOBVLO SALVTEM. Divine admodum constituit divus Claudius consultissimus princeps parens noster, ut iactura causae adficerentur ii, qui sibi potentiorum patrocinium advocassent, ut hoc proposito metu iudiciariae lites potius suo Marte discurrerent, quam potentiorum domorum opibus niterentur. (1.) Quem palam est in tantum provincialium [questionibus][57] esse commotum, ut huius sanctionis rectores provinciarum custodes et contemptae rei vindices fecerit, scilicet ut in actores seu procuratores in subsidia negotiorum vel usurpatos gratia vel redemptos severa sententia vindicarent. (2.) Quare cum intersit et universe omnium et praecipue tenuiorum, qui saepe importunis potentium intercessionibus opprimuntur, inter litigatores audientiam tuam impertire debebis: nec metuas, ne praeiudices clarissimis viris, cum divus Claudius huius rei rectorem provinciae et disceptatorem et, si res postularet, ultorem specialiter fecerit. D. IIII ID. SEPT. AA. CONSS.

DIOCLETIAN AND MAXIMIAN AUGUSTUS AND THE CAESARS TO ARISTOBULUS, GREETINGS. The deified Claudius, that most prudent prince, Our parent, divinely ruled that those who had summoned the patronage of the powerful be punished by the loss of their case, so that by setting this fear before them judicial disputes might proceed on their own strength, rather than rely on the means of the houses of the powerful. (1.) It is manifest that Claudius was moved to such a pitch by the [complaints] of the provincials that he made the provincial governors the protectors of this decree and its avengers, should it be igt-

54. SHA *Ant. Phil.* 10.2; *Ver.* 3.4, 3.5; *Sev.* 4.1; *Alex. Sev.* 2.4; *Aurel.* 25.6.

55. Letter no.22 in Corcoran, *ET*², 130.

56. See chapter 7 on "*Relations* and Potentiores."

57. I tentatively suggest *questionibus* (complaints, "complainings") here for *quaestionibus,* which Krüger prints. Mommsen proposed *questibus.*

> nored, namely so that they punish with a harsh sentence those litigants or agents or procurators who have been employed through favor or bribed to bolster their cases. (2.) Therefore, since it is of interest both universally to all and particularly to the poor, who are often overwhelmed by the brazen interference of the powerful, you will be obliged to share your ear between the litigants: and do not be afraid to rule against men of senatorial rank, for the deified Claudius made the provincial governor particularly both judge and, if matters so demand, avenger in this matter. GIVEN 10 SEPTEMBER (293) IN THE CONSULSHIP OF THE AUGUSTI.

The first sentence sets a tone of dignity and majesty, which is maintained in the following by several eloquent turns of phrase. The emperors make an etymological pun on *divus* and *divine,* an adverb that casts the decree of Claudius and its provisions in the best light. The divine (i.e., deified) Claudius divinely (i.e., ingeniously) regulated the matter at hand. Claudius is further complimented by the superlative *consultissimus,* which at once implies both juristic and authorial approval of his ruling. Disputes at law are personified as doing battle (*iudiciariae lites . . . suo Marte discurrerent*), lending dramatic force to the clash of weak and powerful. The connecting relative pronoun *quem* in the second section resumes the story of Claudius, who was "so greatly moved" (*in tantum . . . commotum*) by the complaints of the provincials that he charged provincial governors to defend them and punish wrongdoers. The sentence is shaped by two specimens of elegant parallelism, one of objective genitives: *provinciarum custodes et contemptae rei vindices;* the other of perfect passive participles: *vel usurpatos gratia vel redemptos.* Parallelism is continued in the third sentence by the adverbs and genitives dependent on *interesse: cum intersit et universe omnium et praecipue tenuiorum.* The first instance of parallelism noted above is reprised with the words *huius rei . . . et disceptatorem . . . et ultorem* in the direct instructions to the governor.

The emperors advertise their awareness that the balance of power in the provinces might often lean to the side of powerful citizens against the governor. It is conceivable that Diocletian and Maximian may have been seeking to inspire confidence in their addressee, Aristobulus, proconsul of Africa,[58] by recalling in impressive language the legislation of Claudius. Conversely, since Aristobulus would doubtless have referred to this imperial letter in a confrontation with senatorial *potentiores,* the solemnity of the

58. Barnes, *NE,* 97.

letter may also have been calculated to impress them. The emperors may also have anticipated an opportunity to forestall the machinations of such men by virtue of the publication of their letter upon receipt. Such speculation aside, the circumstances of the letter and the reason why it differs so strikingly from all other extant letters of this period, are unknown.[59]

As with the rescripts on gifts between spouses, it is also possible to compare administrative letters of Diocletian and Constantine. In the pair below, both Diocletian and Constantine touch on the *Caesariani,* agents of the *res privata* notorious for corruption. CJ 10.1.5, incidentally, has been identified as one of the most "rhetorical" of Diocletian's letters.[60]

CJ 10.1.5 (a. 284/292)[61]

EXEMPLVM SACRARVM LITTERARVM DIOCLETIANI ET MAXIMIANI AA. AD FLACCVM. Prohibitum est cuiuscumque bona, qui fisco locum fecisse existimabitur, capi prius, quam a nobis forma fuerit data. (1.) Et ut omni provisionis genere occursum sit Caesarianis, sancimus licere universis quorum interest obicere manus his, qui ad capienda bona alicuius venerint, qui succubuerit legibus, ut, etiamsi officiales ausi fuerint a tenore datae legis desistere, ipsis privatis resistentibus a facienda iniuria arceantur. (2.) Tunc enim is, cuius interest bona alicuius non interpellari, officialibus volentibus ea capere debet adquiescere, cum litteris nostris cognoverit non ex arbitrio suo Caesarianos ad capiendas easdem venisse facultates, sed iustitiae vigorem id fieri statuisse.

A COPY OF THE SACRED LETTER OF DIOCLETIAN AND MAXIMIAN AUGUSTUS TO FLACCUS. It is forbidden to seize the property of anyone who is deemed to have made room for the *fiscus* before a document has been given by Us. (1.) And so that the *Caesariani* may be resisted with every manner of foresight, We decree that it is permitted to all interested parties to lay hands on them, who have come to seize the property of someone who has succumbed to the laws, so that, even though the officials dare to stray from the tenor of the established law, they shall be kept from wrongdoing by the resistance of private citizens. (2.) For then he, whose interest it is that someone's property not be

59. Cf. Corcoran, *ET*², 130 n. 25.

60. Simon, *Konstantinisches Kaiserrecht,* 47 n. 214; Simon considers only CJ 10.1.5 and 9.9.27 (on which, see below) to be very rhetorical in style; less rhetorical, CJ 2.13.1 and 9.9.25.

61. Corcoran, *ET*², letter no. 18, pp. 129, 347–48, and 349–52. Also on the *Caesariani:* edict no. 36, p. 191 (= Inscr. Cret. 1.189, CIL 5.2781, ll. 31–34; Bruns, *Fontes*⁷, no. 95). See now Corcoran, "Galerius' Jigsaw Puzzle," 221–50; cf. Delmaire, *Largesses Sacrées et* res privata. *L'aerarium impérial et son administration du IVe au VIe siècle* (Rome, 1989), 215.

troubled, should yield to the officials who desire to seize it, since he will learn from Our letter that the *Caesariani* have not come to seize the property of their own accord, but that the force of justice has decreed that it be done.

CTh. 10.8.2 (319)

[IMP. CONSTANTINVS] A. AD PRISCVM RATIONALEM. Ne principali liberalitate praeventa dominium quis rei alienae affectet, iubemus, quotiens iure suadente aliquorum bona ex officio tuo fuerint occupata, breves eorum plenissimos ad virum perfectissimum comitem et amicum nostrum mitti, ne fraudibus Caesarianorum inminuantur vel petentibus aliquid abiuretur; poena contra rationalem et officium eius proposita, si petitorem ante possidere permiserint id quod ei donatum est priusquam praedicti breves commeaverint. DAT. V ID. MAR. SIRMIO CONSTANTINO A. V ET LICINIO CAES. CONSS.

[EMPEROR CONSTANTINE] AUGUSTUS TO PRISCUS, RATIONALIS. So that the imperial generosity may not be prevented and someone affect ownership of something not belonging to him, We order that whenever, at the counsel of the law, someone's property is seized by your staff, extensive briefs on that property be sent to the *vir perfectissimus* and Our friend, the *comes* (*rei privatae*), so that the property is not reduced through the frauds of the *Caesariani* or anything is alienated from the petitioners; a penalty has been set against the *rationalis* and his staff, if they permit a petitioner to take possession of the property granted to him before the aforementioned briefs have arrived. GIVEN AT SIRMIUM 11 MARCH (319) IN THE CONSULSHIP OF CONSTANTINE AUGUSTUS, CONSUL FOR THE FIFTH TIME, AND OF LICINIUS CAESAR.

The confiscations of the loathed *Caesariani* furnish good material for dramatic elaboration. Diocletian states unequivocally that the *Caesariani* cannot confiscate property without a certificate from the imperial chancellery (a *forma* or *litterae*). So as to check the *Caesariani* (*ut . . . occursum sit Caesarianis*) he writes that property holders may "lay hands on them" to prevent them from wrongdoing but must acquiesce if the *Caesariani* produce an imperial notice. The formulation of CJ 10.1.5 is otherwise unremarkable. Repetition of the word *interest* with the genitive (*quorum, cuius interest*) is a particularly pedestrian specimen of legalese, but the linguistic restraint of Diocletian emerges most clearly from comparison with Constantine.

Constantine too speaks disparagingly of the *Caesariani,* citing their habitual "frauds" that diminish properties granted to petitioners. That Constantine is speaking of imperial grants must be inferred from *principalis liberalitas* in the colorful ablative absolute construction with which the fragment begins. One might compare Diocletian's use of the humble phrase *locum fisco facere* (although it is alliterative) and the plain verb *capere* to refer to confiscation. The phrase *principali liberalitate* itself, denoting imperial grants, appears in only two other constitutions of the Codex Theodosianus.[62] The phrase *iure suadente* is unique but resembles a common construction found in fourth-, fifth-, and sixth-century constitutions whereby an abstraction, alone or dependent on *ratione,* is used with *suadente* to indicate motive.[63] The fondness for obscure and lengthy ablative absolute clauses on display here will be familiar to any reader of late antique constitutions. Use of the ablative absolute construction with *poena proposita* to append a penalty clause is a common trick of fourth- and fifth-century constitutions.[64] *Commeare* too is a favorite word of imperial constitutions from Constantine on, used not in its classical frequentative sense but as a recherché synonym for *ire, venire,* and the like.[65] Finally, the use of *abiurare,* normally meaning, "to deny something on oath," in the sense "to deprive someone of ownership of a thing" (for *alienare*) is unattested in the lexica; a parallel can be found however, in a constitution of Theodosius II.[66]

CJ 9.9.27, also considered one of the most rhetorical letters of Diocletian,[67] contains language surprisingly hostile to the Roman legal tradition.[68] The emperors posture as placing *pudor* above legal riddles and introduce their emendation of the law in a single sweeping period. The concluding sentence reiterates the indignity of sacrificing modesty (*pudor*) to legal sleight of hand:t

---

62. CTh. 12.11.1.2: *qui vero aliquid ex eiusdem bonis principali liberalitate fuerint consecuti;* CTh. 5.7.1: *sive in aliquem principali liberalitate transfusa sunt.*

63. CTh. 8.1.3: *utilitate suadente;* CTh. 10.18.3: *suadente numine;* CTh. 13.11.16: *aequitatis ratione suadente;* CTh. 11.36.12: *publica utilitate suadente;* CTh. 12.1.177 pr: *soli genitalis amore vel liberalitatis cupiditate suadente;* CJ 8.51.3.2: *pietatis ratione suadente.*

64. Cf. CTh. 2.18.3; CTh. 4.13.3; CTh. 5.6.3; CTh. 8.4.20. By the reign of Theodosius II *poena proposita* has made its way into the nominative case (CTh. 11.30.60).

65. Compare the usage in CJ 10.40.2 (Alexander Severus on a father who frequently visits his son overseas) with CTh. 8.5.16 pr, CTh. 8.8.7, CTh. 12.12.10, CTh. 15.2.1 (used of aqueducts!), CTh. 16.2.15.2, Sirm. 4. In contrast, CTh. 6.29.6, CTh. 8.5.23.3, and CTh. 13.5.27, all concerning commerce, use *commeare* in the classical sense as in Caesar, *BG* 1.1.3: *minimeque ad eos mercatores saepe commeant.* CJ 4.63.2, on merchants, is also classical.

66. CTh. 10.21.3: *nec est, ut quisquam de abiurato pretio conqueratur. TLL* s.v. *abiuro* 2 translates both these passages as *praestare nolle, retinere.* The sense *alienare* is not found in the *OLD* or in Lewis and Short.

67. Simon, *Konstantinisches Kaiserrecht,* 47 n. 214.

68. Corcoran, *ET*^{2}, 70; cataloged as letter no. 31, p. 132.

CJ 9.9.27 (a. 295)

[IMPP. DIOCLETIANVS ET MAXIMIANVS AA. ET CC. CONCORDIO PRAESIDI NVMIDIAE. Ita nobis pudor cordi est, ut removeamus prisci iuris ambages et constituamus in adulterii quaestione abolitis de medio ceteris praescriptionibus praeter quinquennii temporis et lenocinii quod marito obicitur exceptionem, illam etiam, quae post solutum prius matrimonium ante denuntiationem nuptae competit, fidem criminis nosci. Indignum est enim, ut ultionem pudoris praestigiae versuti iuris excludant. PP. K. IVN. TVSCO ET ANVLLINO CONSS.

DIOCLETIAN AND MAXIMIAN AUGUSTUS AND THE CAESARS TO CONCORDIUS, GOVERNOR OF NUMIDIA. We have such concern for modesty that We remove the ambiguities of former law and, having abolished utterly all limitations besides that of five years and the exception of pimping that may be alleged against a husband, as well as the limitation that affects a bride after the dissolution of her marriage and before her denunciation, We decree that the reliability of the allegation must be ascertained. For it is outrageous that the tricks of cunning law should prevent vengeance on behalf of modesty. POSTED 1 JUNE (295) IN THE CONSULSHIP OF TUSCUS AND ANULLINUS.

The style of this text recalls the tetrarchic edicts more than any letter. It recalls particularly the edict on incestuous marriages (Coll. 6.4), promulgated only month earlier. In the edict against incest, *ius Romanum* and *leges Romanae* are cited with the greatest reverence.[69] The important adjective *Romanus* is absent from CJ 9.9.27. When something is affirmed, Diocletian celebrates his adherence to Roman tradition; when something is annulled, it is a triumph of imperial equity. *Pudor,* on the other hand, is a theme of both texts.[70]

Corcoran notes that the opening words of CJ 9.9.27 suggest a general disposition, but he classifies the text as a letter according to its addressee, the governor of Numidia.[71] Perhaps CJ 9.9.27 is a letter version of an edict similar to Coll. 6.4 that had been forwarded to the governor. It is either an unusual specimen of the epistolary style of the Diocletianic chancellery or perhaps, together with the letter concerning the *potentiores* (CJ 2.13.1), indicative of a shift in style as the tetrarchy matured. An earlier letter to Pompeianus concerning adultery is, by contrast, markedly restrained:

69. Coll. 6.4.1 and 3–4.
70. Coll. 6.4.2: *sine ullo respectu pudoris;* 6.4.6: *pudoris observatio.*
71. Corcoran, *ET*^{2}, 132.

CJ 9.9.19 (a. 287)

IMPP. DIOCLETIANVS ET MAXIMIANVS AA. AD POMPEIANVM. Quamvis indubitati iuris sit, quotiens adulterii crimen intenditur, praesentiam accusatoris procedere oportere, tamen quoniam ex litteris tuis cognovimus Materiam praepositi Viatoris uxorem habitis quaestionibus cum Iuliano quondam adulterium commisisse detectam sub ipsa prolatione sententiae Viatoris ipsius praesentiam postulasse, non putavimus confecto paene in iudicio facinore et iam agitata quaestione convicto praepositum ab excubiis limitis revocandum. [S. D.] NON. DEC. AA. CONSS.

EMPERORS DIOCLETIAN AND MAXIMIAN AUGUSTUS TO POMPEIANUS. Although it is indisputably the law that whenever a charge of adultery is made, the presence of the accuser is first required, since We have learned from your letter that Materia, wife of the *praepositus* Viator, was found over the course of interrogation to have committed adultery with Julianus and then demanded the presence of Viator as the very sentence was being delivered, We do not think that the *praepositus* should be recalled from his station on the frontier, since the trial had virtually been concluded and the crime already proven during the interrogation. [UNDATED] DEC. (287) IN THE CONSULSHIP OF THE AUGUSTI.

The emperors go so far as to grant an exception to the law of adultery, which requires the presence of the husband to act as plaintiff, yet there is no indignation perceptible in their reasoning. CJ 9.9.25,[72] also an alleged specimen of Diocletianic rhetoric,[73] is nothing more than a detailed set of instructions for pursuing a case of adultery complicated by the uncertain status of the adulterer. Bald description of an affair between a slave and a married woman merely as a *flagitium* is symptomatic of the general indifference of the Diocletianic chancellery in expressing the moral judgments in official letters.[74]

---

72. Letter no. 21 in Corcoran, *ET*², 130.

73. See n. 60 above.

74. CJ 9.9.25 (293): *sin vero eum servum esse cognoveris . . . in adulterium crimen protinus debebis inquirere ac, si eum detectum in eo flagitio esse perspexeris, poenam decernere, quam in adulterii crimen legum sanctio statuit.* The word *flagitium* is frequently used by classical jurists to denote such liaisons: e.g., Dig. 4.2.7.1 (Ulpian), 17.1.50.1 (Celsus), 26.2.17.1 (Ulpian), 45.1.123 (Papinian). Contrast the edict of Constantine on such affairs: CTh. 9.9.1; cf. G. Ries, *Prolog und Epilog in Gesetzen des Altertums* (Munich, 1983), 195–96, noting departures from the strict juristic style, which will be examined below.

Tetrarchic Antecedents

A shift in style, however, appears to have occurred by the year 300. If one considers the letters concerning *potentiores* (CJ 2.13.1) and adultery (CJ 9.9.27) typical, such a transition may have been under way at the creation of the tetrarchy. The extant official letters after 300 generally exhibit the grand or ornate style previously reserved for edicts (see below). The earliest specimen is CJ 3.3.3, dated 25 March 300, concerning *iudices pedanei* appointed by a governor:[75]

CJ 3.3.3 (a. 300)

EXEMPLVM SACRARVM LITTERARVM [IMPP. DIOCLETIANI ET MAXIMIANI] AA. ET CC. AD SERAPIONEM. Placet, ut iudicibus, si quos gravitas tua disceptatores dederit, insinues, ut delegata sibi negotia lata sententia determinent: nec in his causis, in quibus pronuntiare debent et possunt, facultatem sibi remittendi patere ad iudicium praesidale cognoscant, maxime cum, et si iudicatio alicui litigatorum parti iniusta videatur, interponendae provocationis potestas a sententia ex omni causa prolata libera litigatoribus tribuatur. D. VIII K. APRIL. ANTIOCHIAE CC. CONSS.

A COPY OF THE SACRED LETTER OF THE SAME AUGUSTI (SC. EMPERORS DIOCLETIAN AND MAXIMIAN) AND CAESARS TO SERAPIO. We decree that you should inform the judges whom Your Gravity appoints to hear trials that they shall resolve the cases delegated to them by the delivery of a ruling: and let them know that the power of remitting those cases, in which they should and can pronounce (a verdict), to the gubernatorial court is closed to them, especially because, even if the judgment should seem unjust to some part of the litigants, the free power of registering an appeal from a ruling delivered in any case is conferred on the litigants. GIVEN 25 MARCH (294 [300]) AT ANTIOCH IN THE CONSULSHIP OF THE CAESARS.

The diction and phraseology of this letter is strikingly reminiscent of letters preserved in the Codex Theodosianus. For example, the emperors use *determino* in the pleonastic phrase *lata sententia determinent* to mean "adjudicate," not "to establish the boundaries of a place" or "to fix a time" or

75. Corcoran, *ET*^{2}, 134, imperial letter no. 35. The transmitted date 294 is incorrect; a different letter potentially to the same addressee (CJ 3.28.26) is dated to 304.

"limit by time" as the classical jurists in the Digest use the word.[76] The complicated sentence, *nec in his causis . . . facultatem sibi remittendi patere . . . cognoscant,* is a model of the late antique legislative style and (juristically speaking) is interrupted by unnecessary comment on the duty and ability of *iudices pedanei* to reach a decision. The emperors could have said as much with the words, for example, *nec ad praesidem remitti possit.* The author takes considerable pains to avoid using the same word twice: judges are *iudices* and *disceptatores* in the first sentence; the act of delivering a ruling is variously described as *sententia lata determinent, pronuntiare, iudicatio,* and *sententia prolata;* lawsuits are *negotia* and *causae.* The boring verb *possum* is studiously avoided by means of artful abstraction: *facultatem remittendi, interponendae provocationis potestas.* The curious partitive genitive *alicui litigatorum parti* stands out as a somewhat infelicitous mixture of two constructions: *si . . . cui litigatori/parti* and *si . . . cui litigatorum/partium* (*partes* in the sense of parties to the dispute). The result of this experiment is ambiguity: to some part of the litigants (i.e., one half?) or to one party of (i.e., among) the litigants. The reader of the Codex Justinianus need only skip up one constitution to CJ 3.3.2 to compare this letter with the purple prose of an edict issued by Diocletian in 294.

Other letters of this period give the same impression.[77] The most famous is the letter concerning the Manichaeans, sent to the proconsul of Africa in 302.[78] This letter is identical in tenor and style to the equally famous edict of 295 on incestuous marriage and to the edict of toleration issued by Galerius in 311.[79]

The edicts of the tetrarchs are the constitutions that most clearly anticipate the Latin style of the legislation of Constantine.[80] The convoluted lan-

---

76. E.g., Dig. 1.1.11 (Paul) of land and 3.1.8 (Papinian) of time.

77. CJ 5.73.4 (a. 303); 3.3.4 (a. 303); 6.9.7 (a. 305), 3.12.1 (a. 305) (these last two are letters issued by Constantius); P.Lips. 44 (probably a. 305); *FIRA*^{2} vol. 1, no. 92 (= CIL 3.6866 = ILS 6090 = Bruns^7, no. 34). The Brigetio Tablet (*FIRA*^{2} vol. 1, no. 93 = *AE* 1937.232), issued in 311 by Licinius, is an excellent specimen; Corcoran, *ET*^{2}, 145–48.

78. Coll. 15.3; Corcoran, *ET*^{2}, 135–36.

79. Corcoran, *ET*^{2}, 173–74, on Coll. 6.4 (imperial edict no. 3). Galerius (edict no. 26): Lact., *DMP* 33.11–35; Eus., *HE* 8.17.1–11.

80. Ries, *Prolog und Epilog,* 186–92; cf. E. Volterra, "Il problema del testo delle costituzioni imperiali," in *La critica del testo,* vol. 2 (Florence, 1971), 912–13; G. Matino, "Innovazioni linguistiche nei testi giuridici tardoantichi," in *Le trasformazioni della cultura nella tarda antichità. Atti del convegno tenuto a Catania, Università degli studi, 27 Sett.–2 Ott. 1982* (Rome, 1985), 109–18. The tetrarchic edicts and those of Constantine up to 324 have been cataloged by Corcoran, *ET*^{2}, 170–98; for epigraphic witnesses, D. Feissel, "Les constitutions des Tétrarques connues par l'épigraphie. Inventaire et notes critiques," *AntTard* 3 (1995), 33–53.

guage of tetrarchic edicts has long been adduced as the most compelling evidence against a stylistic rupture between Diocletian and Constantine, but the late letters of the tetrarchy strongly suggest that already at the time of the elevation of Constantine both imperial edicts and official letters were composed in the grand, ornamental style that would remain standard throughout late antiquity. The Edict of Maximum Prices, of all the constitutions of Diocletian the best and best-known example of what can fittingly be described as the late antique legislative style, had been issued just five years earlier.[81]

No attempt will be made here to quantify the Latin style of individual constitutions in the hope of divining their authorship.[82] It cannot be assumed that any constitution is the work of a single *magister libellorum* or *epistularum* (or *memoriae*), who, after all, presided over a *scrinium* of assistants.[83] The role of the emperor himself in the drafting of imperial constitutions generally can only be surmised. Serena Connolly has recently revived the argument that private rescripts were composed by a team of men under the supervision of the *a libellis* or *magister libellorum*.[84] The emperors cannot have been deeply involved in the composition of private rescripts. Serious doubt has been cast even on the role of *quaestor sacri palatii* under Constantine.[85] The letters and especially the edicts of Constantine

---

81. Corcoran, *ET*², 178–79 (edict no. 11) and 207–13; Eich and Eich, "Genese," 82–84.

82. On the stylometric method of Tony Honoré, see B. Frier, "Law on the Installment Plan," review of *Ulpian*, by T. Honoré (Oxford, 1982), *Michigan Law Review* 82 (1984), 856–68; F. Millar, "A New Approach to the Roman Jurists," *JRS* 76 (1986), 272–80; A. Watson, review of *Tribonian*, by T. Honoré, *Law Quarterly Review* 94 (1978), 459.; A. Watson, review of *Ulpian*, by T. Honoré, *Times Literary Supplement* (18 February 1983), 164; further in "An Open Letter to D. C.," *Rechtshistorisches Journal*, 3 (1984), 286–90 (with a response by Honoré, pp. 290–305); least charitable of all, the review, or rather lampoon, by M.-T. Fögen, "Massenmord an Texten," *Rechtshistorisches Journal*, 17 (1998), 6–11, in response to T. Honoré, *Law in the Crisis of Empire 379–455 AD. The Theodosian Dynasty and its Quaestors* (Oxford, 1998).

83. *Magistri scriniorum: Not. Dig. Occ.* and *Or.* i. and *Occ.* ix. On the duties of the *magistri: Not. Dig. Or.* xix (cf. *Occ.* xvii). See Jones, *LRE*, 367–68 with nn. 3 and 4, pp. 1143–44. The *magister memoriae*, who according to the *Notitia* (*Occ.* xvii, *Or.* xix) also responded to petitions (*respondet tamen et precibus*), destroys the tidy attribution of all private rescripts to the *magister libellorum*. On this official, see M. Peachin, "The Office of the Memory," in *Studien zur Geschichte der römischen Spätantike: Festgabe für Professor Johannes Straub* (Athens, 1989), 168–208.

84. S. Connolly, *Lives behind the Laws: The World of the* Codex Hermogenianus (Bloomington & Indianapolis, 2010), 55–57 and 155–58. Most legal historians never assumed that rescripts were written by the emperors and not by professional jurists, e.g., Ehrhardt, "Religionspolitik," 391: "Denn daß der Kaiser sie nicht alle selbst redigieren konnte, sollte auf der Hand liegen." Ehrhardt, in turn, refers to Vernay, "Note" (1913), etc.

85. Zos. 5.32 says Constantine created this office; J. Harries, "The Roman Imperial Quaestor from Constantine to Theodosius II," *JRS* 78 (1988), 148–72; cf. Jones, *LRE*, 1144 n. 3 (to p. 368); G. de Bonfils, *Il comes et quaestor nell'età della dinastia costantiniana* (Naples, 1981). The recon-

often betray a distinctly personal style, and some of the most characteristic specimens will be discussed in the following chapters. It is impossible to measure where the voice of Constantine begins and where it ends in such documents, but the interpretation of his edicts and most of his official letters offered here presumes the engagement, if not always the authorship, of Constantine himself. Edicts and letters, which were produced far less frequently than private rescripts, need not represent the *ipsissima verba* of Constantine to serve as evidence of a peculiarly Constantinian vision of government and justice.

This work is not the place to attempt an exhaustive philological survey of the constitutions of Diocletian and Constantine; the remarks above are admittedly impressionistic and general in nature. Owing to the state of the legal sources, there may never be consensus on the respective qualities of the rescripts and official letters of Diocletian and Constantine.[86] It would be irresponsible, though, not to make an assessment on the basis of what evidence is available. The examples given above are intended to illustrate how the author has been led to the following assessment of the respective constitutions of Diocletian and Constantine.

First, the impression of stylistic divergence in the constitutions in the Codex Theodosianus and Codex Justinianus is essentially correct; it must, however, be refined. Although the edicts of the tetrarchs and Constantine show remarkable similarity, the style of the rescripts and administrative letters of the tetrarchs before circa 300 differs substantially from that of Constantine. The rescripts of Diocletian consistently conform to what may be described as a classical legal style; that is to say, they continue the usage of the often spare, technical Latin encountered in the writings of the jurists and moreover in the rescripts of the High Empire.[87] Only twenty-five pri-

---

struction by W. E. Voß, *Recht und Rhetorik in den Kaisergesetzen der Spätantike* (Frankfurt, 1982), 22–39, is methodologically flawed: Voß infers what the procedure of drafting constitutions was from reforms introduced by Theodosius II in 446 (CJ 1.14.8); he then posits the hypothetical procedure before the reform under Constantine (25–28). Voß's conclusions were warmly welcomed by T. Honoré, "The Making of the Theodosian Code," *ZRG* 103 (1986), 136–44, and his study is frequently cited in English-language scholarship, but see the devastating review by R. Vigneron, *ZRG* 102 (1985), 637–44 ("Wir stehen vor einem romanistischen Scherbenhaufen").

86. The hypercriticism advocated by Volterra, "Il problema del testo delle costituzioni imperiali," 1094–97, errs in the other extreme.

87. See Eich and Eich, "Genese," 75–81, for an excellent analysis of the "normative" and "representational" styles of the Principate; for comparison, cf. H. Honsell, "Der Gesetzstil in der römischen Antike," in *Sodalitas: Scr. Guarino*, vol. 4 (Naples, 1984), 1659–73, on the defects of the ("schwerfällig, umständlich und pedantisch," p. 1665) legislative style of the Roman Republic.

vate rescripts are extant from the years 295–305; whether the transition to the late antique style in private rescripts took place during this period or was introduced by Constantine is a question that cannot yet be answered. The edicts of the tetrarchs, however, are consistent models of the late antique legislative style.[88]

The official correspondence of Diocletian and his colleagues seems to bear witness to the adoption of a new form of communication between the emperors and their officials. The administrative letters of Diocletian at first adhere to the familiar standard of his predecessors, but it appears that a decision of policy was made, perhaps at the foundation of the tetrarchy, whereby the emperors began to address their officials in the same ceremonial language with which they addressed the Roman people in their edicts.

The purpose served by the legislative style that proliferated under the tetrarchs and Constantine is complex. It would be appropriate to speak of several purposes, insofar as the ceremonial language of the legislation was used in different kinds of enactments before different audiences. One reason must have been the need for persuasion: like the panegyrics delivered before the emperors, the style of which the imperial constitutions closely emulate,[89] the documents composed for the population of the empire were persuasive texts. The emperors seek not only to command but also to convince, and they do so in a language that by its very elegance and sonority should win the approval of their subjects.[90] The need of the imperial regime for approval, palpable in the legislation of the late third and fourth centuries, was heightened, it has been argued, by the burdens imposed on the general population in consequence to the administrative reforms of Diocletian. The greater pervasiveness of the imperial government, and above all a system of taxation imbued with new rigor, had to be compensated by greater intensity of communication.[91] The laws not only command, but also explain and justify. The preface to the Edict of Maximum Prices epitomizes the deployment of persuasive rhetoric to justify the enactment of a law that by its very nature was both invasive and dirigiste.[92] In the words of Clifford

88. See further Eich and Eich, "Genese," 81–91.

89. E.g., Gaudemet, "La constitution 'ad populum,'" 12–22. (= *Droit et Société* [1992], 126–36).

90. On panegyrics as constitutive of consent and on their broad circulation, see the illuminating observations of C. Ando, *Imperial Ideology and Provincial Loyalty in the Roman Empire* (Berkeley, 1999), 127–28; cf. M. Maas, *Die Darstellung des Kaisers in der lateinischen Panegyrik* (Stuttgart, 1994), 53–54 and 225–26.

91. "Eine höhere Kommunikationsintensität" in the words of Eich and Eich, "Genese," 99.

92. See ibid., 91, on the apologetic tone of late antique legislation.

Ando, "the rulers of the empire perpetually sought to found their actions on the *consensus* of their subjects."[93] Persuasion was one means of inspiring such consensus.

It would be an exaggeration, however, to argue that mere awareness of the potential unpopularity of a measure led the emperors to blunt the resentment of their subjects with preemptive, apologetic rhetoric. A great many imperial constitutions composed in the same exalted style betray no concern for argumentation or apology. Rhetoric does more than provide the means with which to present legislation: it provides the means with which to present the emperor himself. The emperors of the late third and early fourth centuries—Diocletian and in particular Constantine—completed the transformation of the person of the emperor from civil *princeps* to godlike *dominus,* a process under way since the inception of the empire. The tetrarchs rose to claim semidivine status, an immediate relationship with the gods.[94] The disguise of the simple citizen, long obsolescent, was exchanged for a shroud of ceremony and ritual. This new imperial style, which conveys the solemnity and majesty of the emperor, finds its visual expression in art already by the end of the third century.[95] The verbal expression of the exaltation of the emperor, the ceremonial language of the legislation, developed apace.

The elaborate language of the imperial constitutions not only raised the emperor above his humble subjects. An inconceivable distance had long stood between emperors and the provincials. The vast population of the empire was affected by changes in ceremonial and ritual only at second hand.[96] The imperial administration, from the praetorian prefects and court bureaucrats to the petty provincial governors, who administered twice as many provinces of greatly reduced size—the functionaries of the imperial administration itself experienced at first hand the metamorphosis of the court. The emperor was exalted in the first instance over those who stood nearest to himself, from whom he had the most to fear.

Peter Brown has demonstrated how representatives of the imperial government elaborated a language of power calculated to win the loyal support,

---

93. Ando, *Imperial Ideology,* 338; cf. p. 48.

94. F. Kolb, "Praesens Deus: Kaiser und Gott unter der Tetrarchie," in *Diokletian und die Tetrachie. Aspekte einer Zeitenwende,* ed. A. Demandt et al. (Berlin, 2004), 27–37.

95. Garnsey and Humfress, *Evolution,* 25–33.

96. In part, by the concurrent elevation of the status of certain high officials: Garnsey and Humfress, *Evolution,* 33, citing R. Lim, *Public Disputation, Power, and Social Order in Late Antiquity* (Berkeley, 1995), 24; cf. Eich and Eich, "Genese," 89–90 and 101–2.

the *devotio,* of provincial notables, and how such provincials used the same language to influence or manipulate the representatives of the emperor.[97] Brown identifies a "seeming dissonance" between the refined, cultured norms of elite society and the coercive authoritarianism of the central government, which threatened to sweep them away.[98] Brown disarms the threat of power by reference to persuasion, the means of interaction embraced both by imperial officials and by provincial grandees, founded on a common culture of *paideia.* Although both provincial elite and imperial officials might pretend to *paideia,* Brown illustrates best the defensive potential of persuasive rhetoric, as employed by provincials to temper the demands of the imperial administration. The rhetorical education of the provincial elite gave them a means of blunting the force of official violence.[99] Despite the education of imperial officials, which is necessary if *paideia* is to have any effect on them, the imperial government as an institution seems to Brown to stand apart from the cultured norms of the provincial elite: "Those who exercised power, by contrast, are virtually mute."[100] On the contrary, emperors like Diocletian and Constantine were hardly mute: through their legislation, they strove to inspire approval and awe—not only in their humblest subjects, but also in the most cultured, and in the ranks of the imperial bureaucracy itself.[101]

In countless official communications, the emperor exhorts and cajoles, all the while expressing himself with transcendent majesty. The exaltation of the emperor was realized even in the language with which he addressed his officials. Official correspondence also demonstrated the supremacy of the emperor, and the regular publication of such documents served to instill in members of the imperial bureaucracy both fear and awe. Ando argues that

97. P. Brown, *Power and Persuasion in Late Antiquity: Towards a Christian Empire* (Madison, 1992), 3.

98. Ibid., 8.

99. Ibid., 48: "The education of a notable, however, provided the basis for dealing with a grimmer aspect of late Roman politics—with the increased impingement of official violence, directed against members of the upper class. The ideals associated with *paideia* were invoked, with great urgency, to check such violence."

100. Ibid., 43: "Once there was a danger that the common code of formalized speech, and all that this stood for, might be brushed aside, the notables of the Greek world had to face a degree of vulnerability to the power of the emperor and his servants to which they had no intention of allowing themselves to become habituated." The quotation above is from p. 13.

101. My discussion of Brown's *Power and Persuasion* and the persuasive force of the late antique legislation is inspired by the insightful review by the late Marie-Theres Fögen, "Die Macht der Sprache und die sprachlose Macht," *Rechtshistorisches Journal* 13 (1994), 95–100.

"the charismatic power of the imperial office guaranteed the orderly functioning of the Roman bureaucracy."[102] "Guaranteed" is too strong a word, but the language of legislation and official correspondence was certainly calculated to inspire *devotio.* If the expression of the imperial will could not guarantee the obedience of the bureaucracy, other means might be found: Constantine lent authority to public acclamations, introduced checks on imperial officials, and reformed the system of appeal.[103] These will be the subjects of later chapters. The authority of the emperor might even facilitate the execution of administrative tasks; he could provide his officials with a redoubtable weapon of words; for example, an imperial letter at once elegant, majestic, and persuasive—or thunderous and terrifying—with which the cultivated appeals of recalcitrant provincial grandees, as illustrated by Brown, could be countered.[104]

The proliferation of the mannered, elaborate rhetorical mode of expression in the legislation of the tetrarchy demonstrates that it was not a consequence of the conversion of Constantine; the exalted style cultivated by the Constantinian chancellery was not in itself an innovation. The changes that legislative style underwent in the final years of the reign of Diocletian were inherited, not by Constantine alone, but by all members of the tetrarchic college. It appears that Constantine took the final step in employing the grand style even in private rescripts; the old hypothesis of Ehrhardt, that Constantine filled his *scrinium libellorum* with Gallic rhetors from Trier, may have some merit to it after all, but it cannot be proven.[105] With the change, one of the last resorts of technical language in a rhetorical world was at last modernized.

In his study of language in late antiquity, Erich Auerbach observes that the traditional correspondence of style and subject matter could not be adopted by Christian authors: "The Christian speaker does not know of any gradation of subject matter. . . . The subject matter of the Christian speaker is always the revelation, and this is never a middle or low subject."[106] A sim-

---

102. Ando, *Imperial Ideology,* 410, reprising the argument developed pp. 362–72.

103. Acclamations are discussed with differing emphasis by Brown, *Power and Persuasion,* 149–50, and by Ando, *Imperial Ideology,* 199–205; 362–64 on bureaucracy; and 373–74 on appeal.

104. Brown, *Power and Persuasion,* 35–70.

105. Ehrhardt, "Religionspolitik," 393–97. There is much to criticize in the details. Cf. Wieacker, *Textstufen klassischer Juristen,* 429–30 n. 14.

106. E. Auerbach, *Literatursprache und ihr Publikum in der lateinischen Spätantike und im Mittelalter* (Bern, 1958), 30: "Der christliche Redner kennt absolute Abstufungen der Gegenstände nicht . . . Der Gegenstand des christlichen Redners ist stets die Offenbarung, und diese ist niemals ein mittlerer oder ein niederer Gegenstand." See further, Auerbach's remarks pp. 43–44 and 187.

ilar principle is at work in the imperial legislation of the age. The theme of the fourth-century legislator is always a species of self-revelation: the very act of legislating becomes both the assertion and confirmation of the supremacy of the imperial will. The connection of religious fervor to rhetorical abundance made by Auerbach lends itself well to late antique emperors, for pagans and Christians alike. The tetrarchs justify their actions by invoking the immortal gods; the palinode of Galerius, and his appeal to Christians to pray for their emperor, is an attempt to create a new religious consensus that admitted, and in a sense naturalized, the god of the Christians alongside those that had always sanctioned imperial rule. The undercurrent of divine sanction that pervades the legislation of this period and accounts for much of its solemn urgency would take a new direction with the ascendancy of the first Christian emperor. Constantine shares the obsession of his colleagues with moralistic exposition, solemn language, and divine sanction.[107] Yet the edicts preserved by Eusebius and other documents reveal a significant break. His pagan counterparts once spoke of the immortal gods and their *Romanitas* in mutual solidarity; Constantine, standing alone, proclaims his God before the provincials of the empire, on whose prosperity and unity his own salvation appears to depend.[108]

107. Av. Cameron, "The Reign of Constantine, A.D. 306–37," *CAH* XII^2, 95.

108. See chapter 4, pp. 97–107, on CTh. 9.1.4; Ando, *Imperial Ideology,* 397–98, rightly stresses the distinctness of Constantine's preoccupation with the divine; cf. J. Wienand, "Der Kaiser als Sieger. Untersuchungen zur militärischen Repräsentation Constantin I.," PhD diss., Konstanz, 2010, 305–7 and 310–13.

4
The Propagation of Justice

Edicts and the Ideals of Justice

The universal edict was the natural vehicle to convey the pretensions of the Constantinian regime to the masses of the empire.[1] Imperial edicts were heard with awe.[2] These constitutions indeed suggest that just governance and the integrity of imperial officials ranked among the foremost ambitions of Emperor Constantine. It was, of course, their purpose to suggest this. Edicts to the Roman people, the inhabitants of the empire, amply attest how justice was advertised and promised under Constantine's rule.

The constitutions in this and in the following chapters are a distillation of what may appropriately be called the aspirations of the Constantinian regime.[3] Constantine answers administrative abuse and corruption with scathing rebukes and violent denunciations; he prohibits and protects in bold, sweeping statements—and punishes. The edicts of Constantine portray an emperor locked in a contest, not with barbarian invaders or domestic criminals, but with the very administration that serves in his name. This spectacle is a kind of populist absolutism; the spectators, those who read or hear the edicts of Constantine throughout the empire, are rallied to the cause of their ruler. Indeed, the religious sanction of the tetrarchs is trans-

1. Cf. A. Eich and P. Eich, "Genese des Verlautbarungsstils der spätantiken kaiserlichen Zentrale," *Tyche* 19 (2004), 84 n. 31 and 85–87.

2. C. Kelly, "Emperors, Government and Bureaucracy," *CAH* XIII, 143, citing Joh. Chrys., *Hom. in Gen.* 14.2, 44.1; *Hom. in Matth.* 1.8; cf. Lib., *Or.* 1.157; Basil, *Ep.* 3.1.

3. Aspirations: Jones, *LRE,* viii. See also the introduction to chapter 6 below.

formed by Constantine into a relationship of service: the salvation of the emperor himself appears to rest on the success of his earthly mission.[4]

The ferocity of Constantine's edicts is characteristic, seldom equaled by his successors. That is not to say that the declarations of Constantine were mere verbiage. Constantine does not expatiate on the vices of his administrators in toothless sermons; he decrees punishment and elaborates means of its realization. The channels through which corrupt governors and other officials may be called to account are consistently illustrated both for offender, the bureaucracy, and victim, the provincials of the empire. The need for administrative oversight after the provincial reorganization of Diocletian is met in part by the deployment of high officials throughout the empire, who were endowed with the legal authority of the emperor himself. Direct delegation might enable the emperor to be present in every province. The path of redress proceeded from the provincial governor to the men closest to Constantine, the praetorian prefects and *comites provinciarum*, and from thence to Constantine himself. This system of control is reflected in the hierarchy of appellate jurisdiction established by Constantine, which is the subject of chapter 8. The same approach is taken in cases of corruption and abuse. As we shall see, the edicts of Constantine loudly make this vicarious accessibility known to all.

Licinius the Tyrant

The conquest of the East in 324 made Constantine sole ruler of the Roman world, which had been shaken by the rival claims of the successors of the failed tetrarchic experiment. The acquisition of the populous and wealthy provinces of the Roman East set Constantine before a challenge of communication. It was naturally desirable to denigrate the Licinian regime, but in order to transform victory over Licinius into the triumph of all inhabitants of the East, Constantine presented a vision of government to his new subjects that advertised the restoration of liberty and the rule of law. Part of Constantinian liberty was, as is well known, religious: documents preserved by Eusebius show that Constantine wasted no time in declaring both general tolerance and personal favor for the Christian religion; the policies of Licinius that had disadvantaged it were reversed. The first years after the conquest of the East witnessed several edicts addressed by the emperor to

4. C. Ando, *Imperial Ideology and Provincial Loyalty in the Roman Empire* (Berkeley, 1999), 397–98; cf. the conclusion of chapter 3 above and the discussion of CTh. 9.1.4 below.

his new subjects, in which he expressed and defended his religious convictions.[5]

Constantine did not, however, limit his public pronouncements to matters of the spirit. Fragments of constitutions preserved in the Codex Theodosianus attest to the broad legislative and governmental ambitions entertained by Constantine. In several edicts after 324, the declared principles of the Constantinian regime receive their most emphatic formulation and convey well the determination to enforce not only religious toleration but also the rule of law throughout the East and the empire at large; such, at least, is the impression they make. The rhetorical triumph of Constantinian rule of law relied heavily on the vilification of Constantine's defeated opponent.

Under Constantine, the removal and execution of a rival brought with them the inevitable suppression of his memory. Such was the fate of Maximian, Maxentius, Licinius, and even Constantine's own son Crispus.[6] This act of suppression extended to the laws of the fallen. After the defeat of Licinius, Eusebius asks, "What need is there to recall each and every one of the deeds of this man hated by God, or how this most lawless of men devised illegal laws?"[7] The annulment of the legislation of Licinius was among the first things done in 324. Constantine effected it with more zeal than forethought:[8]

5. Eus., *VC* 2.24–42 (epistolary edict to the provincials of the East); Eus., *VC* 2.46.1–3 (letter to Eusebius, bishops encouraging them to approach provincial governors for the repair of church buildings); Eus., *VC* 2.48–60 (epistolary edict to the provincials of the East, attack on polytheism); cf. Barnes, *CE*, 208–12; T. D. Barnes, "The Constantinian Settlement," in *Eusebius, Christianity, and Judaism*, ed. H. W. Attridge and G. Hata (Leiden, 1992), 649–50.

6. Maximian: Lact., *DMP* 42.1; Maxentius: Eus., *HE* 8.13.15; for examples of the *damnatio memoriae* of Licinius and Crispus, see boundary stones 1 and 2 in P. Salama, "Anniversaires impériaux constantino-liciniens à Djémila," *Institutions, société et vie politique dans l'empire romain*, in ed. M. Christol et al. (Rome, 1992), 137–59; further, E. R. Varner, *Mutilation and Transformation: Damnatio memoriae and Roman Imperial Portraiture* (Leiden, 2004), 214–24; J. Wienand, "Der Kaiser als Sieger. Untersuchungen zur militärischen Repräsentation Constantins I.," PhD diss., Konstanz, 2010, 264–66.

7. Eus., *HE* 10.8.11: τί δεῖ τῶν καθ' ἕκαστα καὶ κατὰ μέρος τῷ θεομισεῖ πεπραγμένων μνημονεύειν ὅπως τε νόμους ἀνόμους ὁ παρανομώτατος ἐξεῦρεν; cf. Eus., *VC* 1.50–55, with 2.1; Praxagoras, *FGrH* II 219 T1.5–6. On the legislation of Licinius: S. Corcoran, "Hidden from History: The Legislation of Licinius," in *The Theodosian Code*, ed. J. D. Harries and I. Wood (Ithaca, 1993), 97–119; Corcoran, *ET*², 274–92; Gaudemet, "Constantin, restaurateur de l'ordre," in St. Solazzi (Naples, 1948), 664–73 (= *Études*, vol. 2 [1979], 85–94).

8. On the date: Seeck, *Regesten*, 174.

CTh. 15.14.1

IMP. CONSTANTINVS A. AD CONSTANTIVM PRAEFECTVM PRAETORIO. Remotis Licini tyranni constitutionibus et legibus omnes sciant iuris et statutorum nostrorum observari debere sanctionem. PROPOSITA XVII KAL. IAN. CRISPO III ET CONSTANTINO III CAESS. CONSS.

EMPEROR CONSTANTINE AUGUSTUS TO CONSTANTIUS, PRAETORIAN PREFECT. Since We have removed the constitutions and laws of Licinius the tyrant, let all know that the regulations of Our statutes must be observed. POSTED 16 DEC. (324) IN THE CONSULSHIP OF CAESARS CRISPUS, CONSUL FOR THE THIRD TIME, AND CONSTANTINE, CONSUL FOR THE THIRD TIME.

The *inscriptio* of this constitution identifies it as a letter to the praetorian prefect Constantius, who then presided over the East.[9] Its content, however, suggests that an edict preceded it: the annulment of the laws of Licinius affected every inhabitant of the East; the words *omnes sciant* recall the publication orders of edicts, as seen in chapter 2. Moreover, an edict was issued soon afterward to correct an important lapse in the annulment of the legislation of Licinius (see below): it is likely that the lapse itself had been made in an edict. The letter to Constantius, therefore, probably accompanied a lost edict to the provincials of the East.

In terms of substance, the letter to the prefect and the edict it presumably accompanied were straightforward: the constitutions and laws of the Licinius were annulled; those of Constantine supplanted them. The way, however, in which these changes are described and its probable derivation from the lost text of a general edict make the letter to Constantius an extremely important document of the legal pretensions of Constantine.

Constantine brands Licinius with the injurious designation *tyrannus*. This can hardly have presaged well for Licinius, who was living under custody in Thessalonica when the letter was issued.[10] The tyrant, the perennial target of schoolboy declamations, embodied virtually all species of vice, but autocratic lawlessness comes most readily to mind in the context of laws and legislation evoked by Constantine. It is at first glance mildly surprising that Constantine attributes "laws" and "constitutions" to Licinius "the

9. Barnes, *NE*, 131; *PLRE* I, Fl. Constantius 5.

10. D. Kienast, *Römische Kaisertabelle. Grundzüge einer römischen Kaiserchronologie* (Darmstadt, 1996), 294–95, for the relevant dates. Licinius's death: Eutrop., 10.6.1 (Socrates Scholasticus, *HE* 1.4.4, portrays Licinius as inciting barbarians prior to his execution).

tyrant" at all, forcing Constantine to resort to the terms "law" and "statutes" (*ius, statuta*) when referring to his own legislation to avoid repetition. On the other hand, had Constantine cited merely crimes or outrages committed by Licinius (e.g., *scelera, facinora*), the purpose of the text would have been obscured.

Attribution of the terms "law" and "statutes" to Constantine proves to be a felicitous compromise. At first glance, the pair of terms evokes the modern distinction made between *ius* and *leges*, in essence the writings of the jurists and imperial constitutions, or statutory law.[11] *Ius* here, however, is something broader; it evokes existing law and embraces both the writings of the jurists and the constitutions of past emperors. Licinius is denied any part in the law of the Roman Empire. *Ius*, moreover, is something of which Constantine does not claim authorship. His constitutions, *statuta nostra*, stand alongside this body of legal literature and legislation. Constantine annuls what Licinius has imposed on the body of Roman law, restoring pristine *ius* and introducing his own legislation in the East. He presents himself not only as the liberator of the East and the restorer of order but also, in marked contrast to Licinius (so Constantine), the champion of Roman law.

A glance back at the enactments of Constantine after the defeat of Maxentius shows the consistency of Constantine's aspirations as tyrant-slayer and his approach to the legislation of his defeated enemies. The champion of justice and law was a role much coveted by Constantine, who regularly branded his fallen enemies "tyrants," a word that would develop into a late antique *terminus technicus* for "usurper."[12] He had dealt with Maxentius in this way early in 313:[13]

CTh. 15.14.3

[IMP. CONSTANTINVS] A. ANTIOCHO PRAEFECTO VIGILVM. Quae tyrannus contra ius rescribsit non valere praecipimus, legitimis eius rescriptis minime

11. J. Gaudemet, "'Ius' et 'leges,'" *Iura* 1 (1950), 223–52 (= *Études*, vol. 1 [1979], 439–70).

12. V. Neri, "L'Usurpatore come tiranno nel lessico politico della tarda antichità," in *Usurpation in der Spätantike. Akten des Kolloquiums "Staatsreich und Staatlichkeit" 6.–10. März 1996 Solothurn/Bern*, ed. F. Paschoud and J. Szidat (Stuttgart, 1997), 73–75.

13. T. D. Barnes, "Christentum und dynastische Politik (300–325)," in Paschoud and Szidat, *Usurpation*, 106–8; Gaudemet, "Constantin, restaurateur de l'ordre," 655–57 (= *Études*, vol. 2 [1979], 76–78); M. Amelotti, "Da Diocleziano a Costantino. Note in tema di costituzioni imperiali," *SDHI* 27 (1961), 261–63. On the date: Seeck, *Regesten*, 160. Licinius's name has been restored in the *subscriptio*. On the recipient: *PLRE* I, Antiochus 15.

inpugnandis. DAT. VIII ID. IAN. ROMAE CONSTANTINO A. III [ET LICINIO III] CONS[S].

[EMPEROR CONSTANTINE] AUGUSTUS TO ANTIOCHUS, PREFECT OF THE WATCH. We ordain that the rescripts issued by the tyrant against the law are invalid; his legitimate rescripts are not to be challenged. GIVEN AT ROME 6 JAN. (313) IN THE CONSULSHIP OF CONSTANTINE AUGUSTUS, CONSUL FOR THE THIRD TIME, [AND OF LICINIUS, CONSUL FOR THE THIRD TIME].

As in 324, so in 313 Constantine evokes *ius* as a body of law that exists alongside the legislative interventions of the rulers that modify it. This letter, however, addresses a narrower range of imperial legislation than its successor in 324: Constantine invalidates the rescripts of Maxentius that violate (*contra*) or merely alter existing law. The rescripts of Maxentius might be private or administrative; it is unclear whether one category, and if so which, or both are meant. It is further unknown, though not improbable, whether Constantine invalidated other enactments of Maxentius, such as edicts.

With respect to the rescripts of Maxentius, the earlier constitution contains an important qualification missing in the later one. The edict of 324 apparently abolished the enactments of Licinius in their entirety, as the wording of the letter to the praetorian prefect suggests: *Remotis Licini tyranni constitutionibus et legibus.* This formulation appears excessively simplistic. The annulment of every Licinian constitution and law would have had serious legal consequences, yet it appears that the legislation of Licinius was indeed annulled in these broad terms. Although exception had been made in 313 for the *legitima rescripta* of Maxentius, a similar exception remarkably seems to have been overlooked in 324. An edict issued in February 325 both reveals and corrects the omission:

CTh. 15.14.2

[IMP. CONSTANTINVS] A. AD VNIVERSOS PROVINCIALES. Tyranni et iudicum eius gestis infirmatis nemo per calumniam velit quod sponte fecit evertere nec quod legitime gestum est. DAT. PRID. ID. FEB. PAVLINO ET IVLIANO CONSS.

[EMPEROR CONSTANTINE] AUGUSTUS TO ALL PROVINCIALS. Now that the acts of the tyrant and his governors have been invalidated, let no man seek to overturn by frivolous argument what he himself willingly did, nor what was legally done. GIVEN 12 FEB. (325) IN THE CONSULSHIP OF PAULINUS AND JULIANUS.

This second edict strongly suggests that Constantine had addressed the people in 324 in approximately the same wording as in the letter to the praetorian prefect. Absolute annulment of the acts of Licinius permitted disingenuous provincials, and perhaps also imperial officials, to cancel legitimate transactions or to disregard rulings of Licinius that conformed to established law and the legislation of Constantine.[14] Constantine appears to have found himself compelled to stop such crass manipulation of the law in a new edict with the threat of harsh punishment. The words *per calumniam* in this second edict capture the frivolous nature of attempts to renege on valid transactions concluded under Licinius. The phrase moreover provided imperial officials and judges with legal grounds for punishing offenders. They could be prosecuted as *calumniatores* and, if convicted, compelled to reimburse the trial costs and even suffer the punishment that their frivolous claims would have inflicted on the other party.[15]

The enactments in the East after 324 clearly reprise the posture assumed by Constantine after the conquest of Italy. The choice of the terms with which Constantine presents himself and his actions permits him to achieve several ideological ends. Invasion and conquest are justified by the vice of the enemy, the tyrant, and the plight of his subjects. The removal of the tyrant at once leads to the restoration of law and the introduction of the legislation of the liberator. The enactments of the tyrant are pruned away like an unnatural growth on the body of the law. Constantine's enactments of 324 and 325 suggest a legislative purge on a grand scale.

The analysis of CTh. 15.14.1–3 suggests that the legislation of Licinius was declared void in 324, remarkably, without qualification. Such careless legislation by a ruler who had been in power already almost twenty years,

---

14. Gaudemet, "Constantin, restaurateur de l'ordre," 664, comments on CTh. 15.14.1: "ces formules absolues d'une brutalité trop simpliste"; 673 (= *Études*, vol. 2 [1979], 85 and 94): "Inspirées par le désire de rétablir la justice, les mesures prescrites par Constantin en termes aussi généraux ne purent se réaliser sans entraîner un trouble profond de la législation et des situations privées."

15. *Calumnia* encompassed both frivolous accusation and defense. CTh. 15.14.2, *velit quod sponte fecit evertere,* most readily suggests the latter crime, whereby a defendant might dispute his obligations to the plaintiff with the argument that the contract, or whatever legal arrangement was at dispute, had been invalidated with the Licinian legislation. *Calumnia:* Kaser-Hackl §40.IV, pp. 284–85 (High Empire) and §97, pp. 630–32 (Late Antiquity). On the principle of *talio* in cases of *calumnia,* cf. CTh. 9.10.3: *non ignarus eam se sententiam subiturum, si crimen obiectum non potuerit conprobare, quam reus debet excipere* (here in the case of a frivolous suit concerning land).

who had handled an identical situation once before, is nothing if not startling. Had Constantine simply dictated the terms of the annulment, or had a member of the chancellery overlooked their implications? However it came about, the blunder is an excellent illustration of the impetuousness that often characterizes the legislation of Constantine.[16] The legislative enactments of Constantine consistently place message before content. In most cases, the laws will have been clear enough. The details of the annulment of what must have been a considerable body of Licinian legislation in 324/5 appear, however, to have been lost in the exultation of triumph.[17] The consequences of this lapse not only will have complicated the administration of justice throughout the East, but also conspicuously contradict the pretensions of Constantine as the restorer of justice and law after the overthrow of tyranny. It is unsurprising, then, that Constantine moved quickly to clarify and enforce the terms of the annulment of the legislation of Licinius.

Personal Insult and Retribution

The conquest of the East in 324 secured for Constantine not only the territory of Licinius, but also the administrative apparatus with which he had governed it. It was not enough merely to abrogate the acts of the defeated emperor and advertise the restoration of Roman law, the return of justice, and the introduction of the conqueror's statutes. The realization of such claims required the participation of the provincial administration at all levels. Constantine declared not only his religious policy by edict[18] but also his vision of government. Not long after Constantine amended the annulment of the legislation of Licinius, he traveled to Nicaea, where he had summoned the bishops of the empire to resolve the Arian controversy. Upon retiring to Nicomedia, where he remained until mid-September, Constantine issued the following edict to the inhabitants of the empire:[19]

CTh. 9.1.4

[IMP. CONSTANTINVS] A. AD VNIVERSOS PROVINCIALES. Si quis est cuiuscumque loci ordinis dignitatis, qui se in quemcumque iudicum comitum amicorum vel palatinorum meorum aliquid veraciter et manifeste probare posse

---

16. His innovations in private law are briefly discussed.
17. A taste of this exultation may be found in CTh. 7.20.1, discussed.
18. Above, n. 5.
19. On the date: Seeck, *Regesten,* 9; Barnes, *NE,* 76.

confidit, quod non integre adque iuste gessisse videatur, intrepidus et securus accedat, interpellet me: ipse audiam omnia, ipse cognoscam et si fuerit comprobatum, ipse me vindicabo. Dicat, securus et bene sibi conscius dicat: si probaverit, ut dixi, ipse me vindicabo de eo, qui me usque ad hoc tempus simulata integritate deceperit, illum autem, qui hoc prodiderit et conprobaverit, et dignitatibus et rebus augebo. Ita mihi summa divinitas semper propitia sit et me incolumem praestet, ut cupio, felicissima et florente re publica. PROPOSITA XV KAL. OCTOB. NICOMEDIAE PAVLINO ET IVLIANO CONSS.

[EMPEROR CONSTANTINE] AUGUSTUS TO ALL PROVINCIALS. If there is any man of any position, station, or rank who believes that he can truthfully and manifestly prove against any one of My judges, *comites,* friends, or *palatini* something that appears not to have been done honestly and justly, let him fearlessly and confidently approach and address Me: I Myself will hear, I Myself will judge everything, and if the allegation is proven, I Myself will avenge Myself. Let him speak—let him speak with confidence and good conscience: if he proves (what he says), I, as I have said, will avenge Myself upon him who has deceived Me up to that time with feigned integrity, but I will increase the rank and wealth of the man who makes known and proves this (crime). May the supreme deity thus always be propitious and preserve Me, and, so I desire, may the state be most blessed and prosperous. POSTED AT NICOMEDIA 17 SEPT. (325) IN THE CONSULSHIP OF PAULINUS AND JULIANUS.

This edict illustrates in exemplary fashion many traits of the Constantinian legislation that are encountered singly in other constitutions. It illustrates above all the peculiar fashion in which Constantine urges his subjects to turn to him to control the imperial administration.

Foremost is the mistrust Constantine harbors against members of imperial administration itself. The list of *iudices, comites, amici,* and *palatini* comprises the higher levels of the civil administration most likely to come into contact with the provincials. Only vicars and the praetorian and urban prefects have been omitted. The *iudices* mentioned are provincial governors, whom, as we shall see in subsequent chapters, the emperor advised and ordered in numerous constitutions throughout his reign to follow correct procedure in trials, referrals, consultations, and appeals. *Comites* include members of the *comitatus* of Constantine itself, to which the *amici* and certainly the *palatini,* who staffed the imperial *scrinia,*[20]

20. Cf. CTh. 6.35.1 (discussed above, pp. 54–55).

also belong.[21] It is moreover probable that Constantine also intended for the *comites* who fulfilled the duties of vicars in the provincial administration, of whom the *comes Orientis* would become a lasting fixture.[22]

The emperor invites, even encourages, the provincials to report administrative abuse to him personally. The provincial subject should approach the emperor fearlessly and confidently (*intrepidus et securus*); he should state with confidence and good conscience (*securus et bene sibi conscius*) the wrong that he has come to beseech the emperor to right. Constantine makes no distinctions of rank. The edict is addressed *ad universos provinciales* in the widest sense: the emperor will hear men *cuiuscumque loci ordinis dignitatis*. Moreover, should one prove his case, the emperor promises both rank and riches in reward. As we shall see in further constitutions, Constantine was very eager to hear of the deeds and misdeeds of his administrators, sometimes through novel channels.[23]

Constantine's emphatic declaration of readiness to hear, judge, and avenge the crimes of his ministers personally makes this constitution one of the most remarkable of all preserved. The temporary abandonment of the royal We in the text alone catches the eye. Solemnly repeating words of his appeal, Constantine attests his personal readiness to protect his subjects and to avenge—not them—but himself: "I Myself will hear everything, I Myself will judge, and if (the crime) is proven, I Myself will avenge Myself" (*ipse audiam omnia, ipse cognoscam et si fuerit comprobatum, ipse me vindicabo*). Constantine stresses vengeance twice: "If he proves it, as I said, I will avenge Myself" (*si probaverit, ut dixi, ipse me vindicabo*).[24]

Similarly forceful wording and the promise of personal intervention appear in a letter preserved by Athanasius.[25] Constantine had written to Athanasius with the request that he publicly read a letter composed against

21. An *amicus* and *comes* might be one and the same; e.g., CTh. 10.8.2: *virum perfectissimum comitem et amicum nostrum* (here, the *comes rei privatae*). Since even higher officials, such as the prefects, might also be styled as *amici* of the emperor, it is conceivable that they too might be held to account under this edict, as for example in CTh. 11.1.16 (a. 367): *Rufini viri clarissimi et illustris praefecti praetorio parentis amicique nostri;* and in c. *Quantum consulente* (a. 443, printed by Mommsen with the *Gesta senatus*, CTh., p. 4): *vir inlustris praefectus urbi, parens amicusque noster.*

22. Jones, *LRE*, 104–5.

23. See pp. 121–36 on public acclamations; pp. 113–18, on imperial agents; and pp. 192–96 on *breves.*

24. On vengeance, Y. Rivière, "Pouvoir impérial et vengeance. De *Mars Ultor* à la *divina vindicta* (Ier–IVe siècle ap. J.-C.)," in *La vengeance, 400–1200*, ed. D. Barthélemy, F. Bougard, and R. Le Jan (Rome, 2006), 7–42. See also Wienand, "Der Kaiser als Sieger," 291–93, on vengeance in the poems of Optatian.

25. *Apol. c. Arianos*, 68.6 (= Silli, no. 45).

the Melitian heresy.[26] Constantine threatens the Melitians as follows: "Let them know that I have made My judgment and am of this opinion: if they take any action of the sort, I myself will personally hear the case, no longer according to the laws of the Church but according to the laws of the state."[27] The future participle ἀκροασόμενον corresponds precisely to the Latin *audiam* above in the legal sense of "hold a hearing," and the words αὐτὸν με δι' ἐμαυτοῦ match the emphatic use of *ipse . . . me* in the Latin edict.[28]

The vehemence of Constantine's edict should not distract the reader from the fact that emperors had heard accusations against officials since the beginning of the empire.[29] The emperor had long been perceived as the ultimate source of justice; Constantine, then, is telling his subjects what they should already know. The emphasis that Constantine places on his personal involvement and his repeated use of the first person might be an effort to encourage popular scrutiny of the administration, about which Constantine may not have been perfectly informed. A personal role in hearing and judging such cases would in theory obviate the danger of corruption and collusion within the administration. With his thunderous claim to hear and judge provincial complaints of maladministration personally, Constantine portrays himself as an emperor on whom his subjects can rely for redress; on closer consideration, however, the same edict suggests an emperor who fears to be isolated from his subjects by the very administration he commands. The edict presumes that both Constantine and the provincials have an interest in the just administration of the empire; it is the bureaucracy that threatens to pervert justice, and which must be controlled by direct communication between emperor and subject.

Constantine does not take direct responsibility for the actions of his officials, but rather the responsibility of punishing them. Constantine construes the crimes of his officials as betrayal, as violation of his trust. Constantine not only succors the victim but also becomes a victim who must

---

26. Athanasius and the Melitians: Barnes, *CE*, 229–40; Barnes, *Athanasius and Constantius: Theology and Politics in the Constantinian Empire* (Cambridge, MA, 1993); H. A. Drake, *Constantine and the Bishops: The Politics of Intolerance* (Baltimore, 2000), 261–63.

27. *Apol. c. Arianos*, 68.6: γινωσκέτωσαν οὕτω με κεκρικέναι καὶ ταύτης εἶναι τῆς προαιρέσεως· εἴ τι τοιοῦτον κινοῖεν, μηκέτι λοιπὸν κατὰ τοὺς τῆς ἐκκλησίας ἀλλὰ κατὰ τοὺς δημοσίους νόμους αὐτὸν με δι' ἐμαυτοῦ τῶν πραγμάτων ἀκροασόμενον.

28. Cf. Optatus, App. V: *habeo . . . ex me ipso*, and the violent language in the letter to Alexander (Gelasius, *HE* 3.15.1–5 = Silli, no. 31). The letter to Celsus in Optatus, App. VII, likewise bristles with threats of personal intervention: e.g., *sum diligentissime quaesiturus idque iudicaturus . . . nam nequaquam me aliter maximum reatum effugere posse credo.*

29. See Millar, *ERW*^{2}, 516–27, esp. 526–27 (citing CTh. 9.1.4).

vindicate his own good name. He describes the wrongdoer as one who has deceived him with feigned honesty: *qui me usque ad hoc tempus simulata integritate deceperit.* This is as much as to say that he appoints only officials in whose *integritas* he has complete confidence. Constantine thereby reassures his subjects that appointments are made with their interests at heart, and only by an act of deception and dissimulation could an appointee abuse the favor of the emperor by preying on the population.

What punishment Constantine had in store for corrupt officials is not stated in CTh. 9.1.4. We are probably to understand that the emperor reserved himself the right to punish governors and other eminent persons as he saw fit, in consideration of both the crime committed and the rank of the guilty.[30] The grounds for accusation, as suggested in the phrase *non integre adque iuste gessisse,* are so wide that to promise a specific penalty would have produced punishments incommensurate with the crimes. The ability to determine an appropriate punishment from case to case rather than inflicting one automatically was also an opportunity. The emperor could derive strength from his ability to negotiate and to decide such cases affecting the imperial bureaucracy. The threat of prosecution and uncertainty of the outcome might well dissuade an imperial official from disobedience. As the edict implies, a report of administrative abuse could subject an official to the scrutiny of Constantine himself.[31]

It would be absurd to see in the words of the edict an attempt to monopolize the punishment of imperial officials for maladministration and injustice. Rather, the edict reaffirms the principle that all subjects had the right to bring their claims before the emperor. In this, Constantine contrasts with later sentiment, enunciated, for example, by the praetorian prefect of Valens, that the minutiae of private cases were beneath the imperial majesty.[32] Evidence for imperial hearings under Constantine is scarce, but enough survives to lend credibility to the declared readiness of Constantine to try cases personally. The best example is CTh. 8.15.1, an excerpt of records of proceedings.[33] Constantine, speaking in Latin, interrogates a

---

30. Constantine similarly reserves himself the right to decide how most appropriately to punish delinquent governors in CTh. 1.5.1 and 11.30.16 (see below, pp. 108–13): *ad nos referri necesse est, ut digno supplicio puniatur;* cf. CTh. 1.16.3: [*iudex*] *neglegens coercitionem incurrat.* Constantine threatens a *rationalis* and his *officium* with an unspecified *poena* in CTh. 10.1.2 and 10.8.2; cf. chapter 6.

31. Cf. Kelly, "Emperors, Government and Bureaucracy," 153–56.

32. Amm. Marc. 30.4.2: *adserente, quod infra imperiale columen causarum essent minutiae privatarum.* The speaker is Modestus, *PLRE* I, Domitius Modestus 2.

33. Corcoran, *ET*^{2}, 259–60.

woman, who responds in Greek, about property that allegedly had been acquired from a third party who was in public office.[34] The personal involvement of Constantine in ecclesiastical disputes brought before him is amply attested.[35] It would be unwise, however, to presume that Constantine neglected ordinary litigation and devoted himself solely to religious controversy. The interest of the church historians in documenting their conflicts ensured the transmission of the judicial involvement of the emperor in ecclesiastical matters. The interest of the compilers of the Codex Theodosianus (and, probably, their sources, too), by contrast, was to gather constitutions that enshrined principles of law.[36] Individual cases heard by the emperor were less important, and it is doubtful whether records of them may have survived the century between Constantine and Theodosius II. The excerpt of proceedings preserved in CTh. 8.15.1 is a felicitous exception to most constitutions collected in the Codex Theodosianus.

The final sentence of the excerpt preserved in the Codex Theodosianus deserves special attention: *Ita mihi summa divinitas semper propitia sit et me incolumem praestet, ut cupio, felicissima et florente re publica.* In what is in essence a prayer to the *summa divinitas,* Constantine acknowledges a god-given responsibility for the well-being of the inhabitants of the empire. By means of the little word *ita,* the fulfillment of Constantine's prayer is made to depend on the fulfillment of the preceding promises: the *divinitas* will be *semper propitia* so long as Constantine maintains justice in the empire, appointing just men and punishing those found unworthy, granting access and hearings to his subjects, and rewarding them for their help in the governance of the empire.[37] Constantine predicates his personal safety (*et me incolumem praestet*) on the fulfillment of this duty, as well as on the prosperity of the empire.[38] So long as Constantine rules justly, the empire shall flourish; so long as the empire flourishes, Constantine shall enjoy the favor

---

34. On this source: Millar, *ERW*², 237 and 536; C. Dupont, "La vente dans les constitutions de Constantin," *RIDA*³ 2 (1955), 254–56; M. Bianchini, "L'imperatore Costantino e una certa Agrippina. Riflessioni su CTh. 8. 15. 1," in *Sodalitas: Scr. Guarino,* vol. 3 (Naples, 1984), 1191–1206.

35. Millar, *ERW*², 536 and 600–607; cf. Drake, *Constantine and the Bishops,* 309–14, on Athanasius at the imperial court.

36. On *generalitas,* see chapter 1, pp. 24–27.

37. Constantine connects justice, divine favor, and personal salvation in the letter preserved in Optatus, App. V (a. 314): *Sed non profuit apud eos recta diiudicatio neque in eorum sensus ingressa est divinitas propitia; revera enim non inmerito ab his procul abscesserit Christi clementia, in quibus manifesta luce claret huiusmodi esse, ut eos etiam a caelesti provisione exosos cernamus;* Wienand, "Der Kaiser als Sieger," 322–23 and 328–29, discusses related statements from the same period.

38. Gothofredus, *ad* CTh. 11.30.6, interprets the obscure phrase *sub sacramenti observatione* as a reference to oath made precisely in this sense.

of God.[39] The formulation of the prayer in CTh. 9.1.4 reprises the theological legitimation of the conquest of the East. Divine sanction, according to Constantine, manifests itself in success; displeasure, in failure.[40] In war, victory proved the power and support of the deity; in peacetime, divine favor is predicated on the merit of the ruler. Constantine founds his worthiness to rule in CTh. 9.1.4 on the justice of his reign.

It is singularly felicitous that the editors of the Codex Theodosianus did not omit this final part of the edict. Prayers occur frequently in the letters and edicts of Constantine preserved elsewhere. Shortly after he restored the rights of Christians in his edict to the provincials of the East, Constantine issued a second edict that attacked the error of polytheism. In this text, too, Constantine invokes God as the guarantor of prosperity: "I now call on You, greatest God: may You be mild and well-disposed to Your Easterners,[41] may You be so to all Your Provincials, oppressed by long calamity, offering healing through me, Your servant."[42] In the following, Constantine justifies his prayer by reference to his own deeds. As in CTh. 9.1.4, Constantine portrays himself as the instrument of God that sustains the empire; it is Constantine himself, as intermediary, who conciliates God on behalf of his subjects.

The dynamism of CTh. 9.1.4 impressed ancient readers, as well. An edict of Theodosius the Great, promulgated in 386, closely imitates Constantine's appeal to the inhabitants of the empire.[43] Compared directly to its Constantinian forebear, however, the Theodosian edict seems flat, though it is elegant enough. Perhaps most striking is the prevalence of "We" in the later edict, a necessity of joint rule, but an obstacle to individual charisma.[44]

---

39. I disagree with Ando's assessment (*Imperial Ideology,* 397 n. 286) of the ablative absolute *felicissima et florente re publica* as an "afterthought."

40. Eus., *VC* 2.24–42 *passim,* esp. 24.3: πίστιν δὲ τῷ ῥηθέντι καὶ τὰ ἔργα δίδωσιν. Constantine relies heavily on this thought in the letter to Shapur, Eus., *VC* 4.9–13, going so far as to cite the example of Valerian, who died in Persian captivity.

41. Eus., *VC* 2.55.1: τοῖς σοῖς ἀνατολικοῖς, i.e., inhabitants of *Oriens,* the eastern provinces. Constantine similarly speaks of "our eastern provinces" in the first edict; cf. above, p. 47.

42. Eus., *VC* 2.55.1: Σὲ νῦν τὸν μέγιστον θεὸν παρακαλῶ· εἴης πρᾶός τε καὶ εὐμενὴς τοῖς σοῖς ἀνατολικοῖς, εἴης πᾶσι τοῖς σοῖς ἐπαρχιώταις ὑπὸ χρονίου συμφορᾶς συντριβεῖσι, δι' ἐμοῦ τοῦ σοῦ θεράποντος ὀρέγων ἴασιν, etc.

43. CTh. 9.27.6: EDICTVM AD PROVINCIALES. *Iubemus hortamur, ut, si quis forte honoratorum decurionum possessorum, postremo etiam colonorum aut cuiuslibet ordinis a iudice fuerit aliqua ratione concussus, si quis scit venalem de iure fuisse sententiam, si quis poenam vel pretio remissam vel vitio cupiditatis ingestam, si quis postremo quacumque de causa inprobum iudicem potuerit adprobare, is vel administrante eo vel post administrationem depositam in publicum prodeat, crimen deferat, delatum adprobet, cum probaverit et victoriam reportaturus et gloriam.*

44. Cf. pp. 178–80: CTh.13.5.17 (a. 386) repeats CTh. 13.5.5 almost verbatim.

No prayer appears in this text, which the Theodosian compilers include in the title dedicated to provincial corruption, CTh. 9.27, *Ad legem Iuliam repetundarum*. It is impossible to know whether Theodosius also imitated Constantine's prayer in the original.

It is likely that prayers and references to God appeared in many Constantinian constitutions that now survive in abridged form in the Codex Theodosianus. This may be observed, for example, in the complete constitution preserved as Sirm. 4, sent to the praetorian prefect Felix in 336. There Constantine concludes (the passage is unfortunately corrupt): "Therefore, by the love of the deity, We believe that (such a person?) [will be protected?] in all the Roman world if due veneration (for Us?) is observed."[45] Similarly, in a letter to the Christian proconsul Anullinus, Constantine writes that neglect of the Christian faith poses a danger to the state. He concludes, "If they do the utmost service to the divine, it seems this will benefit common affairs (i.e. the empire) the most."[46] The unanimous practice of the Christian religion would benefit the empire, but it was the responsibility of Constantine to find the means to induce the Christians of Africa, divided by the Donatist controversy, to worship God in harmony.

The most striking statement of Constantine's relationship to God survives in a letter to the vicar of Africa in 314, Aelafius:

Optatus, App. III

Nam cum apud me certum sit te quoque dei summi esse cultorem, confiteor gravitati tuae, quod nequaquam fas esse ducam, ut eiusmodi contentiones et altercationes dissimulentur a nobis, ex quibus forsitan commoveri possit summa divinitas non solum contra humanum genus sed etiam in me ipsum, cuius curae nutu suo caelesti terrena omnia moderanda commisit, et secus aliquid hactenus incitata decernet. Tunc enim revera et plenissima potero esse securus et semper de promptissima benivolentia potentissimi dei prosperrima et optima quaeque sperare, cum universos sensero debito cultu catholicae religionis sanctissimum deum concordi observantiae fraternitate uenerari. Amen.

---

45. "Such a person" i.e., Jews who have converted to Christianity. Sirm. 4: *Quare divinitatis affectu confidimus ipsum in omni orbe Romano †qui nostri debita veneratione servata.* Mommsen, *ad loc.*, notes that *tutum fore* or a similar phrase is required for *qui. Nostri* also seems corrupt, since Constantine would then say that veneration is due him, not the *divinitas.*

46. Eus., *HE* 10.7.2: ὤνπερ μεγίστην περὶ τὸ θεῖον λατρείαν ποιουμένων πλεῖστον ὅσον τοῖς κοινοῖς πράγμασι συνοίσειν δοκεῖ.

For since I am certain that you too are a worshipper of the highest God, I confess to Your Gravity that I should never think it right[47] to conceal[48] such strife and disputes, by which the highest Divinity might be angered not only against humankind but even against myself, to whose care by his heavenly decree he has entrusted the government of all things on earth, and, thus provoked, decree some calamity. Only then indeed most truly will I be able to be free from care and able to hope always for what is the most prosperous and best from the unstinting benevolence of all-powerful God, when I see that all (Christians) worship the most holy God with the appropriate rites of the Catholic faith and with harmonious brotherhood in practice. Amen.

As in the letters to Felix and Anullinus above, Constantine justifies his actions with the belief invoked in the edicts to the provincials. With apparent candor before a fellow Christian, Constantine anticipates the very formulation encountered in his edict to the provincials, CTh. 9.1.4, promulgated over a decade later. Constantine defines his task as that of an intermediary who rules over the world by heavenly decree. The power of God and Constantine is neatly contrasted by the apposition of *caelestis* and *terrena*. Constantine does not, however, rule in tandem with God, but as a subordinate, whose own safety is contingent on the benevolence of God. This divine favor proceeds in turn from the success of Constantine's earthly rule. Although, in contrast to the edict CTh. 9.1.4 of 325, Constantine here addresses a religious dispute, sentiment is the same in both texts: Constantine imposes on himself a responsibility that he must fulfill, or he risks the displeasure of God. The task of resolving the controversy in the African church is but one aspect of the universal competence (*terrena omnia moderanda*) that Constantine holds by divine decree (*nutu suo caelesti*). Constantine stresses the solemnity of his mission with the word *amen*, with which he concludes his prayer and the letter itself.

The tetrarchs had also made prominent references to the gods. Such references suggest themselves naturally in legislation dedicated to religion and morality. So, for instance, in the edict of Diocletian on incest, the emperors state, "For thus there is no doubt that the immortal gods themselves shall,

47. The word *fas* is significant for its religious undertone.

48. Cf. Coll. 6.4.1, the Diocletianic edict on incest, for an almost identical sentiment: *dissimulare ea, quae a quibusdam in praeteritum nefarie incesteque commissa sunt, non oportere credimus.* M. Edwards, *Optatus: Against the Donatists* (Liverpool, 1997), 183, mistakenly translates "concealed from us."

as they have always been, be favorable toward the Roman people and appeased, if We perceive that all people living under Our rule conduct a pious, religious, peaceful and chaste life in all things."[49] The sentiment is thoroughly traditional. The favor of the gods is contingent on the maintenance of the *pax deorum;* the suppression of incestuous marriage, which in origin entailed religious pollution,[50] should guarantee that the gods remain *placati.* The emperors nowhere advertise the precariousness of divine approval of their rule.[51] The tetrarchs also make mention of the immortal gods in the letter authorizing the persecution of the Manichaeans in Africa. The emperors ascribe to the gods an active part in the invention of "what is good and true," which in turn is confirmed and preserved "by the counsel of many good, outstanding, and most wise men."[52] The emperors aspire to join this distinguished company of the enlightened Romans, who have maintained the purity of the rites devised, according to this theology, by the gods. The sanction of the gods pertains to the Roman people and empire as a whole; it is not mediated by the persons of the emperors, nor are their persons exposed to imminent divine wrath should their subjects refuse to obey.

We find a closer association of the health of the emperor and the favor of the gods in the edict of toleration issued by Galerius. Galerius, then on his deathbed, urges the Christians to pray to their god "for his health, for that of the State, and for their own, so that in every quarter the State (*res publica*) may be kept sound, and they (i.e., the Christians) may live untroubled in their abodes."[53] Galerius stands to benefit from the favor of the Christian god, but he does not insert himself between the deity and his sub-

49. Coll. 6.4.1: *Ita enim et ipsos inmortales deos Romano nomini, ut semper fuerunt, faventes atque placatos futuros esse non dubium est, si cunctos sub imperio nostro agentes piam religiosamque et quietam et castam in omnibus mere colere perspexerimus vitam.*

50. Klingmüller, s.v. "Incestus," *RE* 9.2 (1916), 1246–49, esp. 1246–47 on the religious derivation of the crime. Cf. S. Remijsen and W. Clarysse, "Incest or Adoption? Brother-Sister Marriage in Roman Egypt Revisited," *JRS* 98 (2008), 53–61.

51. Likewise, Coll. 6.4.6: *nihil enim nisi sanctum ac venerabile nostra iura custodiunt et ita ad tantam magnitudinem Romana maiestas cunctorum numinum favore pervenit, quoniam omnes leges suas religione sapienti pudorisque observatione devinxit.* The emperors claim to conform to venerable tradition; the Roman people rose by divine favor because their laws were founded on piety and modesty.

52. Coll. 15.3.2: *Sed dii inmortales providentia sua ordinare et disponere dignati sunt, quae bona et vera sunt ut multorum et bonorum et egregiorum virorum et sapientissimorum consilio et tractatu inlibata probarentur et statuerentur.*

53. Lact., *DMP* 34.5 (30 April 311): *Unde iuxta hanc indulgentiam nostram debebunt deum suum orare pro salute nostra et rei publicae ac sua, ut undique versum respublica praestetur incolumis et securi vivere in sedibus suis possint.*

jects. The personal investment of Galerius in the benevolence of the Christian god anticipates Constantine, but the relationship constructed is far less personal and intense. The god of the Christians is to be appeased as any other: by acknowledging Christian cult, Galerius grants that the Christian god must be reckoned among the gods embraced in the *pax deorum*, the maintenance of which guarantees the stability of the empire.

The prayers of Constantine are a striking adaptation of tetrarchic practice. The nature of the relationship between Constantine and his chosen god is necessarily personal: Constantine speaks only of one god, whose chosen servant he alone is—a claim strengthened after the demise of Licinius in 324. The *summus deus* of Constantine is interested not only in matters of ritual, religion, or cult. Correct worship is eminently represented in the extant writings of Constantine, and the harmony of the Christian community ranked among his foremost concerns. It is not, however, the exclusive concern of the Christian god. The god of Constantine, as Constantine portrays him, demands righteousness and justice of the ruler who rules by his grace.[54]

Constantine cites divine favor in his enactments, both general edicts and administrative letters, as the tetrarchs before him. He goes beyond his predecessors, though, by invoking his god in explicit prayers inserted into these legal texts. The relationship of Constantine and his god, which he parades before the Roman world, is intensely personal. Constantine's god is not wholly appeased by the worship of his followers; as portrayed by Constantine, god takes an interest in the governance of the empire, and more specifically in the actions of his chosen ruler, Constantine himself. The advertisement of the relationship between Constantine and his god seems calculated to inspire, if not conversion, at least appreciation of Constantine's convictions. Constantine magnifies the earnestness of his administrative purpose: not merely the welfare of his subjects but his own security is made to depend on the achievements of his rule. The constitutions of Constantine depict his relationship with his god with remarkable consistency over time, after the conquest both of Italy and the East, and across genre, both in edicts to the provincials and in letters to administrators. The relationship of Constantine to his provincial administrators, which will be examined in the following, will prove to be a reflection of the relationship between Constantine and his god.

54. Cf. the discussion by Wienand, "Der Kaiser als Sieger," 310–13.

The Praetorian Prefects as Conduits to the Emperor

Constantine's appeal to all provincials in the edict CTh. 9.1.4, in which he urges them to report to him personally any misconduct on the part of his officials, arouses understandable skepticism. It would have cost the emperor considerable time to hear provincial allegations of misconduct in person. Administrators numbered in the thousands throughout the empire; the other tasks of the emperor were innumerable. Constantine omits mention of the prohibitive difficulty of reaching the imperial court for most of his subjects; the length and expense of a journey across the empire must have discouraged most from undertaking it. By pledging to hear cases of administrative corruption, Constantine exaggerates both his own and his subjects' ability to play their parts in the process. Circumstances will seldom have conspired to make such a hearing possible.

If one assumes that Constantine was aware of the physical barriers to realizing his pledge, the universal edict CTh. 9.1.4 might be read purely as a calculated statement of policy and a cynically flattering projection of the character of the emperor; but Constantine could afford to exaggerate the possibility of a personal hearing at the imperial court. His declared readiness to hear cases of administrative corruption personally followed upon a reform of praetorian prefecture that placed men throughout the empire who dispensed justice with the supreme authority of the emperor himself.[55] Until 324, Constantine and Licinius had each retained one praetorian prefect, with a third prefect attached to the Caesar Crispus. After the conquest of the East, Constantine multiplied their number. The reign of Constantine witnessed the first appointment of a praetorian prefect both independent of an emperor and (temporarily) in a designated territory. Constantine assigned several praetorian prefects to accompany his young Caesars and consistently appointed others to rule the diocese of Africa.[56] Constantine also modified the nature of praetorian prefecture itself: the office became open to men of senatorial rank, but this opportunity for the aristocracy was compensated by the redistribution of sensitive tasks to newly created offi-

55. Barnes, *NE,* 131 and 138; Jones, *LRE,* 101–3; cf. B. Palme, "Die *Officia* der Statthalter in der Spätantike," *AntTard* 7 (1999), 97–98, with n. 65. Extensive bibliography in F. Arcaria, "Sul potere normativo del prefetto del pretorio," *SDHI* 63 (1997), 333 n. 146. On the reform of the praetorian prefecture: P. Eich, *Zur Metamorphose des politischen Systems in der römischen Kaiserzeit. Die Entstehung einer "personalen Bürokratie" im langen dritten Jahrhundert* (Berlin, 2005), 211–41; cf. P. Porena, *Le origini della prefettura del pretorio tardoantica* (Rome, 2003), 567–75.

56. Overview of attested praetorian prefects after 324: Barnes, *NE* 131–34.

cials. The military responsibilities of the praetorian prefects passed to the *magister militum;* oversight of the bureaus of the central administration passed to the *magister officiorum.*[57]

In the civil administration, the praetorian prefects gained significant new powers. With respect to the suppression of administrative abuse, the praetorian prefects were firmly established in a position superior to most provincial governors of the empire (excepting the proconsuls, who answered directly to the emperor). The praetorian prefects become the preferred channel through which imperial pronouncements were disseminated to the provincial administration.[58] While this practice is first recorded under Diocletian, it becomes customary under Constantine and is well attested in the Codex Theodosianus from the year 324.[59]

Constantine relied on the praetorian prefects not only to convey legislation and orders to the lower strata of the provincial administration. Information might also flow in the other direction, to the imperial court. The praetorian prefects were charged with the important task of facilitating the central control of the administration. Several constitutions preserved in the Codex Theodosianus illustrate how Constantine informed the population of the empire of the new means of recourse constituted by the praetorian prefects. One such a constitution, according to the date in its *subscriptio,* anticipated the edict CTh. 9.1.4 by perhaps two weeks. The constitution in question is a letter to the praetorian prefect of the East, Flavius Constantius:[60]

CTh. 1.5.1

IMP. CONSTANTINVS A. AD CONSTANTIVM PRAEFECTVM [PRAETORIO].[61] Edicto omnes provinciales monemus, ut, si interpellantes proprios praesides contempti fuerint, gravitatem tuam interpellent, ut, si id culpa vel neglegentia praesidum admissum esse constiterit, ilico ad scientiam nostram referat gravitas tua, quo possint congrue coerceri. DAT. IIII K. SEPT. ANTIOCHIAE PAVLINO ET IVLIANO CONSS.

EMPEROR CONSTANTINE AUGUSTUS TO CONSTANTIUS, [PRAETORIAN] PREFECT. We advise all provincials by edict to call upon Your Gravity, if they have been ignored when calling upon their own governors, so that, if it is de-

57. Eich, *Metamorphose,* 234–35.
58. See chapter 2.
59. Eich, *Metamorphose,* 235–37.
60. *PLRE* I, Fl. Constantius 5 (perhaps identical to Constantius 1).
61. Mommsen, *ad loc.*

termined that it occurred through the fault or negligence of the governors, Your Gravity may immediately bring the matter to Our attention, so that they may be suitably punished. GIVEN 29 AUG. (325) AT ANTIOCH IN THE CONSULSHIP OF PAULINUS AND JULIANUS.

The text has been printed as it appears in Mommsen's edition. In chapter 2, it was noted that the content of CTh. 1.5.1 indicates it was an accompanying letter to an edict. Seeck presumes that the edict must have been CTh. 9.1.4,[62] but the relationship between the two texts is specious. In CTh. 1.5.1, Constantine informs the praetorian prefect that he has advised provincials to approach the prefect if their governor unjustly refuses to hear a case. The praetorian prefect, in turn, should establish the truth of their claims, and if he finds a governor guilty, he must report his name to the emperor for appropriate punishment.[63] The edict of 325, CTh. 9.1.4, refers to no such process. Governors are mentioned, but together with several imperial officials.[64] Refusal to hear a legitimate complaint might, in the wording of the edict, might make one guilty "of having done something dishonestly and unjustly" (*non integre adque iuste gessisse*),[65] but these words embrace administrative corruption broadly. The abuse addressed in CTh. 1.5.1 is the refusal of the governor to take any action at all. Most telling against identifying CTh. 1.5.1 as the *Begleitschreiben* to CTh. 9.1.4 is the fact that the latter pronouncement fails to mention the praetorian prefects. Constantine advises the provincials not to approach the prefects, but himself.[66] The letter to the prefect Constantius (CTh. 1.5.1) corresponds to the tenor of the edict to the provincials of September 325 (CTh. 9.1.4) but not to its content. The constitution CTh. 1.5.1 should then be the accompanying letter to a further edict that addressed negligence in provincial jurisdiction. The two edicts, that preserved (CTh. 9.1.4) and that postulated (in CTh. 1.5.1), complement one another. The earlier edict is symptomatic of the misgovernment that provoked the violent language of the later.

---

62. Seeck, *Regesten*, 115, 175; cf. Barnes, *NE*, 76.

63. CTh. 1.5.1: *si id culpa vel neglegentia praesidum admissum esse constiterit, ilico ad scientiam nostram referat gravitas tua, quo possint congrue coerceri*; cf. K. L. Noethlichs, *Beamtentum und Dienstvergehen. Zur Staatsverwaltung in der Spatantike* (Wiesbaden, 1981), 162.

64. CTh. 9.1.4: *quemcumque iudicum comitum amicorum vel palatinorum meorum.*

65. CTh. 9.1.4: *quod non integre adque iuste gessisse videatur.* Cf. Dig. 1.18.6.4 (Ps.-Ulpian): *Neque licita negotiatione aliquos prohiberi neque prohibita exerceri neque innocentibus poenas irrogari ad sollicitudinem suam praeses provinciae revocet.*

66. CTh. 9.1.4: *interpellet me: ipse audiam omnia, ipse cognoscam et si fuerit comprobatum, ipse me vindicabo.*

The letter to the praetorian prefect in CTh. 1.5.1 reflects a consistent policy of the Constantinian regime: Constantine employed the praetorian prefects not only to disseminate legislation but also to hear allegations of maladministration and, when warranted, report guilty parties to the emperor for punishment. CTh. 1.5.1 closely resembles a section of an important edict issued 1 August 331 and posted in Constantinople 1 September:[67]

CTh. 11.30.16

Quod si victus oblatam nec receptam a iudice appellationem adfirmet, praefectos adeat, ut aput eos de integro litiget tamquam appellatione suscepta . . . si vicerit, contra eum iudicem, qui appellationem non receperat, ad nos referri necesse est, ut digno supplicio puniatur.

If the defeated party asserts that his appeal was made but not accepted by the governor, let him go to the prefects, so that he may litigate before them as if his appeal had been received. . . . If he prevails, it is necessary that a report against the governor who did not receive the appeal be sent to Us, so that he may be punished suitably.

In both CTh. 1.5.1 and CTh. 11.30.16, it is the duty of the praetorian prefect to hear complaints lodged by provincials who have been rebuffed by their governor. The circumstances described in each constitution do not correspond exactly. In CTh. 1.5.1, the wronged provincials are described as *interpellantes* their governor. CTh. 11.30.16 concerns appeal; the provincials would be described as *appellantes.* The words *appellare* and *interpellare* indicate in fact two different legal acts.[68] Constantine assumes in the letter to Constantius that a provincial's attempt to initiate litigation (*interpellare*) has been unjustly rejected; in the edict of 331, he assumes that a provincial has been convicted but the governor has ignored a legitimate appeal (*appellare*). The words of the letter to Constantius and the edict of 331, however, attest the same path of redress: Constantine bids the wronged provincial approach the praetorian prefects (*praefectos adeat*).[69] The praetorian prefect

67. The fragments are collected in Mommsen, *Proleg.*, ccxxi.

68. Pharr, *ad loc.*, mistakenly interprets *interpellantes* in CTh. 1.5.1 as a reference to appeal, leading others astray (e.g., D. Slootjes, *The Governor and His Subjects in the Later Roman Empire* [Boston, 2006], 41).

69. *Adire,* the right to proceed directly to the next instance, if appeal was rejected by the judge in the first instance, was available to the appellant but subject to a degree of risk: according to CTh. 11.30.16 (a. 331), a litigant who brought his case to the praetorian prefect and lost suffered *infamia.*

should review the case and, if the provincial governor is found guilty, report his name to the emperor for punishment (*ad nos referri necesse est / ilico ad scientiam nostram referat gravitas tua*). The final clause in both documents conveys the same thought in different words: *ut digno supplicio puniatur / quo possint congrue coerceri.* Constantine reserves himself the right to set an arbitrary punishment proportional to the crime, which is conveyed by the word *dignus* in the first text and *congrue* in the second. The praetorian prefects serve in both constitutions as intermediaries between the emperor and the provincials.

CTh. 1.5.2 offers a last, colorful example in which Constantine instructs the praetorian prefect to review provincial complaints against their governors:

> [IMP. CONSTANTINVS] A. AD MAXIMVM PRAEFECTVM PRAETORIO. Qui de statutis praesidalibus conqueruntur, cum ea in detrimentum legum prolata arbitrantur, ad tuae auctoritatis iudicium pervenire faciant, ut fractis atque convulsis quae perperam inpressa sunt ne nomen quidem sententiae possint retinere. DAT. XII K. FEB. CONSTANTIO ET MAXIMO CONSS.
>
> [EMPEROR CONSTANTINE] AUGUSTUS TO MAXIMUS, PRAETORIAN PREFECT. Those who lodge complaints concerning the rulings of governors, when they believe they have been made to the detriment of the laws, shall make (them?) come to the tribunal of Your Authority, so that what has been wrongly decided may be broken and demolished and not retain even the name of a ruling. GIVEN JAN. 21 (327) IN THE CONSULSHIP OF CONSTANTIUS AND MAXIMUS.

At first glance, this constitution appears to pertain to the appellate jurisdiction of the praetorian prefects, but since no mention of appeal is made, it seems instead to concern litigants whose appeals have been rejected. As in the constitutions discussed above, CTh. 1.5.2 identifies the praetorian prefect as the instance to which the provincials may turn when their governors have failed them. In all cases, the praetorian prefect serves to guarantee justice by reporting delinquent governors for punishment.[70] The jurisdiction

---

In CTh. 1.5.3, issued shortly afterward, the punishment appears to have been raised to a two-year term of relegation for *honestiores* or of hard labor in the mines for *humiliores;* on this constitution, see chapter 8.

70. Cf. the Donatist controversy in F. Morgenstern, "Die Kaisergesetze gegen die Donatisten in Nordafrika (Mitte 4. Jh. bis 429) im Zusammenhang mit dem antidonatischen Wirken des Augustinus von Hippo," *ZRG* 110 (1993), 121.

of the praetorian prefects was furthermore supplemented by that of the *comites provinciarum,* dispatched by Constantine from the court, and the diocesan vicars whom they intermittently replaced. The importance of the *comites* in the Constantinian provincial administration will be addressed below.

"Missi Dominici"

If threat of punishment, *metus legum,* did not suffice to discourage imperial officials from wrongdoing, Constantine had yet other means of securing the obedience of his administrators. Perhaps most unpredictable and unpleasant to the rogue official was the dispatch of agents who reported directly to the emperor. Little trace of such officials under Constantine remains in the Codex Theodosianus. The compilers could find in allusions to such missions no principles of law to record. Yet a handful of passages have survived. It is generally believed that Constantine created the *agentes in rebus* to control the public post, perhaps as early as 319.[71] In CTh. 6.35.2, Constantine orders the proconsul of Africa to protect members of the palatine bureaus who had been sent "to conduct state affairs or on some other mission" from paying the *collatio equorum.*[72] These *agentes* under Constantine still seem to be irregularly appointed officials who were dispatched from the court on a variety of missions.

CTh. 15.1.2, a letter sent in 322[73] to Menander, then either praetorian prefect or *comes* of Africa, presents us with further evidence of officials sent to investigate imperial administrators. Again, we are indebted to chance: this constitution is preserved in the Codex Theodosianus under the title "Concerning Public Works" (CTh. 15.1, *de operibus publicis*). The Theodosian compilers failed to remove the entire preface of the law:

CTh. 15.1.2 (a. 322)

[IMP. CONSTANTINVS] A. MENANDRO. Propter neglegentiam iudicum, qui imperialia praecepta differunt, ad diversas provincias diversos misimus, qui ad

71. C. Kelly, "Bureaucracy and Government," in *The Cambridge Companion to the Age of Constantine,* ed. N. E. Lenski (Cambridge, 2006), 188–89 and 202 n. 30.

72. CTh. 6.35.2: *Si ex memorialibus vel ex palatinis nostris aliquis ad agendas curas rei publicae vel alterius officii fuerit destinatus, minime ab eo repraesentatio postuletur equorum.* On the *collatio equorum,* see p. 186. CTh. 6.35.3.3, which mentions *agentes in rebus* explicitly, is in fact a constitution of Constantius'.

73. See Barnes, *NE,* 129, on the date.

scientiam nostram referant, quae vel diligentia promota viderint vel desidia corrupta culpaverint. Monendi autem iudices sunt, qui instaurare publica opera debent, ut de effectis eis potius quam inchoatis ad nostram scientiam referant, nisi forte iusta ratione petendum sit aliquos, si forte defuerint, impensarum titulos provideri. De rebus autem praecipuis maximisque, non de quibuscumque vilissimis nostrum debent interpellare consilium. DAT. III ID. APRIL. SIRMI CRISPO II ET CONSTANTINO II CC. CONSS.

[EMPEROR CONSTANTINE] AUGUSTUS TO MENANDER. Because of the negligence of governors who put off imperial commands, We have sent various men to various provinces to bring into Our knowledge what things they have found to have been carried forward with diligence or spoiled by sloth. All judges, however, who ought to undertake public works are to be advised that they should report completed works to Our knowledge rather than those begun, unless it is by chance and for good reason necessary to request that funds for the expenses should be provided, if they be lacking. They ought, though, to request Our counsel about special and very important matters, not about any kind of triviality. GIVEN 11 APRIL (322) AT SIRMIUM IN THE CONSULSHIP OF CRISPUS CAESAR, CONSUL FOR THE SECOND TIME, AND OF CONSTANTINE CAESAR, CONSUL FOR THE SECOND TIME.

The opening sentence of this fragment has no legal content and apparently was retained by Theodosius' compilers by an oversight. The exact purport of the statement is obscured by the loss of what originally preceded it. In the present state of the text, it is impossible to discern the relationship between the first sentence concerning the agents of the emperor and the following one concerning public works. *Autem* in the opening words of the second sentence (*Monendi autem iudices*), indicates a transition, but whether to a new subject (e.g., that of public works) or merely to a different aspect of the same topic, as with the second *autem* in the third sentence (*de rebus autem praecipuis*), it is impossible to say. We are thus ignorant of the breadth of the assignment given these men and of the nature of the *praecepta* imposed on the governors. At the least, though, the constitution remains valuable evidence of administrative control beyond mere recitation of penalties.[74]

The identity of the men dispatched is unknown, but their presence in "diverse provinces" suggests *comites provinciarum.* If that were so, Menan-

74. Cf. CTh. 8.5.3, in which Constantius writes to his praetorian prefect Acindynus concerning the *cursus publicus: Quae res si neglecta fuerit, vobis aestimationis vestrae notam incurrentibus praesides periculum sustinebunt, cum super hac re exploratores iam missi sint.*

der himself could be identified as praetorian prefect, and CTh. 15.1.2 would be further evidence of the function of the Constantinian *comites* in policing the provincial governors, which would sit well with their role alongside the prefects as officials to whom the provincials are instructed in many constitutions to bring their complaints against governors. It is, however, impossible to be certain; the men dispatched by Constantine could also have been much lower in rank, such as ordinary *palatini.* In either case, such agents were expected to be unswervingly loyal and able to obtain and convey accurate information about provincial administrators back to the court.

Notice of the dispatch of agents appears often in the letters of Constantine preserved by ecclesiastical writers. In a fragment of a letter delivered to Athanasius by two such *palatini,* Constantine writes:

Athan., *Apol. c. Arianos* 59.6 (ca. 328)[75]

Ἔχων τοίνυν τῆς βουλήσεως τὸ γνώρισμα ἅπασι τοῖς βουλομένοις εἰς τὴν ἐκκλησίαν εἰσελθεῖν ἀκώλυτον παράσχου τὴν εἴσοδον. ἐὰν γὰρ γνῶ ὡς κεκώλυκάς τινας αὐτῶν τῆς ἐκκλησίας μεταποιουμένους ἢ ἀπεῖρξας τῆς εἰσόδου, ἀποστελῶ παραχρῆμα τὸν καὶ καθαιρήσοντά σε ἐξ ἐμῆς κελεύσεως καὶ τῶν τόπων μεταστήσοντα . . .

Now that you know my wish, grant all who wish to enter the church unimpeded entry, for if I learn that you have blocked some of those converting from the church or have kept them from entering, I will immediately send someone to depose you at my behest and remove you from the place . . .

Similar action was taken in preparation to the Synod of Tyre. Constantine threatens bishops who refuse his summons in terms identical to those offered Athanasius:

Eus., *VC* 4.42.4

ἐὰν γάρ τις, ὡς ἐγὼ οὐκ οἴομαι, τὴν ἡμετέραν κέλευσιν καὶ νῦν διακρούσασθαι πειρώμενος μὴ βουληθῇ παραγενέσθαι, ἐντεῦθεν παρ᾽ ἡμῶν ἀποσταλήσεται, ὃς ἐκ βασιλικοῦ προστάγματος αὐτὸν ἐκβαλὼν ὡς οὐ προσῆκεν ὅροις αὐτοκράτορος ὑπὲρ τῆς ἀληθείας ἐξενεχθεῖσιν ἀντιτείνειν διδάξει.

For if, what I think unlikely, someone should even now try to evade Our command and refuse to appear, then someone will be sent by Us who by imperial

75. Silli, no. 41. On the date and context, see Barnes, *Athanasius and Constantius,* 20–21.

decree will expel him, so that he will learn that it is wrong to strive against the bounds set by the emperor on behalf of truth.

Constantine evidently sought to make such harsh measures unnecessary, for afterward one of the emperor's men arrived personally in the vicinity, bearing with him an imperial letter, to urge prospective participants to make haste.[76] The identity of this person is unknown, as is that of the distinguished men of the court who accompanied the *notarius* Marianos, who presided.[77]

It is regrettable that the record of the administration of Constantine depends almost wholly on the legal sources, which often exclude references to administrative acts in preference to the principles that underlie them. The ecclesiastical sources offer at least a plausible analogy: the emperor might at any time cut through the veil of bureaucracy by sending trusted men to enforce his will.[78] Therein lay the particular value of extraordinary administrators such as the *comites provinciarum* in contrast to the more mundane vicars established by Diocletian. The employment of confidants from the court to investigate and monitor provincial administrators facilitated the enforcement of existing and new rules; it moreover strengthened Constantine's own power—provided that the men on whom he relied proved worthy of that trust.[79]

That it was not always so, even Eusebius testifies: Constantine reminds

76. Eus., *VC* 4.43.1: Ἐπεὶ δὲ δι' ἔργων ἐχώρει τὰ προστεταγμένα, κατελάμβανεν ἄλλος βασιλικὸς ἀνήρ, ἐπισπέρχων τὴν σύνοδον σὺν γράμματι βασιλικῷ, σπεύδειν μηδὲ ἀναβάλλεσθαι τὴν ἐπὶ τὰ Ἱεροσόλυμα παρορμῶν γε πορείαν.

77. Courtiers: Eus., *VC* 4.43.4: . . . παρῆν δὲ τούτοις ἅπασι βασιλική τις ὑπηρεσία, ἄνδρες τ' ἐξ αὐτῶν βασιλείων δόκιμοι κατεπέμποντο φαιδρῦναι τὴν ἑορτὴν ταῖς βασιλέως χορηγίαις. Marianos: Eus., *VC ceph.* ad 4.44; *VC* 4.44.1: ναὶ μὴν καὶ ὁ τούτοις ἅπασιν ἐφεστὼς βασιλεῖ δεξιὸς ἀνήρ, πίστει καὶ εὐλαβείᾳ λόγων τε θείων ἐμπρέπων ἀσκήσει, ὃς δὴ καὶ ταῖς ὑπὲρ εὐσεβείας ὁμολογίαις κατὰ τὸν τῶν τυράννων καιρὸν λαμπρυνόμενος εἰκότως τὴν τῶνδε διάταξιν ἐπιστεύετο. Cf. T. D. Barnes, "Constantine, Athanasius and the Christian Church," in *Constantine: History, Historiography, and Legend*, ed. S. N. C. Lieu and D. Montserrat (London, 1998), 8–11, on the role of Dionysius at the Council of Tyre, a. 335.

78. Cf. Kelly, "Emperors, Government and Bureaucracy," 159–62, on the later fourth century.

79. For comparison, cf. CTh. 1.10.2 (a. 385), in which *palatini* of the *comes sacrarum largitionum* oversee provincial governors, detaining them until they perform the duty of collecting debts; cf. Noethlichs, *Beamtentum und Dienstvergehen*, 84. On the *agentes in rebus*, see W. Liebeschuetz, review of W. Blum, *Curiosi und Regendarii: Untersuchungen zur geheimen Staatspolizei der Spätantike*, *JRS* 60 (1970), 229–30; cf. C. Humfress, *Orthodoxy and the Courts in Late Antiquity* (Oxford, 2007), 244, on Constantine's reference to "men of mine" (*direxi meos homines*) in Optatus, App. V.

his officials, "the Supreme God had entrusted to him rule over the earth, and he, in imitation of the Greater One, had entrusted the governance of its parts to them." They all would one day be called to account before God, but, "they scorned his words out of greed." Constantine seems even to have paraphrased Cicero's *First Catilinarian* in rebuking one such official: καὶ μέχρι τίνος, ὦ οὗτος, τὴν ἀπληστίαν ἐκτείνομεν?[80] Eusebius does himself credit when he feels compelled to concede that the provincial administration under Constantine was criticized because governors failed to prosecute wrongdoers:

Eus., *VC* 4.31

Ἐπεὶ δ' οὐκ ἦν θανάτου φόβος ἀπείργων τοὺς κακοὺς τῆς μοχθηρίας, βασιλέως μὲν ὅλου πρὸς τὸ φιλάνθρωπον ἐκδεδομένου, τῶν δὲ καθ' ἕκαστον ἔθνος ἀρχόντων μηδαμῇ μηδαμῶς μηδενὸς τοῖς πλημμελοῦσιν ἐπεξιόντος, τοῦτο δὴ μομφὴν οὐ τὴν τυχοῦσαν τῇ καθόλου διοικήσει παρεῖχεν . . .

Since, though, no fear of death prevented the wicked from evil and the emperor was wholly given over to kindness, and since not one of the governors in each province even once punished wrongdoers, this brought no unwarranted disrepute on the entire administration.

Had Constantine's provincial governors not punished even one wrongdoer? Eusebius's claim could not be more forceful: μηδαμῇ μηδαμῶς μηδενός! That Eusebius should make such an exaggerated charge in his laudatory *Life of Constantine* is surely significant. Had the governors of Palestina failed him, or had some other official? It is distinctly possible that Eusebius had not merely specific administrators in mind, but also specific Christians. When he mentions the wickedness of those who exploited Constantine's forbearance once more, he connects their greed with feigned Christian belief.[81] "But," he adds, "it was not long before divine justice overtook them."[82] What might be described as "divine justice" certainly overtook many in the aftermath of Constantine's death: there was the massacre of the descendants of Constantius and Theodora in 337, and of further nobles in 338—the

80. Eus., *VC* 4.29.5–30.1; Constantine said something perhaps like this: *Quo usque tandem, O nescioquis, cupiditatem extendemus?* Eusebius has suppressed the name of the addressee.

81. Eus., *VC* 4.54.2–3.

82. Eus., *VC* 4.55.1.

most notable victim being none other than Constantine's former praetorian prefect, the Christian Ablabius.[83]

Even if Eusebius discredits the entire administration because of some person or persons whom he declines to name, he raises a valid caveat: even the closest advisors of the emperor were not wholly immune to the temptations of power and influence, and they certainly were not saints. One is reminded of Ammianus's magnificent sketch of Petronius Probus, who like Ablabius rose to the office of praetorian prefect—an office he held four times.[84] Ammianus represents him as driven into office by the greed of his innumerable clients; he was a good enough man never to order a client or slave to do wrong, but he would defend them to the last against Justice herself.[85] Yet Ammianus also tells us that once Probus had resolved to harm someone, he was utterly implacable and unforgiving.[86] Then Probus played the part of prosecutor, while another undertook the defense. Either way, it was precisely this game of patronage and rivalry that enabled Constantine and his successors to maintain a semblance of order in a vast empire.[87]

The punishments described in public edicts and in official correspondence might be imposed at any time on an official whose misconduct had been discovered by the emperor's men. The presence of long-term delegates in the provinces, to whom provincials might turn when failed by local administrators, provided Constantine with the means of retaining the loyalty of the population and asserting control over the bureaucracy. The disciplining of minor officials could be accomplished through correspondence with their superiors, men like Ablabius and Probus; even provincial governors might be called to account before a vicar, *comes*, or praetorian prefect. Beyond the official hierarchy, extraordinary delegates could confront any official in the empire with the authority of the emperor himself.

83. D. S. Potter, *The Roman Empire at Bay, AD 180–395* (New York, 2004), 462–63; Barnes, *CE* 262; cf. *PLRE* I, Ablabius 4. Jerome, *Chron.* 338, records: *Ablabius praefectus praetorio et multi nobilium occisi.*

84. *PLRE* I, Probus 5.

85. Amm. Marc. 27.11.4: *Namque fatendum est: numquam ille magnanimitate coalitus clienti vel servo agere quicquam iussit illicitum, sed si eorum quemquam crimen ullum compererat admisisse, vel ipsa repugnante Iustitia non explorato negotio sine respectu boni honestique defendebat.*

86. Ibid., 11.6: *ita implacabilis et directus, ut si laedere quemquam instituisset, nec exorari posset nec ad ignoscendum erroribus inclinari.*

87. Rightly emphasized by Kelly, "Emperors, Government and Bureaucracy," 182–83.

5

Constantine and the Provincials

The Paradox of the Bureaucracy

An edict that survives in two fragments looms heavily over the following discussion. It ranks among the most vehement denunciations of judicial corruption produced by the Later Roman Empire.[1] Among other things, this edict to the provincials famously forbids the exaction of fees for legal services. Only a generation later, the Roman emperors yielded to the prevalence of illegal fees that plagued the judicial system, and acknowledged and attempted to regulate them. Constantine, however, was not prepared to do so, but instead both reminds officials of their culpability in threatening words and instills in his subjects a righteous expectation of free access to Roman justice.

Constantine's edict against the imperial bureaucracy is in many ways typical of his paradoxical hostility to his own representatives. Throughout much of his legislation, Constantine portrays the provincial bureaucracy as something alien. Indeed, much of it was alien to a ruler who succeeded his father as a tetrarch but ended as emperor of a unified empire. Beginning in Rome in 312, Constantine extended his power by seizing the territory of his rivals: first Italy and Africa from Maxentius; then the Balkans and Greece from Licinius in 316, and finally in 324 the rest of the East. Each of these conquests necessitated administrative change and multiplied the number of provincial governors, their staffs, and further officials who answered to Constantine. Constantine wisely retained prominent officials even of his

1. CTh. 1.16.6–7.

enemies in the highest offices,[2] but he regarded the provincial administration itself with great suspicion. As Lactantius, the tutor of his eldest son, describes, the division of the provinces into "bits" (*frusta*) under Diocletian made governors and their *officia* seem to menace almost every tract and city.[3] Even when these same men became his own governors and clerks, Constantine hardly regarded them less charily. Constantine did, however, begin to dispatch different men to govern. Well before the conquest of the East, Constantine had taken the noteworthy step of recruiting provincial governors from within the Roman senate.[4] Once he had defeated Licinius, he repeated this experiment in the East and created a new senate in Constantinople to do it. The need to assemble a body of men through whom Constantine might govern the Eastern Empire must have contributed to the decision to found this second senate.[5] By appointing Senators to gubernatorial positions and by promoting other officials to senatorial status, Constantine had raised the prestige of the provincial government generally; he also raised the terms of reward for the men who represented him throughout the Roman world. He sought thereby to lend them greater authority to govern in the provinces while tying them more closely to himself. At least, if they acted in accordance with his will, they were his men and represented his governance; but if they did wrong, they were disowned utterly and publicly.

Constantine took measures to ensure that he could keep a close watch on his provincial governors. He represents himself in his edicts as prepared to hear the pleas of his subjects personally. Constantine recognized that the victims of administrative corruption were vulnerable precisely because they lacked the means to inform him. The crimes of the imperial administration were perpetrated against the voiceless; one way in which Constantine gave them a voice was to give official sanction to public acclamations. Constantine not only required the officials closest to himself to pay heed to public outcry; he urged his subjects to approach even his own imperial majesty. As expressions of political strategy, the edicts of Constantine cultivate the favor of the population precisely with the deficiencies of the imperial govern-

2. For example, Rufius Volusianus, praetorian and urban prefect of Maxentius, ordinary consul in 314 and Julius Julianus, praetorian prefect of Licinius, ordinary consul in 325: Barnes, *NE,* 100 and 102.

3. Lact., *DMP* 7.4.

4. M. T. W. Arnheim, *The Senatorial Aristocracy in the Later Roman Empire* (Oxford, 1972), 52–63; examples in his Fasti (e.g., Domitius Zenophilus, v.c. *consularis Numidiae,* p. 203 = *PLRE* I, Zenophilus).

5. P. Heather, "Senators and Senates," *CAH* XIII, 185–86.

ment. Constantine proposes means of redress but moreover justifies himself and lays responsibility for abuse on the shoulders of his own administrators.

The following discussion will trace the proclamation of these policies in the remains of the legislation of Constantine. Since the political history of Ammianus has been lost, and there was little other impetus to record details of the administration of Constantine, ecclesiastical sources must supply lacunae in the record of the legislation. The religious conflicts that beset the empire after the official recognition of Christianity also tested the determination of Constantine. His efforts to mend the rifts in the Christian community were not unlike his approach to government, but were recorded by the Church Fathers who participated in the controversies.

Trial Procedure and Public Acclamations

An edict on appellate procedure issued in August 331, CTh. 11.30.16, was one of a series dedicated to jurisdiction and administrative corruption that were promulgated late in the year after the dedication of Constantinople. Constantine refined the procedure of *aditio,* whereby a litigant approached the praetorian prefects directly instead of making a regular appeal, in an important letter to the praetorian prefect Bassus already in October 331.[6] He addressed judicial corruption at the gubernatorial level in a vociferous edict *ad provinciales* issued 1 November 331. Two fragments of this edict are preserved in the Codex Theodosianus, placed consecutively under the title *De officio rectoris provinciae.*[7] In the first fragment, Constantine reaffirms fundamental principles of trial procedure. We learn how a governor should conduct a trial, permitting all litigants to bring their complaints before him. Constantine then turns his attention to the provincials themselves, granting them the extraordinary power to praise or blame their governors publicly:

CTh. 1.16.6

[IMP. CONSTANTINVS] A. AD PROVINCIALES. Praesides publicas notiones exerceant frequentatis per examina tribunalibus, nec civiles controversias audituri secretariis sese abscondant, ut iurgaturus conveniendi eos nisi pretio facultatem impetrare non possit, et cum negotiis omnibus, quae ad se delata fuerint,

6. CTh. 1.5.3. See chapter 8, pp. 239–41.
7. On this edict, see De Marini Avonzo, "Giustizia I," 1037–62.

exhibuerint audientiam et frequens praeconis, ut adsolet fieri, inclamatio nullum, qui postulare voluerit, deprehenderit, expletis omnibus actibus publicis privatisque sese recipiant. Iustissimos autem et vigilantissimos iudices publicis adclamationibus conlaudandi damus omnibus potestatem, ut honoris eis auctiores proferamus processus, e contrario iniustis et maleficis querellarum vocibus accusandis, ut censurae nostrae vigor eos absumat; nam si verae voces sunt nec ad libidinem per clientelas effusae, diligenter investigabimus, praefectis praetorio et comitibus, qui per provincias constituti sunt, provincialium nostrorum voces ad nostram scientiam referentibus. PROPOSITA K. NOV. CONSTANTINOPOLI BASSO ET ABLAVIO CONSVL.

[EMPEROR CONSTANTINE] AUGUSTUS TO THE PROVINCIALS. Let governors conduct hearings publicly on tribunals thronged during hearings, and when they intend to hear disputes of civil law, let them not hide themselves in their private chambers, so that a litigant has no opportunity of meeting them except at a price; and once they have given a hearing to all cases brought to them, and the herald's frequent cry, which may usually be heard, discovers no man who wishes to file suit, then, after all public and private records[8] of proceedings have been completed, let them retire. We moreover grant all provincials the power to praise the most just and vigilant judges by public acclamations, so that We may bring them ampler advancements in honor; and on the contrary, the unjust and wicked are to be accused with cries of complaint, so that the force of Our chastisement may annihilate them; for We will carefully investigate whether[9] those words are true and have not been uttered wantonly by clients, as the praetorian prefects and the *comites* who are stationed throughout the provinces bring Our provincials' words to Our knowledge. POSTED 1 NOV. (331) AT CONSTANTINOPLE IN THE CONSULSHIP OF BASSUS AND ABLABIUS.

Constantine reaffirms two principles of trial procedure. First, trials must be held in public.[10] The words *publicas notiones* refer not to criminal proceedings but to proceedings in public.[11] Constantine demanded that his administrators admit the public to judicial proceedings throughout his reign. He had instructed the proconsul of Africa to hear all trials publicly in the first

8. "Public" being those destined for the archives, "private" the copies given to the litigants.
9. "If" in the Latin (*si* for *an* or *utrum*) with an indicative verb!
10. De Marini Avonzo, "Giustizia I," 1041–49, gives a nuanced discussion of the significance of "pubblicità" in Roman procedural law.
11. De Marini Avonzo, "Giustizia I," 1050.

years after the defeat of Maxentius.[12] The letter itself may in origin have been a general directive concerning the duties of provincial governors. Its surviving excerpts, scattered throughout the Codex Theodosianus, strongly resemble the tenor, if not in form, of the edict of November 331. The recurrence of such affirmations in the legislation of Constantine attests both to the importance attached to the transparency of judicial proceedings and to the persistent tendency of provincial judges to withdraw from public scrutiny.

The second principle confirmed by Constantine in CTh. 1.16.6 is that of documentation: the compilation and solemn closing of the records of proceedings. The *acta* served as a record of all that transpired before the court of the governor and could be reviewed by higher officials in the administration, if a complaint or an appeal had been made, or as a means of administrative control.[13] The keeping of records was essential to the success of the judicial and administrative oversight instituted and publicized by Constantine, whether it was a praetorian prefect who ordered an investigation or Constantine himself. The formality of the closing of the *acta* reflects the importance of transparency in proceedings: nothing should transpire in the court of the governor that was not recorded in the *acta* maintained by his official staff.

The steps of trial procedure depicted in the edict are consistent with what is known of the fourth-century *cognitio extraordinaria.* A schoolboy about town might witness all the details mentioned by Constantine:[14]

> (73) Fit hora tertia. Ingrediuntur advocati, causidici, scholastici, evocati in secretarium iudicis sui. Agunt plures causas, quisque ut potest (74) secundum literarum facundiam. Sunt et causae in temporum finem, quas hodie credo terminandas. Exinde descendit praeses ad tribunal custodis sessurus. Sternitur tribunal, conscendit iudex tribunal, et sic voce praeconis iubet (75) sisti personas. Reus sistitur, latro, interrogatur secundum merita; torquetur, quaestionarius pulsat, ei pectus vexatur, suspenditur, †crescit, flagellatur fustibus, vapulat, pertransit ordinem tormentorum, et adhuc negat. Puniendus est: perit poena, ducitur ad gladium. (76) Deinde alter sistitur, innocens, cui adest grande patrocinium, et viri diserti adsunt illi. Hic etenim habebit eventum: ab-

12. CTh. 1.12.1; on the date, Seeck, *Regesten,* 161; cf. Barnes, *NE,* 170; Corcoran, *ET*², 304.

13. See chapter 7; in general, J. Harries, *Law and Empire in Late Antiquity* (Cambridge, 1999), 70–76.

14. The following is an excerpt of the Latin crib for a Greek translation exercise, dated to the fourth century: A. C. Dionisotti, "From Ausonius' Schooldays?" *JRS* 72 (1982), 104–5.

solvitur. (77) Testes bene venerunt in sua causa, sine iniuria absoluti sunt. Haec causa habuit idoneam defensionem, et fidem veritatis apud acta deposuit unus quisque.

(73) It's the third hour. The advocates, pleaders, lawyers, *evocati* enter the court[15] of their judge.[16] They plead many cases, each as best he can (74) according to his skill in letters. There are cases too at the end of the time allowed them to go to trial, which I think must be decided today. Then the governor comes down to the tribunal of the guard[17] to preside. The tribunal is erected; the judge ascends the tribunal, and so by call of the herald orders (75) the parties to be produced before the court.[18] An accused man is produced, a brigand,[19] he is interrogated according to his deserts; he is tortured, the inquisitor beats him, his breast is torn, he is hung up . . . he is whipped with rods, he is flogged, he goes through the order of tortures, and still denies. He is to be punished: he is condemned to death; he is led away to execution (*ad gladium, sc.* by beheading). (76) Then another man is produced before the court, an innocent man, who has a large number of defenders,[20] and eloquent men support him. He will have success: he is acquitted. (77) The witnesses made a good appearance[21] in their case; they are acquitted without injury. This case had a good defense, and each and every one attests to the truth by deposition in the records of proceedings.

In this exercise, the author describes every step mentioned by Constantine with one important refinement. The author begins as various advocates enter the *secretarium* of their respective judges. This, however, does not con-

15. Dionisotti, "From Ausonius' Schooldays," 119, *ad loc.: secretarium* here is the separate court of a *iudex pedaneus.*

16. Dionisotti, ibid., rightly distinguishes this *iudex* from the governor as a *iudex pedaneus* appointed by the governor to hear minor disputes.

17. Dionisotti, ibid., the nature of this *custos* is obscure.

18. *OLD* s.v. *sisto* 2; Lewis and Short, s.v. *sisto* I.C.1. Not "to stand," as translated by R. MacMullen, "Judicial Savagery in the Roman Empire," in *Changes in the Roman Empire. Essays in the Ordinary* (Princeton, 1990), 210.

19. Here I depart from Dionisotti's punctuation. According to the word order, *latro* should be understood in apposition to *reus,* i.e., the text explains (factually) that he is a brigand. Hence he is tortured *ad merita.* Note the parallel to *alter (reus) sistitur, innocens* ("another defendant, an innocent man"). Dionisotti's objection to the summary execution of the first man without a confession (against the instructions of Constantine, CTh. 9.40.1), p. 120, s.v. *negat . . . gladium,* is thus otiose. Cf. the unsophisticated expectation of innocence or guilt in CTh. 9.3.1 (a. 320): *statim debet quaestio fieri, ut noxius puniatur, innocens absolvatur.*

20. Dionisotti, "From Ausonius' Schooldays," 120, *ad loc.,* confuses *patrocinium* with *patrimonium* (apparently understanding the defendant to be a large landholder).

21. *OLD* s.v. *venio* 4a., "To come into court, appear in court."

tradict the edict of Constantine, who forbids the governor to hear cases withdrawn to his private chamber: the judge mentioned first in the school text is already a delegate, a *iudex pedaneus*, appointed by the governor to conduct trials of lesser consequence in side chambers of his court.[22] The governor as judge presides publicly upon his tribunal, as is consistent with the edict of Constantine. The entire scene is imagined as happening in the open, before a temporary tribunal erected for the judge. Constantine's assertion in CTh. 1.16.6 that the person of the governor should be accessible to litigants thus appears to be confirmed by this glimpse of practice.[23]

The elaborate protocol for adjourning court described by Constantine appears to protect the right of litigants to approach the governor. The governor should not close the *acta* and retire until no one brings further claims at the summons of the herald. The principle of free access to the governor was not new, but neither was the temptation to retreat from the public eye. Already Ulpian stresses that the governor should be approachable by all, without distinction of rank.[24] By implication, Constantine too provides for the humble by compelling the governor to hear all persons present.

The significance of one phrase in the edict of Constantine, however, has been the subject of controversy: *nec civiles controversias audituri secretariis sese abscondant, ut iurgaturus conveniendi eos nisi pretio facultatem impetrare non possit.* De Marini Avonzo contends that this phrase is not analogous to the order to hold proceedings publicly, as past Romanists believed.[25] The governor should hear cases outside of his chambers, she argues, not for the sake of ensuring the publicity of trials, but for the sake of guaranteeing litigants free access to his person. In other words, Constantine insists that governors exercise their jurisdiction publicly, lest corrupt *officiales* control access to them through bribery. The contemptuous language, however, with which Constantine describes the retreat of the judges to their chambers, *secretariis sese abscondant,* implies the complicity of the governors in the depredations of their staff members. The blunt description of the corruption of the *officiales* and the suggestion of the dishonesty of governors

---

22. Cf. the definition provided by Julian, CTh. 1.16.8: *pedaneos iudices, hoc est qui negotia humiliora disceptent.*

23. Cf. De Marini Avonzo, "Giustizia I," 1051–52.

24. Dig. 1.16.9.4 (Ulpian): *Observare itaque eum oportet, ut sit ordo aliquis postulationum, scilicet ut omnium desideria audiantur, ne forte dum honori postulantium datur vel improbitati ceditur, mediocres desideria sua non proferant, qui aut omnino non adhibuerunt, aut minus frequentes neque in aliqua dignitate positos advocatos sibi prospexerunt;* Dig. 1.18.19 pr (Callistratus): *Observandum est ius reddenti, ut in adeundo quidem facilem se praebeat, sed contemni non patiatur.*

25. De Marini Avonzo, "Giustizia I," 1051, with n. 60; Kaser-Hackl, §84.I.1, p. 555.

demonstrate to governors and their staffs, as well as to the provincials, that the emperor is aware of such collusion and will not tolerate it.

What follows is still more ominous to the unscrupulous among provincial governors. In the most arresting passage of the edict, Constantine invites the provincials to help moderate their own governors. "We moreover grant all provincials the power," Constantine begins, "to praise the most just and vigilant judges by public acclamations." Constantine exhorts his subjects to pass judgment on their governors en masse, in public acclamations.[26] It is henceforth the duty of the praetorian prefects and *comites provinciarum*, the members of the provincial administration closest to Constantine himself, not only to receive litigants whose suits and appeals have been unjustly rejected,[27] but also to heed public outcry and report acclamations to the emperor himself. Constantine neatly conveys this duty in the ablative absolute construction that concludes the fragment, *praefectis praetorio et comitibus . . . referentibus*. The prefects and *comites* were probably briefed on their role in the collection and report of provincial acclamations in accompanying letters to the edict.[28]

Diocletian once famously remarked, "One must ignore the empty words of the people. Nor may one believe their words when they want a guilty person to be acquitted of a crime or an innocent person to be condemned."[29] Constantine acknowledges in his edict to the people that the pretensions of

26. On public acclamations: J. F. Matthews, *Laying Down the Law: A Study of the Theosodian Code* (New Haven & London, 2000), 35–39; J. H. W. G. Liebeschuetz, *Antioch: City and Imperial Administration in the Later Roman Empire* (Oxford, 1972), 208–19, esp. 216; A. Cameron, *Circus Factions: Blues and Greens at Rome and Byzantium* (Oxford, 1976), 241–42; C. Roueché, "Acclamations in the Later Roman Empire: New Evidence from Aphrodisias," *JRS* 74 (1984), 181–99; R. MacMullen, "The Historical Role of the Masses in Late Antiquity," in *Changes*, 250–76; H.-U. Wiemer, "Akklamationen im spätrömischen Reich," *Archiv für Kulturgeschichte* 86 (2004), 27–73. For the High Empire, see G. S. Aldrete, *Gestures and Acclamations in Ancient Rome* (Baltimore, 1999). Wiemer discusses CTh. 1.16.6 on p. 59.

27. As observed in chapter 4, pp. 108–13.

28. As in CTh. 1.5.1, discussed in chapters 2 and 4, p. 37 and 109–10.

29. CJ 9.47.12: [IMP. DIOCLETIANVS] IN CONSISTORIO DIX[IT]: *Decurionum filii non debent bestiis subici.* CVMQVE A POPVLO EXCLAMATVM EST, ITERVM DIX[IT]: *Vanae voces populi non sunt audiendae. nec enim vocibus eorum credi oportet, quando aut obnoxium crimine absolvi aut innocentem condemnari desideraverint.* SINE DIE ET CONSVLE. This excerpt appears at once to record proceedings of the consistory and public outcry: it is unclear whether both parts, the ruling of Diocletian in the consistory and the subsequent outcry (apparently for the second time: *iterum*), occurred one immediately after the other. Cf. Wiemer, "Akklamationen im spätrömischen Reich," 44–49, on direct confrontations between the people and the emperor in Constantinople.

public sentiment in acclamations may prove to be unreliable. He anticipates above all potential manipulation of the crowd and the danger that powerful persons might use clients or claques (*per clientelas*) to inculpate a governor wrongly. Care must be exercised in evaluating the partisanship of provincial complaints. As Wiemer has shown, the demands made in public acclamations did not necessarily correspond to the desire of the whole people, much less a majority.[30] Yet this same partisanship in provincial politics made acclamations valuable means of administrative control. As long as someone, partisan or no, reported public reaction to an objectionable ruling to higher authorities, the emperor had the chance to correct it. The possibility that a personal enemy might indeed notify a prefect or *comes* could well have discouraged a judge from crossing the crowd with an indefensible ruling.[31]

The authorization of public acclamations against provincial governors accomplished several things at once. Constantine opened a new source of information not only on the opinion of large segments of urban populations but also on the conduct of his own administrators. Constantine, as the ultimate judge of acclamations, could learn of his administrators' disobedience and, as stated in the Nicomedian edict of 325 (CTh. 9.1.4, discussed above), exact vengeance. Excesses of the administration might be checked by the people, and the people owed their allegiance and gratitude to the emperor who welcomed their public demands. Constantine might benefit both by claiming the honest administrators as his own and by disowning and punishing the dishonest: thus the provincial administration was subjected to a new form of scrutiny and the provincials themselves profited from the sympathy of their populist ruler. By empowering his subjects, Constantine could protect them and keep their favor, punish disobedience, and impose his will on the provincial administration that stood between him and the people.

There is evidence that Constantine both duly read and reacted to provincial acclamations relayed to the court. One example is an excerpt of an edict addressed to the provincials of Africa:[32]

30. Wiemer, "Akklamationen im spätrömischen Reich," 40–41, on the basis of the fifth-century acclamations from Edessa.

31. Rivalries in this context: MacMullen, "Historical Role," 260–63.

32. See Millar, *ERW*², 393–94; R. Delmaire, *Largesses Sacrées: et. L* 'aerarium *impérial et son administration du IVe au VIe siècle* (Rome, 1989), 82–83.

CTh. 11.7.4 (a. 328)[33]

[IMP. CONSTANTINVS] A. AD AFROS. Quoniam subclamatione vestra merito postulastis, ne qua his, qui praestationes fiscales differunt, reliquorum laxitas proveniret, specialiter praecipimus observari, ut res eorum, qui fiscalibus debitis per contumaciam satisfacere differunt, distrahantur, conparatoribus data firmitate perpetua possidendi. ETCETERA DAT. XV KAL. IVN. SERDICAE CONSTANTIO ET MAXIMO CONSS.

[EMPEROR CONSTANTINE] AUGUSTUS TO THE AFRICANS. Since you have rightly demanded by your shouts that those who put off their payments to the *fiscus* should receive no leniency in paying their arrears, We specifically order that the property of those who in contempt of the law defer satisfaction of their debts be sold and that the buyers receive firm and permanent right of possession. ETC. GIVEN 18 MAY (327 [328]) AT SERDICA IN THE CONSULSHIP OF CONSTANTIUS AND MAXIMUS.

The *subclamatio* of the provincials to which Constantine refers is generally interpreted as an acclamation recorded at the provincial *concilium*.[34] Such an acclamation would have resembled the chants recorded in the minutes of the Roman Senate meeting that confirmed the Codex Theodosianus.[35] Acclamations on the part of provincial *concilia* will likely have numbered among the sources of information on the basis of which Constantine assessed the conduct of his administrators. Such acclamations would have been delivered to the imperial court in the form of provincial decrees or letters. The procedure for the delivery of provincial decrees, however, established by Constantine himself, entailed their inspection and approval by the provincial governor, which would have been counterproductive in the event that the *concilium* objected to the conduct of the governor.[36] The acclamations of provincial councils are not likely to be those intended by Constantine in CTh. 1.16.6, the edict to the provincials. The virtue of ap-

33. Corrected from 327 by Seeck, *Regesten*, 69; Barnes, *NE*, 77.

34. Millar, *ERW*², 393–94: "protest"; Pharr, 299: "modest entreaty"; n. 12: "reported by a delegation sent by the Africans to the emperor."

35. Esp. *Gesta Senatus* 5; Matthews, *Laying Down the Law*, 37–50; Wiemer, "Akklamationen im spätrömischen Reich," 29–35.

36. CTh. 1.16.2: *Decreta provincialium non prius ad comitatum perferri oportet, quam singuli quique iudicantes ea inspexerint atque probaverint suaque adscriptione signaverint. Si quid fiat contrarium, competens ultio exerceatur.* Cf. CTh. 12.12.4. Both these passages are cited by De Marini Avonzo, "Giustizia I," 1055–56, but they are not relevant to the acclamations intended in CTh. 1.16.6.

pealing directly to the people lay precisely in their independence: it was hoped that acclamations might offer a genuine reflection of the will of the people.[37]

The *subclamatio* cited in CTh. 11.7.4 is difficult to dismiss as a reference to a formal acclamation of the provincial council of Africa. The word *subclamatio* itself is suggestive of a popular acclamation. *Subclamatio* occurs in the Codex Theodosianus only in the present constitution. Constantine himself, however, provides a useful parallel that has been preserved independently in the *Fragmenta Vaticana:*

> FV 35.5[38]
>
> . . . cum longe sit melius, sicuti diximus, ut luce veritatis, fidei testimonio, publica voce, subclamationibus populi idoneus venditor adprobetur, quo sic felix comparator atque securus aevo diuturno persistat.
>
> . . . since it is by far better, as we have said, that a suitable seller be approved by the light of truth, the testimony of honesty, the voice of the public, and the shouts of the people, so that the buyer may remain thus happy and carefree for all time.

This excerpt derives from an extensive revision of the law of sale, as described in a letter addressed to the praetorian prefect and forwarded to the *corrector Piceni.*[39] The passage follows upon the stipulation that a sale and by implication conveyance[40] (of land) be solemnly performed in the presence of neighbors.[41] Constantine is at pains to make such sales as public as possible to prevent fraud and impersonation.[42] With the word *subclamatio,*

---

37. Contra De Marini Avonzo, "Giustizia I," 1056, who interprets CTh. 1.16.6 only with respect to provincial *concilia.*

38. The date of this law is uncertain: the full text in the FV is dated as issued 28 Aug. 313; a fragment of it preserved as CTh. 3.1.2 bears the date 4 Feb. 337; cf. Corcoran, *ET*², 160–62. It seems very probable that these texts give the contents of an edict. The closing phrase (FV 35.7) asks for the obedience of *cuncti* and speaks of regulating *universae successiones.*

39. Huschke *ad* FV 35.7 in *Iurisprudentiae anteiustinianae reliquiae,* ed. E. Seckel and B. Kübler, vol. 2 (Leipzig, 1911), 216. Cf. "Edicts" in chapter 2.

40. E. Levy, *West Roman Vulgar Law* (Philadelphia, 1951), 128–29; summarized, 134.

41. FV 35.4: *Id etiam volumus omnibus intimari nostrae clementiae placuisse neminem debere ad venditionem rei cuiuslibet adfectare et accedere, nisi eo tempore, quo inter venditorem et emptorem contractus sollemniter explicatur, certa et vera proprietas vicinis praesentibus demonstretur.*

42. E.g., FV 35.6: . . . *ne forte, cum aliquis venditor suum esse dicat, quod esse constat alienum;* 35.7: *Ita ergo venditionum omnium est tractanda sollemnitas, ut fallax illa fraudulenta venditio penitus sepulta depereat.*

he evokes a scene of neighbors cheering or deriding a potential seller, almost as if he were a governor appearing in a theater. The most important circumstance is that the neighbors react in unison, which corresponds to the presumed unanimity of public acclamations.[43] *Subclamatio* here is not merely a shout, but a cry that expresses the wish of a united people, their *consensus*.

Such a cry might be attributed equally to a people or to a provincial council. The content of CTh. 11.7.4, however, suggests that this text was an edict in response to the cries of a broad public rather than a letter prompted by the "modest entreaties" of the provincial council of Africa. One might expect that the populace of Africa would welcome the cancellation or postponement of the payment of arrears, but a pertinent passage of Ammianus proves this would be mistaken. In his explanation why Julian never forgave arrears, Ammianus reveals that it was the rich few who stood to benefit, not the many poor:

> Amm. Marc. 16.5.15
>
> Denique id eum ad usque imperii finem et vitae scimus utiliter observasse, ne per indulgentias quas appellant tributariae rei concederet reliqua. Norat enim hoc facto se aliquid locupletioribus additurum, cum constet ubique pauperes inter ipsa indictorum exordia solvere universa sine laxamento conpelli.
>
> Lastly, we know that he maintained the beneficial policy unto the very ends of the empire and the end of his life of never forgiving tax arrears through so-called indulgences. For he knew that by doing this (i.e., remitting arrears) he would be giving something to the rich, since it is well known that the poor everywhere are forced to pay everything in full at the very beginning of the indictions without any reprieve.

Only moneyed, well-connected landholders could hope to procure indulgences from the imperial officials: the poor enjoyed no such advantages. While the wealthy enjoyed reprieves, the burden of covering the loss to the *fiscus* would inevitably fall on the backs of the poor. It is easy to imagine such a practice leading to public outcry.[44]

---

43. Wiemer, "Akklamationen im spätrömischen Reich," 40–41.

44. K. F. Stroheker, "Der spätrömische Kaiser und das Volk," in *Transformations et conflits au IVe siècle après J.-C.* (Bonn, 1978), 15–31, citing Salvian, *de gub. dei* 4.31; P. Brown, *Power and Persuasion in Late Antiquity: Towards a Christian Empire* (Madison, 1992), 28–29. Arrears: Jones, *LRE*, 205–6, and 466–67; H. Ziche, "Making Late Roman Taxpayers Pay: Imperial Government Strategies and Practice," in *Violence in Late Antiquity: Perceptions and Practices*, ed. H. A. Drake (Aldershot, 2006), 135–36.

Constantine's edict to the Africans, CTh. 11.7.4, should be interpreted accordingly: public outcry against "tax indulgences" had reached the ears of the emperor, who was moved to respond in a strongly worded edict. There is no reason to read behind the inscription of CTh. 11.7.4, *Ad Afros,* a confused reference to the provincial council. Wealthy men such as those who made up provincial councils would have been dismayed, if we believe Ammianus or Julian, that the emperor condemned the leniency of his tax officials. In fact, Constantine bypasses the provincial council altogether.[45] He forbids tax indulgences in an edict pointedly addressed to those who had cried out for the emperor's intervention, the people of the province of Africa. He addresses them directly with the words "you" and "your outcry" (*subclamatione vestra . . . postulastis*).

The writings of the Church Fathers preserve examples of acclamations in ecclesiastical affairs that supplement the sparse evidence of the Codex Theodosianus. Eusebius's *Life of Constantine* preserves three letters sent by Constantine, one to the Christians of Antioch, one to the bishops, and one to Eusebius himself.[46] The occasion of these letters was lingering strife over the replacement of the bishop Eustathius, who had been deposed in 326. Two bishops had since been elected to his see, but both died shortly thereafter. When the see had to be filled anew, probably in 327, strife erupted among the people and threatened to descend into violence.[47] The people of Antioch publicly demanded that Eusebius of Caesarea be appointed their bishop. A synod of bishops in Antioch at the time supported the people and wrote to Constantine in favor of Eusebius's translation from Caesarea to Antioch; Eusebius, however, declined and informed the emperor in a letter of his own.[48] Constantine responded to both letters. Eus., *VC* 3.61 preserves his approving reply to Eusebius; *VC* 3.62, his response to the bishops. Constantine also wrote an epistolary edict to the λαός of Antioch itself, preserved in Eus., *VC* 3.60.

It is the response to the people (or congregation) of Antioch that recalls

45. Cf. Wiemer, "Akklamationen im spätrömischen Reich," 65–66, for his concluding reflections on the potential of acclamations to supplant civic councils as the representatives of cities and their population.

46. Eus., *VC* 3.60–62.

47. Eus., *VC* 3.59.2: τοῦ δὲ κοινοῦ τῆς πόλεως αὐτοῖς ἄρχουσι καὶ στρατιωτικοῖς πολεμίων τρόπον ἀνακινηθέντων, ὡς καὶ ξιφῶν μέλλειν ἅπτεσθαι.

48. For details on Eustathius and the date of his deposition: H. Chadwick, "The Fall of Eustathius of Antioch," *JThS* 49 (1948), 27–35; G. Downey, *A History of Antioch in Syria from Seleucus to the Arab Conquest* (Princeton, 1961), 351–53; D. Woods, "Strategius and the 'Manicheans,'" *CQ* 51 (2001), 255–64.

the process of registering acclamations prescribed in the edict of 331 (CTh. 1.16.6). Constantine informs the Antiochenes that he has read ὑπομνήματα of their acclamations: "I acknowledge that I have read the records in which I saw, by the glorious praise and testimony which you showered upon Eusebius, that you passionately wished to make him your own."[49] The Greek term ὑπομνήματα is the usual translation of the Latin *acta*.[50] Constantine also refers to these ὑπομνήματα in his the letter to the bishops. There we learn that the ὑπομνήματα were brought to Constantine by the *comites* Acacius and Strategius.[51] The part these *comites* played in dispatching the acclamations of the Antiochenes to the court anticipates the edict to the people of 331, CTh. 1.16.6, precisely. The practice of reporting public acclamations thus appears to have been confirmed and encouraged, rather than invented, by the edict.

The letters concerning the acclamations sent to Constantine from Antioch give insight into the risks that encouraging and responding to acclamations might entail. As it happened, the demands of the Antiochenes displeased Constantine; he found himself in a situation in which he must acknowledge the Antiochenes' wishes but bend their will to his own. In the letter to the people in which Constantine responds, he urges the Antiochenes to find another man worthy of the vacant see. Constantine criticizes the fanaticism and strife from which their clamorous nomination of Eusebius resulted; he asks the Antiochenes to retreat from their turbulent demands for the sake of restoring public order, "shutting out all factious and disorderly cries: for such cries are always unjust, and sparks and flames arise from the collision of discordant elements."[52] In this oblique manner, Constantine disputes the unanimity of the people in whose name the acclamations were made. He concludes this moderate rebuke with an ominous appeal to reason: "Therefore have forethought for the enjoyment of all these (blessings), so that We do not a second time find you to have set on a cer-

---

49. Eus., *VC* 3.60.3 (= Silli, no. 36): ὁμολογῶ γὰρ ἀνεγνωκέναι τὰ ὑπομνήματα, ἐν οἷς λαμπραῖς εὐφημίαις τε καὶ μαρτυρίαις, αἷς εἰς Εὐσέβιον εἰσηνέγκασθε . . . ἑώρων ὑμᾶς ἐγκειμένως αὐτὸν σφετεριζομένους.

50. The monks in Apamea use the term in transliteration, ἄκτα, to describe the record of their own acclamations: Wiemer, "Akklamationen im spätrömischen Reich," 43–44, and generally on *acta* of acclamations, 58–59

51. Eus., *VC* 3.62.1: ἐπιγνούς τε τὰ πεπραγμένα σύμπαντα τοῦτο μὲν τοῖς ὑμετέροις γράμμασιν τοῦτο δὲ τοῖς Ἀκακίου καὶ Στρατηγίου τῶν διασημοτάτων κομήτων . . . ("Having learned all that has been done from your letter, on the one hand, and from the Acacius and Strategius the most eminent *comites* . . . ")

52. Eus., *VC* 3.60.8: ἀποκλείσαντες πᾶσαν στασιώδη καὶ ἄτακτον βοήν· ἀεὶ γὰρ ἄδικος ἡ τοιαύτη, κἀκ τῆς τῶν διαφόρων συγκούσεως σπινθῆρές τε καὶ φλόγες ἐξανίστανται.

tain course or to have undertaken something altogether inappropriate because of ill-considered and unprofitable zeal."[53] Constantine was not pleased by the public outcry reported to him, but he nevertheless considered it serious enough to warrant a personal reply to the people in an equally public form. By these means, Constantine strove to placate a multitude that could no longer be controlled by the local elite.[54]

Constantine made no effort to disguise his reaction in his other correspondence. In his reply to Eusebius, Constantine writes that he has answered both the letter from the synod and the people: "I wrote a letter about this to the people, and with the inspiration of God I wrote to the others, your fellow servants, who had also written to me about this."[55] In his letter to the bishops, Constantine describes the letter to the people as follows: "I wrote to the people of Antioch what was pleasing to God and in accord with the Church,"[56] a copy of which he includes for the bishops, "and I ordered that a copy of the letter be attached to this one, so that you might recognize what I, inspired by reason of justice, chose to write to the people."[57] The copy of the letter to the people, and the manner in which Constantine refers to it, can only have been intended as a rebuke. Its contents cannot have been unknown to the bishops.

The strife over the see of Antioch is the best example of the system of reporting and responding to acclamations under the reign of Constantine. Acclamations were both an opportunity and a risk: reports of acclamations might well bring unwelcome news, which denied the emperor the chance to respond as benefactor or vindicator of the people. Even in such circumstances, however, Constantine seizes the opportunity to avow his commitment to justice and the common good. Reports of acclamations enabled the emperor to communicate with his subjects; most probably it was for this reason that Constantine accepted the attendant risks of encouraging provincial acclamations. Acclamations were at once a source of informa-

53. Eus., *VC* 3.60.9: διὸ δὴ νῦν προνοήσασθε τὴν ἀπόλαυσιν τούτων ἁπάντων οὕτως ἔχειν, ὡς ἂν μὴ δεύτερον ἀβούλῳ καὶ ἀλυσιτελεῖ σπουδῇ ἢ καθόλου τι πήξασθαι ἢ τὴν ἀρχὴν ἐπιχειρῆσαι μὴ συμφέρον δοκοίημεν.

54. Cf. the vivid discussion of civic violence in Brown, *Power and Persuasion,* 81ff.

55. Eus., *VC* 3.61.3: περὶ δὴ τούτου πρὸς τὸν λαὸν ἐπιστολὴν ἐποιησάμην, πρός τε τοὺς ἄλλους σου συλλειτουργούς, οἳ καὶ αὐτοὶ περὶ τούτου ἐτύγχανον μοι γεγραφότες . . . αὐτοῖς προτροπῇ τοῦ θεοῦ ἔγραψα. The "letter" to the Antiochenes is in essence an epistolary edict; cf. chapter 2.

56. Eus., *VC* 3.62.1: πρὸς τὸν Ἀντιοχέων λαὸν ἔγραψα ὅπερ ἀρεστόν τε τῷ θεῷ ἦν καὶ ἁρμόζον τῇ ἐκκλησίᾳ.

57. Ibid.: ἀντίγραφόν τε τῆς ἐπιστολῆς ὑποταχθῆναι τοῖς γράμμασι τούτοις ἐνετειλάμην, ὡς ἂν καὶ αὐτοὶ γινώσκοιτε ὅ τί ποτε τῷ τοῦ δικαίου λόγῳ προκληθεὶς πρὸς τὸν λαὸν γράψαι προειλόμην.

tion, a means of administrative control, a gesture of populist engagement, and a channel of unmediated communication between the emperor and his subjects.

The authorization of public acclamations and Constantine's reaction to reports of them attest to his effort to cultivate the approval of the people. They also show his sensitivity to the power of public opinion and the need to communicate his public persona. Further, scattered evidence supports these findings. Eusebius mentions Constantine's dismay at religious strife in Egypt and the disfigurement of his statues.[58] The Arian controversy had divided the peoples of the East (καὶ τὰ πλήθη κατατεμνόμενα), and Christian doctrine was publicly satirized in theaters.[59] In response, Constantine wrote letters both to local bishops and to the people:

Eus., *VC* 3.24.1

> Καὶ ἄλλα δὲ τούτοις ἔγραφεν ἀδελφὰ μυρία πλείστας θ' ὅσας ἐπιστολὰς διετύπου, ἐν μέρει μὲν ἐπισκόποις ὑπὲρ τῶν ἐκκλησιῶν τοῦ θεοῦ τὰ πρόσφορα διαταττόμενος, ἤδη δὲ καὶ αὐτοῖς προσεφώνει τοῖς πλήθεσιν, ἀδελφοὺς ἀποκαλῶν καὶ συνθεράποντας ἑαυτοῦ τοὺς τῆς ἐκκλησίας λαοὺς ὁ τρισμακάριος.
>
> And he, that thrice-blessed man, wrote myriad things in the same vein and composed very many letters, in part issuing appropriate orders to the bishops concerning the churches of God, but he also addressed the masses, too, calling the congregations of the church his brothers and fellow servants.

Imperial letters or epistolary edicts in response to acclamations gave Constantine the ability to address the partisans of a conflict collectively when he could not intervene in person. In a similar situation, Constantine ordered Athanasius to deliver a public rebuke to the people in his stead.[60] Constantine had previously written to the λαός of Alexandria to confirm the appointment of Athanasius to the episcopal see.[61] Finally, once settled in his

58. Eus., *VC* 3.4.1.

59. Eus., *VC* 2.61.5: τοσοῦτον δὲ διήλαυνεν ἀτοπίας ἡ τῶν γινομένων θέα, ὥστ' ἤδη ἐν αὐτοῖς μέσοις τοῖς τῶν ἀπίστων θεάτροις τὰ σεμνὰ τῆς ἐνθέου διδασκαλίας τὴν αἰσχίστην ὑπομένειν χλεύην.

60. Athan., *Apol. c. Arianos*, 61–62 (= Silli, no. 39): τὴν παρ' ἐμοῦ πρόσρησιν αὐτὸν Ἀθανάσιον ὑμῖν διακονῆσαι τὸυ αἰδεσιμώτατον ἀναγκαῖον ἡγησάμην (62.7).

61. Codex Angelicus Gr. 22.36b (= Silli, no. 32).

capital, Constantine addressed cheering crowds with sermons in praise of the "king over all":[62]

Eus., *VC* 4.29.2

Καὶ μὴν τὴν αὐτὸς αὑτοῦ διάνοιαν τοῖς ἐνθέοις συναύξων λόγοις, ἐπαγρύπνους μὲν διῆγε τοὺς τῶν νυκτῶν καιρούς, σχολῇ δὲ λογογραφῶν συνεχεῖς ἐποιεῖτο τὰς παρόδους, προσήκειν ἡγούμενος ἑαυτῷ λόγῳ παιδευτικῷ τῶν ἀρχομένων κρατεῖν λογικήν τε τὴν σύμπασαν καταστήσασθαι βασιλείαν. διὸ δὴ συνεκάλει μὲν αὐτός, μυρία δ' ἔσπευδεν ἐπ' ἀκρόασιν πλήθη φιλοσοφοῦντος ἀκουσόμενα βασιλέως. εἰ δέ πη λέγοντι θεολογίας αὐτῷ παρήκοι καιρός, πάντως που ὄρθιος ἑστὼς συνεστραμμένῳ προσώπῳ κατεσταλμένῃ τε φωνῇ, μυεῖν ἔδοξεν ἂν τοὺς παρόντας σὺν εὐλαβείᾳ τῇ πάσῃ τὴν ἔνθεον διδασκαλίαν, εἶτ' ἐπιφωνούντων βοαῖς εὐφήμοις ἀκροωμένων, ἄνω βλέπειν εἰς οὐρανὸν διένευε καὶ μόνον ὑπερθαυμάζειν καὶ τιμᾶν σεβασμίοις ἐπαίνοις τὸν ἐπὶ πάντων βασιλέα.

And indeed to increase his wisdom with inspired words, he spent sleepless nights, and in his leisure he continually composed sermons, considering it to behoove him that he win over his subjects with his instruction and establish his entire reign upon that reasoning. Therefore he himself would give invitations, and myriads eagerly came to hear the emperor philosophize. And if, as he spoke, he had occasion to speak of God, standing utterly erect with his brow drawn and voice lowered, he appeared to initiate those present with deep reverence in the divine teachings, and when those listening cheered him propitiously, he gestured that they look to the sky and admire and honor with their pious praise the king of all.

It will surprise no one that our record of public demonstrations and imperial response is far more extensive for religious controversy than for secular unrest. Bishops adeptly mustered broad and not infrequently violent support in the name of their beliefs. The actors and their causes were naturally of great significance to ecclesiastical authors, who indeed might themselves have been the instigators of such acclamations. The victims of judicial

62. For a potentially early example, cf. Constantine's reaction to the acclamations of veterans recorded in CTh. 7.20.2 (307?); Matthews, *Laying Down the Law*, 37; Barnes, *NE*, 69; most recently, S. Connolly, "Constantine Answers the Veterans," in *From the Tetrarchs to the Theodosians: Later Roman History and Culture, 284–450 CE*, ed. S. McGill, C. Sogno, and E. Watts (Cambridge, 2010), 93–114, with *comparanda* from the High Empire.

crimes must also have found patrons, although an obvious leader was hardly necessary to produce an enraged crowd.[63]

Public acclamation, though a weapon of the weak, was nonetheless formidable. The successors of Constantine likewise availed themselves of the potential for information, communication, and control offered by public acclamations. As Clifford Ando writes, "Later emperors evidently liked Constantine's legislation."[64] Reports of acclamations circulated regularly between the provinces and the courts of subsequent emperors; by the reign of Valentinian and Valens, provincials were granted use of the public post in order to expedite the delivery of acclamations.[65] Once the report of public acclamations was authorized, there was no return, nor is any such desire to repudiate the system established by Constantine detectable. The proliferation of acclamations and their record in late antiquity is a testament to the changed spirit of the times and of the monarchy itself. Ulrich Wiemer argues that the late antique emperors sought to involve as many of their subjects as possible in as many ceremonies as possible that brought them necessary and highly desired approval, unmediated by the civic elite; the emperors sought to encompass the whole empire in a net of symbolic communication.[66] Constantine was the first to realize the potential of acclamations. His decision to authorize them would shape the relationship of emperor and subject long after his reign.

Judicial Bribery

The juxtaposition of a restatement of the principles of trial procedure and the authorization of public acclamations against the conduct of provincial governors in CTh. 1.16.6 raises the suspicion of judicial corruption. Bribery, above all, might compromise provincial jurisdiction. Appeal was one remedy against venal rulings, but recalcitrant judges might attempt to stall appellate proceedings, too. In a fragment of a letter sent the governor

63. See MacMullen, "Historical Role," 263–64, for examples of secular unrest, and 269–75, of ecclesiastical.

64. C. Ando, *Imperial Ideology and Provincial Loyalty in the Roman Empire* (Berkeley, 1999), 204.

65. Cameron, *Circus Factions*, 241, notes on the basis of CTh. 8.5.32 (a. 371) that the reporting of acclamations "at once became established practice" and that "provincials carrying such reports were permitted free use of the public post."

66. Wiemer, "Akklamationen im spätrömischen Reich," 59–60; Brown, *Power and Persuasion*, 149–50, with reference to Roueché, "Acclamations," observes that public acclamations undermined the traditional, rhetorical communication of the urban elite with imperial administrators, founded on shared *paideia*.

of Corsica, Felix,[67] Constantine addresses judicial corruption as follows: "As for him, though, who has judged falsely, corrupted by a bribe or by influence—vengeance shall be given him whom he has injured, not only at the cost of his (i.e., the judge's) reputation but also through the peril of a trial."[68] Loss of reputation, that is, branding as *infamis,* was but the first humiliation the venal governor must suffer. Both the giving and taking of money to influence the outcome of a trial was punishable under the *lex Cornelia de falsis.* The Sentences of Paul state:

> PS. 5.25.2
>
> Qui . . . iudicem . . . ut sententiam ferat vel non ferat, corruperit corrumpendumve curaverit, humiliores capite puniuntur, honestiores publicatis bonis cum ipso iudice in insulam deportantur.
>
> Whosoever . . . corrupts or procures the corruption . . . of a judge, so that he gives or does not give a certain ruling: *humiliores* are punished by death, *honestiores* are deported to an island with the judge himself, and their property is to be confiscated.

The Sentences of Paul record the same punishment specifically for a judge who accepts a bribe in a capital trial:

> PS. 5.23.11(10)
>
> Iudex, qui in caput fortunasque hominis pecuniam acceperit, in insulam bonis ademptis deportatur.
>
> A judge who accepts money against the person and property of a man is deprived of his property and deported to an island.

Classical texts preserved in the Digest and Codex Justinianus omit punishment of the judge. These texts assert the culpability of the giver of the bribe, who loses his case and may be prosecuted under the *lex Cornelia.*[69] The pre-

---

67. *PLRE* I, Felix 1; perhaps identical to Furius Felix, *PLRE* I, Felix 8.

68. CTh. 1.16.3: *De eo sane, qui pretio depravatus aut gratia perperam iudicaverit, ei vindicta quem laeserit non solum existimationis dispendiis, sed etiam litis discrimine praebeatur.*

69. Mommsen, *StrR.,* 674. Dig. 48.10.1.2 (Marcian): (*poena legis Corneliae adficitur*) *et qui iudicem corruperit corrumpendumve curaverit;* Dig. 3.6.1.3 (Ulpian): *Sed et constitutio imperatoris nostri . . . prohibuit iudici vel adversario in publicis vel privatis vel fiscalibus causis pecuniam dare, et ex hac causa litem perire iussit;* CJ 7.49.1 (Caracalla): *Constitit in quacumque causa sive privata sive publica sive fiscali, ut, cuicumque data fuerit pecunia, vel iudici vel adversario, amittat actionem is, qui diffidentia iustae sententiae in pecuniae corruptela spem negotii reposuerit.*

scriptions of Constantine and the Sentences of Paul thus mark a significant change of perspective. No longer is it enough to dissuade a litigant from bribing a judge; the judge himself must be dissuaded, and punished.

Allegations of misconduct on the part of Felix very probably induced Constantine to allude to the penalties for bribery. The second fragment of Constantine's letter to Felix appears to address a complaint made against Felix specifically:

> CTh. 2.6.2
>
> [IMP. CONSTANTINVS] A. AD FELICEM PRAESIDEM CORSICAE. POST ALIA: Si petitores probaverint, interpellantes se saepius esse dilatos, atque ita labsum temporis incurrisse per negligentiam atque desidiam, gravitate tua audientiam differente, indemnitas petitorum pro modo litis, quae in altercationem fuerit adducta, de tuis facultatibus sarciatur. DAT. VIII. KAL. NOVEMB. SIRMIO CONSTANTINO A. V. ET LICINIO CAES. CONSS.
>
> [EMPEROR CONSTANTINE] AUGUSTUS TO FELIX, GOVERNOR OF CORSICA. after other matters: If the claimants prove that their claims have been repeatedly deferred, and they have thus failed to bring suit within the required time because of (Your) negligence and sloth, because Your Gravity has deferred a hearing, an indemnity for the claimants, according to the amount contested in the suit, will be collected from Your resources. GIVEN 24 OCTOBER (319[318]) AT SIRMIUM, IN THE CONSULSHIP OF CONSTANTINE AUGUSTUS, CONSUL FOR THE FIFTH TIME, AND OF LICINIUS CAESAR.

Felix must have incurred the emperor's displeasure to warrant accusation of *neglegentia* and *desidia,* even presumptively. It is mere delicacy that Constantine raises the possibility of negligence and couches the allegation of bribery, which he probably suspected in earnest, in the language of instruction. Accepting a bribe for refusing to hear a case (or, on the other hand, for initiating proceedings unjustly) was punished as severely as accepting a bribe for delivering a predetermined ruling once proceedings were under way: by deportation.[70]

It would appear that word had reached the emperor, who was then in the Balkans, that the governor of Corsica was delaying proceedings and had potentially been bribed. Constantine's response is blunt: if the charges are true, Felix must pay an indemnity equal to the value of the object of the suit.

---

70. Mommsen, *StrR.,* 675; Dig. 47.13.2.

That the petitioners have the opportunity to prove their allegations against Felix (*Si petitores probaverint*) suggests that the case would be heard by a higher instance, perhaps the *vicarius urbis Romae* or the praetorian prefect of Italy himself, under whose jurisdiction Corsica fell.[71] Nor was Felix the only governor to fall under the shadow of such misconduct. The idleness of governors, whether deliberate or merely negligent, was a recurrent failing. In 325 Constantine issued an edict about it, of which an accompanying letter to the praetorian prefect survives as CTh. 1.5.1, discussed in chapter 4. Constantine there instructs the praetorian prefect to report the names of governors who through *culpa* or *neglegentia* ignore the claims of provincials; offenders are to be "suitably punished."[72] We now know what such punishment might have entailed. The edict of 325 shows us that a chain of control had been established to monitor and discipline inattentive or unscrupulous governors. Considered in light of the reprimand sent to Felix, the edict of 325 attests the determination with which Constantine sought to control provincial administrators.[73]

Corruption of the Judicial Staff

Not only the conduct of provincial governors might occasion public acclamations: the conduct of the provincial *officium*, too, could provoke public outrage, if a governor failed to control his clerks or connived at their indiscretions. In the second fragment of the edict of 1 November 331 (CTh. 1.16.7), Constantine turns his attention to the staff of the governor, the *officiales:*

> **CTh. 1.16.7**
>
> [IMP. CONSTANTINVS] A. AD PROVINCIALES. Cessent iam nunc rapaces officialium manus, cessent, inquam: nam nisi moniti cessaverint, gladiis praecidentur. Non sit venale iudicis velum, non ingressus redempti, non infame licitationibus secretarium, non visio ipsa praesidis cum pretio. Aeque aures iudicantis pauperrimis ac divitibus reserentur. Absit ab inducendo eius, qui officii princeps dicitur, depraedatio; nullas litigatoribus adiutores eorundem officii principum concussiones adhibeant; centurionum aliorumque officialium

71. *Not. Dig. Occ.* ii and xix.

72. CTh. 1.5.1: *quo possint congrue coerceri.*

73. Cf. Harries, *Law and Empire*, 167–71. Contrast the grim picture painted by R. MacMullen, *Corruption and the Decline of Rome* (New Haven, 1988), 132–37, and 142.

parva magnaque poscentium intolerandi inpetus oblidantur eorumque, qui iurgantibus acta restituunt, inexpleta aviditas temperetur. Semper invigilet industria praesidalis, ne quicquam a praedictis generibus hominum de litigatore sumatur. Qui si de civilibus causis quidquam putaverint esse poscendum, aderit armata censura, quae nefariorum capita cervicesque detruncet, data copia universis, qui concussi fuerint, ut praesidum instruant notionem. Qui si dissimulaverint, super eodem conquerendi vocem omnibus aperimus apud comites provinciarum aut apud praefectos praetorio, si magis fuerint in vicino, ut his referentibus edocti super talibus latrociniis supplicia proferamus. DAT. KAL. NOVEMB. CONSTANTINOPOLI BASSO ET ABLAVIO CONSS.

[EMPEROR CONSTANTINE] AUGUSTUS TO THE PROVINCIALS. Let the rapacious hands of the *officiales* now cease, let them cease, I say: for if, now warned, they do not cease, they will be cut off with swords. Let not the curtain of the judge be for sale, let not access (to him) be bought, let not his private chamber be notorious for bidding, let not sight of the governor himself come at a price. Let the ears of the judge be opened to the poorest and to the rich alike. Let there be no plunder made from bringing cases by him who is called the chief of staff; let not the assistants of these chiefs of staff perpetrate any extortion on litigants; may the unbearable assaults of centurions and of other officials demanding things great and small be crushed, and may the insatiable greed of those who compile the records be tempered. The diligence of the governor shall always be on watch lest anything is taken from a litigant by the aforementioned kinds of men. If these men think they have the right to demand anything concerning civil cases, armed chastisement will be at hand, which will lop off the heads and necks (*sic*)[74] of the nefarious. We give all who have been victims of shakedowns the power to inform their governors. If they (*sc.* the governors) dissemble, we open to all men the voice of complaint before the *comites provinciarum* or, if they should be closer at hand, the praetorian prefects, so that instructed by their reports We may deal out punishment for such acts of brigandage. GIVEN 1 NOV. (331) AT CONSTANTINOPLE IN THE CONSULSHIP OF BASSUS AND ABLABIUS.

The violence of the language of CTh. 1.16.7 makes it one of the most remarkable texts in the Codex Theodosianus.[75] For all its luridness, though, the significance of this excerpt of the edict of November 331 remains con-

74. Noel Lenski helpfully suggests that these words be understood as a hendiadys, "their heads, necks and all," but I prefer to leave the bizarreness of the original unmitigated.

75. A. Demandt, "Grenzen Spätrömischer Staatsgewalt," in Paschoud and Szidat, *Usurpation in der Spätantike. Akten des Kolloquiums "Staatsreich und Staatlichkeit" 6.–10. März 1996 Solothurn/*

tested. It is on the one hand clear that CTh. 1.16.7 reiterates the principle of free access to the governor defended in CTh. 1.16.6. The second sentence of the text states in four different ways that access to the governor should not be bought.[76] But the question whether Constantine bans all fees (*commoda* or, more commonly in scholarly literature, *sportulae*) collected by *officiales* for the preparation and performance of various legal procedures has divided scholarly opinion.[77] The most serious objection is that CTh. 1.16.7 forbids only the payment of money for access to the governor and for the copy of the ruling of the judge; *sportulae* in general would still be permitted. On this reading, the *concussiones* described in the edict are additional exactions beyond the *sportulae* sanctioned by the imperial administration.[78]

The schedule of *sportulae* appended to the *ordo salutationis* of Timgad has been cited in support of this interpretation since it was first edited by Mommsen.[79] This text was published by the *consularis* of Numidia, Ulpius Mariscianus,[80] in the reign of Julian, 361–363, and contains a list of fees for various services performed by the *officiales* of the governor. The edict of Mariscianus lists no fees for admittance to the governor or for the delivery

---

Bern, ed. F. Paschoudand J. Szidat (Stuttgart, 1997), 157, mistakenly calls this edict "ein protokollierter Wutausbruch," apparently taking literally a remark made by D. Liebs, "Unverhohlene Brutalität, in der Gesetzen der ersten christlichen Kaiser," in *Romisches Recht in der europaischen Tradition. Symposion aus Anlass des 75. Geburtstags von Franz Wieacker* (Ebelsbach, 1985), 103: "Wie wenig ein solcher Wutausbruch ausrichtet, lehren unsere Gerichtsgebühren."

76. De Marini Avonzo, "Giustizia I," 1057: *Non sit venale iudicis velum, non ingressus redempti, non infame licitationibus secretarium, non visio ipsa praesidis cum pretio.* The *velum* is the curtain that marks off the private chamber, or *secretarium,* of the governor. Cf. Kaser-Hackl, §84.I, p. 555 n. 8. The bidding (*licitationes*) will presumably have been between the litigant and *officiales* for the price of an audience with the governor behind the *velum.*

77. For a complete ban: Jones, *LRE,* 496–97; cf. Jones, "The Roman Civil Service (Clerical and Sub-Clerical Grades)," in *Studies in Roman Government and Law* (Oxford, 1960), 171: "In one of his more hysterical constitutions [Constantine] strives by severe penalties to eradicate the system root and branch. . . . By Julian's reign the imperial government had resigned itself to the inevitable, and *sportulae* were no longer prohibited but regulated"; Kaser-Hackl, §84.V., p. 557: "Die Einhebung von Gebühren für gerichtliche Akte wird noch unter Konstantin als Bestechung streng bestraft" (citing CTh. 1.16.7). Against: T. Mommsen, "Observationes Epigraphicae XL. Ordo salutationis sportularumque sub Imp. Iuliano in provincia Numidia," *Ephemeris Epigraphica* 5 (1884), 639 (= *Gesammelte Schriften,* vol. 8, 490 n. 3); J. Karayannopulos, *Das Finanzwesen des frühbyzantinischen Staates* (Munich, 1958), 176; B. Palme, "Die *Officia* der Statthalter in der Spätantike," *AntTard* 7 (1999), 113 n. 142; De Marini Avonzo, "Giustizia I," 1056–58; cf. C. Kelly, *Ruling the Later Roman Empire* (Cambridge, 2004), 214. De Marini Avonzo discusses the question most cogently. On the salary of *officiales,* see Palme, "Die *Officia* der Statthalter," 111–14. In general on the nature of *sportulae,* including their advantages, see the nuanced discussion "Purchasing Power" in Kelly, *Ruling,* 138–85; MacMullen, *Corruption,* 148–70, by contrast, gives a veritable tour of the dark side of late antique bureaucracy.

78. De Marini Avonzo, "Giustizia I," 1056–57.

79. CIL 8.17896 = Bruns, *Fontes*[7], no. 103.

80. *PLRE* I, Ulpius Mariscianus.

of the ruling. De Marini Avonzo interprets this omission as evidence that Constantine forbids only these two fees, which remained forbidden under Julian; other *sportulae,* such as those listed in Timgad, will have been legal even under Constantine.[81]

This interpretation relies on the terminology used in the edict of Constantine, above all the absence of the term *sportulae.* De Marini Avonzo argues that Constantine does not refer to *sportulae* at all, but to *concussiones;* he thereby distinguishes between *sportulae* as legal and *concussiones* as illegal fees. This interpretation, however, overlooks the fact that the term *sportulae* does not prevail over its synonyms until the later fourth century.[82] By the same reasoning, one might claim that the edict of Mariscianus does not refer to *sportulae* because it uses the term *commoda.*[83] What is more, if *sportulae* were illegal in the time of Constantine, they would indeed properly be denoted *concussiones.* It is further unclear whether the *concussiones* cited in the text should pertain only to access to the governor. That the *princeps* of the *officium* should not exact a fee for an audience is clear from the words, "Let there be no plunder made from bringing cases by him who is called the chief of staff."[84] The *concussiones* of aides, centurions, and other *officiales* appear to be much broader in scope; Constantine himself speaks of "officials demanding things great and small."[85]

We know that the context of the prohibition of *concussiones* in CTh. 1.16.7 is the civil procedure: Constantine writes, "If these men think they have the right to demand anything concerning civil cases, armed chastisement will be at hand."[86] The line immediately beforehand appears to refer a general ban on yet illegal *sportulae:* "The diligence of the governor shall always be on watch lest anything is taken from a litigant by the aforemen-

81. De Marini Avonzo, "Giustizia I," 1058.

82. Mommsen, "Ordo salutationis," 638 n. 1.

83. De Marini Avonzo, "Giustizia I," 1057, cites CTh. 8.10.2 (a. 344) as confirmation of the fact that illegal exactions stood in contrast to *sportulae* sanctioned by the government: *praeter sollemnes et canonicas pensitationes multa a provincialibus Afris indignissime postulantur ab officialibus.* The words *sollemnes et canonicas pensitationes* do not refer to *sportulae,* however, but to annual tax payments. See Lewis and Short, s.v. *canon* II. B., *canonicus* III, and *sollemnis* pr. and I (lacking in the *OLD*). The nature of the fees exacted by the *officiales* in cities is not stated; in rural *mansiones* the officials are described as requisitioning animals and imposing corvee labor. The introduction of the constitution suggests that the *officiales* were entitled to collect nothing (i.e., including *sportulae*) other than the regular taxes.

84. CTh. 1.16.7: *Absit ab inducendo eius, qui officii princeps dicitur, depraedatio.*

85. Ibid.: . . . *nullas litigatoribus adiutores eorundem officii principum concussiones adhibeant; centurionum aliorumque officialium parva magnaque poscentium intolerandi inpetus oblidantur eorumque, qui iurgantibus acta restituunt, inexpleta aviditas temperetur.*

86. Ibid.: *Qui si de civilibus causis quidquam putaverint esse poscendum, aderit armata censura.*

tioned kinds of men."[87] Choice of the verb *sumere,* not *concutere,* would appear to ban all "taking" whatsoever.

It may be more profitable to look beyond the text of CTh. 1.16.7 and to ask what a potential litigant might have accomplished without paying fees, if mere access to the governor was protected. Very little, it appears. The nature of the civil procedure of Constantine's day required legal acts later burdened with *sportulae* simply to initiate proceedings. In CTh. 2.4.2, a letter to the praetorian prefect in the year 322, nine years earlier, Constantine established that *litis denuntiatio,*[88] the initial act of legal proceedings, must be performed before the governor or another high official who could authorize records of the proceedings (*ius actorum conficiendorum*). Apparently, privately made *denuntiationes* had fraudulently named the deceased, persons residing in other provinces, or even fictional persons as witnesses.[89] Consequently, one must go to the governor to perform the *litis denuntiatio.* The result of *litis denuntiatio* was the "simple claim" (*postulatio simplex*), which, if admitted by the governor, would be served by the plaintiff to the defendant, potentially with the aid of an *officialis.*[90]

The same process carries considerable fees in the edict of Mariscianus: 5 bushels of grain to the *exceptores* for the registration of the *postulatio simplex,* 5 to the *scholastici* to present it in court, 5 to the *princeps officii* to issue a summons, and 2½ to the *cornicularius* and *commentariensis* each, with fees for the papyrus used as well.[91] The governor enters into these formalities only after *litis denuntiatio* and the preparation of the *postulatio simplex:* he must approve the *postulatio* before it may be served to the plaintiff. If one follows the edict of Mariscianus, a litigant will already have paid several *sportulae* before he even reaches the governor. When, at the beginning of CTh. 1.16.7, Constantine forbids any exactions for access to the governor, he must mean also these legal acts, which were required before the governor became involved. The demand, "Let the ears of the judge be opened to the poorest and to the rich alike,"[92] would be absurdly disingenuous if Constantine guaranteed the access of poor litigants to the governor, yet they

87. *Semper invigilet industria praesidalis, ne quicquam a praedictis generibus hominum de litigatore sumatur.*

88. On the procedure of the *litis denuntiatio,* see Kaser-Hackl, §86, pp. 566–70.

89. CTh. 2.4.1: *Denuntiari vel apud provinciarum rectores vel apud eos, quibus actorum conficiendorum ius est, decernimus, ne privata testatio mortuorum aut in diversis terris absentium aut eorum, qui nusquam gentium sint, scripta nominibus falsam fidem rebus non gestis adfigat.*

90. Kaser-Hackl, §86.II.1, p. 567.

91. See Kelly, *Ruling,* 139–40 with nn. 6 and 8, pp. 276–77.

92. CTh. 1.16.7: *Aeque aures iudicantis pauperrimis ac divitibus reserentur.*

were obliged to pay fees to his staff in order to accomplish anything by such an audience. The traditional interpretation of CTh. 1.16.7 therefore seems correct: that Constantine forbids all *sportulae,* which he calls *concussiones* precisely because they are illegal. It is even possible that this state of affairs obtained until 344, when Constantine's son Constantius speaks generally of "payments, besides annual taxes, most outrageously demanded by the *officiales,*" though this is not the place to pursue this question.[93]

The chain of control in cases of *concussiones* corresponds to that described in CTh. 1.16.6 for the report of public acclamations against provincial governors. The *comites* and praetorian prefects are the officials to whom wronged provincials should turn, if the governors fail to enforce the law. It was the responsibility of the governor, naturally, to ensure that no abuses took place. The *armata censura* that Constantine conjures to strike down corrupt *officiales* will in the first instance have been the governor's power of *coercitio.* Most arbitrary punishments ordained in late antique constitutions were based on this traditional power of Roman magistrates.[94] It is to the governor that the victims of *concussiones* are to turn first. If the governor ignores their complaints, the provincials are directed to the *comites provinciarum* and the praetorian prefect according to proximity and, it is implied, the convenience of the victim.[95] Once the provincials have approached the *comes* or prefect, whether in person or through a representative, these officials, in turn, are to inform the emperor of cases that warrant punishment.

The punishment of the governor who connives at the crimes of his staff is left to the discretion of the emperor. The punishment of the *officiales* is somewhat ambiguous, though certainly unpleasant. The dramatic opening words of CTh. 1.16.7 seem to decree that *officiales* who persist in exacting illegal fees will have their hands severed.[96] A number of crimes were punished by mutilation in Late Antiquity. Even Justinian, in his revision of the imperial *mandata,* ordered that tax collectors guilty of forging receipts suffer amputation of a hand in addition to a fine.[97] It is perhaps fair to speak of

93. CTh. 8.10.2 (a. 344). See n. 83 above.

94. Cf. the list of such vague references to punishment in C. Dupont, *Le droit criminel dans les constitutions de Constantin. Les Peines* (Lille, 1955), 11–13.

95. CTh. 1.16.7: *apud comites cunctos provinciarum aut apud praefectos praetorio, si magis fuerint in vicino.*

96. Ibid.: *Cessent iam nunc rapaces officialium manus, cessent, inquam: nam nisi moniti non cessaverint, gladiis praecidentur.*

97. See Mommsen, *StrR.,* 982–83 with p. 982 n. 7; Nov. 17.8 (a. 535): ἀπειλῶν αὐτοῖς καὶ ζημίαν μεγάλην καὶ χειρὸς ἀφαίρεσιν, εἰ τὸ παραγγελλόμενον μὲνἀεί, μέχρι δὲ νῦν μὴ φυλαχθέν, μὴ τοῦ

"dramatic effect," however, in CTh. 1.16.7: a few lines down the penalty is clearly beheading.[98] A punctilious governor could, of course, inflict both punishments.

The question of the enforcement of CTh. 1.16.7 leads into the next chapter, a survey of official letters concerning a variety of administrative abuse. With respect to illicit judicial fees, it should not be forgotten that CTh. 1.16.7 was not some showpiece for posterity but law, and circulated throughout the empire. The circumstances of publication would ensure that every provincial governor, in addition to the actual addressees, the provincials, would know of its contents. Who among the governors would defy the emperor? The edict of Constantine went beyond appeals to provincials to denounce corrupt officials.[99]

To what extent CTh. 1.16.7 was enforced, with all its vehemence and publicity, is an insoluble question. The public edicts of Constantine, which bound both subject and official, gave provincial litigants means of asserting their rights. In this sense the "charismatic power" of the emperor regulated the bureaucracy—through his subjects.[100] Yet while the edict of Constantine may have deterred officials from exacting fees from provincial litigants—"have created some impression" in the words of Ando[101]—the emperor's condemnation of the practice was no lasting guarantee. Laws are as certainly broken as they are obeyed. The edict of Constantine against *sportulae* itself was occasioned by the persistence of an illegal practice, and within thirty years, the consular governor of Numidia could openly publish the schedule of legal fees that has survived to our times. It must also be added that Constantine's edict did nothing to improve the chronic under-compensation of provincial officials and clerks, the real value of whose salaries had plummeted in the inflation of the third century.[102]

The battle against the encroachment of legal fees in the provincial judiciary would ultimately be lost, but it is rash to presume that CTh. 1.16.7 was never enforced, at least in the first years after its publication, perhaps even

---

λοιποῦ γοῦν πᾶσι φυλάξαιεν τρόποις. On the proliferation of mutilation in Late Antiquity and its symbolic appeal, MacMullen, "Judicial Savagery," 212 with nn. 39–42. Constantine decreed (CJ 6.1.3, cf. Corcoran, *ET*^{2}, 287–88) that slaves caught fleeing into *barbaricum* could (among other punishments) have a foot amputated.

98. CTh. 1.16.7: *aderit armata censura, quae nefariorum capita cervicesque detruncet.*

99. Ando, *Imperial Ideology,* 367.

100. This is argued explicitly by Ando, ibid., 362–73.

101. Ibid., 362.

102. H. A. Drake, *Constantine and the Bishops: The Politics of Intolerance* (Baltimore & London, 2000), 332.

until the end of Constantine's life six years later. The close association of the prohibition of *sportulae* and the authorization of public acclamations lends the edict the character of an experiment in administrative control: the governor who imposed or condoned legal fees might risk denunciation before the emperor's *comites* and praetorian prefects, personally or in public acclamations that it was the duty of these officials to report. How effective the edict against judicial fees was, or how long it was effective, is a question that can be answered only according to one's opinion of the prevalence of corruption in the bureaucracy of the early fourth century, both on the part of governors as enforcers and on that of *officiales* as delinquents, and the susceptibility of the provincial administration to the pressure of imperial pronouncements and public expectations. With respect to the latter, it is worth noting that the *officiales* of provincial governors were drawn from the local population. They will have had to sleep, so to speak, in whatever bed they had made. The governors themselves spent their terms of office not only within a network of *paideia* and honor,[103] but exposed to the scrutiny of a mass of humble subjects. Constantine tells all these groups that he is aware of the practices of provincial *officiales* and their governors and possesses the power to suppress it. What was the life of an *officialis* worth to a governor, if put in the balance with his prospects, fortune, and potentially his own life? And what was the life of a petty provincial governor worth to Constantine, weighed against his reputation, the approval of his subjects, and potentially—to judge by his prayers—his own salvation? The constitutions of the emperors were law, the penalty for disobedience severe. Time must elapse before enforcement could gradually slacken and exceptions to a law become the rule. But until the harsh measures of an edict such as CTh. 1.16.7 lapsed into obscurity, it was safer to obey.[104]

Episcopalis Audientia

The words of the edict of Constantine state that the prohibition of legal fees served to protect the access of poor litigants to the court of the provincial

103. The social and cultural influences explored by Brown, *Power and Persuasion*, and J. E. Lendon, *Empire of Honour* (Oxford, 1997).

104. Mommsen's reflections (*StrR.*, 1040 n. 4) on the severity of late antique criminal law still seem apt: "Allerdings liegt es im Wesen der Willkürherrschaft, dass die Anordnung bald als unbedingt bindend behandelt, bald ignorirt wird; praktisch werden Vorschriften wie die eben angeführte nicht leicht auf die Dauer eingehalten worden sein und wahrscheinlich um so weniger, je schwerer die auf die Nichteinhaltung gesetzte Strafe war." Contra Kelly, *Ruling*, 214, writing on CTh. 1.16.7: "another example of that 'dramatic exaggeration.'"

governor: "Let the ears of the judge be opened to the poorest and to the rich alike."[105] The suppression of judicial fees is only one example of legislation that was introduced to improve access of ordinary provincials to Roman law. Constantine shows great willingness to innovate throughout his reign, and administrative reform seems to intensify in the years after the conquest of the East. This is only natural at a time when Constantine strove to bring the former territory of Licinius under firm control; the creation of a senate in Constantinople will probably have served foremost to provide suitable administrators.[106]

The reinvention of the local judicial officer known as *defensor civitatis* falls within the same period. Previously a local official that served as an advocate, the *defensor* appears to have received new judicial powers, which were conferred on him by Constantine in a law that is now lost.[107] This change provided humble litigants a judicial instance independent of the provincial governor and his potentially expensive, procedurally cumbersome, certainly busy, court. The *defensor* became a judge who might hear disputes of a very humble nature. One amusing example is attested by a papyrus of the year 336, which records a complaint made by a woman who was attacked by a fellow villager while rescuing two drowning pigs from a canal.[108] The office of the *defensor civitatis* would be greatly enhanced by Valentinian in 368, only a few years after the schedule of fees was published in Timgad under Julian.[109]

The exaction of legal fees by the *officiales* of provincial governors could perhaps be tolerated in later times, because such alternative means of redress for humble litigants had already been devised. The petty court of the *defensor* was not the only new judicial instance to emerge for *pauperrimi* during Constantine's reign. The institution of episcopal jurisdiction in private suits notoriously seems to have been intended to authorize yet another avenue of redress for poor litigants.[110] The literature on episcopal jurisdic-

---

105. CTh. 1.16.7: *Aeque aures iudicantis pauperrimis ac divitibus reserentur.*

106. Heather, "Senators and Senates," 185–86.

107. R. M. Frakes, *Contra potentium iniurias: The defensor civitatis and Late Roman Justice* (Munich, 2001), 43–85, esp. 55; Frakes proposed a date of ca. 319 in an earlier article, "Late Roman Social Justice and the Origin of the Defensor Civitatis," *CJ* 89 (1994), 337–48.

108. P.Oxy. VI 901 (= LIV 3771): Φλαουί[ῳ] Ἰουλιανῷ διοικοῦντι συνδικίαν Ὀξυρυγχίτου παρὰ Αὐρηλίας Ἀλλοῦτος Θωνίου ἀπὸ κώμης Ταμπέμο[υ] πάγου.

109. Further on the *defensor civitatis:* S. Schmidt-Hofner, *Reagieren und Gestalten. Der Regierungsstil des spätrömischen Kaisers am Beispiel der Gesetzgebung Valentinians I.* (Munich, 2008), 71–75; Kaser-Hackl, §82.II, pp. 546–47.

110. This connection was made by W. Waldstein, "Die Stellung der *episcopalis audientia* im spätrömischen Prozeß," in *Festschrift für Max Kaser zum 70. Geburtstag* (Munich, 1976), 533–56;

tion, or *episcopalis audientia*, is extensive.[111] Of the Constantinian constitutions concerning it (CTh. 1.27.1 and Sirm.1), Sirm. 1 in particular has been steeped in controversy; recent scholars, however, now generally admit its authenticity.[112] The present author likewise finds no compelling reason to dismiss Sirm. 1 as a fraud.

The first constitution dates probably to 318, because Crispus Caesar is mentioned in the second place of the consular date.[113] Record of Constantinople as the place of issue must be an error, perhaps best explained as an erroneous expansion of Constantine's name (*Constantino*).[114] The text of the constitution also, unfortunately, seems to have suffered in transmission.

CTh. 1.27.1 (a. 318?)

IMP. CONSTANTINVS A. Iudex pro sua sollicitudine observare debebit, ut, si ad episcopale iudicium provocetur, silentium accommodetur et, si quis ad legem Christianam negotium transferre voluerit et illud iudicium observare, audiatur, etiamsi negotium apud iudicem sit inchoatum, et pro sanctis habeatur, quidquid ab his fuerit iudicatum: ita tamen, ne usurpetur in eo, ut unus ex litigantibus pergat ad supra dictum auditorium et arbitrium suum enuntiet. Iudex enim praesentis causae integre habere debet arbitrium, ut omnibus accepto latis pronuntiet. DATA VIIII KAL. IVLIAS CONSTANTINOPOLI [. . .] A. ET CRISPO CAES. CONSS.

EMPEROR CONSTANTINE AUGUSTUS. A judge shall observe as his responsibility the following: if an appeal is made to the court of a bishop, silence shall be enforced, and if someone should wish to transfer a case to Christian law and abide by that court, he shall be heard, even if the case has already been opened

---

and Frakes, *Contra potentium iniurias*, 195–229; similarly, Drake, *Constantine and the Bishops*, 322–33; Harries, *Law and Empire*, 191–211. On ecclesiastical litigation generally, see C. Humfress, *Orthodoxy and the Courts in Late Antiquity* (Oxford, 2007), and A. Banfi, *Habent illi iudices suos. Studi sull'esclusività della giurisdizione ecclesiastica e sulle origini del privilegium fori in diritto romano e bizantino* (Milan, 2005).

111. In addition to the authors named in the previous note, see W. Selb, "Episcopalis audientia von der Zeit Konstantins bis zur Nov. XXXV Valentinians III," *ZRG* 84 (1967), 162–217; M. R. Cimma, *L'episcopalis audientia nelle costituzioni imperiali da Costantino a Giustiniano* (Turin, 1989); Kaser-Hackl, §100 III, pp. 641–44; N. E. Lenski, "Evidence for the *Audientia episcopalis* in the New Letters of Augustine," in *Law, Society, and Authority in Late Antiquity*, ed. R. Mathisen (Oxford, 2001), 83–97; O. Huck, "À propos de CTh 1, 27, 1 et Sirm 1. 1. Sur deux textes controversés relatifs à l'episcopalis audientia constantinienne," *ZRG* 120 (2003), 78–105.

112. Cimma, *L'episcopalis audientia*, 36–55; Huck, "À propos de CTh 1, 27, 1 et CSirm 1, 85–99.

113. Mommsen, *ad loc.*

114. O. Seeck, "Die Zeitfolge der Gesetze Constantins," *ZRG* 10 (1889), 8 and 20; Seeck, *Regesten*, 56–57, 166; Selb, "Episcopalis audientia," 171 n. 42.

before the judge; and whatever is decided by (bishops) shall be considered sacred. However, there shall be no abuse to the effect that one of the litigants proceeds to the aforementioned court and (the bishop?) pronounces his opinion. The judge should have full discretion in the present case, so that he may give a ruling . . .[115] GIVEN 23 JUNE (318?) AT CONSTANTINOPLE IN THE CONSULSHIP OF [CONSTANTINE] AUGUSTUS AND CRISPUS CAESAR.

The text of the latter half of the constitution seems to be disturbed. Among the uncertainties is the subject of the word *enuntiet:* is it the bishop who declares his (*suum*) opinion? This seems to be implied by the use of *suus;* the litigant who consults the bishop independently would return to the public judge to declare his, that is, the bishop's (*eius*) opinion—or does Constantine consider the ruling the litigant's (*suum*) because it is in his favor? The thrust of the constitution, then, seems to be this: if during proceedings a litigant demands to be heard by a bishop instead of a public judge, he must be accommodated; the case is to be transferred to a bishop. The civil judge then adopts the bishop's ruling as his own. One litigant may not, however, obtain a ruling from a bishop independently, unknown to the other party, and expect the original civil judge to enforce it. It is unclear whether one party can compel the other to go to the bishop's court.[116]

The constitution preserved as CTh. 1.27.1 appears to presume that the ability of litigants to request an episcopal hearing was already established. This is certainly the case in Sirm. 1, dated to 333:

IMP. CONSTANTINVS A. AD ABLABIVM P(RAEFECTVM) P(RAETORI)O. Satis mirati sumus gravitatem tuam, quae plena iustitiae ac probae religionis est, clementiam nostram sciscitari voluisse, quid de sententiis episcoporum vel ante moderatio nostra censuerit vel nunc servari cupiamus, Ablabi, parens karissime atque amantissime. Itaque quia a nobis instrui voluisti, olim promulgatae legis

115. Pharr translates *omnibus accepto latis* as "after full credit is given to all the facts presented," but frankly I fail to see any obvious meaning in these words. Selb, "Episcopalis audientia," 183–84, interprets the phrase as a variant of *acceptum ferre* or *accepto ferri,* "to record as received, acknowledge receipt of" ("'erlassen,' 'quittieren,' 'als empfangen bekennen'") and understands a reference to a settlement between the parties. This financial idiom appears in several constitutions (CTh. 12.6.13.1, 12.6.26, 13.5.32, 15.1.6, 15.1.27–28), but always with clear reference to money or receipts, and never with simple *latus,* much less in an inscrutable ablative absolute construction, e.g., CTh. 12.6.13.1: *in septuaginta duos solidos libra feratur accepto.*

116. Selb, "Episcopalis audientia," 176–77, argues that CTh. 1.27.1 forbids unilateral appeal; Cimma, *L'episcopalis audientia,* 59–62, argues that CTh. 1.27.1, not Sirm. 1 (as Selb argues), is interpolated; Huck, "À propos de CTh 1, 27, 1 et CSirm 1," 101–2, sees "une sorte de privilège d'*exequatur*" indeed conferred on the ruling of the bishop.

ordinem salubri rursus imperio propagamus. Sanximus namque, sicut edicti nostri forma declarat, sententias episcoporum quolibet genere latas sine aliqua aetatis discretione inviolatas semper incorruptasque servari; scilicet ut pro sanctis semper ac venerabilibus habeantur, quidquid episcoporum fuerit sententia terminatum. Sive itaque inter minores sive inter maiores <res?>[117] ab episcopis fuerit iudicatum, apud vos, qui iudiciorum summam tenetis, et apud ceteros omnes iudices ad executionem volumus pertinere. Quicumque itaque litem habens, sive possessor sive petitor vel inter initia litis vel decursis temporum curriculis, sive cum negotium peroratur, sive cum iam coeperit promi sententia, iudicium elegerit sacrosancto legis antistitis, ilico sine aliqua dubitatione, etiamsi alia pars refragatur, ad episcopum personae litigantium dirigantur. Multa enim, quae in iudicio captiosa praescriptionis vincula promi non patiuntur, investigat et publicat sacrosanctae religionis auctoritas. Omnes itaque causae, quae vel praetorio iure vel civili tractantur, episcoporum sententiis terminatae perpetuo stabilitatis iure firmentur, nec liceat ulterius retractari negotium, quod episcoporum sententia deciderit. Testimonium etiam ab uno licet episcopo perhibitum omnis iudex indubitanter accipiat nec alius audiatur testis, cum testimonium episcopi a qualibet parte fuerit repromissum. Illud est enim veritatis auctoritate firmatum, illud incorruptum, quod a sacrosancto homine conscientia mentis inlibatae protulerit. Hoc nos edicto salubri aliquando censuimus, hoc perpetua lege firmamus, malitiosa litium semina conprimentes, ut miseri homines longis ac paene perpetuis actionum laqueis implicati ab improbis petitionibus vel a cupiditate praepostera maturo fine discedant. Quidquid itaque de sententiis episcoporum clementia nostra censuerat et iam hac sumus lege complexi, gravitatem tuam et ceteros pro utilitate omnium latum in perpetuum observare convenit. DATA III NONAS MAIAS CONSTANTINOPOLI DALMATIO ET ZENOFILO CONS.

EMPEROR CONSTANTINE AUGUSTUS TO ABLABIUS, PRAETORIAN PREFECT. We are quite surprised that Your Gravity, which is full of justice and right

117. I tentatively conjecture that *res* has fallen out of the text after *maiores* or *minores* because of an eyeskip. Pharr and others interpret the phrase *sive . . . maiores* as a reference to minors and adults, but this seems unlikely on reflection. First, one expects *minores* and *maiores* to be qualified in some way, e.g., *minores aetate* or *natu* or *annis.* Reference to age is not obvious. Second, the thought of minors litigating against one another is unusual, while that of adults litigating against one another otiose. Third, reference to the importance of the litigants, of the judges, or of the litigation is more likely than reference to the age of the litigants. For example, Constantine says (CTh. 11.30.12) that the term "appeal" should be used in *important* cases: *appellationis . . . verbum in maioribus rebus dici oportet.* For a similar distinction of the importance of cases, cf. CTh. 11.36.5; for distinctions of rank between litigants, cf. CTh. 6.35.14; for distinctions of rank between judges, cf. CTh. 6.30.4, CJ 1.3.32pr, 1.22.6, 1.40.5, 1.51.11, 3.1.14.1–4, 12.1.18, 12.25.4pr.

religion, wished to inquire of Our Clemency either what Our Moderation decreed concerning the rulings of bishops or what We now wish to be observed. Since then you wished to be informed by Us, We again, by Our salutary power, make known the contents of the law previously promulgated. For We decreed, as the text of Our edict declares, that the rulings of bishops should be kept inviolable and uncorrupted forever, no matter how they were made and without any distinction of age; namely, they should be considered sacred (*pro sanctis*) and venerable forever, whatsoever has been decided by the ruling of bishops.[118] Therefore, whether a case concerning trifling or important matters is decided by bishops, We desire that the enforcement of the ruling fall upon you and upon all other judges. Therefore, whosoever is involved in litigation—whether possessor or petitioner, whether at the outset of litigation or at the end of the prescribed time, whether the case is being concluded or the ruling has just begun to be delivered—if he chooses the judgment of the priest of the holy law, straightaway, without any hesitation, even if the other party protests, the litigants shall be directed to the bishop. For the authority of the sacrosanct religion investigates and reveals many things that the treacherous pitfalls of legal privilege (*praescriptio*) do not allow to be raised in (an official) court. All cases, then, that hinge on praetorian or civil law, once closed by the rulings of bishops, shall be ratified by the eternal law of validty, nor may a case that the ruling of bishops has decided be reopened subsequently. Moreover, every (official) judge shall accept without hesitation testimony given even by one bishop, nor shall another witness be heard, if the testimony of a bishop has been pledged by any party. For what the conscience of a sacrosanct man of untainted thoughts has produced—that is founded on the authority of truth; that is incorruptible. This We formerly decreed by Our salutary edict; this We confirm by eternal law, stifling the wicked seeds of strife, so that wretched men, who have been entangled in the lengthy and almost unending snares of actions at law by wicked suits or by perverse greed, may leave at a timely end. Thus, whatsoever Our Clemency had decreed, and which We have now covered in this law, it behooves Your Gravity and (all) others to observe as enacted for all time for the benefit of all. GIVEN 3 MAY (333), IN CONSTANTINOPLE, IN THE CONSULSHIP OF DALMATIUS AND ZENOFILUS.

Virtually every line of this constitution is noteworthy. The addressee, Ablabius, was a Christian, whom Constantine had elevated by degrees

---

118. The Latin leads the reader to expect a plural subject of the relative clause where the singular *quidquid* stands. Constantine is perhaps following the original phrasing of his edict too closely; cf. the almost identical language in CTh. 1.27.1, *quidquid ab his fuerit iudicatum.*

through several imperial posts to the lofty office of praetorian prefect.[119] Constantine writes that he is surprised evidently because it seems paradoxical that Ablabius should require clarification about something that, as a Christian, he should support and, as an imperial administrator, he should already know. Hence, Ablabius is reminded of his own abundance of "justice and right religion."

Most scholars have seen a dispute involving minors as the original context of this constitution.[120] The words *sive inter minores sive inter maiores* are usually translated, "between minors or between adults" (Pharr), but reference to minors is not obvious. It seems to me more likely that Constantine here is stressing that the rulings of bishops cannot be questioned regardless of the importance of the case or litigants.[121] Interpretation of the phrase *sine aliqua aetatis discretione* as "without any distinction as to age (of the litigants)" (Pharr) is to read into these words the interpretation of the passage concerning *minores*. The *aetas* to which Constantine refers must be that of the rulings of the bishop, which, he says, are to be "kept inviolable and uncorrupted for ever."[122] In other words, such rulings are inviolable no matter *how* they were made (*quolibet genere latas*) or *how long ago* they were made (*sine aliqua aetatis discretione inviolatas*). This interpretation, moreover, is recommended by the parallelism of the Latin itself, whereby two sonorous past participles, *latas* and *inviolatas*, are paired with modifying phrases. Ablabius's request for clarification may well have derived from a specific case, but it was not necessarily one that concerned minors, and his question to Constantine was general, as is Constantine's reply.

Notoriously, Constantine affirms in Sirm. 1 that even a unilateral demand to be heard by a bishop must be respected, even if the other party protests. This clause of the original edict is compatible with CTh. 1.27.1, in which Constantine states, "if someone should wish to transfer a case to Christian law and abide by that court, he shall be heard." In both CTh. 1.27.1 and Sirm. 1, civil proceedings are to halt if appeal to the bishop is made. These conditions correspond to what the later church historian Sozomen writes (*HE* 1.9.5):

119. *PLRE* I, Ablabius 4.

120. Pharr; Barnes, *CE*, 51; Drake, *Constantine and the Bishops*, 326–27; cf. Selb, "Episcopalis audientia," 196; Huck, "À propos de CTh 1, 27, 1 et Sirm 1," 82 n. 6.

121. See n. 117 above, concerning the text.

122. Similarly, Selb, "Episcopalis audientia," 196; Huck, "À propos de CTh 1, 27, 1 et Sirm 1," 82 n. 6: "hors de toute considération de temps."

τῶν δὲ ἐπισκόπων ἐπικαλεῖσθαι τὴν κρίσιν ἐπέτρεψε τοῖς δικαζομένοις, ἢν βούλωνται τοὺς πολιτικοὺς ἄρχοντας παραιτεῖσθαι· κυρίαν δὲ εἶναι τὴν αὐτῶν ψῆφον καὶ κρείττω τῆς τῶν ἄλλων δικαστῶν ὡσανεὶ παρὰ τοῦ βασιλέως ἐξενεχθεῖσαν, εἰς ἔργον δὲ τὰ κρινόμενα ἄγειν τοὺς ἄρχοντας καὶ τοὺς διακονουμένους αὐτοῖς στρατιώτας.

He permitted litigants to appeal to the judgment of bishops, if they wished to avoid the civil magistrates: their ruling would be valid and greater than that of other judges, as if it had been made by the emperor himself, while the magistrates and the soldiers seconded to them would enforce the rulings.

Sozomen rightly identifies the most significant power conferred on the bishops—which is sometimes overshadowed by the ratification of unilateral appeal—namely that the rulings of bishops were to be inappellable, like those of the emperor himself. In both CTh. 1.27.1 and Sirm. 1, Constantine states that the rulings of bishops are to be considered *pro sanctis.* This is an unusual phrase, and the translation given above, "considered sacred," captures only part of its meaning. While the word *sanctus* is generally recognized as an adjective ("holy," "sacred," etc.), it is also the past participle of the verb *sancire.* In late antique usage, it was the emperor whose business it was to *sancire:* it is the Latin verb par excellence used to describe the decrees of the emperor (θεσπίζειν in Greek). For example, Constantine himself says of his earlier edict in Sirm. 1, *sanximus,* "We decreed that . . ." In effect, Constantine has given bishops the same judicial power as he gave to the high imperial officials who presided *vice sacra,* in the place of the emperor and with his inappellable jurisdiction.[123] Constantine conferred permanent jurisdiction *vice sacra* on a number of high officials some time after circa 314; the conferral of similar jurisdiction on bishops will probably have occurred at the same time, and certainly before 318, the date of CTh. 1.27.1.

Constantine was not attempting to undermine Roman law, nor had he determined to deliver the empire wholesale to the Church: *episcopalis audientia* was one of many innovations whereby Constantine sought to overcome the real deficiencies of ordinary provincial justice. The declared purpose of Sirm. 1 is indeed to help litigants, *pro utilitate omnium.*[124] The

123. So already Waldstein, "Stellung der *episcopalis audientia,*" 556: "Aus alledem ergibt sich, daß Konstantin die *episcopalis audientia* wohl als vom Kaiser delegierte Sondergerichtsbarkeit eingeführt hat."

124. Rightly emphasized by W. Waldstein, review of *L'episcopalis audientia,* by M. R. Cimma, *Gnomon* 65 (1993), 746.

reforms most closely related to *episcopalis audientia* are the multiplication of instances of appeal, the conferral of jurisdiction *vice sacra* on high-ranking members of the provincial administration, and the introduction of an expedited appeals process by means of official correspondence, *appellatio more consultationis.* These reforms will be discussed in chapter 8. If one considers later edicts, such CTh. 9.1.4, promulgated in 325 to encourage the report of wrongs committed by imperial officials; and also CTh. 1.16.6–7, promulgated in 331, authorizing public acclamations to the same effect and forbidding the exaction of judicial fees—then Constantine's lost edicts on *episcopalis audientia* and jurisdiction *vice sacra* attest a remarkable dedication to the improvement of the access and reliability of justice throughout the Roman Empire, spanning almost the entire period for which there is legal evidence, circa 314 to 333.[125]

The Roman legal system was fundamentally biased in favor of those who had status and wealth.[126] Status was indeed recognized and affirmed,[127] but the subtle power of lucre was not.[128] The reforms of Constantine were intended above all to protect poor citizens from abuse of their very poverty. *Episcopalis audientia* as defined in Sirm. 1 is certainly radical, but it strikes at the greatest weakness of the legal system: if one allows that *sportulae* were permitted, it is taken for granted that a poor man challenged at law by a rich man would have to proceed at his expense or lose his case; and even if fees were still prohibited, the poor man simply could not compete if the rich man appealed—and in both these scenarios it is presumed that the judge delivers a just ruling in the first instance. Constantine attempts to reverse this bias: by his law, if the poor man demands justice before a bishop, at no expense, Constantine insists that even the rich man must comply, and whatever the bishop ruled would be final.

One must not, however, confuse dedication to a cause with success. The success of the institution as outlined in Sirm. 1 depended in the first instance on the integrity of the bishops. Constantine seems to regard the sanctity of their decisions with the same deference that he showed the councils convened to hear the Donatists or the Council of Nicaea itself:

125. H. A. Drake, "Firmicus Maternus and the Politics of Conversion," in *Qui Miscuit Utile Dulci: Festschrift Essays for Paul Lachlan MacKendrick,* ed. G. Schmeling and J. D. Mikalson (Wauconda, IL, 1998), 133–49, plausibly interprets Firmicus Maternus's denunciation of the legal system as an attempt to recommend himself for employment by appealing to Constantine's sense of justice.

126. The *locus classicus* remains Jones, *LRE,* chapter 14, "Justice."

127. For example, Constantine orders in CTh. 11.39.3, *ut honestioribus potius fides testibus habeatur.*

128. Or not quite yet, as Kelly, *Ruling,* chapter 4, "Purchasing Power," 138–85, ably demonstrates.

"For what the conscience of a sacrosanct man of untainted thoughts has produced—that is founded on the authority of truth; that is incorruptible" (Sirm. 1).[129] Constantine's faith in bishops recalls that placed in his closest officials and the highest provincial administrators, the praetorian prefects and *comites.* It is surprising that between 318 and 333 Constantine had not yet discovered that even the servants of God might entertain widely divergent views of truth and justice; and yet Constantine was not dissuaded from reaffirming the extraordinary judicial power he had conferred on them. Ablabius, it would seem, had good reason to ask Constantine to reconsider his position. At least one striking novelty of Sirm. 1—that a single bishop sufficed as witness, whereas at least two witnesses were normally required—was annulled already in 334.[130] By the date of the next law preserved concerning *episcopalis audientia* (CJ 1.4.7, a. 398), unilateral appeal to the bishop's court has lapsed, and the consent of the parties is required.

Sirm. 1 appears to preserve a failed experiment, one perhaps already nearing its end, in which Constantine attempted to transform Christian bishops into agents of imperial justice. That the radical privilege of unilateral appeal to a bishop's court could not be upheld beyond Constantine's reign (or at the very latest, by Julian's)[131] must have resulted as much from the intransigence of unwilling litigants as from the bishops who found themselves charged with the unpleasant task of adjudicating such cases. Several scholars have shown how *episcopalis audientia* far more resembles a burden than a boon; it was even an "infliction of powers."[132] The institution itself, however, survived as an established form of arbitration founded on the consent of both parties, much to the benefit of litigants—even wealthy litigants[133]—a fact that even the greatest of jurists could appreciate.[134]

---

129. Cf. Eus., *VC.* 4.27.2: παντὸς γὰρ εἶναι δικαστοῦ τοὺς ἱερεῖς τοῦ θεοῦ δοκιμωτέρους.

130. CTh. 11.39.3; Selb, "Episcopalis audientia," 188; Drake, *Constantine and the Bishops,* 344–45.

131. Julian, *Ep.* 52 (Bidez no. 114 [437a], p. 194): describes bishops as ποθοῦντες δὲ τὴν προτέραν δυναστείαν ὅτι μὴ δικάζειν ἔξεστιν αὐτοῖς καὶ γράφειν διαθήκας καὶ ἀλλοτρίους σφετερίζεσθαι κλήρους καὶ τὰ πάντα ἑαυτοῖς προσνέμειν . . . If bishops were deprived of their power to sit as judges (μὴ δικάζειν ἔξεστιν αὐτοῖς), this must refer to civil litigation.

132. "Infliction of powers": Harries, *Law and Empire,* 191; cf. Drake, *Constantine and the Bishops,* 346–47; Lenski, "Evidence," 93–94; Huck, "À propos de CTh 1, 27, 1 et Sirm 1," 89–90.

133. Harries, *Law and Empire,* 208–10.

134. Kaser, *Das römische Privatrecht,* vol. 2, §192 II.3, p. 13, writes: "Wirksame Hilfe im Dienst der Gerechtigkeit hat die bischöfliche Gerichtsbarkeit (*episcopalis audientia*) geleistet. Sie arbeitete im ganzen sachlicher und unbestechlicher als die staatliche und konnte den einzelnen zuweilen wirksam auch gegen Übergriffe der Staatsbeamten und sonstigen Machthaber schützen."

6

Constantine and the Imperial Bureaucracy

The Efficacy of Imperial Legislation

The edicts to the provincials in September 325 and November 331 are a testament to the value perceived in communication under the reign of Constantine. By means of universal edicts, Constantine could inform both administrators and subjects of the law, of his expectations of the imperial bureaucracy, of available legal remedies, and of the consequences of disobedience. His edicts communicate power, and the messages they disseminated sought to inspire loyalty and demonstrate and strengthen the authority of the emperor. The personal, populist strain of the edicts of Constantine conveys this message above all.

A recurring question asked of such documents is whether the principles enunciated therein in words were realized in fact. The famous assessment of A. H. M. Jones in the preface to *The Later Roman Empire* captures the uneasiness felt by many scholars who have pondered the efficacy of late antique legislation: "The laws, in my view, are clues to the difficulties of the empire, and records of the aspirations of the government and not its achievement."[1] Subsequent scholarship has indeed become ever more sensitive to the limitations of normative texts as historical evidence. Each constitution, taken alone, gives us no direct evidence of its enforcement. There is often no sign, positive or negative, by which to judge whether imperial constitutions were obeyed.[2] We have no evidence, for example, that any

1. Jones, *LRE,* viii.

2. See the discussion by S. Schmidt-Hofner, *Reagieren und Gestalten. Der Regierungsstil des spätrömischen Kaisers am Beispiel der Gesetzgebung Valentinians I.* (Munich, 2008), 21–35; still valuable: J. Gaudemet, "La législation du IVème siècle programme d'enquête," *AARC* 1 (1975), 143–59.

provincial ever approached Constantine to denounce a high official, as described in the edict CTh. 9.1.4, discussed in the preceding chapter. This uncertainty attaches most notoriously to the repetition of various ordinances, whether by later emperors or even by the emperor who first instituted them. The interpretation of such repetitions largely follows the optimism or pessimism of the interpreter. Where earlier scholars considered the repetition of the imperial legislation a sign of its ineffectiveness,[3] recent scholars see in it a confirmation of the vigor of the law and consistency of policy.[4]

Where proof fails, plausibility warrants a hearing. The edicts of the preceding chapter show clearly that *metus legum,* fear of the laws and the threat of punishment, ranked high among the means with which Constantine sought to intimidate his administrators into doing right.[5] The texts of this chapter are of a different nature. The reservation expressed by Jones—that the preserved laws are records of the aspirations of the government, not its achievement—is most appropriate to public edicts. Although edicts are constitutive of law, they remain statements. Most imperial constitutions preserved in the Codex Theodosianus are official letters, which were issued in response to the inquiries of imperial officials themselves.[6] If these consti-

---

3. E.g., De Marini Avonzo, "Giustizia II," 1062 with n. 107: " . . . la ripetizione delle stesse o di analoghe direttive è palese riprova della loro inefficacia"; C. Dupont, "Constantin et les constitutions impériales," in *St. Volterra,* vol. 1 (Milan, 1971), 554–55; J. Gaudemet, "Quelque aspects de la politique législative au Ve siècle," in *St. Volterra,* vol. 1 (Milan, 1971), 225–34 (= *Études,* vol. 1 [1979], 201–12); J. Gaudemet, "Recherches sur la législation du Bas-Empire," in *St. Scherillo,* vol. 2 (Milan, 1972), 693–715 (= *Études,* vol. 1 [1979], 213–37), concluding (693/215): "Mais il est évident que le rappel d'une mesure antérieure, son renouvellement par le législateur prouvent que celui-ci y tient et, sans doute, que la société l'observait peu ou mal"; K. L. Noethlichs, *Beamtentum und Dienstvergehen. Zur Staatsverwaltung in der Spätantike* (Wiesbaden, 1981), 109–10; A. Demandt, "Grenzen Spätrömischer Staatsgewalt," in *Usurpation in der Spätantike. Akten des Kolloquiums "Staatsreich und Staatlichkeit" 6.–10. März 1996 Solothurn/Bern,* ed. F. Paschoud and J. Szidat (Stuttgart, 1997), 155–63; most recently, D. Slootjes, *The Governor and His Subjects in the Later Roman Empire* (Leiden and Boston, 2006), 61 (with reference to Jones, *LRE,* 502).

4. Above all J. Harries, *Law and Empire in Late Antiquity* (Cambridge, 1999), 77–98; J. Karayannopulos, *Das Finanzwesen des frühbyzantinischen Staates* (Munich, 1958), 228–34; E. Lo Cascio, "The Emperor and His Administration: General Developments," *CAH* XII^2, 131–36; Schmidt-Hofner, *Reagieren und Gestalten,* 74–80, offers the most recent and nuanced discussion of late antique corruption, also discussing C. Kelly, *Ruling the Later Roman Empire* (Cambridge, 2004), 138–39, 144–45, and 158–65, concerning legal fees and the sale of office.

5. Constantine nowhere appears to regard punishment as a means of moral improvement; prevention through fear, retribution (*talio*), and vengeance predominates in his laws: Dupont, *Peines,* 81–83; on *talio* in late antique legislation: E. Levy, *West Roman Vulgar Law* (Philadelphia, 1951), 250–63.

6. According to A. J. B. Sirks, *The Theodosian Code. A Study* (Friedrichsdorf, 2007), 86, such letters constitute approximately 94 percent of all constitutions in the Codex Theodosianus; cf. chapter 2.

tutions responded directly to the inquiries of officials, it is inherently plausible that these same officials will have executed the commands of the emperor. A constitution that establishes or affirms punishment, for instance, might be an example of the infliction of that punishment.

A general observation is no replacement for individual analysis, but it seems unduly pessimistic to presume that the orders contained in imperial letters, however harsh, were never executed at least by the officials to whom they were addressed. On the contrary, it is probable that the officials concerned did precisely what the emperor prescribed; the text of an imperial letter and the authority of the emperor that it embodied were might override the complaints even of powerful provincials.[7] Given that a single report might occasion a circular letter to many administrators, the possibility that it might have even greater effect should not summarily be dismissed.[8]

The real culprits behind the reaffirmation of countless points of law and procedure were the ignorance and insecurity of imperial administrators themselves.[9] It should not surprise us if, over the years between one constitution and the next, doubts persisted and old rules must be reaffirmed. Time was the enemy of the imperial legislation, as seemingly new exceptions emerged and rules themselves insensibly slipped into desuetude. There was no systematic codification of law (in the modern sense) that permitted imperial officials to review the laws applicable in a given situation. The administration had to adapt as best it could, relying on the experience of its members, the diligence of advocates, and the supremacy of the imperial court itself as regulations were issued, repealed, supplanted, and amended. That is not to deny the menace of corruption and the deliberate subversion of regulations. These too are the subject of numerous restatements of administrative law.

This chapter offers a survey of imperial constitutions sent as official letters; these letters attest ordinary interventions by Constantine in cases of corruption and administrative irregularities. The majority of these constitutions are not programmatic in themselves but accord with the programmatic denunciation of corruption in the edicts of Constantine. Responses

---

7. See the discussion of *potentiores* in chapter 7, pp. 196–202.

8. M. Bianchini, "Orientamenti di politica normativa nelle due partes imperii all'indomani della codificazione teodosiana," *AARC* 4 (1981), 299–304, concludes that the chancelleries of both East and West issued general laws in response to specific problems. Most innovative enactments of Valentinian were inspired by individual cases: Schmidt-Hofner, *Reagieren und Gestalten,* 33–34.

9. J. E. Lendon, *Empire of Honour: The Art of Government in the Roman World* (Oxford, 1997), 8–9.

to individual cases do not attest corruption that was perceived to endanger the state; programmatic enactments, such as the edict of Constantine against irregular trial procedure and judicial fees, the authorization of public acclamations on the conduct of provincial governors (CTh. 1.16.6–7), or the dramatic modification of the office of the *defensor civitatis* under Valentinian I (CTh. 1.29.1), are more likely to indicate deficiencies in the administration that were perceived to require direct and immediate intervention.[10] The grievances that appear in the following constitutions should not be misconstrued as symptomatic of rampant corruption. Rather, they show that Constantine rigorously took measures to protect provincials from abuse at the hands of officials. Our inability to quantify the extent of corruption and the imperial response is compensated in part by analysis of the communication between Constantine and his officials and subjects. The imperial letters of this chapter complement the imperial edicts of the last. In the following analysis, the language of the constitutions and the concepts of government and policy that may be won from them shall be considered. Regulation of the administration was an occasion for communication. Official letters, too, were registered in the *acta* of the governor and published on site: publication at the local level made official letters also means of cultivating loyalty and exercising authority, of advertising beneficence and sternness, and of facilitating the functioning of government. The coercion of the imperial administration was a public event from which all parties—other than the guilty—might profit.

The Character of Imperial Officials

Before the conduct of officials is examined more closely, it is apposite to ask what qualities officials should exhibit. In his edict to the provincials of the empire, CTh. 9.1.4, Constantine construes administrative abuse as an act of deception against himself: he declares, *ipse me vindicabo de eo, qui me usque ad hoc tempus simulata integritate deceperit,* a statement that conveys several messages at once. As noted in chapter 4, Constantine implies that it is personal integrity and honesty that induce him to appoint someone to administrative office. If the choice proves mistaken, Constantine sees himself among the victims: the corrupt official has deceived him—at least "up to

10. Schmidt-Hofner, *Reagieren und Gestalten,* 79–80. Schmidt-Hofner cites the replacement of *curiosi* with *protectores* in the supervision of the *cursus publicus* (CTh. 8.5.30) as an example of such a programmatic initiative under Valentinian I.

that time." Constantine eschews personal responsibility for the conduct of his officials but embraces accountability by punishing them. Constantine overshadows the real, or immediate, victims whose sympathy he solicits; the victims of corrupt officials should draw comfort from the righteous anger of the emperor. The indignation of Constantine, however, is conspicuously self-centered. The failure of corrupt officials to fulfill his expectations displaces whatever crime they had committed against the provincials. Integrity becomes a species of loyalty and obedience to the emperor, who is the sole arbiter and source of justice.

The record of the legislation of Constantine fortuitously permits comparison of the construction of integrity in the edict CTh. 9.1.4 with another formulation in an imperial letter. The peculiarly Constantinian conception of the *fides* of imperial officials was not limited to public edicts published for consumption by the masses. Constantine speaks of the virtues demanded of officials in a letter to the praetorian prefect Pacatius in 334.[11] The letter specifically concerns tax officials, and the emperor begins with an apology, as if legislation on the *fiscus* itself were an unpleasant task and an impediment to his patronage of his subjects: "Even though We favor the cause of private citizens over the protection of the *fiscus*, We nonetheless order . . ."[12] The question posed is to whom preference should be given among several candidates for the position of *advocatus fisci*, the advocates who represented the interests of the *fiscus* in court. Constantine rules that the man *melior innocentia, potior litteris, pollentior reliquis examinata fide* should be appointed, even if he obtained his certificate of appointment after his competitors.[13] The meaning of the qualities *innocentia* and *litterae* is obvious: blamelessness or probity and a traditional education in literature and rhetoric.[14] *Fides* is more complex. In several late antique constitutions, especially those regulating fiscal matters, *fides* and its derivatives connote honesty in administrative tasks.[15] *Fides* also, however, expresses loyalty. The

11. CTh. 10.15.2.

12. CTh. 10.15.2: *Etsi potior aput nos privatorum causa est quam fisci tutela, praecipimus tamen . . .*

13. On the recruitment of financial offices, see R. Delmaire, *Largesses Sacrées et* res privata. *L'*aerarium *impérial et son administration du IVe au VIe siècle* (Rome, 1989), 133–38; on *probatoriae*, B. Palme, "Die *Officia* der Statthalter in der Spatantike," *AntTard* 7 (1999), 101 with n. 87, and Jones, *LRE*, 576.

14. See P. Brown, *Power and Persuasion in Late Antiquity: Towards a Christian Empire* (Madison, 1992), ch. 2, "*Paideia* and Power," esp. 41–47, on the governmental advantages credited to a rhetorical education.

15. E.g., CTh. 1.12.2 (whether documents prepared by the *officium* are *fidelis*); 1.16.3 (*quis iudicum . . . fidelem operam praestiterit*); 2.26.1 (the *fidelis inspectio* of a land surveyor); 6.35.5 (the *fidele obsequium* of *palatini*); 11.30.8 pr (of a *rationalis*). This usage remains common after Con-

examinata fides of advocates of the *fiscus* might encompass "proven integrity" or "loyalty." The expression captures the ambiguity of loyalty to an emperor whose words wear the mask of justice. Constantine demands a high standard of integrity among his officials; the official letters, however, represent this integrity as obedience or, as shall be seen, as adherence to the *mandata* of the emperor, which defined the responsibilities of administrators.[16]

Iniuste Gesta *and Their Consequences*

An administrative letter to the *vicarius Urbis*, CTh. 10.4.1, contemporary with the edict CTh. 9.1.4, demonstrates the risk taken by officials who disappointed the expectations or disobeyed the commands of Constantine. This letter, issued from the East in 326[17] in the aftermath of the defeat of Licinius, attests the brutality with which Constantine might punish corrupt officials and presents a terrifying example to any deliberating similar crimes:

CTh. 10.4.1

IMP. CONSTANTINVS A. AD PHILIPPVM VICARIVM VRBIS. Si quis ab actore rerum privatarum nostrarum sive a procuratore fuerit vexatus, super eius calumniis vel depraedationibus deferre querimoniam non dubitet. Quae res cum fuerit conprobata, sancimus, ut idem, qui contra provincialem quidquam moliri fuerit ausus, publice concremetur, quoniam gravior poena constituenda est in hos, qui nostri iuris sunt et nostra debent custodire mandata. DAT. III. NON. MART. HERACLEAE, CONSTANTINO A. III. ET LICINIO III. CONSS.

EMPEROR CONSTANTINE AUGUSTUS TO PHILIPPUS, VICAR OF THE CITY (OF ROME). If anyone is harassed by an agent or procurator of Our private property, he shall not hesitate to bring complaint about such false accusations or depredations. If the allegation is proven, We decree that that man, who dared plot anything against a provincial, be publicly burned alive, because a harsher

stantine. Derivatives of *fides* (such as *fidelis*) do not appear in the Digest in this sense (I have not checked all occurrences of *fides* itself), except in a fragment of Marcian, *De iudiciis publicis*, in which he describes a clause of the provincial edict of Antoninus Pius, then proconsul of Asia: Dig. 48.3.6.1, *si diligenter ac fideliter hoc fecerit* . . .

16. See below, pp. 166 and 171–72. Cf. Libanius, *Or.* 45.32–33, who tells the emperor he must consider magistrates who disregard the law as rebels; Slootjes, *Governor*, 58–59.

17. Seeck, *Regesten*, 51; *PLRE* I, Philippus 2 (p. 695); Barnes, *NE*, 77; Corcoran, *ET*^{2}, 292 n. 158.

penalty must be established for those who are under Our power and ought to observe Our instructions. GIVEN 5 MAR. (313 [326]) AT HERACLEA IN THE CONSULSHIP OF CONSTANTINE AUGUSTUS, CONSUL FOR THE THIRD TIME, AND OF LICINIUS, CONSUL FOR THE THIRD TIME.

The recipient of this letter, the *vicarius Urbis,* was the deputy of the praetorian prefect of Italy; the governors of southern Italy, Sicily, Sardinia, and Corsica answered to him.[18] The duties of the vicar were as diverse as those of the prefect to whom he answered, but it is unusual that the letter sent to him concerns corruption among the agents of a separate imperial department, the *res privata.* The administrators of the *res privata* were entrusted with the management and collection of rents on imperial properties. One would expect a constitution concerning such persons to have been addressed to a diocesan administrator, a *rationalis* or *magister rei privatae.* Of the agents mentioned, the *procuratores rei privatae* were subordinate to the *rationales,* assigned perhaps to specific tracts of royal property (*saltus*).[19] The *actores rei privatae* stood beneath the *procuratores,* as "officials on the spot" for small numbers of estates.[20] They were all free men, in contrast to other *actores.*[21] A version of Constantine's letter must also have been addressed to the *rationalis* (or *procurator*) of Italy, who stood over the (lesser) *procuratores* and *actores* threatened with retribution. Constitutions addressed to *rationales* in the Codex Theodosianus are much rarer than those to vicars, and it is conceivable that this bias might account for the preservation of the constitution sent to the *vicarius Urbis.*[22] Administrative practicality might also have justified bringing the constitution to the attention of the *vicarius Urbis* and potentially other administrators of large territories. A provincial would have lodged a complaint (*querimoniam deferre*) naturally before the provincial governor (designated *corrector* and later *consularis* in Italy) under whose jurisdiction he lived.

The object of the provincial's complaint—the wrong suffered—is not

---

18. Jones, *LRE,* 46–47 (Diocletian), 373–74 (generally) and 481 (appellate jurisdiction); in detail: J. Migl, *Die Ordnung der Ämter: Prätorianerpräfektur und Vikariat in der Regionalverwaltung des Römischen Reiches von Konstantin bis zur Valentinianischen Dynastie* (Frankfurt am Main, 1994); cf. *Not. Dig. Occ.* i and xix.

19. Jones, *LRE,* 413. Jones also discusses potential regional *procuratores;* the *procuratores* in CTh. 10.4.1 appear to be lesser magistrates, comparable to the *agentes.*

20. Jones, *LRE,* 414; Karayannopulos, *Finanzwesen,* 62–72, *actores* mentioned p. 67.

21. Delmaire, *Largesses Sacrées,* 679–80.

22. Compare the lists compiled by Mommsen, *Proleg.,* cxcv–cxcix (*vicarii*) and ccii–cciii (*rationales*).

expressed in CTh. 10.4.1 with juristic clarity. The letter specifically cites *calumniae* and *depraedationes* perpetrated by agents of the *res privata*. The *calumniae* with which the financial officials harass (*vexare*) provincials may be described more precisely as false accusations, which might result in the loss of rents paid by provincials or even in the loss of the property for which the provincials were liable.[23] A successful fiscal suit brought against a provincial, even against a provincial obligated to the *res privata* in no way at all, could result in the confiscation of his property, an abuse that Constantine combats elsewhere.[24] So, for example, in CTh. 10.15.1 (a. 313),[25] Constantine writes to the proconsul of Africa that an advocate of the *fiscus* faces punishment if "he should dare to make false accusations in the name of the *fiscus* against private citizens without any legal basis."[26] Similar extortions are likely intended with *depraedationes*.[27] One might compare the numerous deprecations of abuses perpetrated by the *Caesariani*, petty officials who served on the staff of the *rationales*.[28] The *Opiniones* of Ps.-Ulpian suggest further abuses, including forced sales and declarations of debt made under duress, among other crimes.[29]

---

23. Cf. PS. 1.5.1: *Calumniosus est qui sciens prudensque per fraudem negotium alicui comparat.*

24. Cf. CTh. 10.1.1: *Si quid a fisco fuerit occupandum vel a nobis de cetero pro unius cuiusque meritis obsequiisque donandum vel ab eodem distrahendum, intra annum, omnibus vel a petitione vel a conparatione se abstinentibus ii, qui putant iniuste res proprias a fisco esse comparatas, contra eundem agere contendant . . .*

25. Mommsen, *ad loc.;* Seeck, *Regesten*, 78–79 and 161; Barnes, *NE*, 71; Corcoran, ET^2, 304.

26. CTh. 10.15.1: . . . *nullo negotio existente fisci nomine privatis audeat calumnias commovere.* PS. 5.12.7 forbids the *fiscus* to bring suit *in perniciem privatorum* and judges to hear such cases. Compare Constantine's cynicism in CTh. 10.1.3: *Iustas etiam et quae locum habent fisci actiones praecipimus concremari ob hoc solum, quod suis temporibus prolatae non sunt. Iam calumniae privatorum eo saltem arceantur exemplo, quo iustas fisci lites silere praecipimus.* Constantine hopes that his subjects will refrain from "calumnious" actions, seeing that he has ordained the burning of the documents containing legitimate claims of the *fiscus* not made at the appropriate time.

27. Justinian, combining part of a constitution of Honorius (CTh. 10.26.1) and the final words of this constitution (*gravior poena . . . mandata*) elaborates on the ways in which *conductores hominesve augustissimae domus* might interfere with the course of justice in a trial concerning imperial property, CJ 11.72.1: *nec aliorum litigatorum negotio intercedant nec sententiam iudicantium aut illicito patrocinii sui fomite iura conturbent, nullive executionis suae turbulentum ministerium audeant commodare: non privatis se negotiis, non publicis misceant: nec quiescentem domum delatio ulla sollicitet, ne eos inconsultae pertinaciae sero paeniteat.* To draw a comparison from the administration of the *fiscus*, PS. 5.12.5 preserves a rule according to which no man may administer a fiscal office in the province of his birth *ne aut gratiosus aut calumniosus apud suos esse videatur*, that is, lest he use his office either to help old friends or to settle old scores. These abuses are useful illustrations of the sort of corruption Constantine deprecates.

28. Cf. CTh. 10.1.5, in which Constantine cites their *consuetudo fraudium, quibus praedicti omnia temerare consuerint;* see further chapter 3, pp. 76–78.

29. Dig. 1.18.6 pr (Ps.-Ulpian): *Illicitas exactiones et violentia factas, et extortas metu venditiones et cautiones vel sine pretii numeratione prohibeat praeses provinciae. Item ne quis iniquum lucrum*

While the crimes described in CTh. 10.4.1 are conventional, the punishment ordained for them and the reasoning behind it are of extraordinary interest. The official whose *calumniae* and *depraedationes* have injured the provincials faces the full wrath of the emperor in the form of public immolation, "because a harsher punishment should be established for those who are under Our control and ought to observe Our instructions."[30] The word "harsher" is an understatement; there was no punishment harsher than *crematio.* Constantine decreed immolation for a number of offenses, all of which numbered among the most offensive to public or certainly imperial sensibilities.[31] Death by fire would be imposed by the successors of Constantine for many more crimes,[32] and still further examples are found in the Sentences of Paul.[33] It might be said in general that execution by fire was reserved for the servile and those who earned the special displeasure of the emperor.[34]

The petty financial official is a surprising addition to this rogue's gallery. The immolation of a public official for such a crime is unprecedented. Even after Constantine, in 349, Constantius decreed that provincial governors should henceforth inflict on agents of the *res privata* the same penalties as those inflicted on provincials, but he names only imprisonment, torture, and beheading.[35] The closest parallel is the public immolation of the *praepositus sacri cubiculi* of Valentinian, Rhodanus, recorded by John Malalas, who names Rhodanus as only one of many officials executed by Valentin-

---

aut damnum sentiat, praeses provinciae provideat. The expression, *ne quis iniquum lucrum . . . sentiat* ("The governor should ensure that no one suffers . . . unfair profit") appears to be a sign of inept abridgment.

30. According to the PS. 5.12.6, agents of the *fiscus,* who *occupant, describunt vel sub observatione esse faciunt* (*facere* with an infinitive is a good indicator of late origin) someone's property before a judgment had been rendered, are to be delivered to the praetorian prefects for punishment.

31. See D. Liebs, "Unverhohlene Brutalität in den Gesetzen der ersten christlichen Kaiser," in *Römisches Recht in der europäischen Tradition. Symposion aus Anlass des 75. Geburtstags von Franz Wieacker* (Ebelsbach, 1985), 89–116 (*passim*); Dupont, *Peines,* 18; O. F. Robinson, "Roman Criminal Law: Rhetoric and Reality. Some Forms of Rhetoric in the Theodosian Code," in M. Zabłocka et al., eds., *Au-delà des frontières. Mélanges de droit romain offerts à Witwold Wołodkiewicz,* vol. 2 (Warsaw, 2000), 771–72.

32. In addition to Liebs, "Unverhohlene Brutalität," see Gothofredus, *paratitlon ad* CTh. 10.4 and *ad* CTh. 10.4.1; R. MacMullen, "Judicial Savagery in the Roman Empire," in *Changes in the Roman Empire. Essays in the Ordinary* (Princeton, 1990), 213; Harries, *Law and Empire,* 135–52.

33. MacMullen, "Judicial Savagery," 209–10 with n. 26.

34. T. Mayer-Maly, s.v. "vivicomburium," *RE* 9A.1 (1961), 497–98.

35. CTh. 2.1.1 (a. 349): *Iudices provinciarum volumus vim debitae auctoritatis adsumere, ut una actores ceterosque rei privatae nostrae, quae provinciales teneat disciplina. Sceleratos convictosque carcer teneat, tormenta dilacerent, gladius ultor interimat.*

ian.[36] The severity of Valentinian in punishing officials is celebrated by Ammianus, who gives a handful of examples.[37] Rhodanus may have been executed by fire because, as *praepositus sacri cubiculi,* he was also a eunuch.[38] His punishment would thus have been appropriate to his base and servile status. If only the incident had inspired a constitution that could have been preserved in the Codex Theodosianus! The gravity of the penalty imposed on the agents of the *res privata* by Constantine suggests a specific, similarly outrageous case. Perhaps Constantine was stirred to wrath by the doings of a particular official, whom he ordered to be burned alive. His orders in CTh. 10.4.1 nevertheless appear general in nature. The preserved text of CTh. 10.4.1 would, then, have been a general statement looking forward to future cases.

The inclination to restrict the application of CTh. 10.4.1 with reference to the limited jurisdiction of its recipient, the *vicarius Urbis,* should perhaps be resisted. Although the power of other diocesan officials and the prefects eclipsed that of the vicar, the extent of the territory administered by him was great, embracing much of Italy and the surrounding islands. CTh. 10.4.1 could also have been applied even beyond these bounds. The fact that a version of the text was issued to an official outside the immediate orbit of the *res privata* suggests broad circulation. Given the extraordinary punishment, a particular case may have inspired the response of Constantine, but nothing obvious detracts from the likelihood that the constitution was disseminated throughout Italy and perhaps even the empire at the diocesan level.

The exceptional violence visited upon delinquent agents of the *res privata* may be traced to the intensification of the relationship between emperor and imperial official, which the paternalism of Constantine raised to new heights. Even in the early third century, the jurist Ulpian wrote that the acts of fiscal procurators were regarded as acts of the emperor himself.[39] The edict of Constantine CTh. 9.1.4 perpetuates this notion: the misdeeds of imperial officials are not merely an embarrassment to the regime of Constantine but an outrage against the person of the emperor and imperil the prosperity of the empire. By describing the officials who managed the *res*

36. John Mal. 13.31; Schmidt-Hofner, *Reagieren und Gestalten,* 37–38.
37. Amm. Marc. 31.14.2, 29.3; cf. 28.1.21–57; Schmidt-Hofner,*Reagieren und Gestalten,* 37–39.
38. He is also described as ἀρχιευνοῦχος; *PLRE* I, Rhodanus.
39. Dig. 1.19.1 (Ulpian): *Quae acta gestaque sunt a procuratore Caesaris, sic ab eo comprobantur, atque si a Caesare gesta sunt.*

privata as *nostri iuris*, Constantine assumes personal responsibility for their conduct and with it the duty to punish them for their wrongs, just as an ancient paterfamilias might punish children in his *potestas*.[40] In the case of the financial official, what constituted a wrong was laid out in the imperial *mandata* delivered to him upon his appointment. The *mandata* issued in Constantine's name were no mere suggestions of conduct, but sacred and binding, and their breach demanded vengeance.[41] If Constantine embodies justice, the fiscal procurator who acts contrary challenges the authority of the emperor himself. Punishment avenges not only the suffering of the provincials but also the insult to the emperor.

In the event of conviction, a provincial governor was bound, under the threat of deportation at the least, to follow CTh. 10.4.1 as an administrative ordinance.[42] The punishment stipulated—immolation—might strike the modern interpreter as grotesque and inconsistent with the precepts of Christianity.[43] It is rather beside the point to project the expectations of a later age onto fourth-century Christianity and a man whose religious fervor and deficient theology are both well documented. Drastic action was, moreover, fully within the realm of action of a Roman emperor who considered himself both the servant of God and protector of his subjects.[44] Public execution by fire was a brilliant stroke of imperial and populist vindication. The provincials might watch with satisfaction the fiery spectacle provided by their predator and think on the righteous emperor who thus punished those who betrayed his trust and violated his subjects.[45] The im-

40. E.g., L. Junius Brutus (Livy, 2.4–5), Sp. Cassius (Livy, 2.41.10), T. Manlius Torquatus Imperiosus (Livy, 8.7).

41. Cf. CTh. 8.4.2 (a. 315): *coram mandatum est, ut, si extra modum aliquid extorserint, sciant se capite puniendos* (see below).

42. PS. 5.25.4: *Iudex, qui contra sacras principum constitutiones contrave ius publicum, quod apud se recitatum est, pronuntiat, in insulam deportatur.*

43. Liebs, "Unverhohlene Brutalität," 92: "Wie schlimm die Strafpraxis gerade bei der Christenverfolgung aber auch immer gewesen sein mag, so wenig wütete noch unter Diokletian die Gesetzgebung selber. Ihren im 1. und 2. Jh. entwickelten gemessenen Ton behielt sie zumindest bis Diokletian bei. Das wurde anders, als Konstantin bald nach der Schlacht an der milvischen Brücke die Bühne des Gesetzgebers betrat. In seinen Gesetzen begegnen uns erstmals Orgien der Brutalität, die das ganze Mittelalter hindurch Schule machen sollten." See also MacMullen, "Judicial Savagery"; MacMullen, "What Difference Did Christianity Make?" *Historia* 35 (1986), 322–43; D. Grodzynski, "Tortures mortelles et catégories sociales. Les *Summa Supplicia* dans le droit romain aus IIIe et IVe siècles," in *Du châtiment dans la cité: Supplices corporels et peine de mort dans le monde antique . . .* (Rome, 1984), 361–403; E. Patlagean, "Byzance et le blason pénal du corps," in *Du châtiment*, 405–26.

44. Liebs, "Unverhohlene Brutalität," 116, citing N. Baynes: "Constantine's religious policy issues from his unwavering and passionate conviction that he was 'the man of God.'"

45. On the eagerness of the crowd for blood, see MacMullen, "Judicial Savagery," 206–7.

molation of the guilty official transforms the failure of the administration into a public celebration of the emperor.[46]

Controlling the Agents of Tax Collection

As the execution of the fiscal procurator shows, the collection of taxes, which brought the citizens of the empire into regular and frequent contact with the agents of the administration, furnished ample material for both crime and punishment.[47] Ps.-Ulpian cites it as the governor's duty to prevent illegal exactions and other "unfair losses."[48] Evidence of such irregularities under Constantine commences with the record of his enactments. Early in his reign, Constantine addressed a letter, now preserved in several excerpts strewn throughout the Codex Theodosianus, to the proconsul of Africa concerning judicial procedure and fiscal affairs.[49] Its contents appear to be general regulations. The fragment that interests us here, CTh. 11.7.1, regulates the collection of debts to the *fiscus:* equestrian tax officials must not exact sums from debtors until they receive briefs (*breves*) from the *tabularius* of the debtors' cities, nor should any extortion occur in the course of tax collection.[50] If anyone could prove that he had been forced to pay money he did not owe, or had been otherwise harassed by the financial officials, a "harsh sentence" (*severa sententia*) would be rendered against those responsible.[51] A second letter on the same abuse followed just a week later: anyone who believed he had been injured (financially) by *ducenarii* or *centenarii,* and particularly by advocates of the *fiscus,* should not hesitate to seek redress at the court of the governor; the official, if found guilty, would be punished with "appropriate severity."[52]

---

46. Cf. C. Kelly, "Emperors, Government and Bureaucracy," *CAH* XIII, 162: "memorably horrific penalties."

47. Vividly described by Brown, *Power and Persuasion,* 25–29; cf. the constitutions listed by Noethlichs, *Beamtentum und Dienstvergehen,* 117–18. Noethlichs argues that the provinces were too large to control the tax officials even after the reign Diocletian (cf. pp. 158–59).

48. See n. 29 above.

49. Cf. Corcoran, *ET*², 304.

50. CTh. 11.7.1: *Ducenarii et centenarii sive sexagenarii non prius debent aliquem ex debitoribus convenire, quam a tabulario civitatis nominatim breves accipiant debitorum. Quam quidem exactionem sine omni fieri concussione oportet.* See Karayannopulos, *Finanzwesen,* 90; Jones, *LRE,* 584–85; C. Dupont, *La Réglementation Economique dans les Constitutions de Constantin* (Lille, 1963), 87–90.

51. CTh. 11.7.1: *Si quis in iudicio questus, quod indebite exactus est vel aliquam inquietudinem sustinuit, hoc ipsum probare potuerit, severa in exactores sententia proferatur.*

52. CTh. 8.10.1: *Si quis se a ducenariis vel centenariis ac praecipue fisci advocatis laesum esse cognoscit, adire iudicia ac probare iniuriam non moretur, ut in eum qui convictus fuerit competenti*

We have seen another fragment of the former constitution, preserved as CTh. 10.15.1, in which Constantine threatens the *advocatus fisci* for embezzlement and false accusations of provincials.[53] Constantine there describes the *advocatus fisci* as *poenam metuens.* But what constituted "punishment," a "harsh sentence," or "appropriate severity" for these privileged men, of equestrian rank or otherwise entitled to the rights of *honestiores*? The punishment of such men was often handled with delicacy, at least in prose. The manner of execution for minor officials and egregious offenders might be proclaimed with brutal exactitude; one needed only to suggest conventional punishments for men of rank. The extortion of money by tax officials, once subject to the *repetundae* process of the high empire, was prohibited and punished in Late Antiquity chiefly under the name *concussio.* The official guilty of *concussio,* as an *honestior,* could generally expect deportation, that is, banishment to an island or other deserted place, the loss of his citizen rights, and the confiscation of his property.[54] Deportation was the harshest penalty regularly inflicted on *honestiores,* whose status protected them from corporal punishment, condemnation to the mines, and the death penalty in most circumstances. This form of banishment was nonetheless capital, for it extinguished the *caput* of the guilty party in depriving him of citizenship.[55] It was a "harsh sentence" for a man accustomed to the advantages of wealth and distinction; the emperor's call for "appropriate severity" is more susceptible of interpretation. The *cognitio extraordinaria,* the process under which crimes were prosecuted in Late Antiquity, left the judge wide discretion in fixing punishment, whether he chose to aggravate a penalty or mitigate its severity.[56] The judge of a *concussio* case might, if the crime were less serious in nature, move for relegation, usually a temporary banishment with partial confiscation of the property of the guilty party. The judge could determine both the bounds and the duration of relegation, as well as the proportion of property liable to confiscation; he determined whether relegation was to entail confinement to a place or a

---

severitate vindicetur; cf. Dig. 1.18.6 pr (Ulpian): *Illicitas exactiones et violentia factas, et extortas metu venditiones et cautiones vel sine pretii numeratione prohibeat praeses provinciae. Item ne quis iniquum lucrum aut damnum sentiat, praeses provinciae provideat;* Dig. 1.18.6.3 (Ulpian): *sub specie tributorum illicitas exactiones fieri prohibeat.*

53. CTh. 10.15.1; see above.

54. Mommsen, *Str.R.*, 716–17 and 730–31.

55. O. Robinson, *Penal Practice and Penal Policy in Ancient Rome* (London, 2007), 189.

56. Mommsen, *StrR.*, 1037–41.

ban from the province harmed by the guilty party, as consideration of "appropriate severity" demanded.[57]

The exaction of unauthorized taxes, the second crime mentioned in CTh. 11.7.1, could be prosecuted under the *lex Iulia de vi publica et privata.*[58] The Sentences of Paul give us information on the penalties thereby incurred: the regular punishment for *vis privata* was relegation and the confiscation of one-third of one's property.[59] Conviction of *vis* in the exaction of taxes compelled the offender to restore fourfold the amount seized, as was the punishment for manifest theft.[60] Serious cases could be tried *extra ordinem* and punished more severely, probably by deportation or relegation for men of standing.[61] Conviction for other illicit exactions, without the use of force, obliged the offenders to simple restitution when challenged, but to restitution *in duplum,* twice the amount exacted, if the charge were denied but proven at trial.[62] The admonitions of CTh. 11.7.1 and 8.10.1 seem to envision harsher punishment and read rather as directives to the judge to punish *extra ordinem* by deportation or relegation, if not death.

In later constitutions, Constantine orders officials to inflict severe punishment without regard for the gravity of the crime. Constantine writes to the governor of Aemilia in 321 that anyone who exacts more from the provincials than what is prescribed is to suffer capital punishment.[63] In another constitution, Constantine directs the praetorian prefect of Africa to punish offending contractors (*conductores*) for fleecing provincials. These men were essentially publicans who held leases on imperial land for the collection of tolls (*vectigalia*):[64]

---

57. Robinson, *Penal Practice,* 189. For a list of constitutions in which the emperor leaves the nature of punishment to the discretion of the judge, see J. Gaudemet, "Aspects politiques de la codification théodosienne," in *Istituzioni giuridiche e realtà politiche nel tardo impero (III–V sec. d.C.). Atti di un incontro tra storici e giuristi Firenze, 2–4 maggio 1974,* ed. G. G. Archi (Milan, 1976), 261–279 (= *Études,* vol. 1 [1979], 349–69), 277 n. 58.

58. Mommsen, *StrR.,* 663–64 Dig. 48.6.12 (Paulus): *Qui nova vectigalia exercent, lege Iulia de vi publica tenentur.*

59. PS. 5.26.3.

60. PS. 2.31.13: taking *quadruplum* as equal to the sum *cum poena tripli* in the next note.

61. Dig. 39.4.9.5 (*Pauli Sententiae*): *Quod illicite publice privatimque exactum est, cum altero tanto passis iniuriam exsolvitur. Per vim vero extortum cum poena tripli restituitur: amplius extra ordinem plectuntur: alterum enim utilitas privatorum, alterum vigor publicae disciplinae postulat.*

62. Mommsen, *StrR.,* 664 with n. 1.

63. CTh. 4.13.1: . . . *capitali sententia subiugando, quem plus aliquid, quam statutum est, a provincialibus exegisse constiterit;* Delmaire, *Largesses Sacrées,* 290–91.

64. Delmaire, ibid. and 680; Gothofredus, *ad* CTh. 4.12.1; cf. C. Dupont, "Constantin et la préfecture d'Afrique," in *St. Grosso,* vol. 2 (Turin, 1968), 526 and 529.

CJ 4.62.4 (a. 336)

> IMP. CONSTANTINVS A. AD FELICEM PP. Si provincialium nostrorum querella de conductorum avididate extiterit et probatum fuerit ultra vetustam consuetudinem et nostrae terminos iussionis aliquid eos profligasse, rei tanti criminis perpetuo exilio puniantur. Sub conspectibus autem tuis vel eorum, qui tuae gravitati succedunt, licitationis cura servetur. PP. VII ID. MART. CARTHAGINE.

> EMPEROR CONSTANTINE AUGUSTUS TO FELIX, PRAETORIAN PREFECT: If a complaint of Our provincials about the greed of the tax collectors should arise and it be proven that something beyond ancient custom and the limits established by Our decree has laid them low, the men accused of so severe a crime shall be punished with permanent exile. Let oversight of the auctioning be kept in Your presence or in that of those who succeed to Your Gravity. POSTED 9 MARCH (336)[65] AT CARTHAGE.

It is interesting that Constantine speaks of the provincials as a group; their *querella* might have been incriminating public outcry, to which it was the duty of the prefect to respond. Certainty on this point is impossible. "Permanent exile," a circumlocution for deportation, would constitute a retreat from the severity of the constitution issued in 321 (CTh. 4.13.1), which calls for the death penalty for any excessive exaction.[66] The authenticity of the punishment is not unimpeachable; since CJ 4.62.4 is preserved only in the Codex Justinianus, the text is open to the suspicion of editorial intervention.[67] Against this suspicion, however, it must be observed that the expression *exilium perpetuum* was not a phrase cultivated by the Justinian chancellery. It would be hazardous to guess why Constantine reduced the penalty; simple inconsistency is perhaps the most plausible. A much later constitution of Arcadius attests that Valentinian also imposed the death penalty on tax collectors, which Arcadius confirms; no reference there is made to the punishments established by Constantine.[68] Regardless, deportation was a very harsh punishment for the superexaction of taxes, but the coincidence of justice and the imperial will again justifies its severity. The complaint of the provincials alerts Constantine to the misdeeds of the tax

65. Seeck, *Regesten,* 125–26.

66. Dupont, *Peines,* 52–53.

67. Karayannopulos, *Finanzwesen,* 156, attributes the punishment to Justinian, comparing it with CTh. 4.13.1.

68. CTh. 11.8.1 (a. 397).

collectors, but their crime is conceived foremost as violation of "the limits established by Our decree."

Protection of Regular Tax Collection

The collection of transport duties and tolls regularly conflicted with the interests of the imperial *fiscus*. Tolls were an important source of income, but Constantine perceive the necessity of ensuring that the collection of tolls did not impede the payment of regular taxes. The violence of the measures with which Constantine protected taxpaying landholders amply demonstrates the interest of the emperor. In May 315, Constantine issued an edict to the Africans that touched upon the *stationarii primipilarium*.[69] The *stationarii primipilarium* were apparently soldiers stationed along the *cursus publicus* and answered to the *primipilares;* the latter were men who had held the office of *princeps* on the staff of the governor and had subsequently been promoted to oversee the transport of the *pastus primipili,* that is, military provisions, from the province to the army.[70] Their *stationarii* will presumably have supervised the requisition of transport along the route.[71] The *stationarii primipilarium* further appear to be distinct from *stationarii* seconded from the *officium* of the governor to patrol cities and supervise the collection of tolls on merchandise brought in and out of them.[72]

Constantine declares to the Africans in CTh. 8.4.2, "The *stationarii primipilarium* . . . have been openly told in their *mandata* that they know they will be executed if they extort anything beyond the regular amount."[73] Just as the corrupt fiscal procurator faced immolation if he violated the *mandata* of the emperor, Constantine holds up the imperial *mandata* of the

---

69. CTh. 8.4.2.

70. Jones, *LRE,* 459; cf. 594–95.

71. Gothofredus, *ad* CTh. 8.4.2, equates the *stationarii* with the *curiosi* or *agentes in rebus,* referring to CTh. 6.29.1 (a. 355); the later constitution mentions *curiosi* and *stationarii* together but not as synonyms. As the officials responsible for the *cursus publicus,* the *curiosi* will have collaborated with *stationarii,* but the latter seem to be no more than soldiers attached to individual post *stationes.* In general on the *curiosi:* L. Di Paola, *Per la storia degli "occhi del re." I servizi ispettivi nella tarda antichità* (Messina, 2005).

72. C. Brélaz, *La sécurité publique en Asie Mineure sous le Principat (Ier-IIIème s. ap. J.-C.). Institutions municipales et institutions impériales dans l'Orient romain* (Basel, 2005), 254–63; Delmaire, *Largesses Sacrées,* 287–89; Jones, *LRE,* 521 and 600; Karayannopulos, *Finanzwesen,* 154–55; F. Millar, "Italy and the Roman Empire: Augustus to Constantine," *Phoenix* 40 (1986), 312–13, on *stationarii* in Italy.

73. CTh. 8.4.2: *Stationariis primipilarium . . . coram mandatum est, ut, si extra modum aliquid extorserint, sciant se capite puniendos.*

stationarii (*coram mandatum est*) in affirming the punishment that awaited them. Since the constitution proceeds to describe several other rules of conduct, it appears to have been inspired by an extensive denunciation of abuses. By responding per edict, Constantine publicizes the rights of provincials and the restrictions imposed on the *stationarii*. The victims have recourse to the decree of the emperor to obtain their rights from the *stationarii*, who must likewise acknowledge the words of the emperor.

The penalty of execution conforms to the harsh penalties inflicted on tax collectors seen above. Death instead of deportation might reflect the relatively low status of *stationarii*, but Constantine appears to fix the punishment above all in the name of discipline. Reference to the *mandata* of the *stationarii* underscores the theme of retribution that runs throughout the Constantinian legislation. Constantine avows his own innocence: he has stipulated the legitimate amount that the *stationarii* may requisition in their formal instructions; if they exceed it, the fault is theirs. It is the duty of Constantine to exact the punishment also stipulated in the *mandata*. Disobedience demands punishment, which Constantine pledges to administer with military severity.

A slightly different case concerning urban *stationarii* in Africa elicited two successive constitutions six years later, in the summer of 321, while Constantine resided at Sirmium.[74] The office held by the addressee of the two letters, Menander, is unknown; it may have been that of praetorian prefect or *comes Africae*.[75] Constantine writes that *stationarii* may not exact tolls from provincials who are transporting goods for their own use or for the *fiscus*.[76] Little over two weeks later, Constantine writes again to Menander and adds a penalty to the previous ban. *Stationarii* and other soldiers who exact tolls from country-dwelling provincials transporting goods "necessary to their own purposes or for agriculture" will suffer capital punishment.[77] It appears that the lack of a penalty clause in the first constitution caused the issue of the second. Why this deficiency was not noticed when

74. CTh. 4.13.2–3; Barnes, *NE*, 75.

75. Barnes, *NE*, 129. Dupont, *Réglementation*, 116, favors identification as praetorian prefect.

76. CTh. 4.13.2. Cf. Delmaire, *Largesses Sacrées*, 305.

77. CTh. 4.13.3: *Rusticanos usibus propriis vel culturae ruris [neces]saria revehentes vectigal exigi non sinimus: capitali poe(na pro)posita stationariis et urbanis militibus et Tertiis Augustan[is,] quorum avaritia id temptari firmatur*; cf. CTh. 8.5.1, in which Constantine orders the *stationarii* and overseers of the *cursus publicus* to deliver persons who seize farm animals to the governor for punishment or, in the case of *honestiores*, for report of their name to the emperor; cf. also CJ 1.40.4, in which Constantine orders a governor to report *officiales* of the praetorian prefect who abuse the *cursus publicus*.

the first constitution was issued, or how it was brought to the attention of the emperor and by whom, is difficult to divine.[78] The prohibitions imposed by Constantine on the *stationarii* are consistent with a passage of Ps.-Ulpian forbidding illegal services on the pretext of aiding soldiers.[79] Whereas Ps.-Ulpian merely states "the governor shall ensure" that such crimes not occur, Constantine provides imperial authority to execute offenders.

An edict addressed to all provincials issued in March 314 (CTh. 2.30.1) gives these constitutions an arresting context. Constantine deprecates the practice of governor-appointed *intercessores* who seize field-slaves and oxen as pledges for the satisfaction of debts to the *fiscus,* because the farmers affected are subsequently unable to meet their regular taxes. To protect the interest of the state, Constantine orders his governors to punish with death any *intercessor, creditor, praefectus pacis* (= εἰρήναρχος?),[80] or decurion caught offending against his edict.[81]

The execution of *honestiores,* such as the decurion and the *praefectus pacis,* whose office was numbered among the *munera* performed by decurions, is a surprising stipulation that attests to the priority of ensuring the collection of regular taxes despite outstanding debts to the *fiscus.*[82] *Interces-*

78. The distance between Sirmium and Carthage makes it impossible to suppose that the second text was issued on the recommendation of Menander himself.

79. Dig. 1.18.6.3 (Ps.-Ulpian): *Illicita ministeria sub praetextu adiuvantium militares viros ad concutiendos homines procedentia prohibere et deprehensa coercere praeses provinciae curet;* cf. 1.18.6.5–6: *Ne tenuis vitae homines sub praetextu adventus officiorum vel militum, lumine unico vel brevi suppellectili ad aliorum usus translatis, iniuriis vexentur, praeses provinciae providebit. Ne quid sub nomine militum, quod ad utilitates eorum in commune non pertinet, a quibusdam propria sibi commoda inique vindicantibus committatur, praeses provinciae provideat.*

80. The choice between *pacis* and *pagi* in the constitutions is difficult, as both officials might be involved in the collection of debts to the *fiscus,* but the reading *pacis* in the Codex Theodosianus is the *lectio difficilior.* Mommsen, *ad* CTh. 2.30.1, reads *pacis,* citing the periphrasis *cura pacis* in the *interpretatio* of the Breviarium in preference to the reading *praefectus pagi vel vici* in CJ 8.16.7.1; the latter was presumably altered by Justinian. The *interpretatio ad* CTh. 2.1.8 mentions *mediocres iudices, qui publicam disciplinam observant, id est aut defensores aut adsertores pacis,* a locution similar to *cura pacis;* CTh. 12.1.49.2 mentions *praepositi pacis* along with *susceptores diversarum specierum* (Jones, *LRE,* 726 n. 29, reads *pagis*). The *praepositus pagi* is a known official, responsible for levies and law enforcement in villages or town districts; εἰρήναρχοι were generally "wardens of the peace" in the East: Jones, *LRE,* 725–26, and in detail C. Brélaz, *La sécurité publique,* 90–122.

81. CTh. 2.30.1: *Si quis igitur intercessor aut creditor vel praefectus pacis vel decurio in hac re fuerit detectus, a rectoribus provinciarum capitali sententiae subiugetur;* Karayannopulos, *Finanzwesen,* 185; cf. Dupont, *Réglementation,* 27–29.

82. Cf. Dig. 48.19.15 (Venulius Saturninus): *Divus Hadrianus eos, qui in numero decurionum essent, capite puniri prohibuit, nisi si qui parentem occidissent: verum poena legis Corneliae puniendos mandatis plenissime cautum est;* 48.19.27.1 (Callistratus): *De decurionibus et principalibus civitatum, qui cap-*

sores a iudice dati appear also to have been *honestiores.* The nature of their duties is not entirely clear. In the version of CTh. 2.30.1 preserved in the Codex Justinianus (as CJ 8.16.7) we read *exsecutores,* that is, members of the governor's *officium* charged with the execution of judgments and the collection of debts to the *fiscus.*[83] This interpretation of *intercessor* would accord with the appearance of the word among other civic officials. The context of *pignus* and *creditor,* however, might suggest *intercessio* in private law, whereby a third party "intercedes" in a contractual relationship on behalf of another.[84] In this case, an *intercessor* might demand a pledge (*pignus*) from a debtor as security for assuming his debts, perhaps even debts to a creditor of the *fiscus.*[85] One might then interpret the *intercessores a iudice dati* as men presumably of the curial rank who had been appointed by the governor as liable for the payment of the debts of others to the *fiscus.*

Imposition of Munera

Similar concern for the collection of taxes seems to have led Constantine to devise severe punishment for vicars and governors who when assigning *munera,* by exempting the wealthy, burdened the poor. Provincial governors, Constantine writes to the praetorian prefect, may not permit the principales of the cities, that is, leading decurions, to distribute and assign extraordinary munera.[86]

CTh. 11.16.4 (a. 328)

[IMP. CONSTANTINVS] A. AD AEMILIANVM PPO. Extraordinariorum munerum distributio non est principalibus committenda, ideoque rectores

---

itale admiserunt, mandatis cavetur, ut, si quis id admisisse videatur, propter quod relegandus extra provinciam in insulam sit, imperatori scribatur adiecta sententia a praeside.

83. Berger, s.v. *executores,* identifies *intercessores* as synonymous with these tax collectors; discussion in Karayannopulos, *Finanzwesen,* 173–74; Gothofredus, *ad* CTh. 2.30.1, also concludes that *intercessores* were *exsecutores.*

84. Brief definition in Berger, s.v. *intercessio.*

85. Dig. 48.13.11.2 (Paulus): *Eodem capite inferius scribit* (sc. *Labeo*) *non solum pecuniam publicam, sed etiam privatam crimen peculatus facere, si quis quod fisco debetur simulans se fisci creditorem accepit, quamvis privatam pecuniam abstulerit.* A creditor of the *fiscus* would appear to be an individual who had paid the sum owed by a third party to the *fiscus,* thereby receiving the right to recover that sum from the taxpayer directly.

86. CTh. 11.16.4 (a. 328). Constantine uses the expression *rectores provinciarum monendi sunt* to indicate that the prefect should convey the contents of the letter to the governors under his jurisdiction. Constantine also speaks of *vicariorum tuorum.* On the definition and functions of the *principales:* Jones, *LRE,* 731 and 756–57.

provinciarum monendi sunt, ut eam distributionem ipsi celebrent manuque propria perscribant adque encauto nomina adnectant, ea forma servata, ut primo a potioribus, dein a mediocribus adque infimis quae sunt danda praestentur. Neque umquam sationibus vel colligendis frugibus insistens agricola ad extraordinaria onera trahatur, cum providentiae sit opportuno tempore his necessitatibus satisfacere. Quae res negelecta vicariorum tuorum verecundiam tangit, ad rectorum autem [et][87] officiorum capita venietur. Manu autem sua rectores scribere debebunt, quid opus sit et in qua necessitate per singula capita vel quantae angariae vel quantae operae vel quae aut in quanto modo praebendae sint, ut recognovisse se scribant, exactionis praedicto ordine inter ditiores mediocres atque infimos observando. LECTA VII ID. MAI. ROMAE IANVARIO ET IVSTO CONSS.

[EMPEROR CONSTANTINE] AUGUSTUS TO AEMILIANUS, PRAETORIAN PREFECT. The assignment of extraordinary liturgies is not to be entrusted to the leading decurions; therefore the provincial governors are to be advised that they must perform the assignment themselves and in their own hand write out and in ink add the amounts due.[88] They shall abide by the following order: what must be given shall be provided first by the more suitable persons and then by the middling and the poorest. Nor may a farmer occupied with sowing and gathering his fruits ever be drawn away to perform extraordinary burdens, since it is good foresight to attend to these necessities at the appropriate time. If this rule is neglected, it shall touch the modesty (i.e., reputation) of your vicars, but it will cost the governors [and] their staffs their heads. The governors shall have to write in their own hand what is needed and for what extraordinary purposes for each person, or how many post wagons, or how much personal labor, its nature, or its amount, should be provided; and they shall write that they have confirmed the lists while observing the aforementioned order of collection among the rich, middling, and poor. READ 9 MAY (328) AT ROME IN THE CONSULSHIP OF JANUARIUS AND JUSTUS.

The governors must draft the lists for extraordinary *munera* by hand and assign *munera* to the wealthiest before proceeding to less affluent candidates. Moreover, farmers must not be called upon to perform extraordinary

---

87. Mommsen *ad loc.* adds *et* to the text (rejected by Pharr). Provincial governors, when called *rectores,* are often described as *rectores provinciae/-arum; rectores officiorum* does not occur, and the double genitive *rectorum officiorum* is jarring. The reading *rectores autem provinciarum* might be expected, but other constitutions also pair *rectores* and *officia:* CTh. 7.4.21, 7.6.2, 11.16.11.

88. *Nomina:* in this context, probably "amounts owed, debts" rather than the "names" of the persons affected (so Pharr: "names of the taxpayers").

munera at planting or harvest time.[89] Constantine had stipulated in a text curiously titled "in response to the edict of the Macedonians and Chalcedonians"[90] that the assignment of extraordinary liturgies should be made by governors to protect poorer citizens from the caprice of the rich and powerful.[91] This earlier constitution was issued shortly after the defeat of Licinius and appears to have addressed popular grievances in the newly conquered territory.[92]

The letter sent to the praetorian prefect in Rome (CTh. 11.16.4) seems programmatic in contrast and sets a harsh penalty for disobedience. The practice of permitting the most eminent decurions to fix the division of extraordinary liturgies for their city doubtless extended beyond Bithynia (and Macedonia); Constantine attempts to curb the very practice deplored by Salvian in his *de gubernatione dei*, written in Gaul roughly a century later.[93] Constantine disseminates his instructions and warning through the administrative hierarchy and enforces obedience by establishing punishment for the officials involved, whose interest it then is to control the others. Only the praetorian prefect appears exempt from Constantine's suspicions.

---

89. Cf. the exception made for sowing and harvesting in the establishment of Sunday as a day of rest: CJ 3.12.2 (Gothofredus, *ad* 11.16.4).

90. CTh. 11.16.3 (a. 324): AD EDICTVM CALCHEDONIENSIVM ET MACEDONIENSIVM. CTh. 5.13.1 similarly bears the heading AD EDICTVM [HELIOPOLI]TANORVM (restored from CJ 11.66.1), issued from Antioch to Heliopolis. Mommsen writes *ad loc.* that copyists presumably have substituted this formula for the spare description *edictum*, which occurs in several constitutions; in *Proleg.*, cliii n. 2, he states that either the names of the civic magistrates have been lost (although, even then, it is unclear why the emperor might reply to such an edict) or the preposition *ad* has been misplaced. Gothofredus, *ad* CTh. 11.16.3, suggests that the form *ad edictum* should attest letters written in response to the decrees of cities, provinces, or curias, but such decrees (of deliberative bodies) cannot be equated with *edicta* (of individual magistrates), and the letters of the emperors to cities are otherwise addressed to the citizens themselves (e.g., *ad Antiochenses*, CTh. 16.2.16; *decurionibus Agrippiniensibus*, CTh. 16.8.3) or to the *ordo* (e.g., *ordini Carthaginensium*, CTh. 12.1.41).

91. CTh. 11.16.3: *Quotienscumque aliquam adscribtionem fieri necesse est, rectorum consiliis et dispositione uniuscuiusque civitatis fiat adscribtio, ne libidini et commodo potiorum multitudo mediocrium subiecta gravibus et iniquissimis adficiatur iniuriis.*

92. The suggestion of Gothofredus, *ad loc.*, that *Macedoniensium* may be a corruption of *Nicomediensium* is quite plausible; the more so because, as Mommsen, *ad loc.*, observes, the combination of a province and a city in the inscription of a constitution is very unusual.

93. Salv., *de gub. dei* 5.17–18, 5.28–33; the process is described most vividly in chapter 30: *Veniunt plerumque novi nuntii, novi epistolarii a summis sublimitatibus missi, qui commendantur inlustribus paucis ad exitia plurimorum. Decernuntur his nova munera, decernuntur novae indictiones. Decernunt potentes quod solvant pauperes, decernit gratia divitum quo pendat turba miserorum; ipsi enim in nullo sentiunt, quod decernunt.* Cf. Salv., *de gub. dei* 5.18: *Quae enim sunt non modo urbes, sed etiam municipia atque vici, ubi non quot curiales fuerint, tot tyranni sunt?* See C. Leppeley, "*Quot curiales, tot tyranni.* L'image du décurion oppresseur au bas-empire," in *Crise et redressement dans les provinces européennes de l'Empire (milieu du IIIe-milieu du IVe siècle ap. J.-C.). Actes du colloque de Strasbourg, décembre 1981*, ed. E. Frézouls (Strasbourg, 1983), 143–56.

The penalty clause of this official letter to the prefect is particularly striking: "If this rule is neglected, it shall touch the modesty of your vicars, but it will cost the governors [and] their staffs their heads." The task of vicars in reviewing the lists compiled by the governors attests their jurisdiction over provincial governors in matters affecting the *fiscus*, better known from later constitutions.[94] The threat of punishment in CTh. 11.16.4 presumes that they were accountable for controlling the documents submitted to them by the governors and ensuring that they were drafted in the prescribed fashion. Their punishment would appear to be for connivance at the negligent or unjust assignment of *munera* by the governors under their jurisdiction. The ominous phrase *Quae res neglecta vicariorum tuorum verecundiam tangit* is a veiled reference to the punishment of *infamia*. A constitution of Honorius offers a neat parallel to this usage of *verecundia:* if someone brings groundless allegations against a bishop or other clergyman, he shall suffer *infamia* and thereby lose his own good name, and thus "learn . . . that he may not plot against the modesty (*verecundia*) of someone else with impunity."[95] The *verecundia* of the vicars would certainly have been "touched" by a sentence of *infamia. Infamia* entailed not only removal from office but also exclusion from any further offices, in addition to the usual legal disadvantages to which *personae infames* were subject.[96] *Infamia* often was consequence of still harsher punishment such as relegation or deportation, but the allusive character of the penalty clause for the vicars allows only speculation. As is often true of the punishment of high officials, deliberate vagueness leaves considerable discretion to the potential judge, whether he is the praetorian prefect or the emperor.

Mere loss of rank seems mild when contrasted with the execution of governors and their staffs. Again, however, the phrasing of the penalty clause leaves much open to interpretation. The "heads" (*capita*) cited in the text might be the lives of those involved; the term might also mean their legal status, since common punishments such as deportation carried *capitis deminutio* with them. Constantine moreover makes no distinction between governors and *officiales,* but it is unlikely that they would have been treated

94. E.g., CTh. 1.15.6 (a. 372), 1.15.14 (a. 395), 1.15.15 (a. 400), 1.15.17 (a. 401): *Virum spectabilem vicarium Africae, quem totius conlationis ac transmissionis cura constringit, iudicibus volumus imminere.*

95. CTh. 16.2.41 (a. 412): *Si quis ergo circa huiusmodi personas non probanda detulerit, auctoritate huius sanctionis intellegat se iacturae famae propriae subiacere, ut damno pudoris, existimationis dispendio discat sibi alienae verecundiae inpune insidiari saltem de cetero non licere.*

96. CJ 10.59.1 (Diocletian); CJ 12.1.2: *Neque famosis et notatis et quos scelus aut vitae turpitudo inquinat et quos infamia ab honestorum coetu segregat, dignitatis portae patebunt.*

identically in practice. The vagueness of the penalties in CTh. 11.16.4 seems calculated above all to inspire vigilance on the part of the officials involved with the governor but not directly responsible for the compilation of the registers of *munera extraordinaria.* The vicars at the level above the governor and the *officiales* below him are made liable, if in imprecise terms, for the conduct of the governor in assigning extraordinary liturgies due from single cities. Salvian's vivid description of the unscrupulous conduct of the *principales* naturally owes much to dramatization and hyperbole, but without question the practice was one of the evils to which the imposition of superindictions was prone. Salvian goes on to describe how decurions contested the distribution of liturgies among themselves.[97] By threatening not only the governor, but also the vicars and *officiales* with punishment, Constantine places pressure on the governors from within the imperial administration in addition to that from without: the expectations of the population, whom Constantine encourages to voice their complaints, and even of less influential decurions.

Munera performed on behalf of the state by the *navicularii,* who supplied grain to Rome and later Constantinople, also led Constantine to threaten a series of officials with death:[98]

CTh. 13.5.5 (a. 329)[99]

[IMP. CONSTANTINVS] A. AD ABLAVIVM PPO. Navicularios omnes per orbem terrarum per omne aevum ab omnibus oneribus et muneribus, cuiuscumque fuerint loci vel dignitatis, securos vacuos inmunesque esse praecipimus, sive decuriones sint sive plebei seu potioris alterius dignitatis,[100] ut a conlationibus et omnibus oblationibus liberati integris patrimoniis navicularium munus exerceant. Naves quoque eorum, quantaecumque fuerint, ad aliud munus ipsis invitis teneri non convenit, ad quodcumque litus accesserint; lito-

97. Salv., *de gub. dei* 5.32–33.

98. On Constantine and the *navicularii:* J. Gaudemet, "Les privilèges des 'navicularii' au début du IVe siècle," in *Hommages Besnier* (1980), 99–106 (= *Droit et Société* (1992), 97–104); cf. Dupont, *Réglementation,* 122–32 (though dated). In general, see A. J. B. Sirks, *Food for Rome: The Legal Structure of the Transportation and Processing of Supplies for the Imperial Distributions in Rome and Constantinople* (Amsterdam, 1991); L. De Salvo, *Economia privata e pubblici servizi nell'impero romano. I corpora naviculariorum:* (Messina, 1992).

99. Date emended from 326 by Seeck, *Regesten,* 64; Barnes, *NE,* 132. On the legal import of this constitution, see Sirks, *Food for Rome,* 141–42.

100. Mommsen, *ad loc.,* writes that *alterius* should be deleted or emended to *altiores,* but the former solution seems too drastic and the latter too cumbersome. Perhaps the present reading is the result of confusion of *seu potius altioris dignitatis.*

rum custodibus et vectigalium praepositis exactoribus decurionibus adque rationalibus et iudicibus scituris, quod qui hanc legem violaverit capite punietur. DAT. XIIII KAL. OCTOB. CONSTANTINO A. VII ET CONSTANTIO CAES. CONSS.

[EMPEROR CONSTANTINE] AUGUSTUS TO ABLABIUS, PRAETORIAN PREFECT. We order that all *navicularii* throughout the earth be untroubled, free, and immune from all burdens and liturgies for all time, whatever their station or rank, whether they are decurions or plebeian or another higher rank, so that they may carry out the duty of *navicularius* excused from taxes in kind and in cash with their patrimonies intact. It is also inappropriate that their ships, whatever their size, should be liable for another liturgy against the will of their owners, no matter on which shore they land; the coastal guards and the overseers of the tolls, the tax collectors, decurions, *rationales,* and governors shall know that whoever violates this law will be punished with death. GIVEN 18 SEPT. (326 [329]) IN THE CONSULSHIP OF CONSTANTINE AUGUSTUS, CONSUL FOR THE SEVENTH TIME, AND OF CONSTANTIUS CAESAR.

An eminent scholar of late antique Roman law has dismissed this decree as "mere propaganda"; Constantine will have issued it to win the favor of the shippers, whose services he will have required supposedly for military action on the Danube.[101] Otherwise, we should be unable to explain why immunities were granted again to *navicularii* by an edict of 334, which regulated their organization in Constantinople.[102] Against this view, it must be stressed that however disagreeable the contents of CTh. 13.5.5 are, it is hazardous to presume that petty provincial governors and lesser officials could dismiss Constantine's words—or even knew to distinguish law and propaganda in imperial constitutions. Disobedience, while the law remained in force, was at their peril. The later constitution, CTh. 13.5.7, in which Constantine established the immunities of the freshly organized *navicularii* of Constantinople, may perhaps clash with systematic legal thought, but it should excite little surprise if on the occasion of the creation of a new body of *navicularii* to serve his new eastern capital, Constantine thought it appropriate to issue an edict to proclaim the privileges of that new body.[103] There in fact appears to have been no other law that punished the imposi-

101. D. Liebs, "Privilegien und Ständezwang in den Gesetzen Konstantins," *RIDA*^{3} 24 (1977), 332 ("bloße Propaganda").

102. Liebs, "Privilegien und Ständezwang," 332–33, citing CTh. 13.5.7.

103. Cf. Gaudemet, "Navicularii," 103–6.

tion of illegal *munera* on *navicularii* until 386, when the law of Constantine was reissued almost verbatim by Valentinian II, who decreed the confiscation of the property of the guilty in addition to death.[104]

The wording of CTh. 13.5.5 is certainly calculated to impress listeners. The recurrence of forms of *omnis* underscores the universality of the constitution. The breadth of the exemption from *munera* granted all *navicularii* by Constantine is elaborated by adjective pronouns constructed with the suffix *-cumque* and the conjunctions *vel* and *sive/seu*. The inclusion of persons *cuiuscumque loci vel dignitatis* recalls the edict to all provincials CTh. 9.1.4, in which Constantine encourages all his subjects everywhere to bring their complaints against his officials before him. Two tricola, *securos, vacuos inmunesque* and *sive decuriones sive sint sive plebei seu potioris alterius dignitatis* (*seu potius altioris dignitatis*?), stress the universal immunity of *navicularii* whatever their legal status, decurion, *humilior*, or *honestior*. The concluding sentence unites officials in a chain of increasing importance and eminence, from guards stationed on the coasts to the provincial governor himself, who must all observe the privileges of the shippers. The final verb, the last word of our fragment, remains in the indicative mood despite being in a subordinate clause introduced by *scituris quod* and conveys the certainty of punishment. Constantine's *navicularii* were not to be trifled with. Indeed, according to Eunapius, Constantine had his erstwhile advisor the Neoplatonist Sopater beheaded, because it was alleged by the same Ablabius to whom CTh. 13.5.5 is addressed, that Sopater had "chained the winds" to prevent the grain fleet from reaching Constantinople![105]

Illegal Sales

As it was necessary to protect the privileges of some, so was it necessary to prevent the abuse of privilege against others. The financial officials of provincial governors, the *numerarii*, faced severe punishment for miscon-

---

104. CTh.13.5.17 (a. 386): *Omnes navicularii per omne aevum ab omnibus oneribus et muneribus et conlationibus et oblationibus subleventur, cuiuscumque loci fuerint vel dignitatis. Et quicumque contra istam fecerit legem, seu custos litorum seu vectigalium praepositus seu exactor vel decurio seu rationalis vel iudex cuiuscumque provinciae, exhibitus sublatis universis facultatibus suis capitali sententiae subiugetur.* Constantius (CTh. 13.5.9, a. 357) had set a fine of 10 lb. of gold for those who attempted to harass *navicularii*. He mentions *vis, concussiones*, and *aliquod genus incommodi*, but not *munera*.

105. Eun., *VS* 6.2.9–12. Among the charges that led to the exile of Athanasius in 335 was that he threatened to prevent the grain fleet from sailing (Ath., *Apol. c. Ar.* 9.3). I thank H. A. Drake for both these references.

duct, and the guilty among them naturally sought to evade justice through various subterfuges. A favorite method was the acquisition of high rank, which might shield a *numerarius* from judicial torture. In 334, Constantine wrote of the "rapacious and deceitful plan of the *numerarii*" to the vicar of Asia:

CTh. 8.1.4

[IMP. CONSTANTINVS] A. AD VERONICIANVM VICARIVM ASIAE. Vorax et fraudulentum numerariorum propositum, qui diversis rectoribus obsequuntur, ita inhibendum est, ut[106] et antea sanximus et nunc itidem sancimus, condicioni eos subdi tormentorum et eculeis adque lacerationibus subiacere nec ultra biennium hoc fungi obsequio. ET CETERA. DAT. XIIII KAL. IVN. OPTATO ET PAVLINO CONSS.

[EMPEROR CONSTANTINE] AUGUSTUS TO VERONICIANUM, VICAR OF ASIA. The rapacious and deceitful plan of the *numerarii,* who serve various governors, is to be stopped in such a way, as We have decreed before and now again decree: that they are to be made liable to torture and subject to the rack and flogging, nor may they hold office for more than two years. ETC. GIVEN 19 MAY (334) IN THE CONSULSHIP OF OPTATUS AND PAULINUS.

The precise nature of the scheme of the *numerarii* is revealed in a second fragment of this letter:

CTh. 8.15.2

[IMP. CONSTANTINVS] A. AD VERONICIANVM VIC. ASIAE. POST ALIA: Damus provincialibus facultatem, ut, quicumque sibi a numerariis, qui diversis rectoribus obsecuntur, conquesti fuerint aliquas venditiones extortas, inritas inanesque efficiant et male vendita ad venditoris dominium revertantur, amissione etiam pretii inlicitis ac detestandis emptoribus puniendis. DAT. XIIII KAL. IVN. OPTATO ET PAVLINO CONSS.

[EMPEROR CONSTANTINE] AUGUSTUS TO VERONICIANUS VICAR OF ASIA. AFTER OTHER MATTERS: We grant the provincials the ability, that, whoever should complain that sales have been forced upon him by the *numerarii,* who

106. Anacoluthon at *ut:* since *ut* follows *ita,* one would expect it to introduce a result clause; it serves here however in the sense of "just as," and the sentence concludes with an indirect statement elaborating the content of Constantine's decree (*sancimus*). The translation reflects this inconcinnity.

serve various governors, they may make those sales null and void and the things sold at a loss should revert to the ownership of the seller, while the wrongdoing and detestable sellers will be punished through forfeiture of the price paid. GIVEN 19 MAY (334) IN THE CONSULSHIP OF OPTATUS AND PAULINUS.

Similar constitutions in book 8, title 1 of the Codex Theodosianus suggest that Constantine intended to prevent *numerarii* from impeding prosecution and avoiding judicial torture by acquiring rank or honorary titles.[107]

Punishment by simple restitution of the property and forfeit of the price paid, no doubt well below its real worth, is for Constantine conspicuously restrained, but this mildness is compensated by the degradation of the personal status of the *numerarii* on the staffs of provincial governors. The *numerarii* are said in CTh. 8.1.4 already to have been made subject to judicial torture. The earlier constitution to which it alludes does not survive, but it may have been related to CTh. 8.1.3, issued a year earlier in 333. There Constantine decrees that the counterparts of the *numerarii* in the military administration, the *actuarii* (and *annonarii*) should be subject to torture.

The threat of torture was real. In subsequent constitutions, the successors of Constantine confirmed and expanded the number of *numerarii* subject to judicial torture and prevented them from acquiring immunity by means of higher rank. Constantius strips *numerarii* of various ranks that the legislation of Constantine had forbidden them to hold.[108] Further efforts were made to define the period of liability: Julian, for instance, confirms that *numerarii* may be tortured but limits this period to their terms of office, five years (it had been two under Constantine), and an additional, sixth year during which "their life as private citizens may be easily attacked by the lawsuits of accusers"; if they passed this year honorably, they received the rank of *perfectissimus* and permanent immunity.[109] As in other constitutions, Constantine encourages provincials to bring their complaints against the *numerarii* before higher authorities. The combination of pressure from above and below should guarantee integrity among the ranks of *numerarii.*

---

107. Compare CTh. 8.1.5–8. Jovian colorfully explains in c. 8, *Iubemus omnes numerarios . . . solutos penitus militaribus sacramentis condicionales etiam fieri, ne dignitas fraudibus faciat umbraculum* ("We order all *numerarii,* utterly divested of military oaths, to be made subject to torture, lest rank provide a screen for fraud").

108. CTh. 8.1.5 (a. 357).

109. CTh. 8.1.6 (a. 362): *ut ad incusantium iurgia facilis adpetitu sit vita privata.*

Imperial Grants

Imperial officials who belonged to the departments of finance could, like their subordinates, be called to account for maladministration.[110] In CTh. 10.8.2 (a. 319), Constantine directs a *rationalis privatae rei*[111] to send full briefs to the *comes* (*privatae rei,* presumably) before a petitioner may occupy vacant property granted him by the emperor. A record of the donation of the property would have prevented the lower staff of the *res privata,* the notorious *Caesariani,* from diminishing its value to the petitioner's loss and their own profit. The fragment concludes: "a penalty is fixed against the *rationalis* and his staff, if they should permit a petitioner to occupy what has been donated to him before the aforesaid briefs have arrived."[112] A letter sent the same year to the *rationalis Africae,* again on property granted by the emperor, contains a similar threat. Constantine writes that he wishes such properties "to be held by direct and perpetual right and beyond all question; a penalty has been fixed against the *rationalis privatae rei* and his staff, should they attempt anything to the contrary."[113] The nature of these *poenae* is difficult to determine. The ablative absolute *poena proposita* could refer equally to a penalty already established in a previous constitution or to a penalty to be determined *extra ordinem* by the *rationalis* or *comes rei privatae* or the emperor once guilt is established. The lack of any words qualifying the severity of the punishment might suggest a fine, but this is by no means certain. Severe punishment may lurk behind the allusive words of the emperor. An attack on the claims of the recipients of imperial grants might be well construed as *calumnia* like that committed by the fiscal procurator and punished with immolation in CTh. 10.4.1, with which this chapter began. The vagueness of the penalties mentioned in these laws allows the emperor or his high officials to determine how most appropriately to punish offenders.

---

110. On relations between Constantine and the administrators of the *fiscus,* T. Spagnuolo Vigorita, "*Beneficium lenitatis nostrae.* Conflitto di interessi e munificenza imperiale in una costituzione di Costantino," in *Hommages à Gérard Boulvert, Index* 15 (1987), 357–65.

111. Mention of *Caesariani* in the constitution allows us to conclude that the addressee probably represented the *res privata,* which the *Caesariani* served, and not the *sacrae largitiones.* See Delmaire, *Largesses Sacrées,* 618–19 and 629–30, on this constitution.

112. CTh. 10.8.2: . . . *poena contra rationalem et officium eius proposita, si petitorem ante possidere permiserint id quod ei donatum est priusquam praedicti breves commeaverint.*

113. CTh. 10.1.2: *Haec directo iure atque perpetuo absque omni quaestione volumus obtineri poena contra rationales et magistros privatae rei atque officiales proposita, si quid contra tentaverint.*

Prisons

Constantine is much less discreet in fixing the punishment of officials who oversaw prisons. CTh. 9.3.1 (a. 320), a letter to the *rationalis* Florentius, concerns prison conditions:[114]

CTh. 9.3.1

IMP. CONSTANTINVS A. AD FLORENTIVM RATIONALEM. In quacumque causa reo exhibito sive accusator exsistat sive eum publicae sollicitudinis cura perduxerit, statim debet quaestio fieri, ut noxius puniatur, innocens absolvitur. Quod si accusator aberit ad tempus aut sociorum praesentia necessaria videatur, id quidem debet quam celerrime procurari. Interea vero exhibito non ferreas manicas et inhaerentes ossibus mitti oportet, sed prolixiores catenas, ut et cruciatio desit et permaneat fida custodia. Nec vero sedis intimae tenebras pati debebit inclusus, sed usurpata luce vegetari et, ubi nox geminaverit custodiam, vestibulis carcerum et salubribus locis recipi ac revertente iterum die ad primum solis ortum ilico ad publicum lumen educi, ne poenis carceris perimatur, quod innocentibus miserum, noxiis non satis severum esse cognoscitur. (1.) Illud etiam observabitur, ut neque his qui stratorum funguntur officio neque ministris eorum liceat crudelitatem suam accusatoribus vendere et innocentes intra carcerum saepta leto dare aut subtractos audientiae longa tabe consumere. Non enim existimationis tantum, sed etiam periculi metus iudici imminebit, si aliquem ultra debitum tempus inedia aut quocumque modo aliquis stratorum exhauserit et non statim eum penes quem officium custodiae est adque eius ministros capitali poena subiecerit. DAT. PRID. CAL. IVL. SERDICAE CONSTANTINO A. VI ET CONSTANTINO CAES CONSS.

EMPEROR CONSTANTINE AUGUSTUS TO FLORENTIUS, RATIONALIS. In any case in which a defendant has been summoned, whether his accuser is present or the responsibility of public office has brought him, a hearing should be given immediately, so that the guilty may be punished, the innocent acquitted. If, though, the accuser is away at the time or the presence of partners appears necessary, that should be arranged as swiftly as possible. Meanwhile, the defendant in custody should not be put in iron shackles that cling to his bones but in looser chains, so that there is no torture but his custody remains secure. Nor should he be forced to endure the darkness of the innermost cell, but he should be invigorated by the enjoyment of light; and when night doubles the watch

114. Cf. CTh. 9.3.2; also CTh. 11.30.2; cf. below, chapter 8, pp. 241–42.

over him, he should be taken to the entrances of the cells and healthy places, and when day returns he should be brought forth right at sunrise to the light of public; thus, he shall not perish from the punishment of imprisonment, which, as is known, is wretched for the innocent, not harsh enough for the guilty. 1. This too shall be observed: that neither those who serve as *stratores*[115] nor their assistants may sell their cruelty to accusers and let innocent men perish within the confines of the prisons or deprive them of a hearing and let them be consumed by long wasting away. For fear not only for his reputation but also of danger shall loom over the judge, if one of his *stratores* should fatigue anyone long past the proper time by starvation or by any other means and he (the judge) does not immediately inflict capital punishment on the official responsible for the prison and his assistants. GIVEN 30 JUNE (320) AT SERDICA IN THE CONSULSHIP OF CONSTANTINE AUGUSTUS, CONSUL FOR THE SIXTH TIME, AND CONSTANTINE CAESAR.

Prisoners in Late Antiquity depended wholly on the benevolence of their guards and the care of friends and family.[116] Constantine attempts to ameliorate the condition of prisoners by forbidding abuses and inhuman conditions; to illustrate why he must intervene, he gives a lurid description of late antique incarceration: persons accused should be tried immediately, not left to languish; prisoners should be put in loose chains that bind securely yet do not torment, not in iron shackles that "cling to their bones"; prisoners should be brought into the light of day, and at night they should be confined in the entrance of the prison and in healthy places, not banished to the depths of the prison. The emperor reasons that prisoners "should not perish from the punishment of imprisonment, which, as is known, is wretched for the innocent, not harsh enough for the guilty."[117] Constantine addresses specifically the *stratores*, the officials whom he holds responsible for such abuse and grim conditions. The name of these officials derived from the *stratum*, a "saddle" or rather a saddlecloth.[118] *Stratores* were in Late Antiquity low-ranking members of the *officium*, whose position descended from

115. Pharr translates "prison guards."

116. Living conditions in ancient prisons: J.-U. Krause, *Gefängnisse im Römischen Reich* (Stuttgart, 1996), 271–304. On evidence of prison conditions from Egyptian papyri, see S. Torallas Tovar, "Violence in the Process of Arrest and Imprisonment in Late Antique Egypt," in *Violence in Late Antiquity: Perceptions and Practices*, ed. H. A. Drake (Aldershot, 2006), 103–12.

117. CTh. 9.3.1 pr: *ne poenis carceris perimatur, quod innocentibus miserum, noxiis non satis severum esse cognoscitur.*

118. *OLD* s.v. *stratum* 2.

that of the governor's "horsemen" once held by seconded soldiers. They were charged with the collection of a tax known as the *collatio equorum*[119] and are attested on the staff of proconsuls and other high officials.[120]

It is remarkable that Constantine speaks of *stratores* as if they routinely oversaw provincial prisons. The official on the gubernatorial staff normally responsible for the custody of accused persons was known as the *commentariensis*.[121] The earliest text in the Codex Theodosianus to associate the *commentariensis* with prisons dates to 364;[122] subsequent laws in the title *de custodia reorum* (9.3) mention the *commentariensis* as the official overseer of prisons exclusively.[123] The text under consideration, CTh. 9.3.1, suggests that this had not always been true. Constantine mentions an official responsible for the prison at the end of the constitution without naming his title (*eum penes quem officium custodiae est*), but it seems unlikely that Constantine means someone other than a *strator*. Constantine describes this official as managing *ministri* in the penalty clause of the constitution, just as the *stratores* are described as presiding over *ministri* at the beginning. It is possible that the relationship of the *stratores* to the *commentariensis* was not initially one of subordination, at least with respect to prisons. The third-century *Acta Cypriani* present a *strator* as the overseer of a proconsular prison: Cyprian is arrested by an *equistrator* who holds the office of *a custodiis* under a proconsul.[124] The manner in which Constantine speaks of the *stratores* might plausibly be explained if *stratores* frequently oversaw the prisons of proconsular governors until this duty was transferred to the higher-ranking *commentariensis* at some point between 320 and 364.

The penalty clause of CTh. 9.3.1 threatens both governor and staff: the governor must fear not only *infamia* (*metus existimationis*) but also greater punishment (*periculi*), should he fail to execute the overseer of the prison and his assistants under whom the offence was made. Constantine similarly decrees the punishment of "exile" for *assessores* who illicitly sign *libelli* in the name of the governor. He requires the praetorian prefect to report the name of the offending governor to himself, "so that he (the governor) may

119. Karayannopulos, *Finanzwesen*, 172–73; Palme, "Die *Officia* der Statthalter," 95 ("Stallmeister"); see CTh. 6.31.1 (a. 373) with Schmidt-Hofner, *Reagieren und Gestalten*, 41–42.

120. Jones, *LRE*, 372–73 and 593 n. 71; cf. the dedication of an ex-strator, ILS 1357a.

121. Palme, "Die *Officia* der Statthalter," 109; Krause, *Gefängnisse im Römischen Reich*, 265 (264–70 in general on the organization of prisons in Late Antiquity); Jones *LRE*, 521–22, 587 and 593.

122. CTh. 9.40.5; further evidence in Jones, *LRE*, 587 n. 58.

123. CTh. 9.3.5–7.

124. *Acta Cypr.* 2.2; Krause, *Gefängnisse im Römischen Reich*, 253.

be punished more severely."[125] A fine, perhaps even *infamia* with loss of office and privileges of rank, would appear to be the lightest punishment for such governors.

Constantine's letter to the *rationalis* in CTh. 9.3.1 was anticipated by an extensive edict *ad populum* dated to early 320.[126] This edict contains similar regulations on the imprisonment and treatment of debtors of the *fiscus:*

CTh. 11.7.3

[IMP. CONSTANTINVS] A. AD POPVLVM. Nemo carcerem plumbatarumque verbera aut pondera aliaque ab insolentia iudicum repperta supplicia in debitorum solutionibus vel a perversis vel ab iratis iudicibus expavescat. Carcer poenalium, carcer hominum noxiorum est. [*desunt nonnulla*] . . . officialium, et cum denotatione eorum iudicum, quorum de officio †coherciti citatiores† esse debebunt, qui contra hanc legem admiserint.[127] Securi iuxta eam transeant solutores: vel certe, si quis tam alienus ab humano sensu est, ut hac indulgentia ad contumaciam abutatur, contineatur aperta et libera et in usus hominum constituta custodia militari. Si in obdurata nequitia permanebit, ad res eius omnemque substantiam cives eius accedant, solutionis obsequio cum substantiae proprietate suscepto. Qua facultate praebita omnes fore credimus proniores ad solvenda ea, quae ad nostri usus exercitus pro communi salute poscuntur. DAT. [PR.] KAL. FEB. CONSTANTINO A. VI ET CONSTANTIO CAES. CONSS.

[EMPEROR CONSTANTINE] AUGUSTUS TO THE PEOPLE. Let no man fear prison and the blows of leaden rods or weights or other punishments devised by the wantonness of governors for the payment of debts, nor should any man take fright at bitter or angry governors. Prison is for criminals, for guilty persons [*some words are missing*] . . . for *officiales,* with the brand of *infamia* for those judges, from whose staff they who contravene this law †should be punished (?)†. May taxpayers pass in safety according to this law: or certainly, if someone is so bereft of human sense as to abuse this indulgence contemptuously, let him be held in the open and free military custody that has been humanely established. But if he should persist in stubborn iniquity, his (fellow) citizens shall

125. CJ 1.51.2 (a. 320): *Praesides non per adsessores, sed per se subscribant libellis. Quod si quis adsessori subscriptionem inconsultis nobis permiserit, mox adsessor qui subscripsit exilio puniatur: praesidis vero nomen ad nos referri iubemus, ut in eum severius vindicetur.* Dupont, *Peines,* 52, inclines to interpret *exilium* here as *relegatio.*

126. Seeck, *Regesten,* 59; Barnes, *NE,* 74; and Corcoran, *ET*², 194.

127. See immediately below on the textual uncertainties of this sentence.

come into his belongings and all his property, receiving with ownership of the property the obligation of payment. Having given this opportunity, We believe that all men will be more disposed to pay what is required by Our army for the common welfare. GIVEN 31 JAN. (320) IN THE CONSULSHIP OF CONSTANTINE AUGUSTUS, CONSUL FOR THE SIXTH TIME, AND OF CONSTANTIUS CAESAR.

The edict bristles with indignation. Constantine conjures images of imprisonment, beatings, and pressing in the opening sentence of the fragment. These and other forms of torture "devised by the wantonness" of provincial governors may not be inflicted on debtors of the *fiscus.* Constantine attributes excesses of such governors to bitterness and wrath, vices unbecoming magistrates of the Roman people and delegates of the Roman emperor. The prison, Constantine declares with passion, is for criminals, for wrongdoers, not, as the context suggests, insolvent debtors of the state.

Taxpayers should not be subjected to such treatment at the hands of the provincial governors. If, however, someone should fail to make good his debt, negligence that Constantine construes as a species of madness, he may be held in "open" custody. Constantine uses the paradoxical phrase *aperta et libera custodia,* which appears to mean imprisonment outdoors and without chains, or perhaps with light chains, as befits a free man—free by birth, that is. Constantine prescribes light chains and orders that prisoners be permitted to enjoy daylight in his letter to the *rationalis* (CTh. 9.3.1). This later letter seems to elaborate how "humanely established" incarceration as demanded in the edict might appear.

The debtor who persists in his refusal to pay is unreasonably stubborn: Constantine avoids all mention of the contingency that a debtor to the *fiscus* might be unable to pay. It is presumed that the debtor should possess enough property to satisfy the claims of the state, and it is from this property that his fellow citizens (presumably, all are decurions) must pay his debt. The compilers of the Codex Theodosianus fortuitously neglected to prune away the final sentence of CTh. 11.7.3, in which Constantine explains why he has resolved to introduce these measures: he believes that by providing this opportunity or ability, taxpayers will be more willing to satisfy their obligations. It is ambiguous, however, whether the *facultas* which Constantine cites should refer to the prohibition of the excesses of incarceration or to the potential property of the debtor.

The punishment of the provincial governors and their officials, if they violate the terms of the edict of Constantine, is regrettably described in a passage riddled with textual difficulties. With the reference to the constitution CTh. 9.3.1, we might infer that the punishment of *officiales* who abuse their power to incarcerate is death, which punishment it is the responsibility of the governor to impose. The punishment of the governor himself fortunately can still be discerned in the text of CTh. 11.7.3: Constantine threatens *denotatio,* which must mean *infamia.* Although rare, the verb *denotare* is used in the sense of "censure" already in the Digest;[128] its etymology moreover recalls the "brand" of *infamia* or the *nota* to which the imperial constitutions frequently refer.[129] Constantine alludes to this punishment in CTh. 9.3.1 by describing the fear of the governor for his reputation, *existimatio;* the penalty prescribed in CTh. 11.7.3 with *denotatio* should correspond to *infamia,* which would have subjected the governor to all the legal disadvantages endured by *infames personae.* Most importantly, *infamia* would have stripped the governor of his office and made it impossible for him to hold another of any kind. A guilty governor would not only remain liable to perform curial duties,[130] but he would also lose his status as an *honestior* and become subject to torture and harsher penalties.[131]

The Stay-at-Home Materfamilias

In a last example in this survey of crimes and punishments, we find Constantine informing Domitius Celsus, vicar of Africa, of a special prohibition regarding distraint made on the property of a materfamilias. CTh. 1.22.1 forbids, with threat of the direst consequences, any provincial governor to send an *officialis* to evict a materfamilias whose house is under distraint. The violent language of the fragment merits full citation:

CTh. 1.22.1 (a. 316)

IMP. CONSTANTINVS A. AD DOMITIVM CELSVM VICARIVM. Nemo iudex officialem ad eam domum, in qua materfamilias agit, cum aliquo praecepto aes-

---

128. Dig. 30.54 pr (Pomponius): *Turpia legata, quae denotandi magis legatarii gratia scribuntur, odio scribentis pro non scriptis habentur.*

129. E.g., two constitutions of Constantine's, CTh. 2.19.1: *quibus inustas constiterit esse notas detestabilis turpitudinis;* and CTh. 2.19.3: *per turpitudinem aut aliquam levem notam.*

130. CJ 10.58.1 (Diocletian): *Infames personae, licet nullis honoribus, qui integrae dignitatis hominibus deferri solent, uti possunt, curialium tamen vel civilium munerum vacationem non habent.*

131. Constantine formulates this in CJ 12.1.2: *Neque famosis et notatis et quos scelus aut vitae turpitudo inquinat et quos infamia ab honestorum coetu segregat, dignitatis portae patebunt.* On *infamia* in Late Antiquity, see Kaser, *Das römische Privatrecht,* vol. 2, §206 IV, p. 115.

timet esse mittendum, ut eandem in publicum protrahat, cum certum sit, debita eius, quae intra domum considerato sexu semet contineat, domus eius vel cuiuscumque rei habita distractione, publicis necessitatibus posse servari. Quod si quis in publicum matremfamilias posthac crediderit protrahendam, inter maximos reos citra ullam indulgentiam, capitali poena vel exquisitis potius exitiis suppliciis plectatur. DAT. III. ID. IAN. TREVIRIS, SABINO ET RVFINO COSS.

EMPEROR CONSTANTINE AUGUSTUS TO DOMITIUS CELSUS, VICAR. Let no governor deem it necessary to send an *officialis* to the home of a materfamilias on some order, so that he drags her into public, since it is certain that the debts of a woman who out of consideration of her sex keeps herself inside the house can be preserved for the needs of the state, should her house or any other thing be subject to confiscation and distraint. If anyone hereafter should think a materfamilias should be drawn into public, let him suffer capital punishment or rather an exquisite demise and execution as one of the gravest offenders, without any mercy. GIVEN 11 JANUARY (316) AT TRIER IN THE CONSULSHIP OF SABINUS AND RUFINUS.

We have encountered other constitutions that bear the stamp of the impetuosity of the first Christian emperor. The particulars of a case, if they offended against his principles, might move Constantine to drastic, decisive action. Constantine intervenes here in defense of the dignity of the traditional Roman matron, the materfamilias, which persists even in the face of financial embarrassment. The constitution, addressed to a vicar, has been preserved midway on its journey from the imperial court to the provincial governors to whom it applied. The term *iudex* in this instance may also include *rationales,* who maintained their own *officium.* The vicar would ensure that the decree of the emperor reached all those who must obey it. It seems moreover fair to suppose that the enforcement of this measure was also entrusted to the vicar, whose position, like that of the provincial *comites* also favored by Constantine, included not only the supervision of subordinates but also the report of their crimes to the emperor.

The penalty clause of CTh. 1.22.1 deserves particular notice: the words *capitalis poena* could indicate ambiguously death or deportation, which was capital insofar as it extinguished the *caput* of the guilty as a Roman citizen. Yet Constantine corrects himself, adding *vel exquisitis potius exitii suppliciis.* This phrase can only indicate the death penalty, and it indeed suggests an aggravated form, such as crucifixion (later banned by Constantine himself) or immolation.[132] The tone of the constitution leaves the reader to believe that the harshness of the penalty was commensurate, not to the offense, but rather to the indignation of the emperor. It seems reasonable to assume that the notorious handling of a materfamilias prompted the wrathful condemnation of Constantine.

132. Contra Dupont, *Peines,* 16 and 26, who interprets *supplicia exquisita* as torture.

7

Control and Consultation: *Breves, Relationes, Consultationes*

Breves

Several of the constitutions discussed in previous chapters illustrate evidence of a further means of controlling the administration, namely the traffic of reports. Official correspondence between provincial administrators, whether gubernatorial, fiscal, or military, and the imperial court was brisk. The Codex Theodosianus addresses at great length the forms of correspondence peculiar to judicial matters—*relationes* and *consultationes.* These forms of correspondence lead to the subject of the next chapter, appeal, which was partly modeled on the procedure of the *consultatio.* Besides correspondence generated by judicial business, a steady flow of reports, frequently in the form of lists, from lower to higher officials in the administrative hierarchy and eventually to the emperor was fostered under the Constantinian regime.[1] Such briefs (*breves*) could be, and often were, used to monitor the actions of various officials throughout the empire.[2]

The delegation of authority, from emperor to praetorian prefect, to *comes* or vicar, facilitated the collection of reports and distributed the burden of their review. In CTh. 10.8.2, Constantine instructs the *rationalis* Priscus to send *breves* to his superior, the *comes* (*rei privatae*), when property has been confiscated by *Caesariani,* the clerical officials who served on the staff of the *rationalis.* These *breves,* the emperor states, are to be *plenis-*

1. See n. 44 below.
2. Cf. the discussion in S. Schmidt-Hofner, *Reagieren und Gestalten. Der Regierungsstil des spätrömischen Kaisers am Beispiel der Gesetzgebung Valentinians I.* (Munich, 2008), 64–68.

simi: the detail of the description of the property affected should prevent spurious claims to it or peculation perpetrated, as it seems, by the *Caesariani.* Since the property subsequently would have been granted to a petitioner or lavished on some other favorite by the emperor or in his name, it lay in the imperial interest to maintain such potential gifts intact for their future recipients. The *rationalis* is thus called upon to protect the interests of both emperor and imperial beneficiary by guaranteeing the integrity of his staff. One should not assume a priori that the emperor's wish had little prospect of fulfillment. The *rationalis* served for a short time, over a staff of career clerks. It would be hasty to suppose that there existed such solidarity between him and his clerks that he might connive at their indiscretions at his own peril. The *rationalis* looked to the *comes rei privatae* and ultimately to the emperor for advancement and reward. That he should have ensured that full documentation of confiscated property reached his superiors in order to retain their favor is much more credible than the alternative—that he should sacrifice due procedure and expose himself to punishment for the sake of enriching an underling. *Caesariani* may indeed have persisted in attempts to profit from the manipulation of such confiscations, but the diligence of the *rationalis* in reporting the extent of confiscated property will have prevented the diminution of imperial grants without the knowledge, and before the arrival, of the grantee.

Reports of judicial proceedings might also be demanded of provincial governors in the form of *breves.* This is shown in CTh. 1.16.3, one of the fragments of the letter addressed to Felix, governor of Corsica.[3] Constantine instructs Felix to send reports of all cases to the praetorian prefect after six months of his governorship have elapsed:

> Cum sex menses transcurrerint, breves omnium negotiorum ab officio tuo descripti commeent ad scrinia eminentissimae praefecturae, ut his recensitis et ad scrinia nostra perlatis pandatur, quis iudicum et in quibus discingendis causis fidelem operam praestiterit, quo vel dignus praemium mereatur vel neglegens coercitionem incurrat.

> After six months have passed, reports drafted by your *officium* of all cases shall go to the bureaus of most eminent (praetorian) prefecture, so that once they have been reviewed and forwarded to Our bureaus, it may be shown which judges, and in which cases they have heard, have acted honestly, so that either the worthy earn his reward or the negligent meet with punishment.

---

3. Seeck, *Regesten,* 57.

The reports were prepared by the *officium* of the governor, not by the governor himself. Constantine again exploits the potential for antagonism between an official and his permanent staff, his *officium,* that appears in CTh. 10.8.2. Constantine assumes that the records drafted by the *officiales* will accurately reflect the legal business conducted at the court of the governor, so accurately even as to incriminate the governor. Tampering with the public records would have been subject to heavy punishment, and members of the *officium* may well not have sought complicity in such acts. The drafting of the *acta* was a public act conducted during judicial proceedings before the governor. Constantine evokes this scene in his edict to the provincials, CTh. 1.16.6: *expletis omnibus actibus publicis privatisque sese recipiant.* Only after the *acta* have been compiled may the judge retire. The record of the *acta* could even have borne witness to irregularities of which the governor himself was ignorant and have provided a constructive means of improving the administration of justice.

The procedure imposed upon the staff of Felix in CTh. 1.16.3 may not have been unique. The language of the letter to Felix suggests that Constantine expected the praetorian prefect to receive and review judicial reports from provincial governors generally. According to the text, Felix must send reports to the prefect "so that once they have been reviewed and forwarded to Our bureaus, it may be shown which *judges,* and in which cases *they* have heard, have acted honestly."[4] It is impossible that reports sent by the *officium* of Corsica illustrated the conduct of other provincial governors, which is presupposed by words *quis iudicum.* The abrupt shift to the plural may be the result of an omission made by the compilers of the Codex Theodosianus. Alternatively, the role of the praetorian prefect in reviewing the records of proceedings from the provinces under his jurisdiction may have led the drafter of the constitution to speak of judges generally, despite the fact that the letter is concerned with reports from *officium* of Felix (*ab officio tuo*) specifically. This interpretation seems more plausible, since it is otherwise unclear how the general statements of CTh. 1.16.3 may be reconciled with the rebuke of Felix in CTh. 2.6.2. Delmaire goes so far as to suggest that precisely such reports of judicial activity were among the sources drawn upon by the compilers of the Codex Theodosianus; this hypothesis on the sources of the Codex Theodosianus is unlikely, but the practice of

4. CTh. 1.16.3: *ut his recensitis et ad scrinia nostra perlatis pandatur, quis iudicum et in quibus discingendis causis fidelem operam praestiterit . . .*

submitting reports to the praetorian prefects appears to have been widespread.[5]

The institution of semiannual reports by Constantine recalls other measures of control. As seen in CTh. 1.5.1, Constantine relies on information from the praetorian prefects to punish provincial governors who have refused to hear legitimate claims.[6] The procedure described in this later constitution effectively supplements the review of *acta* ordered in CTh. 1.16.3, for the cases of provincials whose claims were rebuffed out of hand would have failed to appear in the *acta*. Constantine accordingly instructs provincials in such straits to approach the praetorian prefects, who are to investigate the veracity of their complaints. The praetorian prefect plays the same part in both processes, reporting to the emperor if he uncovers wrongdoing committed by a provincial governor. The praetorian prefects and *comites* likewise serve as the intermediaries between the people and the emperor in reporting acclamations, as seen most prominently in CTh. 1.16.6.

The circulation of reports not only was an instrument of positive administration but also of preventative character. The duty of collecting and reviewing reports should be regarded as one of the most important control functions assigned to the praetorian prefects and *comites provinciarum*. *Breves* were compiled also at the lower levels of the imperial administration, especially in matters of taxation, and flourished after Constantine.[7] The institution as it emerges from the constitutions of Constantine exploits the latent antagonism that must have existed both between *officium* and governor and between governor and praetorian prefect or whichever superior administrator, proconsul, vicar, or *comes*, to whom supervision fell whether by proximity or some other circumstance. It would be rash to envision the imperial administration merely as a parasitical junta united in its persecution of provincial victims. Governors served briefly, usually for only a year; the members of their *officia*, who derived from the area in which they served, would stay on and literally had to live with the consequences of corruption perpetrated against their townsmen.[8] Likewise, there is no reason

5. R. Delmaire, introduction to *Les lois religieuses des empereurs romains de Constantin à Théodose II (312–438)*, vol. 1: *Code Théodosien livre XVI*, ed. T. Mommsen, J. Rougé, and R. Delmaire (Paris, 2005), 16–17.

6. See chapter 4.

7. Seeck, s.v. "brevis," *RE* 3.1 (1897), 832; N. E. Lenski, *Failure of Empire: Valens and the Roman State in the Fourth Century A.D.* (Berkeley, 2002), 296–97, describes Valentinian and Valens as obsessed with the compilation of *breves*.

8. A. H. M. Jones, "Roman Civil Service," 174–75; cf. the discussion of "small-town societies" by C. Kelly, *Ruling the Later Roman Empire* (Cambridge and London, 2004), 145–52, esp. 151–52.

to imagine all too extensive friendship between petty provincial governors and the prefects to whom they answered.

Relationes and *Potentiores*

Ps.-Ulpian writes, "It is one of the duties of the provincial governor to see that powerful men do not inflict injuries on the weak or their defenders persecute the innocent with false accusations."[9] In late 328, Constantine wrote to the praetorian prefect Maximus not because this duty of the provincial governor had lapsed, but because the means of fulfilling it might prove elusive.

CTh. 1.16.4

[IMPERATOR CONSTANTINVS] A. AD MAXIMVM. Praesides provinciarum oportet, si quis potiorum extiterit insolentior et ipsi vindicare non possunt aut examinare aut pronuntiare nequeunt, de eius nomine ad nos aut certe ad gravitatis tuae scientiam referre, quo provideatur, qualiter publicae disciplinae et laesis minoribus consulatur. ET CETERA. DAT. IIII K. IAN TREVIRIS IANVARINO ET IVSTO CONSVL.

[EMPEROR CONSTANTINE] AUGUSTUS TO MAXIMUS. If some powerful person should prove intractable, and the provincial governors themselves cannot punish, investigate, or deliver a ruling, they must report his name to Us or surely to the knowledge of Your Gravity, so that it may be determined in what way to protect public discipline and the less powerful who have been injured. ETC. GIVEN 29 DECEMBER (328) AT TRIER IN THE CONSULSHIP OF ANUARINUS AND USTUS.

It is salutary to recall that as early as the reign of Constantine provincial governors might be impeded in the prosecution of their duties by the presence of *potentiores,* men whose influence might overshadow the restricted and transitory power of their nominal governors. The governor might not be the most powerful man in the diminutive civilian provinces of Late Antiquity. *Potentiores* could subject a governor to illegal or extralegal pressure and even challenge or ignore his authority. The scope of their interference

9. Dig. 1.18.6.2: *Ne potentiores viri humiliores iniuriis adficiant neve defensores eorum calumniosis criminibus insectentur innocentes, ad religionem praesidis provinciae pertinet.*

was wide and the steps enumerated in the constitution with the words *vindicare, examinare,* and *pronuntiare* give the impression that the governor was vulnerable at every stage of litigation. CTh. 1.16.4 thus anticipates rise of the *potentiores* to prominence and the burden they placed on provincial jurisdiction in the later fourth and fifth centuries.[10] It also illustrates the channels of communication that were employed to concert resistance against the resources of the powerful.

As briefs (*breves*) and other reports served to control the excesses of administrators, official letters or *relationes* voluntarily offered by officials were equally vital to the efficacy of the legal system and the imperial administration. Constantine affirms the responsibility of the praetorian prefect for the receipt of correspondence from the provincial governors—now as their protector rather than punisher. In a world in which the representatives of the emperor no longer ruled as the most powerful men in the provinces, someone was needed to whom governors could turn when their position was challenged or their weakness exposed. As formulated in CTh. 1.16.4, the emperor stands before the prefect ready to intervene in cases complicated by the interference of private power. As a matter of fact, however, it was probably a question of proximity whether a provincial governor first informed the emperor or his prefect, or perhaps even a vicar or *comes provinciarum,* all of whom possessed jurisdiction *vice sacra,* notionally equal to that of the emperor.

CTh. 1.16.4 alleges two purposes for notifying the emperor or prefect. First, public discipline required it; the authority of the provincial governor in his province must be upheld. Second, those whose recourse to justice was imperiled must receive aid. The declared intentions and administrative actions of Constantine demanded the deliverance of the weak. No inconsiderable advantage accrued to Constantine from realizing the claims of his public edicts. Constantine at once consolidated his authority among the population by vindicating the weak in the name of justice; he confirmed his power as supreme arbiter even over powerful individuals, whose titles depended on the continuance of imperial favor; and the provincial governors

10. A. Wacke, "Die *potentiores* in den Rechtsquellen Einfluß und Abwehr gesellschaftlicher Übermacht in der Rechtspflege der Römer," *ANRW* II.13 (1980), 562–607; A. Wacke, "The *potentiores:* Some Relations between Power and Law in the Roman Administration of Justice," in *Estudios de derecho romano y moderno en cuatro idiomas* (Madrid, 1996), 69–86; J. Gaudemet, "Les abus des 'potentes' au Bas Empire," *Irish Jurist* 1 (1966), 128–35 (= *Études,* vol. 3 [1979], 433–42); R. MacMullen, *Corruption and the Decline of Rome* (New Haven and London, 1988), 104–18.

themselves remained dependent on his supreme authority. Their letters informed the emperor and provided him material for intervention on behalf of his subjects.

Another constitution, CTh. 1.15.1, gives some insight into one way in which Constantine sought to guarantee lawful hearings when the balance of justice preponderated unfairly to the side of the powerful, not for virtue of their cause but by the added weight of money, might, or influence:

CTh. 1.15.1

IMP. CONSTANTINVS A. AD SILVIVM PAVLVM MAGI [VICARIVM] ITALIAE. POST ALIA: Ne tua gravitas occupationibus aliis districta huiusmodi rescriptorum cumulis oneretur, placuit has solas causas gravitati tuae iniungere, in quibus persona potentior inferiorem aut minorem iudicem premere potest aut tale negotium emergit, quod in praesidiali iudicio terminari fas non est, vel quod per eosdem praesides diu tractatum apud te debeat terminari. DAT. V K. MART. NICOMEDIAE PAVLINO ET IVLIANO CONSVL.

EMPEROR CONSTANTINE AUGUSTUS TO SILVIUS, MASTER [VICAR] OF ITALY. AFTER OTHER MATTERS: That Your Gravity, already intent on other business, not be burdened by heaps of rescripts of this sort, We have decreed to impose on Your Gravity only those cases in which a powerful person can oppress a weak or inferior judge or such a dispute arises that may not rightly be decided in a provincial court, or one, long handled by the same governors, that ought to be settled before you. GIVEN 25 FEBRUARY (325) AT NICOMEDIA IN THE CONSULSHIP OF PAULINUS AND JULIANUS.

As in CTh. 1.16.4, this letter addresses cases in which provincial governors find themselves unable to resolve a dispute because of the interference of a *persona potentior.*[11] CTh. 1.15.1 gives additional reasons that might necessitate the transfer of a case from a lower to a higher instance. One appears to be propriety: certain cases, for reasons of judicial competence or jurisdiction, ought not to be decided at the provincial level—*quod . . . terminari fas non est.* The other reason is expediency: cases that have been fruitlessly disputed at the provincial level should be brought before a higher judge.

---

11. Cf. Dupont, "Constantin et les constitutions impériales," in *St. Volterra,* vol. 1 (Milan, 1971), 564. For a social and cultural perspective, see P. Brown, *Power and Persuasion in Late Antiquity: Towards a Christian Empire* (Madison, 1992), 22–23.

The addressee of CTh. 1.15.1, Silvius Paulus, is described as *mag*[i] (i.e., *magister*) *Italiae*. This is almost certainly a corruption of *vic*(*arius*) *Italiae*. Inclusion of the constitution in the Codex Theodosianus under the title *de officio vicarii* (CTh. 1.15) would be inexplicable otherwise. The ostensible purpose of the letter to Silvius is to inform him that the emperor has decided to impose on him only cases concerning powerful private citizens. It appears that Constantine will decide which cases to mandate (*iniungere*) to the vicar. CTh. 1.15.1 is consistent with CTh. 1.16.4, in which Constantine decrees that provincial governors should bring cases involving *potentiores* to his notice. Constantine may choose cases to remit to a vicar or resolve by personal intervention.

Relationes and the replies they necessitated were not indiscriminately welcomed. A mountain of correspondence might bury the administration in minutiae best settled by provincial authorities. In CTh. 1.15.1, Constantine is concerned that a vicar not be "burdened by heaps of rescripts of this sort." The *relationes* that occasioned these rescripts were, apparently, of a trifling sort. Constantine uses similar language in CTh. 11.29.1, in which he urges the *corrector Lucaniae et Bruttiorum* to consult him concerning only few cases that the *corrector* cannot decide, lest he distract Constantine from other, more pressing business:[12]

CTh. 11.29.1

IMP. CONSTANTINVS A. AD CLAVDIVM PLOTIANVM CORRECTOREM LVCANIAE ET BRITTIORVM. POST ALIA: Super paucis, quae iuridica sententia decidi non possunt, nostram debes consulere maiestatem, ne occupationes nostras interrumpas, cum litigatoribus legitimum remaneat arbitrium a sententia provocandi. DAT. VI KAL. IAN. TREVIRIS, ACC. VIII ID. FEB. REGIO CONSTANTINO A. III ET LICINIO III CONSS.

EMPEROR CONSTANTINE AUGUSTUS TO CLAUDIUS PLOTIANUS, CORRECTOR OF LUCANIA AND BRUTTIUM. AFTER OTHER MATTERS: You should consult Our Majesty on few matters that cannot be decided by a legal ruling, so you do not interrupt Our other business, for there remains to litigants the appropriate legal choice of appealing the sentence. GIVEN 27 DECEMBER (314/15)[13] AT TRIER, RECEIVED 6 FEBRUARY AT REGIUM IN THE CONSUL-

12. Cf. Dupont, ibid., 558.
13. On the date, see Corcoran, *ET*[2], 305.

SHIP OF CONSTANTINE AUGUSTUS, CONSUL FOR THE THIRD TIME, AND OF LICINIUS, CONSUL FOR THE THIRD TIME.

The documents in CTh. 11.29.1 differ from those in CTh. 1.15.1 and 1.16.4. In CTh. 1.15.1, Constantine describes replies to the governors as *rescripta,* yet the text supposes greater involvement on the part of the vicar than the mere answering of requests for counsel. In CTh. 1.16.4, Constantine decrees that governors send (*referre*) the names of intransigent parties to himself or to the praetorian prefect. Such reports from the governor are a form of *relatio.*

CTh. 11.29.1, in contrast, concerns a special form of the common *relatio* known as a *consultatio,* or in legal literature *consultatio ante sententiam.* The *consultatio* was not merely a report (e.g., of someone's name) or request for aid or counsel on a single point, but the administrative equivalent of the layman's private rescript. This form of correspondence was subject to particular conventions. In a *consultatio,* the governor sent the emperor all documents and evidence concerning a case in anticipation of a ruling. The emperor reached a decision on the basis of the documents sent him and conveyed his answer to the governor by imperial rescript. The *rescripta* described as burdening the vicar in CTh. 1.15.1 may have been responses to such inquiries sent directly to the vicar; the word might also refer, perhaps more probably, to paperwork that the vicar must draft in response to ordinary *relationes* delegated to him by the emperor. The substance of CTh. 1.15.1 is that Constantine leaves to the vicar only cases prompted by requests of provincial governors for assistance against *potentiores.* The *consultatio,* by contrast, was the preserve of the emperor.

Proper Occasions for Consultationes

Judges presiding over a *cognitio extraordinaria* had previously enjoyed extensive judicial discretion in their courts. Over time, however, this judicial freedom eroded in favor of regularity and consistency imposed by the central government. In the legislation of Constantine, numerous rules affecting court procedure emerge already, it appears, fully developed.[14] The *consultatio* is the first of such procedures that is strictly regulated by Constantine.

When a provincial governor was unable to reach a decision, he might present the case to the emperor, whose decision, in theory, was final and inappellable. Constantine appears to assume that simple lack of experience

14. Kaser-Hackl, §77.II, pp. 520–21.

was the usual cause for *consultationes:* "Let him (*sc.* the judge) consult Our Knowledge about that which he deems to be uncertain."[15] The *consultatio* was not to be exploited, however, as a means of shirking judicial duties, nor should a governor try to rid himself of unpleasant cases, whether for lack of patience or confidence. Constantine admonishes the *corrector Lucaniae et Brittiorum* that he must limit his *consultationes* to questions of law to which he could find no answer: "You should consult Our Majesty about few things, which cannot by decided by (your) judicial ruling."[16] While Constantine acknowledges the right of his administrators to appeal to his judgment for counsel, he also demands that they restrict their inquiries to essential matters of law—*super paucis*—for he had enough business to which to attend. It was of vital importance that Constantine remained accessible both to his subjects and to his administrators, and this access was greatly facilitated by the forms of correspondence continued, encouraged, and introduced during his reign, but the system of judicial instances, over which Constantine presided, was promoted to handle matters in which Constantine did not need to intervene. To guarantee his own ability to react, Constantine could not permit his administrators to resort to unwarranted *consultationes.* To protect the channels of appeal and preserve the efficacy of responses to *relationes* and *consultationes,* by which Constantine could augment his authority far more than by signing myriad trifling inquiries, it was necessary to divert these to the appropriate instances within the judicial hierarchy.

Constantine also sought to check the issuing of *consultationes* by judges after sentence had been passed. This was an important procedural rule. Judges eager to intimidate potential appellants sent or threatened to send *consultationes* after they had already delivered a ruling. Such unnecessary *consultationes* not only burdened the imperial chancellery but also undermined the credibility of provincial jurisdiction and the success of the appellate system. Constantine accordingly decrees, "If a judge has passed sentence, he should in no way afterward terrify litigants with the threat of a *relatio* to prevent an appeal against his judgment."[17] The exploitation of *con-*

15. CTh. 11.29.2 (a. 318): *super quo haesitandum putaverit* [sc. *iudex*], *nostram consulat scientiam.* On the date of this text, cf. Corcoran, *ET*², 308, following Seeck, *Regesten,* 57, against Barnes, *NE,* 74, who retains the MS date of 319. On the juristic helplessness of Symmachus as urban prefect, see T. Honoré, "The making of the Theodosian Code," *ZRG* 103 (1986), 174–75.

16. CTh. 11.29.1: *super paucis, quae iuridica sententia decidi non possunt, nostram debes consulere maiestatem.* Cf. F. Pergami, *L'appello nella legislazione del tardo impero* (Milan, 2000), 91–94.

17. CTh. 11.29.2: *si* [sc. *iudex*] *tulerit sententiam, minime postea, ne a se provocetur, relatione promissa terreat litigantes.* On this constitution, see Pergami, *Appello,* 57–59. See chapter 8.

sultationes to stifle appeals was a recurrent abuse. Constantine later complains in a letter to the urban prefect that lower judges send him "unnecessary and insolent" *relationes* to hinder appeals that would normally proceed to the urban prefect.[18] This abuse will be discussed in the next chapter.

The Procedure of the Consultatio

The purpose of a *consultatio* was to request judicial counsel, by its nature authoritative, on how to decide a case. The case itself was not transferred to the jurisdiction of the emperor; that occurred upon appeal. Since the response of the emperor was equivalent to a statement of law, a *consultatio* produced rulings reached by the emperor and executed by the provincial judge. The judge had to ensure that the facts of the case correspond to those assumed by the response of the emperor. The *consultatio* thus remained a resource that might be employed only prior to a ruling. Constantine states as much explicitly: "If any judge should consider a *consultatio* necessary, let him not pass sentence, but rather consult Our Knowledge on what he believes he must hesitate (sc. to make a ruling)."[19] A *consultatio* sent to the emperor after a sentence had been delivered violated this principle and infringed on the procedure of appeal.[20]

The *consultatio* must also be issued after the judge had conducted a preliminary investigation of the facts of the case, generically called *cognitio.* Both parties must be heard: *cognitis utrisque actionibus* ("having examined both arguments," CTh. 11.30.1).[21] Constantine paints an idealized picture of this inquest in CTh. 2.18.1, a fragment of a letter sent to the urban prefect:[22]

---

18. CTh. 11.30.13 (a. 329); date according to Seeck, *Regesten,* 64; Barnes, *NE,* 78; cf. Pergami, *Appello,* 59–60.

19. CTh. 11.29.2 (a. 318): *Si quis iudicum duxerit esse referendum, nihil pronuntiet, sed magis super quo haesitandum putaverit, nostram consulat scientiam.*

20. Cf. CTh. 11.30.13 and 11.30.18, in which the *relatio* and *appellatio* procedures are contrasted.

21. *Actio* is here translated as "argument" because both parties are obviously intended in the context of the passage. The word *actio* in late antique legal texts often merely indicates the "claim" of the plaintiff and had no procedural consequences in *cognitio extra ordinem;* Kaser-Hackl, §88.I.1–2, pp. 577–78 and I.3, p. 580; cf. §73.I, pp. 485–86, on *cognitio extraordinaria.* By a further dilution of the meaning of *actio,* Constantine here describes the claims both of the plaintiff and of the defendant as *actiones.*

22. On the date: Seeck, *Regesten,* 61 and 100; Barnes, *NE,* 75.

CTh. 2.18.1 (a. 321)

IMP. CONSTANTINVS A. AD MAXIMVM [PV]. Iudicantem oportet cuncta rimari et ordinem rerum plena inquisitione discutere, interrogandi ac proponendi adiciendique patientia praebita ab eo: ut, ubi actio partium limitata sit, contentiones non occursu iudicis, sed satietate altercantium metas conpresserint, saepius requiratur et crebra interrogatione iudicis frequentetur, ne quid novi resideat, quod adnecti allegationibus in iudiciaria contentione conveniat, cum ad alterutrum hoc proficiat, sive definienda sit causa per iudicem sive ad nostram scientiam referenda . . . DAT. PRID. ID. [IVN.] SIRMIO CRISPO II ET CONSTANTINO II CC. COSS.

EMPEROR CONSTANTINE AUGUSTUS TO MAXIMUS, [URBAN PREFECT]. A judge must examine everything and investigate the facts of the case through exhaustive inquiry, permitting (the litigants) to ask questions, lay out (their cases/evidence), and make additions; in such a way that when the pleading of the parties is finished, and their litigation has concluded not through the interference of the judge, but because of the satisfaction of the litigants, the judge may ask frequently and repeatedly whether there remains any new evidence that ought to be included in the materials cited in litigation, since this is useful both whether the case is to be concluded by the judge or referred to Our Knowledge . . . GIVEN 12 [JUNE] (321) AT SIRMIUM IN THE CONSULSHIP OF CAESARS CRISPUS, CONSUL FOR THE SECOND TIME, AND CONSTANTINE, CONSUL FOR THE SECOND TIME.

That a judge must reach his decision through evaluation of testimony and evidence presented in the course of a trial was, or should have been, self-evident, and it is curious that Constantine lectures the urban prefect on elementary trial procedure. It seems plausible that this lesson in judicial propriety was occasioned by the prefect himself or, perhaps, a judge under his jurisdiction, who had conducted a trial in a brusque and high-handed manner. The second fragment of this letter to Maximus, concerning appeal, will occupy us below. A complaint seems to have reached the imperial court—how, we regrettably cannot know. If the offender was in fact a lesser judge, Constantine may have intended his letter to the urban prefect for further distribution among his subordinates in Italy; the fragment preserved in CTh. 11.30.11 strongly suggests that Maximus himself or perhaps other *iudices vice sacra* were at fault.

Constantine's depiction of a hearing in his letter to the urban prefect conforms to his encouragement of legal documentation and presupposes the remedies in the second instance fostered under his rule. The reasons for conscientiousness on the part of his judges are above all pragmatic: a thorough hearing would produce the documents necessary not only for reaching and justifying a ruling but also for preparing and sending a *consultatio*, should the case prove too difficult for the judge himself to decide; the material collected would also support an appeal to the emperor, which we will discuss below.

The *consultatio* was subject to further rules besides its timing and intent. Once the judge had heard both parties and determined that he could not resolve the controversy, he had to declare his intention to consult the emperor in full court.[23] Both litigants had to be apprised of this decision; by compelling the judge to make this declaration publicly, the submission of *consultationes* at an improper time and without the knowledge of one or both of the parties could be prevented.

After declaring his intention to consult the emperor, the judge composed the *consultatio* itself, which formally was no different from any other *relatio*. It was distinguished by its content, which concerned a specific legal dispute. Among the letters of Pliny to Trajan are excellent early examples of this kind of communiqué;[24] later examples can be found among the letters of Symmachus.[25] The *relatio* requested by Constantine in CTh. 1.16.4, for example, when a judge found himself unable to prosecute a powerful person, would have differed from a judicial *consultatio* in that it did not request that the emperor make a provisional ruling.

Once the judge had composed his *consultatio*, he was required to make it available to the litigants by registering it in the *acta* drafted by his staff. A copy would be made available to the parties within ten days of the declaration of intent to write to the emperor.[26] If a litigant was dissatisfied with the written statement of the judge, he might, within five days of the posting of

---

23. Constantine uses the word *pronuntiaverits* in CTh. 11.30.1 and *promiseris* in 11.30.5 and even calls the judge's declaration a *sententia* in 11.30.8 pr; cf. *spoponderit* in 11.29.5, a constitution of Valentinian and Valens. This declaration is technically an *interlocutio*, since the delivery of the sentence would ensue only once the emperor's response to the *consultatio* had been received; thus Ulpian writes, Dig. 49.1.1.2, *si quis* [sc. *iudex*] *forte interlocutus fuit principem se consultaturum*. See Kaser-Hackl, §74.I.1, p. 495; Berger, s.v. *interlocutio;* D. Nörr, "Zu einem fast vergessenen Konstitutionentyp: *de plano interloqui*," in *St. Sanfilippo*, vol. 3 (Milan, 1983), 519–43.

24. E.g., Plin., *Ep.* 10.31 and 10.96; summary in A. N. Sherwin-White, *The Letters of Pliny* (Oxford, 1966), 546–51.

25. E.g., Symm., *Rel.* 16 and 19; D. Vera, *Commento storico alle* relationes *di Quinto Aurelio Simmaco* (Pisa, 1981), 128–31 and 142–47, respectively.

26. CTh. 11.30.1: *consultationis exemplum litigatoribus intra decem dies edi aput acta iubeas.*

the *consultatio,* submit a *refutatio,* also called *libelli refutatorii* or *preces refutatoriae.*[27] The *consultatio* of the judge must include full records of proceedings before his own court and before any others, for instance at an earlier stage of litigation.[28] Constantine expressly forbids any litigant to include in his statement material not declared (and scrutinized) before the judge.[29] This is only reasonable, when one considers that review of the *consultatio* at the imperial court could not determine the reliability of evidence that had not already been examined by the judge. In the interest of avoiding the review of cases already decided by imperial rescript, Constantine required not only a full statement by the litigants but also the full cooperation of the governor: "if a full . . . statement is produced by the litigant in court, and complete documentation is included in the composition of the *consultatio,* the decisions Our court renders per rescript will stand valid and accurate."[30]

Instructio Plena: *Full Documentation*

It was the duty of the provincial governor to include everything pertinent to a case in his dispatches to higher instances. Constantine persistently urges governors to include full documentation (*instructio*) in all judicial correspondence: he recommends a thorough inquisition before the governor's tribunal as conducive to the production of such extensive documentation. As seen above in CTh. 2.18.1, Constantine concludes his ideal description of how a judge ought to conduct a trial with the observation that a thorough interrogation of the parties may be of use should the judge later decide to refer the case to the emperor. He adds, "nor may anything be sent to Us that lacks full documentation."[31] After describing the procedure that judges are to follow in sending *consultationes,* Constantine orders the *corrector Lucaniae et Bruttiorum* "to append everything that was done in your court or in others' concerning the case, along with the statements of the litigants."[32]

27. CTh. 11.30.1: *si cui forte relatio tua minus plena vel contraria videatur, is refutatorias preces similiter tibi aput acta offerat intra dies quinque.*

28. CTh. 11.30.1: *omnia, quae aput te vel aput alios gesta fuerint in eo negotio, consultationi tuae cum refutatoriis litigantis adnectere.*

29. CTh. 11.30.11.

30. CTh. 11.30.11 pr: *Nam si plena, ut iubemus, adsertio per litigatorem in iudiciis exeratur et integra instructio in consulti ordinem conferatur, stabit ratum ac fidele, quod iudicia nostra rescripserint.* Cf. the summary of the *consultatio* procedure in Dupont, "Constantin et les constitutions impériales," 561–63.

31. CTh. 2.18.1: *Nec ad nos mittatur aliquid, quod plena instructione indigeat.*

32. CTh. 11.30.1: *omnia, quae aput te vel aput alios gesta fuerint in eo negotio, consultationi tuae cum refutatoriis litigantis adnectere.*

Constantine speaks of the preparation of such dossiers for appeal as traditional already in 316: "according to previous statutes and after observance of the traditional formalities, let all records be sent to the imperial court."[33] "All documents cited by the parties, the complete court records, and copies of all documents should be sent," Constantine writes in 321.[34] Even in fiscal cases, Constantine repeats in 329, "let everything be sent to Our knowledge."[35]

The demand for "all records" brings out an important terminological point. The *instructio* consisted of several documents, all of which should have been recorded in the official proceedings of the court, the *acta* or *gesta,* by the *officium* of the presiding judge. The precise form that this case dossier might take seems to have been flexible. Constantine describes the documents produced by the litigants as *indita actis vel subiecta* in CTh. 11.30.9. *Indita actis* suggests that the documents were recorded in the *acta* themselves (as by *insinuatio*); *subiecta,* on the other hand, indicates that copies of the litigants' documents might be appended to the relevant excerpt of the court proceedings. Yet the entire *instructio* of a case was registered and recorded in the *acta* of the court; thus Constantine also speaks casually of sending *acta* or *gesta* alone, as in CTh. 11.30.5: *gesta ad comitatum omnia dirigantur* ("let all records be sent to the imperial court"); he also speaks of the *instructio* as itself inserted in the *acta,* as in CTh. 11.30.9: *instructiones . . . actis inseri praecipimus* ("We order that the documentation be inserted in the proceedings/records"). The *instructio* of a case might contain or itself be considered *acta* or *gesta;* every document required of the litigants and the records of previous hearings were registered in the *acta* of the judge in one way or another. Thus the *instructio* is described sometimes as the *acta* of the judge who prepares it and at other times as a dossier to which the judge attaches additional material, whether *acta* or other documents provided by the litigants.

The efficacy of the *consultatio* procedure depended wholly on the availability of all materials relevant to the case. In 319, Constantine established twenty days as the time by which "whatever belongs in the documentation

33. CTh. 11.30.5: *iuxta priora statuta sollemnitatis more expleto gesta ad comitatum omnia dirigantur.*

34. CTh. 11.30.11 pr: *omnes igitur partium allegationes acta universa scribturarumque exempla omnium dirigantur.* On the date, see Seeck, *Regesten,* 61 and 100; Barnes, *NE,* 75.

35. CTh. 11.30.18: *universa ad nostram scientiam referantur.* On the date, see Seeck, *Regesten,* 48; Barnes, *NE,* 78.

of the case" (*quaecumque ad instructionem pertinent causae*) must be brought to the imperial court, whether for an appeal or *consultatio*.[36] He threatens the *officium* of a judge who failed to provide a full *instructio* within twenty days with a fine equal in value to the case, to be exacted within the next twenty days. The amount of the fine was to be determined by the *rationalis*, whose absolute honesty in the assessment was demanded on pain of death. The judge himself, at least in cases of appeal, might face a charge of *sacrilegium*, if by denying a litigant a copy of his ruling, which made appeal impossible, he forced a litigant to resort to *supplicatio*, irregular appeal directly to the emperor.[37]

The inclusion of all materials relevant to a case in a *consultatio* or appeal was intended to guarantee the applicability of Constantine's response. So too were private rescripts valid under the proviso that the judge found the circumstances of the case to correspond to those assumed in the rescript. Constantine elaborates this point at length in a letter written to the vicar Severus:

CTh. 11.30.9

[IMP. CONSTANTINVS] A. AD SEVERVM VICARIVM. Ne causas, quae in nostram venerint scientiam, rursus transferri ad iudicia necesse sit, instructiones necessarias plene actis inseri praecipimus. Nam cogimur a proferenda sententia temperare, qui sanximus retractari rescribta nostra ad opiniones vel etiam relationes iudicum data non oportere, quoniam verendum est, ne lis incognito negotio dirimatur adempta copia conquerendi. Quare perennibus inuretur iudex notis, si cuncta, quae litigatores instructionis probationisque causa recitaverint, indita actis vel subiecta non potuerint inveniri. DAT. X KAL. IVL. AQVILEIAE CONSTANTINO A. V ET LICINIO C. CONSS.

[EMPEROR CONSTANTINE] AUGUSTUS TO SEVERUS, VICAR. So that it should not be necessary to remit cases that have come into Our knowledge back to the courts, We order that the necessary documentation be inserted completely in the records. For We are forced to abstain from delivering a verdict, as We have ordained that Our replies (*rescripta*) made on the rulings or even *con-*

36. CTh. 11.30.8 pr: *intra vicensimum diem quaecumque ad instructionem pertinent causae, ad comitatum nostrum properantissime volumus adferri.* This holds whether for an appeal or *consultatio: ex eo die, quo fuerit quaestio terminata vel ex quo relationem iudex per sententiam promiserit.*

37. CTh. 11.30.6. Pergami, *Appello*, 94–95, overlooks the punishment of the judge and accordingly believes this constitution handles the situation when a judge declares an appeal unfounded.

> *sultationes* of judges must not be reexamined, because it is to be feared that a dispute might be decided with the case unknown and the ability to protest removed. Therefore, a judge will be branded with permanent marks (of infamy), if everything that the litigants have cited by reason of documentation and proof cannot be found inserted in or attached to the records. GIVEN 22 JUNE (319 [318])[38] AT AQUILEIA IN THE CONSULSHIP OF CONSTANTINE AUGUSTUS, CONSUL FOR THE FIFTH TIME, AND OF THE CAESAR LICINIUS.

Constantine rightly considers it improper to reopen cases that should have been resolved by imperial rescript. The rulings of the emperor were supposed to be unassailable and absolute, and their appeal was normally disallowed. Imperial rulings founded on false or incomplete information not only threatened the course of justice but imperiled the authority of the emperor. Thus in a letter to the urban prefect, Constantine writes that his rescript to a *relatio* (i.e., *consultatio*) will be sound and accurate "if a full statement is produced by litigants in court and complete documentation is included in the *consultatio*."[39] The emperor concludes, "Thus let all statements of the parties, all records, and copies of all documents be sent."[40] The entire system of consultation and appeal depended on the authority of the emperor: it was vital that this authority not be called into question in any circumstances.

The punishment of the judge in CTh. 11.30.9 evinces the importance attached by Constantine to the finality of his rulings. Constantine threatens the judge guilty of suppressing evidence with *infamia* (*perennibus inuretur notis*). *Infamia* may have been merely the consequence of still harsher punishment: the contemporary Sentences of Paul record that the suppression of documents fell under the purview of the *lex Cornelia testamentaria* (also called *de falsis*). The punishment recorded there, for *honestiores*, is deportation to an island.[41]

---

38. On the date, see Seeck, *Regesten*, 56 and 62; Barnes, *NE*, 144; cf. Pergami, *Appello*, 96–99.

39. CTh. 11.30.11 pr: *Nam si plena, ut iubemus, adsertio per litigatorem in iudiciis exeratur et integra instructio in consulti ordinem conferatur, stabit ratum ac fidele, quod iudicia nostra rescribserint neque ullus querimoniae locus dabitur nec occasio supplicandi, ut convelli labefactarique iubeamus quae ad relationem eius sanximus, qui neque vera neque universa suggessit.*

40. CTh. 11.30.11 pr: *Omnes igitur partium allegationes acta universa scribturarumque exempla omnium dirigantur.*

41. PS. 5.25.1: *Lege Cornelia testamentaria <tenetur>, qui testamentum quodve aliud instrumentum falsum sciens dolo malo scripserit recitaverit, subiecerit suppresserit amoverit deleverit . . . honestiores quidem in insulam deportantur, humiliores autem aut in metallum dantur aut in crucem tolluntur, servi autem post admissum manumissi capite puniuntur.*

The rules guiding the process of the *consultatio* were not elaborated all at once. The extant legislation shows how they were refined even under Constantine. Further legislation was required in 319 to introduce a deadline for the dispatch of the *consultatio* to the imperial court, alongside the deadlines for the publication of the *relatio* and the delivery of the *refutatoriae* of the litigant, already established in CTh. 11.30.1 (a. 314/15).[42] Hostile judges had apparently frustrated litigants simply by omitting to send the *consultatio* promised. A constitution of Julian attests that certain *officiales* on the staff of the governor were responsible for bringing the *consultatio* to the imperial court.[43] The introduction of a deadline by which the *consultatio* must be dispatched to the court eliminated this defect.

Suppression of Documents

Late Antiquity witnessed a proliferation of the use of documents in legal transactions, a practice that the regime of Constantine actively promoted.[44] A similar proliferation was under way within the imperial administration itself, and the exchange of documents between litigants and judge afforded corrupt officials new means of perverting justice. As has been observed above, culpable officials might be threatened with the punishment of *infamia*. So in CTh. 11.30.9 (a. 318), Constantine decrees that a "judge should be branded with permanent marks (of infamy)" if he should neglect to include all documents produced by litigants in the *acta* that he must send to the emperor with a *consultatio* or *opinio* (i.e., an appeal).[45] The suppression of documents might also be punished by fine. Constantine threatens the *officium* of a governor in a letter to the urban prefect, CTh. 11.30.8, in which

42. CTh. 11.30.8. On the date of CTh. 11.30.1, Seeck, *Regesten*, 78; Corcoran, *ET*², 305, proposes 314.

43. CTh. 11.30.31: . . . *si promissa relatio intra triginta dies non fuerit sine aliqua ambiguitate transmissa his officialibus, per quos convenit gesta transmitti. Et quia plerumque contingit, ut gerulis litterarum aliquo casu existente tarditatis obstaculum videatur adferri* . . . Julian requires that the day on which the *gesta* are given to the *geruli* be noted in the *acta*, so that the governor cannot be held accountable for delinquency of the letter-bearers. Cf. the fee in the edict of Mariscianus, ll. 21–22 (discussed in chapter 5, pp. 141–44), *si mittendus* (sc. *officialis*) *sit trans mare.*

44. M. Amelotti, "Documentazione privata e prova. Dall'epoca postclassica all'età giustinianea," in *Atti del xvii Congresso internazionale di papirologia (Napoli, 19–26 maggio 1983)* (Naples, 1984), vol. 3, 1161–72. One famous example of this is CTh. 9.1.5 (a. 320), in which Constantine abolishes oral accusations, admissible under the classical Roman law, and requires accusations to be made in writing.

45. CTh. 11.30.9: *Quare perennibus inuretur iudex notis, si cuncta, quae litigatores instructionis probationisque causa recitaverint, indita actis vel subiecta non potuerint inveniri.* The punishment of *infamia* continued to be applied well after Constantine, as evidenced by a constitution of his sons, Constantius and Constans, and by Valentinian and Valens: CTh. 11.30.24 and 11.30.34.

he sets a fine at the value of the disputed object, should the *officium* suppress or fail to process any documents submitted by litigants for an appeal or *consultatio.* The task of establishing the value of the case is entrusted to the *rationalis,* who must "with utmost honesty" (*fidelissime*) assess the sum—on pain of death.[46] Constantine vaguely threatens the *officium* itself with punishment, should it allow a litigant to prosecute a case that is pending on appeal, is awaiting a response to a *consultatio,* or has already been decided by imperial rescript.[47] His justification of this punishment has fortunately been left intact:

> CTh. 11.30.8.1
>
> Nam decreta nostra debet ingerere iudicanti ut ipso etiam dissimulante iudice reluctari et tamquam manibus iniectis eos de iudicio producere ac rationum officio traditos statuti prioris nexibus obligare, quorum desideriis violari nostras prospexerit sanctiones.
>
> For (the *officium*) ought to impose Our decrees on the judge so that it may resist, even if the judge himself dissembles, and, as if laying hands on them,[48] drag those, by whose desires it (i.e. the *officium*) has observed that Our resolutions are being violated, forth from the court and deliver them to the *officium* of the *rationalis,* thus binding them by the snares of the previous statute.[49]

The rulings of Constantine, whether for an appeal, *consultatio,* or *relatio,* were inviolable. It was the duty of the *officiales* to execute imperial decisions; Constantine contends that they must compel even the governor they serve to execute his commands.[50] Constantine thus declares his readiness to defend his imperial dignity by degrading the governor, executing the *rationalis,* and fining the *officium,* if a case should be mishandled at all levels of

46. CTh. 11.30.8 pr: *ab universo officio viginti transactis diebus, quos post latam sententiam placuit supputari, intra viginti alios dies qui sequuntur tantum fisco nostro praecipimus inferri, quanti per aestimationem rationalis emolumentum litis, cuius suppressa fuerat instructio, fidelissime potuerit aestimari. Cui capitale supplicium imminebit, si rigorem legis quocumque modo mollire temptaverit.*

47. CTh. 11.30.8.1: *Eadem poena officio imminente, si quando appellatione vel consultatione pendente vel post decisas nostris responsionibus causas ei, quod ullo modo fuerit impetratum, damnabilem voluerit coniventiam commodare.* The precise nature of the *poena* is somewhat uncertain.

48. An allusion to *manus iniectio;* cf. Berger, s.v. *manus iniectio* and *legis actio per manus iniectionem.*

49. This is CTh. 11.30.6, which sets a fine at the value of the object of the suit.

50. Cf. K. L. Noethlichs, *Beamtentum und Dienstvergehen. Zur Staatsverwaltung in der Spätantike* (Wiesbaden, 1981), 35.

the administration involved. It is the authority of the emperor that is here paramount.

Certain charges in Late Antiquity could be construed in such a way as to justify novel, severe punishment. The reform of the appellate system under Constantine depended to a large extent on the faithful transmission of numerous documents, but this reform was met with some resistance on the part of provincial governors. The suppression of appellate documents by provincial governors imperiled the success of the entire system. Constantine responded in kind, threatening charges of sacrilege against any provincial governor who refused or suppressed the transmission of appellate documents. *Sacrilegium* had an ominously bright future ahead of it. In later time, any breach of imperial commands could be construed as sacrilege, an insult to the sacred majesty of the emperor.[51] As an *honestior,* a governor found guilty of *sacrilegium* might expect deportation, perhaps death in exceptional circumstances.[52] The recorded punishments for *sacrilegium* pertain to temple robbery or to the desecration of graves, the traditional meaning of the word. It seems fair to assume that these punishments were also applied in Late Antiquity to what we may call administrative sacrilege, but still harsher punishment *extra ordinem* might well take their place at the discretion of the emperor.[53] In the constitution that interests us here, Constantine rules that a charge of sacrilege might be brought against any judge who had suppressed appellate documents or denied appellants a copy of his judicial ruling. Constantine writes to Petronius Probianus:

CTh. 11.30.6 (a. 316)

[IMP. CONSTANTINVS] A. PETRONIO PROBIANO SVO SALVTEM. Supplicare causa pendente non licet nisi forte ei, cui opinionis exemplum negatum est vel instructionis universae subpressa transmissio. Quo facto crimen iudici sacrilegii imminebit, qui hoc commisso litigatori supplicandi necessitatem inponit . . . DAT. ID. AVG. ARELATO; PROPOSITA ID. OCTOB. THEVESTE SABINO ET RVFINO CONSS.

[EMPEROR CONSTANTINE] AUGUSTUS TO HIS FRIEND PETRONIUS PROBIANUS, GREETINGS. It is not permitted to supplicate while a case is pending

51. Mommsen, *StrR.*, 569 n. 2 and 760 n. 7; cf. 771; C. Kelly, "Emperors, Government and Bureaucracy," *CAH* XIII, 143.

52. The punishment appears to be flexible; cf. CTh. 9.23.1 pr, in which Constantius writes of counterfeiters: *sacrilegii sententiam subeat et capite plectatur.*

53. Mommsen, *StrR.*, 820–21.

> except to him to whom a copy of the ruling has been denied or the delivery of the complete documentation has been suppressed. Should this occur, the charge of sacrilege shall threaten the judge (governor) who by this deed imposes the necessity of supplication on the litigant . . . GIVEN 13 AUGUST (316) AT ARLES; POSTED 15 OCTOBER AT THEVESTE IN THE CONSULSHIP OF SABINUS AND RUFINUS.

The subject of the letter, *supplicatio,* was an appeal in the last resort made directly to the emperor. *Supplicatio* stood outside the hierarchy of appellate instances and presumes both conviction and the exhaustion of instances of appeal or (as in this case) its unavailability. Constantine and his successors were wary of permitting *supplicationes* to flow to the imperial court unchecked. Such appeals might easily impede other, more urgent business that demanded the attention of the emperor. Many *supplicationes* might be prompted by the callous refusal of the judge to deliver documents necessary to appeal; Constantine sought to reduce the number of such extraordinary appeals by sharpening the punishment decreed for the abuses that could cause them.[54] It was moreover essential to enforce the observation of the new rules of appeal, with which Constantine advertised his effort to improve the administration of the empire and the availability of justice.

The procedure of the *consultatio* developed from that of the *relatio,* the traditional form of correspondence between the emperor and his officials. Alongside appeal, the *consultatio* was one of the most important means of promoting justice under Constantine and of emphasizing the direct dependence of provincial jurisdiction and the entire legal system on the authority of the emperor. The *consultatio* enabled the imperial court to compensate for the ignorance or uncertainty of its governors by providing an authoritative and binding ruling. If provincial judges proved incapable, they and provincial litigants could turn to the emperor, whose authority over both was insensibly confirmed. The procedure was elaborated to permit both judge and litigants to state their positions, and the inclusion of all evidence and pertinent records of the case was intended to ensure that the ruling of the emperor would be as well founded as that of the judge himself. The provincial governor, however, was not expected to resort to *consultatio* in every case of uncertainty. The composition of a *consultatio* had to be justified by the importance of the case or other circumstances that warranted the immediate attention of the emperor. For lesser matters, Constantine

54. Cf. Dupont, "Constantin et les constitutions impériales," 560–61.

stressed the availability of the appellate system, which invariably led to the emperor himself or to officials empowered with his delegated authority. Constantine had multiplied the number of judges competent to hear appeals and completely reformed the procedure of appeal to the imperial court, devising a new system based on the *consultatio*, which he strove relentlessly to enforce. It is to the Constantinian system of appeal that we now turn, but it should be remembered that in cases decided by *consultatio* or by appeal, whatever the outcome for the parties, the emperor always profited.

8

Appellatio

Access to Justice

Appellate jurisdiction may seem a surprising subject with which to conclude a book dedicated to the administration of Constantine the Great. The appellate system under Constantine,[1] however, brings together the separate threads of this study. The provincial administration of the Roman Empire knew no independent judiciary. The men responsible for the civil administration were the same who heard trials. Not only judicial but also broad administrative competence was necessary for the appellate system to succeed. Improvement of the appellate system could improve the availability of justice; by protecting his subjects from mistrial and error, Constantine could both content them and confirm their belief in his righteousness as emperor and source of all law. To ensure access to appeal, Constantine had to ensure the collaboration of his provincial judges. The control mechanisms sketched in the preceding chapters played a large part in compelling this collaboration.

Appeal not only helped to guarantee a just ruling but also checked the conduct of imperial officials. By making the rulings of provincial judges subject to challenge, Constantine induced imperial officials to obey the law—and himself. Not only the provincials of the empire but also Constantine benefited from the availability of appeal: it was to Constantine that

1. For a (largely descriptive) survey of Constantine's appellate legislation, see J. Gaudemet, "Constitutions constantiniennes relative à l'appel," *ZRG* 98 (1981), 47–76 (= *Droit et Société* [1992], 67–96). F. Pergami, *L'appello nella legislazione del tardo impero* (Milan, 2000), 45–119, offers a juristically oriented survey.

everyone looked for justice; it was Constantine who deliberated over the rulings and conduct of his officials; and it was Constantine who ostentatiously dispensed justice and on whom it depended.

Access to appeal guaranteed the subjects of the empire judicial rulings in conformance with the norms of Roman law. To this end Constantine vigorously ordered his administrators to permit and conduct appellate proceedings as prescribed by imperial legislation. Constantine rendered appeal more accessible by multiplying appellate instances throughout the empire, an achievement that was effected by investing the high officials of the tetrarchic reorganization of the empire with permanent imperial authority to hear and decide cases of appeal. Constantine concurrently created a new system of appeal to the imperial court, conducted entirely through official correspondence. The changes introduced to appellate jurisdiction relieved the emperor of the burden of a multitude of complaints yet permitted him to claim ultimate responsibility for the success of the system. It was to the advantage of the emperor that ever more persons turned to him for aid; an effective system of appeal enabled Constantine to appear omnipresent throughout the empire, even if in the person of a delegate, and spared provincials the lengthy and costly journey to the imperial court, wherever it happened to reside.

Appellate Judges of the Provincial Administration

Appellate jurisdiction under Constantine was exercised in the courts of several imperial officials who had been endowed with judicial authority equal to that of the emperor, or in the consistory of the emperor himself. Praetorian prefects, urban prefects, vicars, probably *comites provinciarum*, and proconsuls all were officials whom Constantine integrated into the appellate system known *vice sacra* or *vice nostra*.[2] Under the Principate, and until circa 314, jurisdiction *vice sacra* had been irregularly delegated to a variety of imperial officials. Under Constantine, it became the permanent competence of a chosen circle.[3] Officials who judged *vice sacra* effectively represented the emperor himself. They could receive appeals from provincial governors subordinate to them, and in exceptional circumstances—a possibility often overlooked—might also judge with imperial authority in

2. In general on this subject, M. Peachin, *Iudex vice Caesaris: Deputy Emperors and the Administration of Justice during the Principate* (Stuttgart, 1996).

3. Pergami, *Appello*, 429–32; cf. 425 n. 85; Peachin, *Iudex vice Caesaris*, 188–99.

the first instance.[4] The position of the proconsuls, as both provincial governors and judges *vice sacra,* necessitated this combination of competencies.[5]

The inclusion of vicars among the newly created judges *vice sacra* suggests a hierarchical chain of appeal from governor, to vicar (or *comes*), to praetorian prefect or emperor, but no such hierarchy was strictly maintained. Appellants frequently appealed from their governor directly to a praetorian prefect or to the emperor himself.[6] It was forbidden to appeal to a lower judge, but otherwise the choice of the appellate judge appears to have been left to the discretion of the appellant.

Ordinary Appeal and Appellatio More Consultationis

It is a testament to the extent of the Constantinian legislation that it alone provides evidence for almost every aspect of the procedure of appeal to the emperor in Late Antiquity. Subsequent legislation is dedicated chiefly to the refinement of details. The process of appeal to the imperial court was thoroughly reformed; alongside it, however, another form of appeal—in fact the traditional form—persisted in Late Antiquity. This procedure was followed in appeals from the court of one official to that of another, higher official. No constitution addresses this earlier form of appeal directly, but it is mentioned casually in two constitutions, one of which stems from the chancellery of Constantine.

A brief description of appellate procedure before Constantine will illustrate the novelty of Constantine's own enactments.[7] The constitutions CTh. 11.30.18 and 11.30.61 attest appeal as it existed prior to the reign of Constantine. CTh. 11.30.18, dated to 19 June 329,[8] concerns cases in which a *rationalis* presides over civil suits. Constantine stipulates,

> . . . si a sententia fuerit provocatum, non ad nostram scientiam referendum est, sed apostolis datis, quod iuxta observatam rationem postulari sufficiet, ad au-

4. Pergami, *Appello,* 428.

5. Jones, *LRE,* 481 (Jones considers this double jurisdiction peculiar to the proconsuls).

6. Pergami, *Appello,* 409–12, holds that the sources never indicate the appellate jurisdiction of the vicars as "effettivamente e tassativamente stabilita" (412). Jones, *LRE,* 481, notes the concurrent jurisdiction of the praetorian prefect but holds that the vicars would have heard most appeals from provincial governors in their dioceses.

7. For a synopsis of *appellatio* in the classical *cognitio extraordinaria,* see Kaser-Hackl, §75, pp. 501–10; detailed treatment by W. Litewski, "Die römische Appellation in Zivilsachen (IV)," *RIDA*[3] 15 (1968), 143–283; cf. M. A. von Bethmann-Hollweg, *Der römische Civilprozeß,* vol. 2 (Bonn, 1865), 700–712.

8. Mommsen, *ad loc.,* correcting the MS dating of 339; Seeck, *Regesten,* 48; Barnes, *NE,* 78.

ditorium gravitatis tuae, cui ad vicem nostram delata iudicatio est, partes pervenire oportet.

. . . if his ruling is appealed, the case should not be referred to Our knowledge, but *apostoli* should be given, which it shall suffice to request according to the observed manner, and the parties should proceed to the court of Your Gravity, to whom jurisdiction has been delegated in Our stead.

Sixty-one years later, in the reign of Honorius and Arcadius, a similar procedure is described; in CTh. 11.30.61, the emperors write to the urban prefect:

Sin vero huiusmodi examen arripuerit, in quo sine ullo legis vinculo non tam crimen obicitur quam cuiusdam criminis conflatur invidia lataque sententia appellatione suspenditur, inlustrem sedem tuam editis ex more apostolis sacra vice audientiam praebere sancimus.

If however he (*sc.* the urban vicar) has taken on a trial in which, without the binding support of a law, not so much an accusation is made as notoriety for some crime is drummed up, and the ruling delivered is suspended by appeal, We ordain that Your Illustrious tribunal shall, after *apostoli* have been duly presented, give hearing in the stead of the emperors (i.e., *vice sacra*).

Two things distinguish this form of appeal from the form that shall be examined below: the issuing of *apostoli* by the judge *a quo*[9] and the requirement that the appellant bring these documents personally to the designated court of appeal. Once an appeal had been made, whether orally or in writing (see below), and the judge *a quo* admitted it, he was obliged to compose *litterae dimissoriae,* colloquially called *apostoli,* and to present them to the appellant upon request within thirty days: this document, in which the judge *a quo* stated his position, was addressed to the appellate judge. It was to the court of the latter that the appellant brought the *apostoli,* whether personally or through a representative.[10] The judge *ad quem* then heard the

9. For the sake of brevity, the "judge *a quo*" shall indicate the judge in the first instance; the "judge *ad quem,*" the appellate judge.

10. Cf. Dig. 49.6.1 (Marcian): *Post appellationem interpositam litterae dandae sunt ab eo, a quo appellatum est, ad eum, qui de appellatione cogniturus est, sive principem sive quem alium, quas litteras dimissorias sive apostolos appellant. Sensus autem litterarum talis est: appellasse puta Lucium Titium a sententia illius, quae inter illos dicta est. Sufficit autem petisse intra tempus dimissorias instanter et saepius, ut et si non accipiat, id ipsum contestetur: nam instantiam petentis dimissorias constitutiones desiderant. Aequum est igitur, si per eum steterit, qui debebat dare litteras, quo minus det, ne hoc accipienti noceat.*

case anew on the basis of the *apostoli* of the judge *a quo* and the statements of the party or parties present at his court.[11] His ruling both rescinded and replaced that of the judge *a quo.*

This is in essence the procedure conjured by CTh. 11.30.18 and 11.30.61, which contrasts sharply with the procedure commonly encountered in late antique legislation.[12] In the age of Constantine and in Late Antiquity generally, the traditional appellate procedure continued to be used for appeals made not to the emperor but to high officials endowed with the power to hear appeals *vice sacra.* Constantine authored one significant change to this regime. An edict of Diocletian's, preserved as CJ 7.62.6, required a judge *a quo* to provide *apostoli* even if the appellant should fail to request them.[13] This regulation was no longer observed under Constantine by the year 329, when CTh. 11.30.18 was issued, if not earlier; it was again the task of the appellant to request *apostoli* from the judge *a quo.*[14]

The form of appeal far more prominent in the legislation of Constantine and his successors is generally designated *appellatio more consultationis* by scholars of Roman law, following the nineteenth-century German scholar M. A. von Bethmann-Hollweg, who discussed it in his work *Der römische Civilprozeß.*[15] As the modern name suggests, this appellate procedure closely resembles that of the *consultatio ante sententiam,* which was discussed in chapter 7. *Appellatio more consultationis* dispenses with the *apostoli* of the traditional procedure and their delivery to the judge *ad quem* by the appellant. Instead, the appeal consists of a dossier in the form of a *consultatio* in which all the pertinent documents are brought by official couriers to the imperial court.[16]

Appellatio More Consultationis

In both ordinary appeal and *more consultationis,* once a sentence had been delivered, the defeated party could, if he so desired, immediately make an

---

11. Sources and literature in Kaser-Hackl, §75.IV–V, pp. 507–10.

12. Litewski, IV, 185–86; the objections of Pergami, *Appello,* 450–51, are unconvincing (see below).

13. CJ 7.62.6.6: *Apostolos post interpositam provocationem etiam non petente appellante sine aliqua dilatione iudicem dare oportet;* Pergami, *Appello,* 38–40.

14. CTh. 11.30.18: *apostolis datis, quod iuxta observatam rationem postulari sufficiet;* Pergami, *Appello,* 386–87.

15. Bethmann-Hollweg, *Der römische Civilprozeß,* vol. 3 (Bonn, 1866), 332–38.

16. Litewski, IV, 186–87, on the "Überweisung der Akten von Amts wegen." Such couriers, *geruli,* are explicitly attested in a constitution of Julian, CTh. 11.30.29: *dies, quo gerulis gesta tradantur, fideliter designetur;* cf. CTh. 11.30.31, concerning *consultationes: si promissa relatio . . . non fuerit . . . transmissa his officialibus, per quos convenit gesta transmitti.*

oral appeal. Constantine himself confirmed the right of oral appeal in a constitution of 317:

CTh. 11.30.7

[CONSTANTINVS] A. AD BASSVM PV. Litigatoribus copia est etiam non conscribtis libellis ilico appellare voce, cum res poposcerit iudicata. DAT. VIII ID. IVN. SIRMIO GALLICANO ET BASSO CONSS.

EMPEROR CONSTANTINE AUGUSTUS TO BASSUS, URBAN PREFECT. Litigants have the power of appealing immediately by voice even without composing a petition of appeal (*sc. libelli appellatorii*), when the decision of the case calls for it. GIVEN 6 JUNE (317) AT SIRMIUM IN THE CONSULSHIP OF GALLICANUS AND BASSUS.

Oral appeal had, it seems, fallen out of favor by Constantine's day. Although still permissible, as Constantine states, it would appear that a judge had contested the validity of an oral appeal, which brought this question of procedure to the attention of the emperor. As is suggested by the emphasis of the phrase *etiam non conscribtis libellis,* the usual form of appeal at this date was written, consisting of *libelli appellatorii;* the common expressions *appellationem offerre* and *accipere/recipere* also suggest the giving and receiving of an appeal in written form.[17] All appeals were duly registered in the *acta* of the presiding judge. It follows that an oral appeal must be made immediately after the judge has rendered his decision so as to be taken down in the records of proceedings. For the preparation of a written appeal, the appellant enjoyed a period of two days in which to draft and deliver *libelli appellatorii,* which would subsequently be registered in the *acta* by the *officium* of the judge; a period of three days was granted if the person delivering the appeal were acting on behalf of another.[18]

The *libelli appellatorii* are the first of several documents in the process of appeal, both ordinary and *more consultationis.* The content of *libelli appellatorii,* according to Ulpian, was minimal:

Dig. 49.1.1.4

Libelli qui dantur appellatorii ita sunt concipiendi, ut habeant scriptum et a quo dati sint, hoc est qui appellet, et adversus quem et a qua sententia.

---

17. Pergami, *Appello,* 374.

18. This period appears in the writings of the classical jurists (e.g., Marcian, Dig. 49.1.5.4) and is prescribed by Diocletian in CJ 7.62.6.5; Pergami, *Appello,* 36–37 and 387–88; cf. Litewski, IV, 149–51.

> The petition of appeal to be submitted is to be formulated so that it contains in writing both by whom it is submitted, that is who appeals, and against whom and from what sentence.

The records of proceedings of the trial in which an oral declaration of appeal had been made would presumably have sufficed to clarify all three of these things.

Whether an appellant was required to supplement an oral appeal or *libelli appellatorii* with the reasons for his appeal is disputed. The question hinges on one's estimation of the power of the judge to evaluate and accept or reject an appeal. On the one hand, numerous constitutions appear to require judges to accept virtually all appeals.[19] On the other, the right to appeal was restricted in important ways: an appellant had first to observe several formalities.[20] The appeal had to be delivered within the prescribed number of days.[21] The appellant was also obliged to request and deliver constituent documents, acts vaguely called *sollemnia* in the imperial constitutions.[22] Constantine ruled that failure to fulfill these formalities constituted abandonment of the appeal, so litigants could not abuse appeal to delay the execution of a sentence against them. Failure to request or produce such documents led to the dismissal of an appeal as an *appellatio moratoria*, an appeal intended to delay proceedings.[23] There were further restrictions placed on appeals of interlocutory decisions, appeals made prematurely or late, and appeals in certain criminal cases, all of which will occupy us below.[24]

Beyond such formal requirements and specific restrictions, there is no explicit evidence that a judge *a quo* was entitled to review the legal grounds of an appeal made in his court. Pergami, the most recent authority on ap-

19. Pergami, *Appello*, 392–93.

20. See Litewski, IV, 166–71, for a list of formal grounds for the rejection of an appeal.

21. See preceding page.

22. Pergami, *Appello*, 104–5 and 383–87, rightly argues that the *sollemnia* are formal acts which must be performed by the appellant, not by the judge *a quo*, and embraced the *interpositio appellationis* in the form of an oral declaration or written *libelli appellatorii*, the request for a copy of the *opinio* of the judge, and the presentation of the *preces refutatoriae* (on which, see below, p. 228). Cf. p. 217 above on the request for *litterae dimissoriae* or *apostoli* in the ordinary appellate procedure. I do not believe with Pergami that the *sollemnia* included a presentation of the reasons for the appeal by the appellant (see immediately below).

23. CTh. 11.30.14: *placuit, ut, si intra dies complendis sollemnitatibus praestitutos ad facienda haec appellatoris cura defuerit, deserta ab eo provocatio aestimetur.* Cf. Pergami, *Appello*, 395; Litewski, IV, 269–70; CTh. 11.30.8 with 11.30.1.

24. Pergami, *Appello*, 394–96, offers an overview.

peal in Late Antiquity, postulates that a judge *a quo* must have evaluated the legal basis of an appeal against his ruling.[25] This view, however, seems at variance with the purpose of appeal itself. It was a fundamental principle, for one, that a judge could not try an appeal made against his own sentence.[26] An analysis of the legal grounds of an appeal by the judge *a quo* rather than the judge *ad quem* would amount precisely to such a conflation of the judicial hierarchy and undermine the system of appeal. It is easy to imagine that a judge *a quo*, having already delivered the contested ruling, might not readily be inclined to allow for its erroneousness.[27] The availability of appeal could remedy incorrect verdicts, but an appellant would have had no recourse to it if a judge considered his own verdict watertight.

Nor should we exaggerate the legal expertise of the various officials who acted in the capacity of a judge beneath the emperor. Constantine, for his part, urged judges to refrain from consulting him on matters that could be decided in court precisely because a litigant could invoke the remedy of appeal.[28] If Constantine thus allows for erroneous rulings, we should not presume that he expected his judges seriously to weigh the merits of an appeal made against them, for it was forbidden to consult the emperor once an appeal had been made.

Several constitutions demonstrate that Constantine expected appeals to be received virtually automatically. In a constitution dated to August 329, CTh. 11.30.13,[29] Constantine writes that judges should not send *consultationes* to the imperial court after an appeal has been lodged. The proper time for *consultatio* (not to be confused with *appellatio more consultationis*) was before a ruling had been delivered. Constantine baldly states, "We therefore wish that when their (*sc.* judges of low rank) rulings have been appealed, they should not send a *relatio* to Our Clemency concerning that case, of which they have ceased to be judges upon the submission of an appeal."[30] Although this letter to the urban prefect regulates the use of *consultationes*, which by their nature should be *ante sententiam*, Constantine implies that an appeal normally removed all discretionary power from the

25. Pergami, *Appello*, 391–94, citing (p. 394) R. Orestano, *L'appello civile in diritto romano* (Genoa, 1952), 364ff.

26. Cf. Pergami, *Appello*, 23–24 on CJ 7.62.6 pr.

27. On the hostility of judges to appeal, a very common theme of the Constantinian and late antique legislation in general, see below.

28. CTh. 11.29.1; quoted in chapter 7, pp. 199–200.

29. Date emended to 329 by Seeck, *Regesten*, 64; Barnes, *NE*, 78.

30. CTh. 11.30.13: *Igitur volumus, cum ab eorum sententiis fuerit provocatum, super ea quaestione, cuius appellatione interposita iudices esse desierunt, minime eos ad nostram referre clementiam.*

judge. Constantine clearly preferred that a case be brought to a higher court rather than permit the potential judge *a quo* to weigh the law further.

In CTh. 11.36.1, Constantine gives several grounds on which appeals could be denied by the judge *a quo*, but they appear rather as exceptions to a general principle stated at the beginning of the constitution: "Help must not be denied to those who appeal well."[31] In another fragment of the same constitution, preserved as CTh. 11.30.2, Constantine addresses defendants who must remain in custody while their appeals are pending. He writes, "Moderation is to be observed so that appeals made by those who are not found to have appealed from an interlocutory decision or prior to the examination and conclusion of the case . . . should be received."[32] Read with CTh. 11.36.1, this statement strongly suggests that all appeals, even in criminal proceedings, ought to be admitted, so long as the defendants had not been convicted of specific heinous crimes or convicted by overwhelming evidence or a confession.

Promotion of appeal helped Constantine to check the flood of extraordinary *supplicationes* to the imperial court, the last resort of a defendant after his appeal had been refused. Constantine threatens judges with harsh punishment if they are found to have rejected an appeal that should have been allowed.[33] Elsewhere Constantine urges litigants whose appeals had been disallowed to proceed directly to the praetorian prefects, whereupon their case should be heard "as if their appeal had been admitted."[34] The silence of the sources on the power of the judge *a quo* to evaluate the legal grounds of an appeal and the numerous statements in the imperial constitutions that support the granting of appeals generally leave little doubt that, as in the ordinary appellate procedure, so in *appellatio more consultationis,* the judge *a quo* checked the formal admissibility of an appeal, the judge *ad quem* the legal soundness of its claims.[35]

---

31. CTh. 11.36.1: . . . *bene appellantibus negari auxilium non oportet* . . .

32. CTh. 11.30.2: *Ea custodita moderatione, ut eorum provocationes recipiantur, qui easdem non a praeiudicio interposuisse noscuntur aut etiam ante causam examinatam et determinatam* . . . ; cf. K. L. Noethlichs, *Beamtentum und Dienstvergehen. Zur Staatsverwaltung in der Spätantike* (Wiesbaden, 1981), 167–68.

33. CTh. 11.30.6, discussed in chapter 7, pp. 211–12.

34. CTh. 11.30.16: *Quod si victus oblatam nec receptam a iudice appellationem adfirmet, praefectos adeat, ut aput eos de integro litiget tamquam appellatione suscepta.* Cf. chapter 4.

35. Litewski, IV, 168: "Die Frage der Zulässigkeit einer Appellation war gewöhnlich nicht mit der Frage ihrer sachlicher Rechtsmäßigkeit verbunden, derer Beurteilung zum Appellationsgericht gehörte"; specifically on *appellatio more consultationis,* IV, 262–63: "Eine ausreichende Grundlage bildete die Einlegung einer Appellation an den Kaiser. Die Frage der rechtlichen Zweifel war ohne Bedeutung."

The Opinio Iudicis

The procedure of *appellatio more consultationis* permitted the appellant to present the grounds for appeal against the ruling of the judge *a quo* within a dossier of documents destined for review at the imperial court. The dossier was introduced by a message from the judge to the emperor, called the *litterae* of the judge in one constitution.[36] This "letter," however, should be identified with the *opinio,* by which name the statement of the judge *a quo* is usually called. The term *opinio* appears most commonly with respect to the duty of the judge to prepare a copy of it for the appellant upon request. Several constitutions[37] speak of the "copy of the *opinio*" (*opinionis exemplum*) that the judge *a quo* was obliged to "provide"[38] (usually *edere*) to the appellant. The *opinio* of the judge was included in the dossier for the emperor itself. Although it would have been recorded in the *acta* of his *officium,* from which the appellant could receive a copy, the *opinio* must have served as a kind of cover letter for the entire appellate dossier rather than appear merely in the records of proceedings. Thus Constantine can speak of *rescripta nostra ad opiniones* in CTh. 11.30.9, a statement that shows the prominence of the *opinio* in the appellate dossier.

The appearance of the *opinio* of the judge *a quo* in legal sources that antedate the Constantinian legislation has caused some debate on its real nature. The most important of these sources is an excerpt by the jurist Macer, from the early third century:

> **Dig. 49.5.6 (Macer)**
>
> Sciendum est, cum appellatio non recipitur . . . [eum] qui appellationem non receperit, opinionem suam confestim per relationem manifestare et causam, pro qua non recepit appellationem, eiusque exemplum litigatori edere debere mandatis cavetur.
>
> One should know that, when an appeal is not admitted . . . it is required by the *mandata*[39] that [he] who has not admitted the appeal should immediately make

36. CTh. 11.30.16: . . . *ut appellanti iudex praebeat opinionis exemplum et acta cum refutatoriis partium suisque litteris ad nos dirigat.*

37. CTh. 11.30.6, 11.30.8 pr, 11.30.14, and 11.30.16.

38. Described as *opinionis editio* and *opinione edita* respectively in CTh. 11.30.11.1 and 11.30.18, with *exemplum . . . opinionis . . . exhibere* in CTh. 11.30.8 pr, and with *praebeat exemplum opinionis* in CTh. 11.30.16.

39. I.e., the general instructions of the emperor to provincial governors and other imperial officials. The jurists treat the *mandata* as a traditional body of instructions handed down from reign to reign, although the reigning emperor could modify them *ad libitum. Cf. Berger s.v. mandata principum.*

clear his *opinio* and the reason for which he did not admit the appeal in an official letter (*relatio*) and give a copy of it to the litigant.

The *opinio* of the judge *a quo* in this source appears to be a report on the rejection of an appeal. Macer avoids the word *sententia* ostensibly because a decision by the judge on the admissibility of an appeal does not constitute a ruling whereby a case is decided. *Opinio* is used in its general legal sense; it is the opinion of the judge on a legal question, here on the admissibility of the appeal made by the litigant.[40] A copy of the *opinio* is prepared for the unsuccessful appellant, and there the procedure ends. With this copy of the *opinio,* the party could exercise its right to proceed directly to a higher court (*adire; supplicare* at the court of the emperor) and there contest the ruling.[41]

The second piece of pre-Constantinian evidence for the *opinio* is an important edict of Diocletian, tentatively dated to 294, of which one fragment, CJ 7.62.6, addresses appeal at length.[42]

CJ 7.62.6.3

Super his vero, qui in capitalibus causis constituti appellaverint . . . id observandum esse sancimus, ut inopia idonei fideiussoris retentis in custodia reis opiniones suas iudices exemplo appellatoribus edito ac refutatorios eorum ad scrinia quorum interest transmittant.

We decree that the following shall be observed concerning those who have appealed in capital cases . . . that the judges should provide a copy of their opinions to appellants who are kept in custody for want of a suitable guarantor and send them (*sc.* the *opiniones*) and their (*sc.* the appellants') *refutatorii* to the bureaus to which they pertain.

This passage has been called the first example of *appellatio more consultationis,*[43] but to describe it as such is to overlook several differences from the mature procedure of *appellatio more consultationis* under Constantine. For one, the edict of Diocletian seeks to circumvent a significant limitation of the ordinary appellate procedure, the required presence of the appellant. The text presumes that the appellant not only is unable to secure his release

40. See Berger, s.v. *opiniones.*

41. Litewski, IV, 175–78.

42. For discussion of the formal problems of the fragments and the date of the edict, see Pergami, *Appello,* 15–22.

43. Litewski, IV, 256.

from custody but is also unable to find a third party to plead his case before the appellate court. The procedure outlined in the edict thus applies only to criminal cases in which appellants are unable to appear in person. The phrase *ad scrinia quorum interest* in the final line of the excerpt, as Pergami notes, further reveals that the edict applies to appeals not only to the emperor but to higher officials generally, such as vicars and the urban or praetorian prefects.[44] The procedure imposed by the edict is simultaneously narrower and broader in scope than *appellatio more consultationis* under Constantine.

The *opinio* procedure in the edict of Diocletian departs from that described by Macer. The *opinio* of the tetrarchic edict is not merely notice of the rejection of an appeal. The appeal is treated as if it has been granted; the *opinio* must be a recapitulation of the challenged ruling and, potentially, the arguments of the judge against the appeal. The role of the *opinio* of the judge in the edict of Diocletian closely resembles that played under Constantine. Constantine, however, adopts the *opinio* for appeals to the imperial court generally, not only for certain criminal cases in which the appellant could not secure release from custody.[45] Although appeals to Constantine would have required the composition of an *opinio* regardless, the edict of Diocletian may have remained in force for appellants who appealed to high officials such as the praetorian prefects according to the ordinary procedure. The inclusion of an *opinio* in a *relatio* when an appeal had been refused, as described by Macer, is also compatible with *appellatio more consultationis* and may have remained in use.

Several of the constitutions of Constantine on appeal make mention of the *opinio* of the judge as an integral part of the proceedings. In CTh. 11.30.6, Constantine forbids a litigant to resort to *supplicatio* unless a copy of the *opinio* has been denied him or part of the appeal dossier (*universa instructio*) has been suppressed.[46] The *opinio* of the judge cannot be a mere declaration of inadmissibility, for the judge who "imposes the necessity of supplication on the litigant" faces a charge of sacrilege for violating the or-

44. Pergami, *Appello,* 30.

45. Pergami, ibid., 100–102, suggests that Constantine was also aware of the rule described in Macer but regarded it as a *consuetudo prisca* (CTh. 11.30.18). Pergami finds no reason for the inclusion of the *opinio,* which he interprets as a declaration of inadmissibility, in all appeals: "In sostanza si veniva, così, ad appesantire senza un serio motivo il procedimento di gravame" (102). This redundancy is eliminated, however, if one distinguishes between the procedures *appellatio more consultationis* and ordinary appeal.

46. CTh. 11.30.6: *Supplicare causa pendente non licet nisi forte ei, cui opinionis exemplum negatum est vel instructionis universae subpressa transmissio.*

ders of the emperor.[47] The *opinio* is thus both included in the *instructio* sent to the emperor and made available to the litigant beforehand to facilitate the composition of his counterarguments: *libelli refutatorii.*[48]

CTh. 11.30.8, which addresses the procedures of both *appellatio more consultationis* and *consultatio ante sententiam,* begins with reference to a previous constitution:

> CTh. 11.30.8 pr
>
> Manente lege, qua praescriptum est, intra quot dies opinionis sive relationis exemplum privatis iudex debeat exhibere et refutatorii libelli intra quot dies rursum iudicibus offerendi sint, tam in privatis quam etiam in fiscalibus causis ex eo die, quo fuerit quaestio terminata vel ex quo relationem iudex per sententiam promiserit, intra vicensimum diem quaecumque ad instructionem pertinent causae, ad comitatum nostrum properantissime volumus adferri.
>
> The law remaining in force whereby it is prescribed within how many days a judge should present a copy of his *opinio* or *relatio* to litigants in private suits and, vice versa, within how many days *libelli refutatorii* are to be delivered to the judges, We wish, that everything that pertains to the documentation of a case be brought to Our court within twenty days, reckoning from the day on which the case was decided or from the day on which the judge promised a *relatio* by interlocutory decision, both in private and in fiscal cases.

The law to which Constantine refers has since Gothofredus plausibly been identified as CTh. 11.30.1, but this identification has recently been questioned on the grounds that CTh. 11.30.1 addresses only *consultatio ante sententiam.*[49] This objection loses much of its force, however, if one allows that CTh. 11.30.8 addresses both *consultatio ante sententiam* and *consultatio more appellationis.* This is made clear by the phrase *opinionis sive relationis exemplum* and the words *appellatione vel consultatione pendente* in the following paragraph. Since the procedures were largely identical, it is preferable to assume that the original text of CTh. 11.30.1 originally discussed both the *consultatio* and *appellatio more consultationis.*

Opinio in subsequent constitutions of Constantine's consistently accords with a statement by the judge on the grounds for his ruling and the

---

47. On this law, see chapter 7, pp. 211–12.
48. Contra Pergami, *Appello,* 94–95.
49. Ibid., 96.

merit of the appellant's case. CTh. 11.30.9, written to the vicar of Italy in June 318,[50] stipulates that the dossiers for both consultations and *appellaio more consultationis* should contain all necessary documents in the records of the case.[51] The inclusion of this material guarantees, in principle, that the ruling of the emperor, which cannot be appealed, will be founded on the same information as that available to the judge of the first instance. Pergami interprets the expression *opiniones vel etiam relationes* as reference to two aspects of the activity of the judge. The jurist Macer, writing on the ordinary appellate procedure, noted that the judge should send his reasons for the inadmissibility of an appeal (*opinio*) *per relationem.*[52] Pergami concludes that the passage in question should similarly refer to the *relatio* in which the declaration of inadmissibility, the *opinio,* appears.[53] This solution, however, fails to explain the expression *rescribta nostra ad opiniones vel etiam relationes iudicum data.*[54] If one rejects the existence of *appellatio more consultationis,* there is no explanation. If, on the other hand, one grants the existence of *appellatio more consultationis* as a distinct procedure for appeals to the emperor, the confusion evaporates: by a kind of metonymy (*appellatio more consultationis* has no distinct name in the legal sources),[55] *opinio* merely refers to the statement of the judge on the case, which in the procedure of *appellatio more consultationis* takes the place of the *litterae dimissoriae* of the ordinary appellate procedure. Constantine juxtaposes precisely *appellatio* and *consultatio* in CJ 3.11.5 to refer to these distinct procedures. He begins, "When a rescript in response to an appeal or *consultatio* has been sent . . ."[56] Why would Constantine issue a rescript in response to an appeal, unless he were not physically present?

The importance of the *opinio* of the judge in the procedure of *appellatio more consultationis* is underscored in CTh. 11.30.11 (a. 321).[57] This fragment contains a noteworthy rebuke of the urban prefect Maximus, which

50. See chapter 7, p. 207 for the text.

51. CTh. 11.30.9: *instructiones necessarias plene actis inseri praecipimus.*

52. Dig. 49.5.6, cited above.

53. Pergami, *Appello,* 98.

54. Ibid., 98–99: "Ma resta, allora, inspiegabile . . . "

55. Litewski, IV, 262–63: "[Die *consultatio*] wurde auch mit anderen Ausdrücken bezeichnet, die bei der *consultatio ante sententiam* gebildet worden sind, wie *relatio, opinio, suggestio* entgegen ihrer Benennung keine Anfrage, sondern war ein sachlicher Bericht." Pergami's criticism of Litewski on this point (*Appello,* 98 n. 92) misses the mark.

56. CJ 3.11.5: *Cum a nobis fuerit ad appellationem consultationemve rescriptum* . . . Pergami seems to have overlooked this constitution.

57. Seeck, *Regesten,* 61 and 100, emends the month of the issue of this constitution; Barnes, *NE* 75.

follows another section, preserved as CTh. 2.18.1, describing at length how a judge should conduct a trial[58]:

CTh. 11.30.11.1

> Sane etiam ex eo querimoniae litigantium oriuntur, quod a vobis, qui imaginem principalis disceptationis accipitis, appellationum adminicula respuuntur. Quod inhiberi necesse est. Quid enim acerbius indigniusque est, quam indulta quempiam potestate ita per iactantiam insolescere, ut despiciatur utilitas provocationis, opinionis editio denegetur, refutandi copia respuatur?
>
> Indeed complaints also arise from the fact that the bulwarks of appeal are rejected by you, you who receive the likeness of imperial jurisdiction. This must be stopped. For what is bitterer and more outrageous than that one granted a power should sit idle through arrogance so that the utility of appeal is despised, release of the *opinio* is denied, and the occasion to refute rejected?

The complaints of litigants whose appeals had been rejected by Maximus apparently found their way to the ears of the emperor, perhaps via the praetorian prefects, by supplication, or by personally approaching the imperial court. Although the urban prefect judged *vice sacra* (*qui imaginem principalis disceptationis accipitis*), unlike the rulings of the praetorian prefects, his own remained subject to appeal to the emperor. Such an appeal would have followed the usual procedure of *appellatio more consultationis.* Refusal to provide a potential appellant with the *opinio* would either effectively stall appellate proceedings entirely or make it impossible for the appellant to respond to the ruling of the judge in his own statement, in the *libelli refutatorii.*

CTh. 11.30.14 (a. 327) similarly illustrates the importance of the *opinio* and *libelli refutatorii* (here called *preces refutatoriae*) in the procedure of *appellatio more consultationis.* CTh. 11.30.14, addressed to the *rationalis urbis Romae,* states that debtors of the *fiscus,* who register an appeal against the collection of their debts, yet fail to request the *opinio* of the judge or offer *preces refutatoriae* by the established deadlines, will be deemed to have abandoned their appeal. The thrust of the letter is to prevent the delay of the collection of such debts by moratory appeals (*appellationes moratoriae*). Failure to request the *opinio* of the judge (and consequently to draft one's response) renders the appeal toothless and reveals the true intentions of the

58. Discussed in chapter 6, pp. 202–5.

appellant.[59] The earnestness of an appeal is presumed to appear in the request for the *opinio,* without which the success of an appeal would be jeopardized.

CTh. 11.30.18, which has been discussed in part above, also concerns fiscal trials, establishing an alternative procedure for cases in which a *rationalis* comes to preside over cases of civil law. In strictly fiscal cases, Constantine requires that "the old custom" should be followed, namely that after the *opinio* has been made available, the judge should send all materials pertinent to the case to the imperial court.[60]

Finally, in CTh. 11.30.16, from an important edict of 331 to the provincials of the empire, the *opinio* again is cited as a main feature of appeals to the emperor. Constantine states that appeals are permitted from the proconsuls, *comites,* and vicars, all of whom judged *vice sacra;* the judge should provide a copy of his *opinio* to the appellant and send the *acta,* the *libelli* (or *preces*) *refutatorii* of the litigants, and his own "letter" to the imperial court.[61] The letter of the judge should not be identified as *litterae dimissoriae* of the ordinary appellate procedure; it would appear that the chancellery uses *litterae* to avoid repetition of *opinio,* which also must be sent to the imperial court.[62] *Litterae dimissoriae* figure nowhere in the procedure of *appellatio more consultationis,* for the *opinio* of the judge makes them redundant.

Libelli Refutatorii *and* Acta

The justification of an appeal by the appellant was framed as a response to the *opinio* of the judge and was denoted *libelli refutatorii* or *preces refutato-*

---

59. R. Delmaire, *Largesses Sacrées et res privata. L'aerarium impérial et son administration du IVe au VIe siècle* (Rome, 1989), 85–86.

60. CTh. 11.30.18: *in fiscalibus causis servato priscae consuetudinis more, ut opinione edita universa ad nostram scientiam referantur.*

61. CTh. 11.30.16: *A proconsulibus et comitibus et his qui vice praefectorum cognoscunt, sive ex appellatione sive ex delegato sive ex ordine iudicaverint, provocari permittimus, ita ut appellanti iudex praebeat opinionis exemplum et acta cum refutatoriis partium suisque litteris ad nos dirigat.* The force of *permittimus* is that of the statement of a fact, not of an innovation; cf. M. Balestri Fumagalli, "Il divieto di appello contro le sentenze dei prefetti del pretorio (C. Th. 11, 30, 16)," in *Atti del II Seminario Romanistico Gardesano* (Milan, 1980), 213–30; Pergami, *Appello,* 110–12.

62. Contra Pergami, *Appello,* 100, who interprets the *litterae* of CTh. 11.30.16 precisely as *litterae dimissoriae.* He cannot explain the apparent change in procedure from CTh. 11.30.18, where (under the name *apostoli*) *litterae dimissoriae* are required for appeals in civil suits from the *rationalis* to the urban prefect, in accordance with the ordinary appellate procedure, while the presentation of an *opinio* is required in appeals in fiscal suits from the *rationalis* to the emperor.

riae, mention of which has been made above. This document is essentially identical to the *libelli refutatorii* of the procedure of the *consultatio ante sententiam*, save that the response of the appellant to the judge falls in the context, not of a decision to be made, but of a ruling to be reconsidered by the emperor.[63] On the presumption, discussed in the preceding section, that CTh. 11.30.1 also regulates submission deadlines of the appellate process, the appellant will have had five days to submit his *libelli refutatorii* after receipt of the copy of the *opinio* of the judge. In contrast to the ordinary appellate procedure, new material could not be included in the *libelli refutatorii*.[64] The impossibility of evaluating the veracity of new evidence at the imperial court led Constantine to declare emphatically that litigants should include only material that had been produced before the judge *a quo*.[65]

Libelli refutatorii, like the *opinio* of the judge, occur already in the edict of Diocletian concerning appeals in criminal cases, in which the appellants must remain under custody;[66] they appear to have been introduced to the procedure of *appellatio more consultationis* generally by Constantine. *Libelli refutatorii* are a fundamental element of the procedure and appear in a number of constitutions discussed above.[67] CTh. 11.30.14 illustrates the importance of the preparation of *libelli refutatorii*: as with the petition for a copy of the *opinio* of the judge, failure to compose *libelli refutatorii* is regarded by Constantine as grounds for the dismissal of an appeal as *moratoria*.[68]

The final component of the appellate dossier to be sent to the imperial court is the documentation of the trial itself, the *acta* or *gesta*.[69] Again, *appellatio more consultationis* adheres to the model of the *consultatio ante sententiam* in that full records, variously denoted *instructio plena*,[70] *instructio universa*,[71] *instructiones necessariae*,[72] *integra instructio*,[73] or simply *uni-*

63. On *libelli refutatorii* for *consultatio ante sententiam*, see chapter 7, pp. 204–5.

64. Contra Pergami, *Appello*, 380–82, who considers CTh. 11.30.11 as relevant only to the *consultatio ante sententiam*. The words *consulti ordo* and *relatio*, with which Constantine refers to the documents that prompt his rescripts, apply respectively to both the procedure of *consultatio ante sententiam* and *appellatio more consultationis*.

65. Litewski, IV, 268.

66. CJ 7.62.6.3, cited above.

67. CTh. 11.30.11.1, 11.30.8 pr, 11.30.14, 11.30.16.

68. See above, n. 23 and p. 228.

69. *Gesta*: CTh. 11.30.5; *acta*: CTh. 11.30.9, 11.30.11 pr, 11.30.16. See also chapter 7.

70. CTh. 2.18.1.

71. CTh. 11.30.6

72. CTh. 11.30.9.

73. CTh. 11.30.11 pr.

versa,[74] be sent to the imperial court. Constantine established a period of twenty days from the delivery of a ruling, in the event of an appeal, or from the declaration of the judge to consult the emperor, in the event of a *consultatio ante sententiam*, for everything that pertained to the case to be sent to the imperial court.[75] CTh. 11.30.11 pr gives us a fair picture of the material to be included in the dossier: "Thus all allegations of the parties, all records of proceedings, and copies of all documents should be dispatched."[76]

Such, in broad strokes, was the procedure of appeal to the emperor in the time of Constantine. The emphasis on deadlines, both for appellant and judge *a quo*, suggests that the emperor anticipated an expedited procedure. The judge had ten days to produce his *opinio*, the appellant five to compose his *libelli refutatorii*, and, after twenty days in all, the entire dossier had to be sent *properantissime* to the imperial court.[77] The emperor might also condescend to personal admonishment. In one text, a fragment of a letter to the proconsul of Africa, who presided *vice sacra*, Constantine explicitly orders the proconsul to decide appellate cases *quam maturissime*. This source refers, of course, to the ordinary appellate system, for the proconsul is hearing appeals, not the emperor. Regardless, speed was an element vital to both processes, as attested by the care with which Constantine regulated the appellate system.

Restrictions on Appeal: Supplicatio *and* Praeiudicia

The Codex Theodosianus contains a number of special restrictions on appeals and special circumstances in which appeals may, or may not, be made. In an edict of 331, Constantine forbids all provincials to seek a new ruling by appealing to the emperor through *supplicatio*, if they had failed to register an appeal. Constantine minces no words: whosoever makes such an "impudent" supplication "ought to keep silent for ever." The severe penalty for such a *supplicatio*, deportation, reflects the fervor with which

74. CTh. 11.30.18.

75. CTh. 11.30.8 pr: . . . *ex eo die, quo fuerit quaestio terminata vel ex quo relationem iudex per sententiam promiserit, intra vicensimum diem quaecumque ad instructionem pertinent causae, ad comitatum nostrum properantissime volumus adferri.*

76. CTh. 11.30.11 pr: *Omnes igitur partium allegationes acta universa scripturarumque exempla omnium dirigantur* (sc. *ad nos* vel *ad comitatum*).

77. Ten days for *opinio*, five for *libelli refutatorii*: CTh. 11.30.1 with CTh. 11.30.8 pr; twenty days for the entire dossier: CTh. 11.30.8 pr. See chapter 7 and below for penalties.

Constantine promoted the appellate system generally.[78] In another fragment of the same edict, Constantine declares that the allegation of judicial intimidation cannot justify a supplication after failure to register an appeal.[79] The edict specifically addresses supplications against the rulings of judges who presided *vice sacra*.[80] Constantine orders that the supplicant be deported and his property confiscated in such cases. According to the notional identity of these courts with the imperial court itself, the allegation of intimidation is indirectly made against the emperor himself.[81] It is unclear whether a similar prohibition was in force before the publication of the edict. The edict of 331 appears to supplant CTh. 11.30.6, in which Constantine orders that half the property of the litigant or the object sought in the suit be confiscated, if a supplication was made before final judgment had been reached.[82] However, it seems most plausible to interpret the harshness of the penalty as an attempt to stifle all such supplications made after appeal had been omitted and supplications coupled with allegations of intimidation. The previous penalty in CTh. 11.30.6 will have still applied to pedestrian cases of unlawful supplication made before a final ruling had been delivered.[83]

More prominent than restrictions on the occasions of appeal are those on the object of the appeal; in other words, against whatever particulars the

78. CTh. 11.30.17: *Qui licitam provocationem omiserit, perpetuo silere debebit nec a nobis inpudens petere per supplicationem auxilium. Quod si fecerit, deportationis poena plectendus est.* Justinian reduced this penalty to *ignominia* (CJ 1.21.3).

79. CTh. 11.34.1: *In insulam deportandi sunt cum amissione omnium facultatum, quae fisco addicendae sunt, ii, qui provocatione omissa litem reparare temptaverint contra comitum ceterorumque sententias qui vice nostra iudicaverint, firmantes se per metum appellationis omisisse auxilium. In qua re vel nostrum vel praefectorum praetorio ex nostra erit iussione iudicium.* Cf. the discussion of Pergami, *Appello*, 115–18, on this and the preceding fragment; also C. Dupont, "Constantin et les constitutions impériales," in *St. Volterra*, vol. 1 (Milan, 1971), 560.

80. This appears to be what distinguishes CTh. 11.34.1 from 11.30.17. See Gothofredus, *ad* CTh. 11.30.17, who notes that it concerns *iudices ordinarii*.

81. Cf. CTh. 11.30.3: *Appellationum causas, quae per vos in auditorio nostro, quibus vicem nostri mandamus examinis, diiudicantur;* CTh. 11.30.11 pr: *sublimitatem tuam, qui cognitionibus nostram vicem repraesentas;* CTh. 11.30.11.1: (*vos*) *qui imaginem principalis disceptationis accipitis;* CTh. 11.30.13: *gravitatis tuae, cui nostram vicem commisimus, sacrum auditorium expectari* (*volumus*); CTh. 11.36.3: *causam autem universam . . . sine ulla dilatione discingas, cum in nostro auditorio dari minime dilationem oporteat;* CJ 3.13.4: *appellatione legibus facta ad sacrum auditorium* (sc. *iudicis spectabilis*) *veniat.* CJ 3.11.5 is particularly striking, in which Constantine refuses *dilatio* to be granted to a litigant who has received an imperial rescript in response to an appeal or *consultatio: eadem ratione, qua nec in iudiciis quidem cognitionum nostrarum dilatio tribui solet.*

82. CTh. 11.30.6: *cui aliter supplicanti dimidiae partis rei de qua agitur inponenda est multa.*

83. Cf. De Marini Avonzo, "Giustizia II," 220–21; Dupont, "Constantin et les constitutions impériales," 560.

appellant makes his appeal. Even these limitations are framed as restrictions on the timing of the appeal. Above all, Constantine forbids appeals against *praeiudicia* or *articuli*. The—here, apparently synonymous—terms *praeiudicia* and *articuli* denote interlocutory decisions made by the judge in the course of the trial.[84] *Praeiudicium* is also used of intermediary rulings that might affect the outcome of the principal trial, but in either case, Constantine advertises his confidence that the appellate system could resolve such questions. He prohibits all appeals before the *definitiva sententia*, the final ruling of the judge.[85]

Constantine first mentions the prohibition of appeals against *praeiudicia* in a letter to Catullinus, dated to 313.[86] Constantine forbids appeals *a praeiudiciis* or *ab articulis* in two fragments of this letter, CTh. 11.30.2 and CTh. 11.36.1.[87] In two later constitutions, prohibition of appeal *a praeiudiciis* is coupled with a further prohibition on appeal against the execution of the ruling, *ab executione* or *ab executoribus*. The first constitution, CTh. 11.36.2, sent to the urban prefect and published in Rome in 315, establishes a fine of thirty *folles* for anyone who has appealed an interlocutory decision or the execution of a ruling. Emphasis again is laid on the timing of the appeal, which is described as being made against the executors of "things already established" (*rerum antea statutarum*); petition for the settlement of the case before another judge is described as hastily made (*praepropere*), that is, falling before the definitive ruling of the judge of the first instance.[88]

CTh. 11.36.3, published in Carthage in 315,[89] is directly related to CTh.

---

84. Kaser-Hackl, §93.II.1, p. 608; cf. Berger, s.v. *interlocutio*.

85. The term *definitiva sententia* is postclassical: Kaser-Hackl, §93.II.1, p. 608; Berger, s.v. *definitiva sententia*. Cf. CJ 3.13.4: *Nemo post litem contestataem ordinariae sedis declinet examen, nec prius praefecti praetorio aut comitis Orientis vel alterius spectabilis iudicis imploret auxilium, sed appellatione legibus facta ad sacrum auditorium veniat.*

86. Cf. Corcoran, *ET*², 162.

87. CTh. 11.30.2: . . . *ut eorum provocationes recipiantur, qui easdem non a praeiudicio interposuisse noscuntur aut etiam ante causam examinatam et determinatam* . . . ; CTh. 11.36.1: *Qui de variis litibus causisque dissentiunt, nec temere, nec ab articulis praeiudiciisque . . . provocare debebunt.* Pergami, *Appello*, 67–68, partly following Gradenwitz (68 n. 37), considers this sentence to be an interpolation added by the Theodosian compilers, to accommodate CTh. 11.36.1 to CTh. 11.30.2. This, however, is unlikely, and the unoriginality or redundancy of the sentence itself is not an argument against its authenticity.

88. CTh. 11.36.2: *Qui a praeiudicio appellaverit vel ab executoribus rerum antea statutarum atque alterius auditorii praepropere iudicia poposcerit* . . . The coordinate clause, *atque . . . poposcerit*, properly compliments the first object of the appeal, the *praeiudicium;* appeal against the execution of the ruling should instead have been characterized as late (e.g., *sero*, as used in CTh. 11.36.3: *qui sero ab exsecutoribus provocant*). The words *vel ab executoribus rerum antea statutarum* are perhaps a later edition.

89. Seeck, *Regesten*, 60 and 64.

11.36.2, although the precise nature of the relationship between them is difficult to determine. Seeck argues that both constitutions are different versions of the same imperial decree.[90] Constantine informs the proconsul of Africa of a previous "law on appeals" (*lex de appellationibus data*) that prohibits him from admitting appeals *a praeiudicio vel ab executione;* so too in CTh. 11.36.2 Constantine adjures the urban prefect to follow the protocol "that has already been most evidently established by Us."[91] The edict that contained this regulation of appeal has not survived. Peachin has argued that it was issued some time in 314 and is likely to have been the same edict in which Constantine established the *vice sacra* jurisdiction of the urban and praetorian prefects, the proconsuls, and the diocesan administrators, the vicars and *comites.*[92] The prohibition on appeals against interlocutory decisions will thus have figured prominently in the general reorganization of the appellate procedure itself.

Restrictions on Appeal: Criminal Cases

Other restrictions on appeal were established for persons convicted of certain capital crimes. The earliest constitution to define these crimes, CTh. 11.36.1, antedates even the constitutions that forbid appeals against *praeiudicia.* In this constitution, issued only a year after Constantine had defeated Maxentius, Constantine states that those who "appeal well" should receive help.[93] In context, however, this maxim is the counterpart to those whose appeals are empty and vain.[94] The antithesis justifies the prohibitions that follow:

> **CTh. 11.36.1**
>
> Unde cum homicidam vel adulterum vel maleficum vel veneficum, quae atrocissima facinora sunt, confessio propria vel dilucida et probatissima veritatis quaestio probationibus atque argumentis detexerit, provocationes suscipi non

---

90. Seeck, *Regesten,* 60; cf. C. Dupont, "Le domaine géographique d'application des textes constantiniennes," *IVRA* 18 (1967), 38–39; J. Gaudemet, "Recherches sur la législation du Bas-Empire," in *St. Scherillo,* vol. 2 (Milan, 1972), 696–97 (= *Études,* vol. 1 [1979], 218–19); J. Gaudemet, "Les constitutions constantiniennes du Code Théodosien," *AARC* 5 (1983), 148.

91. CTh. 11.36.2: . . . *observare debebis, quod iam pridem a nobis est evidentissime constitutum.*

92. Peachin, *Iudex vice Caesaris,* 194–96.

93. See above, p. 222.

94. CTh. 11.36.1: *Nam sicut bene appellantibus negari auxilium non oportet, ita his, contra quos merito iudicatum est, inaniter provocantibus differri bene gesta non decet.*

oportet, quas constat non refutandi spem habere quae gesta sunt, sed ea potius differre temptare.

Wherefore, when a personal confession or a clear and with proof and evidence most thoroughly proven investigation reveals a murderer or adulterer or evil-doer or sorcerer,[95] which are the most heinous crimes [*sic*], (their) appeals are not to be admitted, which it is clear have no hope of refuting what has been done (by the court) but attempt rather to delay it.

The conditions for the rejection of such appeals are elaborated further in CTh. 9.40.1, which derives from the same text:

CTh. 9.40.1

Qui sententiam laturus est, temperamentum hoc teneat, ut non prius capitalem in quempiam promat severamque sententiam, quam in adulterii vel homicidii vel maleficii crimen aut sua confessione aut certe omnium, qui tormentis vel interrogationibus fuerint dediti, in unum conspirantem concordantemque rei finem convictus sit et sic in obiecto flagitio deprehensus, ut vix etiam ipse ea quae commiserit negare sufficiat.

He who is about to deliver a ruling should exercise restraint as follows, namely he should not deliver a capital and harsh ruling against anyone until he (*sc.* the defendant) has been convicted of adultery or homicide or sorcery either by his own confession or surely by that of all those who were subjected to torture or interrogation, leading to a unanimous and unvarying conclusion of the case, and is thus caught in the outrage alleged against him so that he himself can scarcely deny what he has done.

The Constantinian regime prosecuted the crimes to which the constitution refers with exceptional zeal; possible motives for this policy have been the subject of much discussion.[96] Relevant here are the circumstances in which a judge is not bound to the policy of admitting appeals that satisfy formal requirements. In both constitutions, despite the indignation of the emperor,

95. These last two terms are generally synonymous, although it is just possible that a difference of method may be implied, the *maleficus* working through incantations, the *veneficus* using potions or herbs. Only *maleficus* appears in CTh. 9.40.1, which belongs to the same original as CTh. 11.36.1.

96. C. Dupont, *Le droit criminel dans les constitutions de Constantin. Les Infractions* (Lille, 1953), 32–36; C. Dupont, *Le droit criminel dans les constitutions de Constantin. Les Peines* (Lille, 1955), 25–26; on adultery, see esp. Evans-Grubbs, *Law and Family,* 205–21.

who calls the crimes "most heinous crimes" (*atrocissima facinora*) and "outrage" (*flagitium*), the judge is constrained to reject appeal only on the most rigorous proof. The trial or investigation (*quaestio*), including torture, receives its own superlative in CTh. 11.36.1 with regard to the proof accumulated against the accused: it must be *probatissima*. In both fragments, the confession of the accused suffices. In CTh. 11.36.1, Constantine emphasizes the role of evidence (*probationes atque argumenta*); in CTh. 9.40.1, he elaborates on the torture and interrogation that undoubtedly would have constituted part of the evidence collected. Yet in CTh. 9.40.1, Constantine stresses the unanimity of even these "witnesses": their testimony must agree in all particulars. These stringent requirements serve to satisfy the presuppositions upon which the denial of appeal rests. As stated in CTh. 11.36.1, it must be established (*constat*) that such appeals have no prospect of success but merely attempt to delay the inevitable; according to CTh. 9.40.1, the evidence in support of conviction should be so great that even the defendant cannot deny his guilt.

Abuse of Appeal from Below

The long exposition of grounds for rejecting appeals preserved in CTh. 11.36.1 and CTh. 9.40.1 shows an appreciation of the delicacy required in limiting an appellate system that otherwise, barring formal errors, universally permitted dissatisfied litigants the opportunity to seek redress before a higher court. Constantine augmented and promoted the appellate system by means of new *iudices vice sacra*, placing a judge with imperial authority in every diocese of the empire. Constantine further expedited appeals to the imperial court itself by streamlining a process that ideally should have provided the emperor with all materials and statements necessary for delivering a ruling per rescript.

Constantine moved to protect this system from abuse and manipulation. The opening words of CTh. 11.36.1 capture his indignation at the perversion of the appellate system: "It is inappropriate to admit moratory and frustratory delays, (which are) not so much appeals as they are mockeries."[97] The appellate system devised by Constantine attempts to reach a compromise between the guarantee of justice embodied in appeal and the protection of the appellate system. The danger that appeals might unjustly

97. CTh. 11.36.1: *Moratorias dilationes frustratoriasque non tam appellationes quam ludificationes admitti non convenit.* On these, see above n. 23 and p. 228.

be denied should not be exaggerated; because admissibility rested on formal criteria, the potential for injustice should not have exceeded that already inherent in the procedure of *appellatio more consultationis.* Confronted with a dossier including the confession of the appellant, the unanimous testimony of witnesses, or an unassailable burden of proof, the Constantinian chancellery would no doubt have confirmed the ruling of the judge. By confining the exceptions to so narrow a circle of crimes and subjecting them to the most stringent evidentiary standards, Constantine could both accelerate the rendering of justice and spare the imperial court unnecessary paperwork.[98] Aside from such lost causes, Constantine encouraged appeals to his court unequivocally. Appeals furnished him ready material to exercise and affirm power and authority. Reform of appeal might indeed benefit provincials, but Constantine also profited from their dependence.

Lest there remain any ambiguity, Constantine outlines the state of evidence when final judgment should be reserved to himself:

CTh. 11.36.1

Quod si reus in homicidii vel maleficii vel adulterii vel veneficii crimine partem pro defensione sui ex testibus quaestioneque proposita possit arripere, parte vero obrui accusarique videatur, tunc super interposita appellatione ab eodem, qui sibi magis, quae pro se faciant, testimonia prodesse debere adfirmat, quam ea, quae adversus ipsum egerint, nocere, deliberationi nostrae plenum arbitrium relinquatur.

If the defendant of a charge of homicide or magic or adultery or sorcery may seize upon part of the witnesses and interrogation for his own defense, but seems in part to be crushed and incriminated (by them), then full discretion should be left for Our deliberation concerning the appeal lodged by him, who asserts that the evidence that is in his favor should benefit him more than that which has worked against him should harm him.

The same unimpeachable evidence is assumed in three other cases in which appeal is forbidden. In 317,[99] Constantine wrote to the proconsul of Africa

98. Mommsen's disdain, *StrR.*, 470, is misplaced, "Es ist dem Unterrichter wenigstens in dem geschärften und verwilderten Prozess der Spätzeit freigestellt, nach abgelegtem Geständniss und sogar bei ausreichend erbrachtem Schuldbeweis ohne dies die Appellation als bloss verschleppend abzulehnen."

99. See Seeck, *Regesten*, 67.

that anyone convicted of *vis manifesta* would no longer be punished by relegation or deportation to an island but would be executed: nor may the offender suspend the sentence delivered against him by registering an appeal.[100] Constantine appears to have abandoned this innovation soon after. CTh. 9.10.3, issued only two years later, prescribes deportation and confiscation of the property of the guilty party, making no mention of the previous enactment. Constantius claims in a later constitution that Constantine "interpreted the words of his law" in other, later enactments, as if CTh. 9.10.3, to which it appears to refer, were such an explanation.[101]

The crimes of counterfeiting and *raptus* were also inappellable, as established in CTh. 9.21.2 (a. 320)[102] and 9.24.1 (a. 320) respectively.[103] Both constitutions encourage the public to denounce offenders with the promise of immunity, presumably from prosecution under Constantine's own prohibitions against delation,[104] and the advancement of legal status for humble accusers.[105] CTh. 9.21.2 denies appeal to *humiliores; honestiores* are to be reported to the emperor.[106] CTh. 9.24.1 flatly forbids the hearing of any appeal made by one convicted beyond the shadow of a doubt (*indubitate*) of *raptus*.[107] This last word, *indubitate*, brings CTh. 9.24.1 in harmony with

---

100. CTh. 9.10.1: *nec interposita provocatione sententiam quae in eum fuerit dicta suspendat.*

101. CTh. 11.36.14: *Plectatur, inquit, qui manifestam detegitur commisisse violentiam. Quae legis suae verba aliis quoque scitis clemens conditor explanavit. Etenim vigorem vindictae differri post totius negotii exitum noluit, scilicet ut, si procacem vesaniam principalis negotii discussio publicasset, convictum reum aut medietatis amissio aut sors deportationis adfligeret;* on CTh. 9.10.1–3: Dupont, *Réglementation,* 57–59.

102. Seeck, *Regesten,* 62, emends the date to 318; Barnes, *NE,* 103, follows *PLRE* I, Ianuarius 1, in making 320 the date of publication in Rome; Corcoran, *ET*², 311, follows Krüger in CJ 7.13.2 and 9.24.1, in dating the publication to 321.

103. On these constitutions in this context, see J. Gaudemet, "De la responsabilité pénale dans la législation post-classique," in *Sodalitas: Scr. Guarino,* vol. 6 (Naples, 1984), 2570–71 (= *Droit et Société* [1992], 232–33).

104. CTh. 10.10.1–3. Comparable exceptions were made for the denunciation of haruspices operating in a private capacity (CTh. 9.16.1) and of women who had sexual relationships with slaves (CTh. 9.9.1). Constantine restricts the denunciation of adulterers to family members in CTh. 9.7.2. On delation under Constantine, J. Gaudemet, "La répression de la délation au Bas-Empire," in *Φιλίας χάριν: Miscellanea de studi classici in onore di Eugenio Manni,* vol. 3 (Rome, 1980), 1065–83 (= *Droit et Société* [1992], 157–73); T. Spagnuolo Vigorita, *Exsecranda pernicies. Delatori e fisco nell'età di Costantino* (Naples, 1984).

105. Roman citizenship (CTh. 9.21.2); Latin status for slaves or full citizenship for Latins (CTh. 9.24.1). Cf. M. Sargenti, *Il diritto privato nella legislazione di Constantino: persone e famiglia* (Milan, 1938), 71–72.

106. CTh. 9.21.2.3: *Appellandi etiam privato licentia denegetur; si vero miles aut promotus huiusmodi crimen incurrerit, super eius nomine et gradu ad nos referatur.*

107. CTh. 9.24.1.3: *Raptor autem indubitate convictus si appellare voluerit, minime audiatur.*

the evidentiary requirements of the constitutions discussed above. It seems reasonable to presume that the same guidelines applied to convictions of counterfeiting.

Punishment for Failed Appeals?

The constitution CTh. 1.5.3 (a. 331) has attracted much attention because Constantine appears to punish unsuccessful appellants indiscriminately, *honestiores* by a two-year sentence of relegation to an island, *humiliores* by two years of hard labor in the mines. Already Bethmann-Hollweg deplored the extreme severity of such a penalty, which Justinian subsequently reduced.[108] The prospect of such a penalty would have stifled the entire appellate system, rendering appeal feasible only to those whose conviction of the merit of their case or confidence in success was unshakeable and absolute. Such consequences for failure would make Constantine's numerous exclamations in support of appeal disingenuous in the extreme.

The interpretation of Bethmann-Hollweg remains dominant,[109] but the text of CTh. 1.5.3 may not in fact refer to appeal.

CTh. 1.5.3

[IMP. CONSTANTINVS] A. AD BASSVM PRAEFECTVM PRAETORIO. Super his, qui a praeside vel a quolibet alio iudice sententiam dictam infirmari deposcunt, sub eo fine sublimitatis tuae succeda<n>t[110] examen, ut, si internis negotii usquequaque decursis ex evidenti claruerit, sententiam a iure iustitiaque discedere, ea penitus explosa controversia de aequitate terminum capiat. Quod si consentanea sit legibus iam prompta sententia, eius pronuntiationis inprobus oppugnator, si patrimonio circumfluit, biennio in insulam relegatione plectatur eiusque bonorum media portio fiscalibus conpendiis addicta cedat: quod si agrestis vitae sit aut etiam egentis, ad biennii tempus in metal-

108. Bethmann-Hollweg, *Civilprozeß*, vol. 3, p. 337.

109. E.g., Kaser-Hackl, §95.I.3, p. 621 n. 38 (citing CTh. 1.5.3: "Justinian übernimmt statt dessen Diocl. C. 7.62.6.4: Der Richter soll nach seinem Ermessen eine mäßige Strafe festsetzen"); C. Kelly, *Ruling the Later Roman Empire* (Cambridge, 2004), 127. Litewski, IV, 305, also notes the penalty set in CTh. 1.5.3, though without comment on its severity. In the citation of CTh. 1.5.3 in Kaser-Hackl, §78.II, p. 52, the crime appears to be considered unrelated to appeal: "Umgekehrt wenden sich die Kaiser auch gegen Querulanten, die grundlos gegen Amtshandlungen anzukämpfen versuchen."

110. Mommsen and Krüger both print *succedat,* which gives the meaning " . . . the inquiry of Your Sublimity shall proceed on this condition . . . " On this emendation, see below.

lum detrudendus est. Quam legem in annotationibus quoque nostris de iterando post sententiam iudicio custodire debebis. DAT. XIII. K. NOVEMB. BASSO ET ABLAVIO CONSS.

[EMPEROR CONSTANTINE] AUGUSTUS TO BASSUS, PRAETORIAN PREFECT. Concerning those who demand that a ruling delivered by a governor or any other judge be annulled, they may approach the tribunal of Your Sublimity on the condition that, if upon perusing the details of the case in every detail, it should become evidently clear that the ruling departs from the law and justice, it should be utterly rejected and the case should reach a decision in accordance with equity. But if the ruling already delivered should correspond to the laws, the wicked assailant of that pronouncement, if he is rich in property, shall be punished with two years' relegation to an island, if he leads a peasant's life or is poor, he shall be cast into the mines for two years' time. You will observe this law also in our annotations concerning the renewal of a trial after a ruling. GIVEN 20 OCT. (331) IN THE CONSULSHIP OF BASSUS AND ABLABIUS.

The usual terms, *appellatio, provocatio,* and their derivatives are conspicuously absent. Had they been present in the text, we should have found it in the title of the Codex Theodosianus on appeal, CTh. 11.30. Constantine here, however, presumes that the litigants have taken it upon themselves to go directly to the praetorian prefect instead of appealing against the sentence of the governor. This practice is usually indicated by the verb *adire* in classical law.[111] Constantine, however, uses the unusual expression *succedant examen,* to indicate that the litigants approach or *go up to* the tribunal (literally his "judgment") of the prefect. The reading *succedant* for *succedat* is not without manuscript support;[112] it moreover eliminates the abrupt change of subject from the litigants to the *examen* of the prefect and makes better sense than *succedat* with *examen* as its subject. Constantine formulates the situation from the perspective of the praetorian prefect: he has the litigants approach the court of the prefect and instructs him how to proceed. Finally, the subject of the *adnotationes* mentioned by Constantine is not appeal but something else. If the law described by Constantine concerned appeal, so should his reference to the title of the pertinent *annotationes* in the possession of the praetorian prefect. In fact, however, Con-

111. Cf. CTh. 11.30.16: *Quod si victus oblatam nec receptam a iudice appellationem adfirmet, praefectos adeat.*

112. It appears as a correction by the scribe of the Gothanus codex of the Breviarium; Mommsen, *ad loc.;* cf. *Proleg.,* lxxii.

stantine refers to a title called *de iterando post sententiam iudicio;* this should be identified with the irregular procedures of *supplicatio* or *aditio,* which bypass the appellate system.[113]

The punishment of two-year relegation or hard labor corresponds neatly to the penalties established for supplicating the emperor after failing to make an appeal. The penalty for such *supplicationes* was deportation generally and deportation and confiscation for supplicating against the sentences of *iudices vice sacra.*[114] As the emperor is greater in majesty, so the punishment in severity. On this view, the purpose of CTh. 1.5.3 is not to punish unsuccessful appellants, thereby depressing the number of appeals, but rather to compel litigants to avail themselves of the appellate system.

Judicial Hostility to Appeal

Constantine knew very well that the success of the appellate system depended on the compliance of administrators, from provincial governors and their staffs to the praetorian prefects. Yet it was no easy matter to compel all imperial officials to cooperate fully with the regulations laid down by the emperor. The hostility of provincial judges to appeal emerges in numerous constitutions. It is clear that Constantine was aware of it and reacted accordingly throughout his reign when word of such abuses reached his ears.

The first constitution to record the indignation of provincial judges, whose sentences had been challenged, is among the earliest extant constitutions of Constantine, CTh. 11.30.2 from the year 313. In a letter that discussed appeal at length,[115] Constantine forbids judges to subject appellants to incarceration, torture, or any other form of *iniuria:*

CTh. 11.30.2

Minime fas est, ut in civili negotio libellis appellatoriis oblatis aut carceris cruciatus aut cuiuslibet iniuriae genus seu tormenta vel etiam contumelias perferat appellator.

It is by no means right that an appellant in a civil case should, after offering his petition of appeal, endure the torment of prison or any kind of injustice or torture or even insults.

---

113. On *adnotationes,* see W. Turpin, "Adnotatio and Imperial Rescript in Roman Legal Procedure," *RIDA*[3] 35 (1988), 285–307.

114. See on CTh. 11.30.17 and 11.34.1 below.

115. Other excerpts are CTh. 9.40.1 and 11.36.1.

These regulations appear to apply also to appellants in criminal cases, with the exception of incarceration required for serious criminal offenses. Incarceration and abuse was one way to intimidate appellants from pursuing their legal right to challenge the ruling of the judge. Incarceration itself might suffice to stifle an appeal, a fact that Constantine shrewdly grasps: once an appellant had applied for appeal by submitting his *libelli appellatorii,* it followed that the judge must reciprocate by presenting the appellant with his *opinio,* if the appeal was to the emperor, or *apostoli,* if the appeal was to another, higher instance. Incarceration guaranteed that the procedure would progress no further, and the conditions of prison alone might well induce a potential appellant to acquiesce. Incarceration would further prevent an appellant from approaching (*adire*) a higher instance personally, where his case could be heard and complaint against the recalcitrant judge registered. As we have seen, such complaints, if justified, had grave consequences for the official who occasioned them.[116] The appellant faced *infamia,* should his appeal prove to have been groundless.[117]

Constantine issued a similar warning to the *praefectus annonae Africae* in 315, reminding him that it was the duty of his staff to receive all petitions for appeal (*libelli appellatorii*) and inflict no *iniuria* upon an appellant.[118] *Iniuria* could be many things in this context: simple suppression of documents as a favor or for a bribe (e.g., from the victorious party),[119] the exaction of illicit fees or other demands,[120] refusal to register the appeal by the prescribed deadline, and so on.

Gothofredus astutely observed that the *praefectus annonae* may have resisted appeals to the urban prefect of Rome.[121] He cites CTh. 11.29.2, also directed to a *praefectus annonae,* which contains the injunction that no

116. See chapter 4; cf. Pergami, *Appello,* 52–55, who believes that Constantine still granted a judge *a quo* the power to evaluate the legal basis of the appeal.

117. CTh. 11.30.16: *Superatus enim si iniuste appellasse videbitur, lite perdita notatus abscedet.* The word *notatus* is merely a colorful way of evoking *infamia.* The interpretation of *notatus* as reference to *ignominia,* so Pergami, *Appello,* 114 n. 118, citing De Marini Avonzo, "Giustizia II," 217, seems anachronistic. Mommsen, *StrR.,* 993 n. 2, holds that the legal effects of *infamia* and *ignominia* (the technical term for soldiers) were identical. Litewski, IV, 177–78, and Dupont, *Peines,* 55–57, interpret *notatus* also as *infamia.* On *infamia* generally, see M. Kaser, "Infamia und ignominia in den römischen Rechtsquellen," *ZRG* 73 (1956), 220–78.

118. CTh. 11.30.4: *Officii cura est, ut omnes omnino appellationes, quaecumque fuerint interpositae, sollemniter curet accipere nec in recipiendis libellis aliquod genus iniuriae inferendum cuipiam existimet.*

119. De Marini Avonzo, "Giustizia II," 219.

120. Cf. the discussion of CTh. 1.16.7 in chapter 5.

121. Gothofredus, *ad* CTh. 11.30.4.

judge should intimidate appellants by declaring that he will send a *relatio* to the emperor.[122] Constantine's reference to "judges" (*si quis iudicum*), however, suggests that this constitution applied not only to the *praefectus annonae;* more probably it reflects a general policy. The proper time for a *consultatio* was before a ruling had been reached. Otherwise the judge must submit to the review of his ruling on appeal.

Incarceration and intimidation were not the only means of impeding the completion of the formal requirements of appeal. A judge might simply refuse to perform his part in the formal procedure. In a letter to the proconsul of Africa, CTh. 11.30.6, Constantine sets a very harsh penalty for withholding the *opinio* from the appellant or suppressing the dossier for the emperor.[123] Such intransigence of the part of the judge would have left the appellant no choice but to apply directly to the praetorian prefect or to resort to *supplicatio,* extraordinary appeal to the emperor himself. Both these options not only inconvenienced the appellant, forcing him or a representative to undertake a journey to another, potentially distant court, but also burdened the court of appeal itself. Litigants who supplicated the emperor without first attempting appeal accordingly faced a fine of half the value of the object of the suit, if their complaint proved unjustified—a penalty that would substantially increase in later years.[124]

CTh. 11.30.9, sent to a vicar in 318, threatens the judge who suppresses documents or evidence submitted by appellants with permanent *infamia.*[125] Constantine orders that all relevant materials be included in the dossiers destined for the imperial court, "lest it be necessary to remit cases that come into Our knowledge back to the courts (i.e., of the first instance)."[126] Constantine implies that accidental omissions would not have escaped the notice of the imperial court. This, of course, would be impossible if a judge had deliberately suppressed material and formulated his *opinio* accordingly, a maneuver that could have had grave consequences for the litigant or appellant. The purpose of insisting on the transmission of all materials is to

---

122. CTh. 11.29.2: *Si quis iudicum duxerit esse referendum, nihil pronuntiet . . . aut, si tulerit sententiam, minime postea, ne a se provocetur, relatione promissa terreat litigantes.* Cf. Dupont, "Constantin," 558–59, who believes the addressee of this letter was guilty of such intimidation.

123. On the nature of the penalty for this crime, characterized as *sacrilegium,* see chapter 7.

124. Cf. CTh. 1.5.2–3.

125. CTh. 11.30.9 (a. 318): *Quare perennibus inuretur iudex notis, si cuncta, quae litigatores instructionis probationisque causa recitaverint, indita actis vel subiecta non potuerint inveniri;* cf. chapter 7.

126. CTh. 11.30.9 (a. 318): *Ne causas, quae in nostram venerint scientiam, rursus transferri ad iudicia necesse sit.*

prevent the issue of an erroneous imperial rescript (whether for *consultatio ante sententiam* or *appellatio more consultationis*), which Constantine himself had declared inappellable.[127] The unfortunate litigant who discovered his judge's deceit upon receipt of the imperial rescript would have had no choice but to hasten to the imperial court.

Many judges greeted appeals with chagrin or outright indignation. Constantine, for his part, encouraged the cultivation of impartiality among his administrators—one might almost say professionalism. In several constitutions, the emperor emphasizes that the remedy of appeal existed for the benefit of the provincials; no judge should have regarded its use as an affront. Various reasons may be imagined why judges might resist appeals. Corruption or collusion with one of the parties to a suit has plausibly been alleged.[128] The words of Constantine himself, however, suggest that mere human frailty was most often to blame: the constitutions allege that spite, bureaucratic self-importance, and intolerance of being challenged most frequently led judges to frustrate the efforts of appellants. Even the urban prefect, it appears, was not immune to such fits of passion. A lengthy letter sent to Maximus, urban prefect in 321, contains not only an idealization of the proper conduct of a judge and a discussion of the materials that should be included in an appeal to the emperor, but also a direct rebuke of the prefect himself.[129] Complaints (*querimoniae*) alleged that Maximus had been rejecting appeals. Constantine assumes the perspective of the appellant and asks, "For what is bitterer and more outrageous than that one granted a power should sit idle through arrogance, so that the utility of appeal is despised?"[130] The fragment concludes with characteristic sarcasm:[131] "As if indeed appeal was invented to insult the judge, not to privilege the litigant; or rather, in appeal, not the fairness[132] of the judge, but the utility to the litigant

127. CTh. 11.30.9 (a. 318): *Nam cogimur a proferenda sententia temperare, qui sanximus retractari rescribta nostra ad opiniones vel etiam relationes iudicum data non oportere, quoniam verendum est, ne lis incognito negotio dirimatur adempta copia conquerendi.* Gothofredus, *ad* CTh. 11.30.9, rightly comments: "Quae omnia rursum argumento sunt, quantopere seu quam enixe Constantinus in hanc rem cautum voluerit." Cf. CTh. 11.30.6 (above, p. 232) and CTh. 1.2.5: *quod autem totius negotii cognitionem tollit et vires principalis negotii exhaurit, sine gravi partis alterius dispendio convelli non potest.*

128. So, e.g., Pergami, *Appello*, 52 n. 15, citing De Marini Avonzo, "Giustizia II," 219.

129. CTh. 2.18.1 and CTh. 11.30.11.

130. CTh. 11.30.11.1: *Quid enim acerbius indigniusque est, quam indulta quempiam potestate ita per iactantiam insolescere, ut despiciatur utilitas provocationis . . . ?* Cf. above, p. 228.

131. Cf. *Epit. de Caes.* 41.16: *Irrisor potius quam blandus.*

132. I.e., whether the ruling is right or wrong is irrelevant; the right of the litigant to appeal is guaranteed.

should be considered."[133] The arrogance alleged by Constantine suggests that Maximus had perhaps identified his jurisdiction *vice sacra* too literally with that of the emperor and boldly considered his own rulings to be as inappellable as Constantine's.

Constantine again cites the indignation of judges whose rulings have been appealed in CTh. 11.30.15, a letter probably issued in response to an embassy from the *concilium Africae.*[134] The excerpt begins, "Judges wrongly believe they are insulted if a litigant, whose case has been wounded by their ruling, appeals from the principal matter, which is neither strange nor foreign to the courts."[135] Recalling CTh. 11.30.2, Constantine forbids judges to intimidate appellants with incarceration or military custody.[136] He affirms the principle that litigants have the right of appeal after a final ruling. Constantine cites the same motive for judicial hostility—indignation—in CTh. 11.30.13. As is likely the case in CTh. 11.30.15, so also in CTh. 11.30.13 his criticism is directed at "judges of lesser rank," presumably provincial governors and others who do not preside *vice sacra:* "Some judges of lesser rank, angry that the remedy of appeal has been invoked against their rulings, bring it about that their unnecessary and uncustomary[137] *relationes* are heaped upon Us."[138] Constantine informs the addressee of this letter, the urban prefect, that judges may not send *consultationes* to the emperor to prevent appeals (cf. CTh. 11.29.2 above) but must allow appeals to be heard at the court of the urban prefect, which he denotes the *sacrum auditorium,* a reference to the prefect's jurisdiction *vice sacra.* It would not be unreasonable to suppose that the prefect distributed copies of this letter at least to the judges in his jurisdiction, for instance the *correctores Italiae,* so that all might be reminded of the impropriety of sending a *consultatio* both after a case has been decided and appeal has been made.[139]

---

133. CTh. 11.30.11.1: *Quasi vero appellatio ad contumeliam iudicis, non ad privilegium iurgantis inventa sit vel in hoc non aequitas iudicantis, sed litigantis debeat considerari utilitas.*

134. Cf. Gothofredus, *ad loc.*

135. CTh. 11.30.15: *Non recte iudices iniuriam sibi fieri existimant, si litigator, cuius negotium sententia vulneratum est, a principali causa provocaverit, quod neque novum neque alienum a iudiciis est.*

136. CTh. 11.30.15: . . . *et iudices observare debebunt, ne appellatores vel in carcerem redigant, vel a militibus faciant custodiri.*

137. I.e., "contra solitum et sic ordinarium ius appellationum" (Gothofredus, *ad loc.*). The word may well have been chosen also to convey the sense "insolent" (cf. *iactantia* in CTh. 11.30.11.1 above).

138. CTh. 11.30.13: *Nonnulli iudicum inferioris gradus a sententiis suis interponi provocationis auxilium aegre ferentes id efficiunt, ut nobis eorum relationes non necessariae et insolentes ingerantur.*

139. Gothofredus, *ad loc.*

The specter of collusion among imperial officials manifests itself in several constitutions. The various *iniuriae* inflicted on potential appellants by members of the *officium* of the judge have been discussed above.[140] Corruption and subterfuge were not the province of imperial officials alone, however. CTh. 11.30.6 describes the "sacrilege" done by a judge who suppresses a litigant's appellate dossier, forcing him to resort to *supplicatio*, but Constantine further notes the penalty for the supplicant who has failed first to appeal: one-half of the value of the object at stake. He then addresses those who attempt to overturn rulings issued by the imperial court itself:

> CTh. 11.30.6
>
> Eo etiam, qui terminatam rescripto vel consultatione quaestionem exquisito suffragio refricare conabitur, quoniam maius crimen admittit, in omnem litis aestimationem protinus condemnando et sub sacramenti observatione omni venia deneganda, si quis contra haec supplicare temptaverit.
>
> He moreover who, having sought out patronage, attempts to reopen a case settled by rescript or *consultatio*, because he commits a greater crime, is forthwith to be condemned for the entire value of the case, and in accordance with (Our?) oath[141] all pardon is to be denied, if someone attempts to supplicate against these (*sc.* rulings).

The attempt to overturn an imperial rescript is a far greater crime, whether issued in response to *consultatio ante sententiam* or *appellatio more consultationis*. In both cases, the ruling of the emperor should be final. With reference to *suffragium*, Constantine conjures up a litigant who attempts (through connections or bribes, or both) to win the support of someone at the court to secure an audience with the emperor.[142] The aggravated punishment reflects the use of deceit in addition to contempt for the inappellability of imperial rulings. Deceit, of course, would have been necessary in such cases; Constantine states in no uncertain terms that he would reject the pleas of a litigant who appeared personally.

CTh. 11.30.8 presents us with a similar case at the provincial level. Constantine holds the *officium* of the judge responsible, if it should connive at

140. See on CTh. 11.30.4 (a. 315) above, pp. 242–43.

141. Cf. chapter 4, p. 102 n. 38.

142. It is also possible that the litigant might seek, through his patron, to obtain a new rescript in the name of the emperor from the imperial chancellery itself.

the efforts of a litigant to take illicit action in a case that is pending on an appeal or *consultatio* or has already been settled by imperial rescript.[143] In the first section of this excerpt, Constantine penalizes the judge who fails to send materials necessary for a ruling. The second section threatens the *officiales* themselves:

CTh. 11.30.8.1

> Eadem poena officio imminente, si quando appellatione vel consultatione pendente vel post decisas nostris responsionibus causas ei, quod ullo modo fuerit impetratum, damnabilem voluerit coniventiam commodare.
>
> The same penalty looms over the *officium,* if at any time while an appeal or *consultatio* is pending or after cases have been decided by Our responses, it should wish to lend its condemnable connivance to what has been obtained by any means whatsoever.

The sentence preceding this citation, at the end of CTh. 11.30.8 pr, decrees the death penalty (*capitale supplicium*) for a *rationalis* who mitigates the fine established for guilty judge. Even given Constantine's penchant for harsh retribution, though, it seems incredible that he intended to put the entire staff of a governor to the sword. Besides the practical consequences of the execution of a permanent body of valuable clerks and officials, a more plausible alternative is the punishment prescribed in the first section of the constitution: that of a fine in value equal to the object of the suit. The words *eadem poena* rather ineptly overlook the intervening punishment of the *rationalis.*

The crime perpetrated by the litigant is the illicit acquisition and use of an imperial rescript or other official document. It is to this that Constantine refers with the words *quod ullo modo impetratum fuerit.* Constantine forbids such rescripts *contra ius* in several constitutions.[144] We learn from the present constitution that the enforcement of the penalty established in CTh. 11.30.6, a fine assessed at the value of the object of the litigant's suit, devolved not only on the judge but also on his *officium.*

---

143. CTh. 11.30.8.1.

144. See especially CTh. 1.2.2: *Contra ius rescribta non valeant;* CTh. 1.2.3: *Quae* [*rescribta*] *postea elicita sunt, nullum robur habeant, nisi consentanea sint legibus publicis;* cf. G. G. Archi, "Il problema delle fonti del diritto nel sistema romano del IV e V secolo," in *St. Grosso,* vol. 4 (Turin, 1971), 34–37; Noethlichs, *Beamtentum und Dienstvergehen,* 49–50.

The Edict of 331

The legislation of Constantine on appeal closes, fittingly, in an edict addressed to the provincials in 331. This edict survives in no fewer than eight fragments preserved in the Codex Theodosianus and Justinianus.[145] Its original extent must have been much greater. Four of the surviving fragments concern appeal; the rest, a wide range of procedural regulations.[146] Of the fragments of the edict of 331 that pertain to appeal, each has been addressed in this chapter: CTh. 11.30.16 confirms the right of appellants to appeal from *iudices vice sacra* with the exception of the praetorian prefects, the right to proceed to the praetorian prefects if appeal is refused, and the penalties for either judge or appellant, whichever in the event proves to have acted injuriously. CTh. 11.30.17 and 11.34.1 forbid *supplicatio* if a litigant has failed to appeal; the penalty is deportation. CTh. 11.34.1 specifies that whoever makes allegations of intimidation against *iudices vice sacra* will suffer the confiscation of all his property. CJ 3.13.4 reiterates that once a litigant has brought his case before an ordinary judge, he may not appeal to a higher official until a ruling has been made.

Almost every regulation is anticipated in earlier legislation of Constantine. The edict of 331 was, in a sense, the culmination of nearly two decades of legislative activity in the field of appeal and other areas of judicial procedure. In the words of De Marini Avonzo, the edict of 331 was neither particularly innovative, nor revolutionary, nor occasional: more than a radical reform of judicial procedure, it was a codification in the sense of a uniform and organic exposition of regulations.[147] Gothofredus rightly called this the edict "in which Constantine sought to provide for the sanctity, integrity,

---

145. CTh. 2.26.3, 3.30.4, 4.5.1, 11.30.16–17, 11.34.1; CJ 3.13.4, 3.19.2. Also CTh. 1.16.6–7 are often considered related to this edict; on these fragments, see De Marini Avonzo, "Giustizia II," 220–21. CTh. 1.5.3, though not an edict, might also be considered a related text.

146. For a reconstruction and discussion of each fragment of this edict, see De Marini Avonzo, "Giustizia II," 171–229. For discussion of the fragments relative to appeal, see Pergami, *Appello,* 109–19.

147. De Marini Avonzo, "Giustizia II," 227: "A me pare certo che l'editto del I agosto non è particolarmente innovatore, nè rivoluzionario, nè occasionale. Si ricordi che quasi ciascuna regola ha dei precedenti: nella stessa legislazione costantiniana, o in quella dioclezianea, o nelle costituzioni imperiali dei primi secoli. Per questo motivo, esso si deve interpretare, piuttosto che come una radicale riforma del processo, come un programma di «cofidicazione» di princìpi già esistenti. Ovviamente, uso questa parola nel senso di esposizione uniforme ed organica, e non in quello di legislazione sistematica e completa."

venerability, and organization of the judges and courts with the greatest effort and passion."[148]

The occasion of the edict of 331 is not known. A year after the ceremonial foundation of Constantinople, Constantine perhaps felt that the time was ripe for an authoritative recapitulation of the important regulations on appeal shaped over the course of his reign. The edifice of the appellate system by this date was truly impressive. The creation of numerous superior judges presiding *vice sacra* throughout the empire vastly increased the availability and feasibility of appeal against the rulings of provincial governors. Appellants now had at least one such judge, and often several, within their diocese and no longer had to traverse the empire to seek out the ever-changing abode of the emperor. The implementation of *appellatio more consultationis* created further options for the appellant. It established a three-tier system for those who wished to appeal from the sentences of judges *vice sacra,* with the exception of the praetorian prefects. The coexistence of *appellatio more consultationis* and the ordinary appellate procedure left the decision to the appellant whether to appeal directly to the emperor on the basis of his and his judge's statements and the records of the case, or to proceed personally to the nearest higher instance. Constantine imposed harsh penalties on imperial officials to guarantee their adherence to the rules of appeal, and on litigants who attempted to circumvent them.[149] *Supplicatio* remained possible, but as the availability of appeal was considered guaranteed, litigants were obliged to use it. The appellate system Constantine founded remained unchanged in its essentials until the time of Justinian, who himself included most of the constitutions collected for the Codex Theodosianus in his own Codex.[150]

Constantine strove publicly both to guarantee justice and to prevent its perversion, but he effected his reforms by exalting his own authority and courting the acknowledgment and favor of his subjects. The imperial bureaucracy was the means with which he pursued this goal. It was necessary

---

148. Gothofredus, *ad* CTh. 1.5.1 (= Mommsen 1.5.3): "quo Constantinus iudicum et iudiciorum sanctitati, integritati, reverentiae, ordinique summa ope, enixoque studio consultum ivit."

149. Gothofredus, *ad* CTh. 11.30.1, assesses the constitutions of Constantine on appeal as follows: "Ex quibus omnibus apparet, ab una parte quatenus iudiciorum retractationi per appellationes deferri voluerit Constantinus in favorem litigantium, ab altera quomodo iniustis appellationibus occursum voluerit."

150. Cf. CJ 7.62. Doubtless the appellate system saw constant use in the time between Constantine and Theodosius II. The title on appeal in the Codex Theodosianus (CTh. 11.30) makes a respectable showing of sixty-eight constitutions, eighteen of which are Constantine's.

to control the administration to enforce the reform of the appellate system; Constantine accordingly instituted several different means of achieving this end. By subjecting the rulings of imperial officials to appeal, Constantine could exercise still greater control over his administration and render it dependent on his authority and approval. The propagation of justice ultimately benefited its author—Constantine.

Conclusion

The Constantinian legislation on appeal, which culminated in the edict of August 331, ties together the separate threads and major themes of this book: the utilization of distinct forms of legislation to communicate with distinct audiences; the practice of addressing the inhabitants of the empire generally in universal edicts, in a manner that goes far beyond the apologetic language exemplified by the edict of Alexander Severus on *aurum coronarium* or the Edict of Maximum Prices; a profound mistrust of the imperial administration, expressed both in edicts and in official letters, that ally the emperor with his subjects against the imperial bureaucracy itself; and, in imperial constitutions generally, the effort of Constantine instill loyalty in his servants and subjects and to affirm and strengthen his own authority.

The edict of August 331 contained not only a lengthy recapitulation of the procedural rules governing appeal under Constantine but also paragraphs devoted to several distinct subjects of law. The thunderous edict *ad universos provinciales,* preserved as CTh. 1.16.6–7, which is treated at length in chapter 4, followed three months later, less than two weeks after the controversial letter *de iterando post sententiam iudicio,* CTh. 1.5.3 treated in chapter 8, was sent to the praetorian prefect. The later edict of 331, preserved in CTh. 1.16.6–7, with its stern insistence on proper procedure and passionate deprecation of illegal judicial fees, seems to crown some twenty years of judicial legislation. There are noticeably fewer constitutions of Constantine's in the Codex Theodosianus after 331. Given that Constantine now resided chiefly in Constantinople, if he had continued to issue constitutions at the rate observed in previous years, one would have expected the Theodosian compilers to have recovered more. Study of the record of Constantine's legislation in the Codex Theodosianus, however, suggests that the compilers gathered Constantine's constitutions from one or more unknown intermediate collections that derived ultimately from Rome and Carthage. It is likely for this reason that the record of Constantine's legislation begins only after he had defeated Maxentius (chapter 1).

The innovations of Constantine were a lasting contribution to the law of the Later Roman Empire, but his constitutions affected not only substantive law. The patterns of communication and control within the imperial administration had been set for the next century. Constantine utilized edicts to address the totality of his subjects, but Constantinian edicts did far more than disseminate new law and procedures that affected the empire: by means of an edict, Constantine could project his voice into the far corners of the empire. Constantine harnessed the publication and dissemination of such edicts by provincial administrators from high to low, from praetorian prefect to provincial governor, to appeal directly to his subjects and court their loyalty. The conventions of Roman edicts were less important than the immediacy of communication with the Roman provincials that Constantine achieved by them. Although Roman edicts were traditionally formulated as declarations, in which the magistrate or emperor avoids familiar forms, such as "you," Constantine frequently uses edicts as letters to entire populations, to represent himself and his goals before the people on whose behalf he acts (chapter 2).

The revelatory style of Constantinian legislation follows important tetrarchic precedents, which should not be overlooked. Already the tetrarchs cultivated a majestic Latin style in their edicts; they appear to have introduced the same style in official correspondence with imperial administrators. Constantine inherited these practices and began to issue even private rescripts in the same grand Latin style. Every imperial utterance became an occasion of ceremony and carefully wrought self-representation. A significant change of emphasis can also be observed in the enactments of Constantine. As Constantine envisioned one god over all, so as ruler he envisioned himself as the sole person responsible for the welfare of his subjects. Constantine's approach to legislation may be adapted from practices in the later years of the tetrarchy, but he invested his legislation with a peculiarly personal vigor. The tetrarchs appealed to the Roman people and the Roman gods behind a mask of uniformity and concord. The tetrarchic "We" was not merely *royal* but an ideal and a statement of policy. As Constantine dispensed with his rivals, so too with their pretensions—and their gods. Whatever alliances he formed, or the formal arrangement of power,

Constantine was always prepared to assert his own autonomy.[1] When occasion called for it, Constantine approached his subjects not with "We" but with "I," and with the blessing of the one *summa divinitas* (chapter 3).

Constantine saw his greatest ally, if perhaps after the Christian god, in his own subjects, the provincials of the empire. The edict was the form of law that by its very nature might reach them in the greatest numbers, and universal edicts play no small part in Constantine's efforts to win the Roman people for himself. Constantine could not only address his subjects, in part or in whole, in such a published pronouncement but also chastise the imperial bureaucracy; he could inform both subjects and officials how the empire should be governed and how justice would be served. The guarantee of a just administration and the vociferous denunciation of the injustices perpetrated by the imperial bureaucracy spoke directly to the interests and sympathies of the Roman people.

The edicts issued after the defeat of Licinius in 324 bear witness to Constantine's pretensions to justice. The legislation of Licinius was utterly abolished; Constantine's succeeded in its place. Licinius was branded a tyrant. No authority was conceded to any act of his—initially. Constantine soon found that he had to allow that legal transactions concluded under Licinius and consistent with law under his own reign were to remain in force. Even this concession, however, permitted Constantine to play the part of the lawgiver and restorer of justice. Constantine also advertised that provincial administrators that governed in his name were to be just: if it were proven that one of them had done wrong, not only the provincials but Constantine, too, were victims. Corruption in the administration and the crimes of officials were not merely unjust but also disloyal—and dangerous. Constantine owed his prosperity to his god, but the blessing of the deity was contingent on the prosperity of the empire. Constantine averred that he chose men to serve with faith in their integrity. If they proved otherwise, he, Constantine, was the victim of deception—but his vengeance would be swift and merciless.

At the same time as Constantine proclaimed his triumph over evil and lawlessness, he began to develop and extend to the Roman East the administrative structures that he had imposed on the West. The provincial reorganization of Diocletian had doubled not only the number of provinces but

---

1. Cf. J. Wienand, "Der Kaiser als Sieger. Untersuchungen zur militärischen Repräsentation Constantins I.," PhD diss., Konstanz, 2010, 95.

also the number of their administrators, who both relied on the Constantine for counsel and authority, and whose conduct might require vigilance. After Licinius had been removed, Constantine appointed several praetorian prefects to accompany his sons and prospective heirs and to administer areas such as Africa; special *comites provinciarum* were dispatched from the court as diocesan administrators and special delegates to oversee the provincial administration. The praetorian and urban prefects, the proconsuls, vicars, and others had been endowed with permanent judicial competence to hold trials in the emperor's stead; now more such officials were installed in the East. The praetorian prefects presided with the final, uncontestable authority of Constantine himself. Constantine had multiplied his authority and put himself, so to speak, within reach of far more of his subjects than ever before. The power of these officials to hear provincial disputes was not exhausted in their competence as judges of the second instance. They were further charged to receive complaints and accusations leveled at lesser officials, above all against provincial governors. By admonishing governors in circulars disseminated by the same high officials who might judge their conduct, and by proclaiming in universal edicts the rules that governors must observe and provincials could demand, Constantine amplified his voice and communicated power to his subjects through the officials vested with his authority. If a Roman provincial had been wronged by his governor, he should seek out the court of a praetorian prefect or *comes,* whose duty it was to help. Further officials frequently dispatched from the imperial court constituted another safeguard. These men traversed the empire on special missions, kept watch on suspect administrators, and fed information directly to the emperor (chapter 4).

The conduct of imperial administrators, for which he believed he would be held to account, was an interest that Constantine shared with his humble subjects, whose lives and livelihoods might depend on the integrity and justice of their governors. The bureaucratic administration of the fourth century was still nascent, and Constantine regarded it warily as a foreign body, despite both his dependence on it and his efforts to expand it. In what seems like a grandiose gesture of goodwill toward the inhabitants of the empire, Constantine declared that public acclamations made for or against provincial governors would henceforth not only be permitted but also welcomed. Constantine enacted this policy ostensibly to contribute to the just governance of the provinces, but there is more to the authorization of public acclamations than concern for equity in the provincial administration. Constantine perceived, cultivated, and exploited in public acclamations a potential for direct communication with his subjects. The authorization of the report of acclamations to the emperor squares admirably with other measures whereby Constantine circumvented both the provincial bureaucracy and the civic elite, in order to subject both to greater control. The highest officials of the provincial administration, the praetorian prefects and the *comites,* were specially charged to record and report public acclamations to the imperial court. The process excluded the provincial governors about whom such acclamations might be made. By means of symbolic communication with the people, Constantine attempted to counteract and undermine the negotiation of power between provincial governors and the local civic elite, described from different perspectives by Brown and Lendon,[2] and transform imperial administrators into reliable instruments of the imperial will. Late Roman justice was obedience, and obedience often had to be compelled; the obedience of the bureaucracy brought Constantine the loyalty of his subjects.

Constantine's impassioned edict against the encroachment of judicial fees, his denunciation of *sportulae* in CTh. 1.16.7, may be understood as a declaration conceived according to such strategies of communication. Constantine condemns the conduct of provincial clerks and petty officials in an edict addressed to the population of the empire; he expresses himself in vehement, indignant language and calls for severe punishment of corrupt officials. In another part of the same edict, CTh. 1.16.6, Constantine authorizes public acclamations against provincial governors. Just as in the edict CTh. 9.1.4 of 325, in which Constantine encouraged his subjects to approach him directly to denounce the misdeeds of imperial officials, in CTh. 1.16.6 of 331 he institutes a process whereby the voice of the crowd might reach him wherever he was. The juxtaposition of this novel measure and the prohibition of judicial fees suggests that Constantine hoped acclamations might curb irregularities before the governor's tribunal and corruption among his official staff. The prohibition of *sportulae* may ultimately have been a lost cause, but Constantine seems at least to have forestalled defeat, which would be conceded by a later ruler. It is perhaps not a coincidence that papyrus records of civil proceedings all but disappear in the mid-fourth century while alternative means of resolving disputes flourish.[3]

Constantine himself formally recognized two alternatives to the ordi-

---

2. Discussed briefly in the introduction.

3. A. Schiller, "The Courts Are No More," in *St. Volterra,* vol. 1 (Milan, 1971), 469–502; T. Gagos and P. van Minnen, *Settling a Dispute: Towards a Legal Anthropology of Late Antique Egypt* (Ann Arbor, 1994).

nary courts. He transformed the official known as the *defensor civitatis* into a judicial official who might resolve minor cases between ordinary litigants. Far more radically, Constantine conferred official sanction to *episcopalis audientia,* a form of trial conducted by Christian bishops. Constantine seems to have regarded bishops with such veneration that he conferred on them judicial powers that approached that of praetorian prefects or his own: the rulings of bishops were considered sacred—*sancta*—and, like the emperor's, inappellable. Constantine had such confidence in the judgment of bishops that he decreed that a case had to be transferred to the bishop even against the wishes of one of the parties. The brashness of this decision and the naive faith placed in Christian bishops seem genuinely Constantinian; the readiness and even the willingness of bishops to be thrust into the ugly arena of worldly litigation has rightly been contested. Episcopal jurisdiction had been established, but it would endure after Constantine as a consensual alternative to the ordinary courts (chapter 5).

The engagement of the people was one way to exert pressure on the imperial bureaucracy; but in addition to control from without the administration, Constantine also imposed control from within. Official correspondence remained essential to communication between the imperial court and administrators throughout the empire. Petitions and embassies that might prompt a letter to an official streamed in from throughout the empire; but far more inquiries and reports, it seems, poured in from the imperial officials themselves. Many such reports concerned other officials, and Constantine consistently strove to make the imperial bureaucracy a self-policing organization. Imperial officials were ordered to observe, control, report, and even punish others. The praetorian prefects frequently channeled imperial indignation downward onto those in the civil administration who had earned it. Other high officials also received orders concerning the fate of subordinates. Constantine exploited the innate tension between different officials and especially between provincial governors and their resident clerical staff to create a culture of fear and obedience in the lower ranks of the provincial administration. Punishment, of course, was a favorite method of encouraging obedience. A severed head or a smoking pyre brought the justice of Constantine before the eyes of his subjects far more vividly than the most violently worded edict (chapter 6).

That is not to say that the relationship between Constantine and his administration was a one-sided tale of crime and punishment. Constantine did much to support his officials. The numerous constitutions sent in response to official inquiries are testament to this policy. In itself, there was nothing new in responding to official letters sent from the provinces. Constantine particularly favored forms of correspondence that made his administrators ever more dependent on his authority even as they relied on it to govern. Constantine promoted the use of *relationes,* reports by letter, when a governor found himself confronted by a recalcitrant provincial grandee; such occasions permitted Constantine to intervene and exercise authority and power. Constantine further regulated the procedure of the *consultatio,* in which a provincial governor consulted the emperor concerning a pending trial; the verdict returned then derived from the decision of the emperor. Constantine shifted responsibility for the ruling, for justice generally, onto himself; the governor had merely to follow correct procedure and ensure that all requisite documents were submitted to the imperial court: the authority of Constantine could suffer no second-guessing (chapter 7).

The procedure of appeal under Constantine unites reform, in the name of justice but in the interest of the emperor, with control of the imperial administration and the affirmation of power and authority. The reform of appeal complements tangible change in the imperial administration with the intangible projection of the imperial persona. Appellate reform appears at first sight to be a popular measure, a reform designed to expedite the rendering of justice for provincials generally, but there is more behind it than zeal for justice. The proper functioning of appeal required first the obedience of administrators to the rules established by Constantine. To effect this, Constantine employed now familiar methods of control. Appeal itself was a means of reviewing the judicial activity of imperial officials and assessing their adherence to the emperor's law. The object of an appeal might well be neglect of imperial statutes: this was naturally of great interest to Constantine. By encouraging appeals and guaranteeing the success of the system, Constantine encouraged and guaranteed an unstinting stream of opportunities to insert himself into legal decisions, by virtue of which his power and authority as supreme arbiter of the Roman world was constantly paraded before the eyes of his subjects. The procedure of *appellatio more consultationis,* in essence appeal by dossier, dispensed even with the need to hear litigants in person. Constantine may have had excessive faith in the reliability and veracity of documents, and his or his ministers' ability to interpret them, but even this shortcoming was more than compensated by the authority that the procedure permitted him to exercise. The more attractive and expeditious appeal to Constantine was, the more often appeals would be made. The threat of easy appeal made the decisions of imperial officials and the outcome of provincial litigation dependent on the will of Constantine (chapter 8).

The constitutions of Constantine often seem to evoke a man whose mission was to render justice to an entire world, but justice for its own sake was not the only motive behind the remarkable legislation of Constantine preserved in the Codex Theodosianus. It is perhaps the personal investment of Constantine in his legislation that has emerged from the present study: justice proves often more necessary than commendable, and it was measured at the discretion of the emperor. From the deathbed of his father Constantius to his own, Constantine grew from a contested to a rightful and righteous ruler with three decades of power and authority to speak on his behalf. Military skill and daring may have brought Constantine to power, but deft manipulation of his subjects and servants maintained him in it—and that in spite of the danger that his peculiar religious convictions might alienate many of both. The Constantine that emerges from his legislation has little in common with the stereotypical picture of a late antique ruler, aloof and serene. Constantine reveals himself in his legislation as greater than a monolith: he is a firebrand, a populist autocrat, more terrible than majestic; a man who in one breath proclaims his devotion to the welfare of his subjects and his wariness of the officials he appoints to govern them. It is a selfish devotion. Constantine's words accompanied genuine legislative and administrative innovation, for which he is justly extolled. By these same decrees, however, Constantine inexorably tightened his grasp on the Roman Empire, on its subjects, and on fleeting power. The mutual slaughter of his kinsmen and sons after his death would be the greatest failure of his naive confidence in the virtue of others; while he lived, though, the same confidence advertised in his subjects, in his closest officials, in Christian bishops, and in himself, helped to impose order and justice, however imperfect, on a vast empire. It was this combination of deeds and words that made Constantine great.

Works Cited

Albanese, B. "L'abolizione postclassica delle forme solenni nei negozi testamentari." In *Sodalitas: Scr. Guarino,* vol. 2 (Naples, 1984), 777–92.

Albanese, B. "Sul programma legislativo esposto nel 429 da Teodosio II." *APal* 38 (1985), 251–69. (= *Estudios de derecho romano en honore de Alvaro D'Ors,* vol. 1 [Pamplona, 1987], 123–40.)

Albertario, E. "Alcune osservazioni sulla legislazione di Costantino." In *Studi di diritto romano,* vol. 5 (Milan, 1937), 255–66.

Aldrete, G. S. *Gestures and Acclamations in Ancient Rome.* Baltimore, 1999.

Alföldi, A. *The Conversion of Constantine and Pagan Rome.* 1st ed. Oxford, 1948. 2nd ed. Oxford, 1969.

Amelotti, M. *Per l'interpretazione della legislazione privatistica di Diocleziano.* Milan, 1960.

Amelotti, M. "Da Diocleziano a Costantino. Note in tema di costituzioni imperiali." *SDHI* 27 (1961), 241–323.

Amelotti, M. "Documentazione privata e prova. Dall'epoca postclassica all'età giustinianea." In *Atti del xvii Congresso internazionale di papirologia (Napoli, 19–26 maggio 1983)* (Naples, 1984), 1161–72, 6299.

Ando, C. *Imperial Ideology and Provincial Loyalty in the Roman Empire.* Berkeley, 1999.

Andreotti, R. "Contributo alla discussione del rescritto costantiniano di Hispellum." In *Atti del I Convegno di Studi Umbri, Gubbio, 26–31 maggio 1963* (Perugia, 1964), 249–90.

Arcaria, F. "Sul potere normativo del prefetto del pretorio." *SDHI* 63 (1997), 301–41.

Archi, G. G. "Il volgarismo e il diritto postclassico, Inchiesta: Quarta puntata." *Labeo* 7 (1961), 210–17. (= *Scritti di diritto romano,* vol. 3 [Milan, 1981], 1672–82.)

Archi, G. G. "Contributo alla critica del Codice Teodosiano. Osservazioni su C. Th. 8, 18, 1 e C. T. 8, 18, 2." In *Symbolae iuridicae et historicae Martino David dedi-*

catae, vol. 1 (Leiden, 1968), 33–44. (= *Scritti di diritto romano*, vol. 3 [Milan, 1981], 1745–57.)

Archi, G. G. "Il problema delle fonti del diritto nel sistema romano del IV e V secolo." In *St. Grosso*, vol. 4 (Turin, 1971), 1–93.

Archi, G. G. "Nuove prospettive nello studio del Codice Teodosiano." In *Istituzioni giuridiche e realtà politiche nel tardo impero (III–V sec. d.C.). Atti di un incontro tra storici e giuristi, Firenze, 2–4 maggio 1974*, ed. G. G. Archi (Milan, 1976), 281–313.

Archi, G. G. *Teodosio II e la sua codificazione*. Naples, 1976.

Arnheim, M. T. W. *The Senatorial Aristocracy in the Later Roman Empire*. Oxford, 1972.

Arnheim, M. T. W. "Vicars in the Later Roman Empire." *Historia* 19 (1970), 593–606.

Auerbach, E. *Literatursprache und Publikum in der lateinischen Spätantike und im Mittelalter*. Bern, 1958.

Balestri Fumagalli, M. "Il divieto di appello contro le sentenze dei prefetti del pretorio (C. Th. 11, 30, 16)." In *Atti del II Seminario Romanistico Gardesano* (Milan, 1980), 213–30.

Banfi, A. *Habent illi iudices suos. Studi sull'esclusività della giurisdizione ecclesiastica e sulle origini del* privilegium fori *in diritto romano e bizantino*. Milan, 2005.

Bardill, J. *Constantine, Divine Emperor of the Christian Golden Age*. Cambridge, 2011.

Barnes, T. D. *Constantine and Eusebius*. Cambridge, MA, 1981.

Barnes, T. D. *The New Empire of Diocletian and Constantine*. Cambridge, MA, 1982.

Barnes, T. D. "The Constantinian Settlement." In *Eusebius, Christianity, and Judaism*, ed. H. W. Attridge and G. Hata (Leiden, 1992), 635–57.

Barnes, T. D. *Athanasius and Constantius: Theology and Politics in the Constantinian Empire*. Cambridge, 1993.

Barnes, T. D. "Christentum und dynastische Politik (300–325)." In *Usurpation*, ed. Paschoud and Szidat (Stuttgart, 1997), 99–109.

Barnes, T. D. "Constantine, Athanasius and the Christian Church." In *Constantine: History, Historiography, and Legend*, ed. S. N. C. Lieu and D. Montserrat (London, 1998), 7–20.

Barnes, T. D. Review of *Constantine and the Bishops: The Politics of Intolerance* by H. A. Drake, *Phoenix* 54 (2000), 381–83.

Baynes, N. H. *Constantine the Great and the Christian Church*. The Raleigh Lecture on History 1929. 2nd ed. Ed. H. Chadwick. London, 1972.

Berger, A. *Encyclopedic Dictionary of Roman Law*. Philadelphia, 1953.

Bethmann-Hollweg, M. A. von. *Der römische Civilprozeß*. Vols. 2–3. Bonn, 1865–66.

Bianchini, M. "Orientamenti di politica normativa nelle due 'partes imperii' all'indomani della codificazione teodosiana." *AARC* 4 (1981), 283–304.

Bianchini, M. "L'imperatore Costantino e una certa Agrippina. Riflessioni su CTh. 8. 15. 1." In *Sodalitas: Scr. Guarino*, vol. 3 (Naples, 1984), 1191–1206.

Biondi, B. *Il diritto romano cristiano.* 3 vols. Milan, 1952–54.

Bleckmann, B. *Konstantin der Große.* Reinbek, 1996.

Bleicken, J. *Constantin der Große und die Christen.* Munich, 1992.

Bowman, A. K., P. Garnsey, and Averil Cameron, eds. *The Cambridge Ancient History, Vol. XII: The Crisis of Empire, A.D. 193–337.* 2nd ed. Cambridge, 2005.

Brandt, H. *Konstantin der Grosse. Der erste christliche Kaiser. Eine Biographie.* Munich, 2006.

Brélaz, C. *La sécurité publique en Asie Mineure sous le Principat (Ier-IIIème s. ap. J.-C.). Institutions municipales et institutions impériales dans l'Orient romain.* Basel, 2005.

Brown, P. *Power and Persuasion in Late Antiquity: Towards a Christian Empire.* Madison, 1992.

Bruns, C. G. *Fontes Iuris Romani Antiqui.* 7th ed. Ed. O. Gradenwitz. Tübingen, 1909.

Burckhardt, J. *Die Zeit Constantins des Großen.* 3rd ed., unaltered repr. of 2nd ed. Leipzig, 1898. (English translation: *The Age of Constantine the Great.* Trans. Moses Hadas. Repr. Berkeley, 1983.)

Cagnat, R., A. Merlin, and L. Chatelain, eds. *Inscriptions Latines d'Afrique (Tripolitaine, Tunisie, Maroc).* Paris, 1923.

Calderone, S. "Problemi di esegesi constantiniana. Una mancata riforma costituzionale?" In *Istituzioni giuridiche e realtà politiche nel tardo impero (III–V sec. d.C.). Atti di un incontro tra storici e giuristi, Firenze, 2–4 maggio 1974*, ed. G. G. Archi (Milan, 1976), 247–60.

Cameron, A. *Circus Factions: Blues and Greens at Rome and Byzantium.* Oxford, 1976.

Cameron, Av. "Constantinus Christianus." Review of *Constantine and Eusebius* and *The New Empire of Diocletian and Constantine*, by T. D. Barnes. *JRS* 73 (1983), 184–90.

Cameron, Av. "The Reign of Constantine, A.D. 306–337." In *CAH* XII^2, ed. Bowman et al. (Cambridge, 2005), 90–109.

Carlà, F., and M. G. Castello. *Questioni: tardoantiche. Storia e mito della "svolta costantiniana."* Rome, 2010.

Castello, C. "Il pensiero politico-religioso di Costantino alla luce dei panegirici." *AARC* 1 (1975), 47–117.

Chadwick, H. "The Fall of Eustathius of Antioch." *JThS* 49 (1948), 27–35.

Chastagnol, A. *La préfecture urbaine à Rome sous le bas-empire.* Paris, 1960.

Chastagnol, A. "Constantin et le Sénat." *AARC* 2 (1976), 49–69.

Christol, M., S. Demougin, Y. Duval, C. Lepelley, and L. Pietri, eds. *Institutions, société et vie politique dans l'empire romain.* Rome, 1992.

Cimma, M. R. *L'episcopalis audientia nelle costituzioni imperiali da Costantino a Giustiniano.* Turin, 1989.

Clauss, M. *Konstantin der Grosse und seine Zeit.* 3rd ed. Munich, 2007.

Connolly, S. *Lives behind the Laws: The World of the* Codex Hermogenianus. Bloomington, 2010.

Connolly, S. "Constantine Answers the Veterans." In *From the Tetrarchs to the Theodosians: Later Roman History and Culture, 284–450 CE,* ed. S. McGill, C. Sogno, and E. Watts (Cambridge, 2010), 93–114.

Corcoran, S. "Hidden from History: The Legislation of Licinius." In *Theodosian Code,* ed. Harries and Wood (London, 1993), 97–119.

Corcoran, S. *The Empire of the Tetrarchs: Imperial Pronouncements and Government, AD 284–324.* Revised paperback ed. Oxford, 2000.

Corcoran, S. "Galerius' Jigsaw Puzzle: The Caesariani Dossier." *AntTard* 15 (2007), 221–50.

Corcoran, S. "The Heading of Diocletian's Prices Edict at Stratonicea." *ZPE* 166 (2008), 295–302.

Crawford, M. H., and J. Reynolds. "The Publication of the Prices Edict: A New Inscription from Aezani." *JRS* 65 (1975), 160–63.

De Bonfils, G. *Il comes et quaestor nell'età della dinastia costantiniana.* Naples, 1981.

De Marini Avonzo, F. "La giustizia nelle province agli inizi del Basso Impero." In *Synteleia Arangio Ruiz,* vol. 2 (Naples, 1964), 1037–62. (= "La giustizia nelle province agli inizi del Basso Impero, I. Princìpi generali del processo in un editto di Costantino," *Studi Urbinati* 31 [1962–63], 291–328.)

De Marini Avonzo, F. "La giustizia nelle province agli inizi del Basso Impero. II. L'organizzazione giudiziaria di Costantino." *Studi Urbinati* 34 (1965–66), 171–229.

De Robertis, F. M. "Un precedente costantiniana alla cosiddetta 'Legge delle Citazioni' del 426 di Teodosio II e Valentiniano III." *SDHI* 64 (1998), 245–52.

De Robertis, F. M. "La constantiniana 'manumisso in ecclesiis' e i gravissimi sviamenti nelle altre forme manomissorie allora correnti." *SDHI* 65 (1999), 145–50.

De Salvo, L. *Economia privata e pubblici servizi nell'impero romano. I corpora naviculariorum.* Messina, 1992.

Delmaire, R. *Largesses sacrées et* res privata. *L'*aerarium *impérial et son administration du IV*[e] *au VI*[e] *siècle.* Rome, 1989.

Delmaire, R. "Étude sur les souscriptions de quelques lois du Code Théodosien: Les lois reçues à Regium." In *Institutions,* ed. Christol et al. (Rome, 1992), 315–28.

Delmaire, R. "Introduction." In *Les lois religieuses des empereurs romains de Constantin à Théodose II (312–438),* vol. 1: *Code Théodosien livre XVI,* ed. T. Mommsen, J. Rougé, and R. Delmaire (Paris, 2005), 13–110.

Demandt, A. "Grenzen Spätrömischer Staatsgewalt." In *Usurpation,* ed. Paschoud and Szidat (Stuttgart, 1997), 155–63.

Demandt, A., and J. Engemann, eds. *Konstantin der Grosse. Geschichte—Archaologie—Rezeption. Internationales Kolloquium vom 10.–15. Oktober 2005.* Trier, 2006.

Demandt, A. *Die Spätantike. Römische Geschichte von Diocletian bis Justinian,*

284–565 n. Chr. Handbuch der Altertumswissenschaft, III.6. 2nd ed. Munich, 2007.
Demandt, A., and J. Engemann, eds. *Konstantin der Grosse. Austellungskatalog. Begleitband zur gleichnamigen Ausstellung in Trier, 2007.* Mainz, 2007.
Dessau, H. *Inscriptiones Latinae Selectae.* Berlin, 1892–1916.
Di Paola, L. *Per la storia degli "occhi del re." I servizi ispettivi nella tarda antichità.* Messina, 2005.
Dickey, E. *Latin Forms of Address from Plautus to Apuleius.* Oxford, 2002.
Dionisotti, A. C. "From Ausonius' Schooldays?" *JRS* 72 (1982), 83–125.
Dölger, F., and J. Karayannopulos. *Byzantinische Urkundenlehre. Erster Abschnitt: Die Kaiserurkunden.* Munich, 1968.
Dörries, H. *Das Selbstzeugnis Kaiser Konstantins.* Abhandlungen der Akademie der Wissenschaften in Göttingen. Philologisch-historische Klasse, 34. Göttingen, 1954.
Downey, G. *A History of Antioch in Syria from Seleucus to the Arab Conquest.* Princeton, 1961.
Dräger, P. *Eusebios. Über das Leben des glückseligen Kaisers Konstantin (De vita Constantini).* Oberhaid, 2007.
Drake, H. A. "Firmicus Maternus and the Politics of Conversion." In *Qui Miscuit Utile Dulci: Festschrift Essays for Paul Lachlan MacKendrick,* ed. G. Schmeling and J. D. Mikalson (Wauconda, IL, 1998), 133–49.
Drake, H. A. *Constantine and the Bishops: The Politics of Intolerance.* Baltimore, 2000.
Dupont, C. *Les constitutions de Constantin et le droit privé au début du IVe siècle. Les personnes.* Lille, 1937.
Dupont, C. *Le droit criminel dans les constitutions de Constantin. Les Infractions.* Lille, 1953.
Dupont, C. "La vente dans les constitutions de Constantin." *RIDA*[3] 2 (1955), 237–62.
Dupont, C. *Le droit criminel dans les constitutions de Constantin. Les Peines.* Lille, 1955.
Dupont, C. *La réglementation économique dans les constitutions de Constantin.* Lille, 1963.
Dupont, C. "Le domaine géographique d'application des textes constantiniennes." *IVRA* 8 (1967), 28–44.
Dupont, C. "Constantin et la préfecture d'Afrique." In *St. Grosso,* vol. 2 (Turin, 1968), 515–35.
Dupont, C. "Constantin et les constitutions impériales." In *St. Volterra,* vol. 1 (Milan, 1971), 549–69.
Edwards, M., trans. *Optatus: Against the Donatists.* Liverpool, 1997.
Eich, A., and P. Eich. "Thesen zur Genese des Verlautbarungsstils der spätantiken kaiserlichen Zentrale." *Tyche* 19 (2004), 75–104.

Eich, P. *Zur Metamorphose des politischen Systems in der römischen Kaiserzeit. Die Entstehung einer "personalen Bürokratie" im langen dritten Jahrhundert.* Berlin, 2005.

Ehrhardt, A. "Constantin des Grossen Religionspolitik und Gesetzgebung." *ZRG* 72 (1955), 127–90. (Repr. in *Konstantin der Grosse,* ed. H. Kraft [Darmstadt, 1974], 388–456.)

Evans-Grubbs, J. *Law and Family in Late Antiquity: The Emperor Constantine's Marriage Legislation.* Oxford, 1995.

Feissel, D. "Les constitutions des Tétrarques connues par l'épigraphie. Inventaire et notes critiques." *AntTard* 3 (1995), 33–53.

Feissel, D. "L'*Adnotatio* de Constantin sur le droit de cité d'Orcistus en Phrygie." *AntTard* 7 (1999), 255–67.

Fögen, M.-T. "Die Macht der Sprache und die sprachlose Macht." Review of *Power and Persuasion in Late Antiquity,* by P. Brown. *Rechtshistorisches Journal* 13 (1994), 95–100.

Fögen, M.-T. "Massenmord an Texten." *Rechtshistorisches Journal* 17 (1998), 6–11.

Frakes, R. M. "Late Roman Social Justice and the Origin of the Defensor civitatis." *CJ* 89 (1994), 337–48.

Frakes, R. M. Contra potentium iniurias: *The* Defensor Civitatis *and Late Roman Justice.* Munich, 2001.

Frier, B. "Law on the Installment Plan." Review of *Ulpian,* by T. Honoré. *Michigan Law Review* 82 (1984), 856–68.

Gagos, T., and P. van Minnen. *Settling a Dispute: Towards a Legal Anthropology of Late Antique Egypt.* Ann Arbor, 1994.

Garnsey, P., and C. Humfress. *The Evolution of the Late Antique World.* Cambridge, 2001.

Gascou, J. "Le rescrit d'Hispellum." *MEFRA* 79 (1967), 609–59.

Gaudemet, J. "Constantin restaurateur de l'ordre." In *St. Solazzi* (Naples, 1948), 652–74. (= *Études,* vol. 2 [1979], 73–95.)

Gaudemet, J. "Droit romain et principes canoniques en matière de mariage au Bas-Empire." In *Studi in mem. di E. Albertario,* vol. 2 (Milan, 1950), 173–96. (= *Études,* vol. 3 [1979], 163–88.)

Gaudemet, J. "'Ius' et 'leges.'" *Iura* 1 (1950), 223–52. (= *Études,* vol. 1 [1979], 439–70.)

Gaudemet, J. "Constantin et le recrutement des corporations." In *Atti del Congresso internazionale di diritto romano e di storia del diritto. Verona, 27–28–29 settembre 1948,* vol. 3 (Milan, 1951), 19–25. (= *Études,* vol. 3 [1979], 445–53.)

Gaudemet, J. "Constantin et les Curies municipales." *IVRA* 2 (1951), 44–75. (= *Études,* vol. 3 [1979], 97–130.)

Gaudemet, J. "Un problème de la codification théodosienne: Les constitutions géminées." *RIDA*[3] 4 (1957), 253–67. (= *Études,* vol. 1 [1979], 301–17.)

Gaudemet, J. "Les transformations de la vie familiale au Bas-Empire et l'influence du Christianisme." *Romanitas* 5 (1962), 58–85. (= *Études,* vol. 3 [1979], 281–310.)

Gaudemet, J. *Le Bréviaire d'Alaric et les Épitomés.* Milan, 1965.
Gaudemet, J. "Les abus des 'potentes' au Bas Empire." *Irish Jurist* 1 (1966), 128–35. (= *Études,* vol. 3 [1979], 433–42.)
Gaudemet, J. "Quelque aspects de la politique législative au Ve siècle." In *St. Volterra,* vol. 1 (Milan, 1971), 225–34. (= *Études,* vol. 1 [1979], 201–12.)
Gaudemet, J. "Recherches sur la législation du Bas-Empire." In *St. Scherillo,* vol. 2 (Milan, 1972), 693–715. (= *Études,* vol. 1 [1979], 213–37.)
Gaudemet, J. "La législation du IVème siècle programme d'enquête." *AARC* 1 (1975), 143–59.
Gaudemet, J. "Aspects politiques de la codification théodosienne." In *Istituzioni giuridiche e realtà politiche nel tardo impero (III–V sec. d.C.). Atti di un incontro tra storici e giuristi Firenze, 2–4 maggio 1974,* ed. G. G. Archi (Milan, 1976), 261–79. (= *Études,* vol. 1 [1979], 349–69.)
Gaudemet, J. "Tendances nouvelles de la législation familiale au IVe siècle." In *Transformations et conflits au IVe siècle après J.-C.* Antiquitas, 29 (Bonn, 1978), 187–207.
Gaudemet, J. *Études de droit romain.* 3 vols. Camerino, 1979.
Gaudemet, J. "La répression de la délation au Bas-Empire." In *Φιλίας χάριν: Miscellanea de studi classici in onore di Eugenio Manni,* vol. 3 (Rome, 1980), 1065–83. (= *Droit et Société* [1992], 157–73.)
Gaudemet, J. "Les privilèges des 'navicularii' au début du IVe siècle." In *Hommages Besnier* (1980), 99–106. (= *Droit et Société* [1992], 97–104.)
Gaudemet, J. "Constitutions constantiniennes relative à l'appel." *ZRG* 98 (1981), 47–76. (= *Droit et Société* [1992], 67–96.)
Gaudemet, J. "Privilèges constantiniennes en faveur des militaires et des vétérans." In *St. Sanfilippo,* vol. 2 (Milan, 1982), 179–90. (= *Droit et Société* [1992], 105–16.)
Gaudemet, J. "La constitution 'ad populum' du 31 Janvier 320." In *Estudos em Homenagem aos Profs. Manuel Paulo Merêa e Guilherme Braga da Cruz* (Coimbra, 1983), 3–22. (= *Droit et Société* [1992], 117–36.)
Gaudemet, J. "Les Constitutions constantiniennes du Code Théodosien." *AARC* 5 (1983), 135–56.
Gaudemet, J. "De la responsabilité pénale dans la législation post-classique." In *Sodalitas: Scr. Guarino,* vol. 6 (Naples, 1984), 2569–74. (= *Droit et Société* [1992], 231–36.)
Gaudemet, J. "Constitutions constantiniennes destinées à l'Afrique." In *Institutions,* ed. Christol et al. (Rome, 1992), 329–52.
Gaudemet, J. *Droit et société aux derniers siècles de l'Empire romain.* Naples, 1992.
Girardet, K. M. *Kaisergericht und Bischofsgericht. Studien zu den Anfängen des Donatistenstreits (313–315) und zum Prozeß des Athanasius von Alexandrien (328–346).* Bonn, 1975.
Girardet, K. M. *Der Kaiser und sein Gott. Das Christentum im Denken und in der Religionspolitik Konstantins des Großen.* Berlin, 2010.

Gothofredus, J. *Codex Theodosianus cum perpetuis commentariis Iacobi Gothofredi.* Ed. A. Maurillius. Leipzig, 1736–45.

Grodzynski, D. "Tortures mortelles et catégories sociales. Les *Summa Supplicia* dans le droit romain aux IIIe et IVe siècles." In *Du châtiment dans la cité: Supplices corporels et peine de mort dans le monde antique. Table ronde organisée par l'École française de Rome avec le concours du Centre national de la recherche scientifique (Rome 9–11 novembre 1982)* (Rome, 1984), 361–403.

Grünewald, T. *Constantinus Maximus Augustus: Herrschaftspropaganda in der zeitgenössischen Überlieferung.* Stuttgart, 1990.

Haensch, R. "Das Statthalterarchiv." *ZRG* 109 (1992), 209–317.

Hall, S. G. "Some Constantinian Documents in the Vita Constantini." In *Constantine: History, Historiography, and Legend,* ed. S. N. C. Lieu and D. Montserrat (London, 1998), 86–103.

Hansen, G. C. *Sokrates Kirchengeschichte.* Berlin, 1995.

Harries, J. "The Roman Imperial Quaestor from Constantine to Theodosius II." *JRS* 78 (1988), 148–72.

Harries, J. "'Sacra generalitas': The Administrative Background to the Theodosian Code." In *Estudios de Historia del Derecho Romano: Homenaje al profesor G. Martínez Díez,* ed. R.P. Bustamonte, vol. 1 (Madrid 1994), 31–42.

Harries, J. "How to Make a Law-Code." In *Modus Operandi. Essays in Honour of Geoffrey Rickman,* ed. M. Austin, J. Harries, and C. Smith (London, 1998), 63–78.

Harries, J. *Law and Empire in Late Antiquity.* Cambridge, 1999.

Harries, J., and I. Wood, eds. *The Theodosian Code: Studies in the Imperial Law of Late Antiquity.* London, 1993.

Heather, P. "Senators and Senates." In *CAH* XIII, ed. Av. Cameron and P. Garnsey (Cambridge, 1998), 184–210.

Heather, P. *The Fall of the Roman Empire.* London, 2005.

Heather, P. *Empires and Barbarians: Migration, Development and the Birth of Europe.* London, 2009.

Heinze, T. *Konstantin der Große und das konstantinische Zeitalter in den Urteilen und Wegen der deutsch-italienischen Forschungsdiskussion.* Munich, 2005.

Herrmann, J. "Diokletians Reskripte zur Landpacht." In *Studien zur antiken Sozialgeschichte. Festschrift Friedrich Vittinghoff* (Cologne, 1980), 453–63. (= *Kleine Schriften zur Rechtsgeschichte* [Munich, 1990], 373–83.)

Hobson, D. W. "The Impact of Law on Village Life in Roman Egypt." In *Law, Politics and Society in the Ancient Mediterranean World,* ed. B. Halpern and D. W. Hobson (Sheffield, 1993), 193–219.

Hofmann, F. "Der Verfall der römischen Rechtswissenschaft." In *Kritische Studien im römischen Rechte* (Vienna, 1885), 1–37.

Honoré, T. *Ulpian.* Oxford, 1982. 2nd ed., 2002.

Honoré, T. "New Methods in Roman Law." *Rechtshistorisches Journal* 3 (1984), 290–305.

Honoré, T. "The Making of the Theodosian Code." *ZRG* 103 (1986), 133–222.
Honoré, T. *Emperors and Lawyers.* 2nd ed. Oxford, 1994.
Honoré, T. *Law in the Crisis of Empire, 379–455 AD: The Theodosian Dynasty and its Quaestors.* Oxford, 1998.
Honoré, T. "Roman Law AD 200–400: From Cosmopolis to Rechtstaat [*sic*]." In *Approaching Late Antiquity: The Transformation from the Early to Late Empire,* ed. S. Swain and M. Edwards (Oxford, 2004), 109–32.
Honsell, H. "Der Gesetzstil in der römischen Antike." In *Sodalitas: Scr. Guarino,* vol. 4 (Naples, 1984), 1659–73.
Huck, O. "À propos de CTh 1, 27, 1 et CSirm 1. Sur deux textes controversés relatifs à l'episcopalis audientia constantinienne." *ZRG* 120 (2003), 78–105.
Huck, O. "Encore à propos des Sirmondiennes . . . Arguments présentés à l'appui de la thèse de l'authenticité en réponse à une mise en cause récente." *AntTard* 11 (2003), 181–96.
Humfress, C. *Orthodoxy and the Courts in Late Antiquity.* Oxford, 2007.
Instinsky, H. U. Review of *Das Selbstzeugnis Kaiser Konstantins,* by H. Dörries, and *Kaiser Konstantins religiöse Entwicklung,* by H. Kraft, *Gnomon* 30 (1958), 125–33.
Jacques, F. "Les moulins d'Orcistus. Rhétorique et géographie au IVe siècle." In *Institutions,* ed. Christol et al. (Rome, 1992), 431–46.
Johnston, D. "Epiclassical Law." In *CAH* XII², ed. Bowman et al. (Cambridge, 2005), 200–207.
Jones, A. H. M. "The Roman Civil Service (Clerical and Sub-Clerical Grades)." In *Studies in Roman Government and Law* (Oxford, 1960), 151–75. (= *JRS* 39 [1949], 38–55).
Jones, A. H. M. Review of *Das Selbstzeugnis Kaiser Konstantins,* by H. Dörries. *English Historical Review* 71 (1956), 136–37.
Jones, A. H. M. *Constantine and the Conversion of Europe.* 1st ed. London, 1948. 2nd ed. New York, 1962.
Jones, A. H. M. *The Later Roman Empire, 284–602: A Social, Economic and Administrative Survey.* Oxford, 1964.
Jones, A. H. M., J. R. Martindale, and J. Morris, eds. *The Prosopography of the Later Roman Empire.* Vol. 1: *A.D. 260–395.* Cambridge, 1971.
Karayannopulos, J. *Das Finanzwesen des frühbyzantinischen Staates.* Munich, 1958.
Kaser, M. "Infamia und ignominia in den römischen Rechtsquellen." *ZRG* 73 (1956), 220– 78.
Kaser, M. *Das römische Zivilprozeßrecht.* 2nd ed. Ed. K. Hackl. Munich, 1996.
Keil, M. *Quellensammlung zur Religionspolitik Konstantins des Großen.* 2nd ed. Darmstadt, 1995.
Kelly, C. "Emperors, Government and Bureaucracy." In *CAH* XIII, ed. Av. Cameron and P. Garnsey (Cambridge, 1998), 138–83.

Kelly, C. *Ruling the Later Roman Empire.* Cambridge, MA 2004.

Kienast, D. *Römische Kaisertabelle. Grundzüge einer römischen Kaiserchronologie.* 2nd ed. Darmstadt, 1996.

Kipp, T. "Edictum." *RE* 5.2 (1905), 1940–48.

Klingmüller, F. "Incestus." *RE* 9.2 (1916), 1246–49.

Kolb, F. "*Praesens Deus:* Kaiser und Gott unter der Tetrarchie." In *Diokletian und die Tetrachie. Aspekte einer Zeitenwende,* ed. A. Demandt, A. Goltz, and H. Schlange-Schöningen (Berlin, 2004), 27–37.

Kraemer, C. J., and N. Lewis. "A Referee's Hearing on Ownership." *TAPhA* 68 (1937), 357–87.

Kraft, H. *Kaiser Konstantins religiöse Entwicklung.* Tübingen, 1955.

Krause, J.-U. *Gefängnisse im Römischen Reich.* Stuttgart, 1996.

Krüger, P. *Geschichte der Quellen und der Literatur des römischen Rechts.* 2nd ed. Munich, 1912.

Krüger, P. *Codex Theodosianus. Fasciculus I, Liber I–VI.* Berlin, 1923. *Fasciculus II, Liber VII–VIII.* Berlin, 1926.

Lee, A. D. "Traditional Religions." In *The Cambridge Companion to the Age of Constantine,* ed. N. E. Lenski (Cambridge, 2006), 159–79.

Lendon, J. E. *Empire of Honour: The Art of Government in the Roman World.* Oxford, 1997.

Lenski, N. E. "Evidence for the *Audientia episcopalis* in the New Letters of Augustine." In *Law, Society, and Authority in Late Antiquity,* ed. R. Mathisen (Oxford, 2001), 83–97.

Lenski, N. E. *Failure of Empire: Valens and the Roman State in the Fourth Century A.D.* Berkeley, 2002.

Lenski, N. E, ed. *The Cambridge Companion to the Age of Constantine.* Cambridge, 2006.

Leppeley, C. "Quot curiales, tot tyranni. L'image du décurion oppresseur au bas-empire." In *Crise et redressement dans les provinces européennes de l'Empire (milieu du IIIe–milieu du IVe siècle ap. J.-C.) Actes du colloque de Strasbourg (décembre 1981),* ed. E. Frézouls (Strasbourg, 1983), 143–56.

Levy, E. *West Roman Vulgar Law: The Law of Property.* Philadelphia, 1951.

Levy, E. *Weströmisches Vulgarrecht. Obligationenrecht.* Weimar, 1956.

Lewis, C. T., and C. Short. *A Latin Dictionary Founded on Andrew's Edition of Freund's Latin Dictionary.* Oxford, 1879.

Liebeschuetz, J. H. W. G. *Antioch: City and Imperial Administration in the Later Roman Empire.* Oxford, 1972.

Liebeschuetz, W. Review of *Curiosi und Regendarii: Untersuchungen zur geheimen Staatspolizei der Spätantike,* by W. Blum. *JRS* 60 (1970), 229–30.

Liebs, D. "Ulpiani Opinionum libri VI." *TR* 41 (1973), 279–310.

Liebs, D. "Römische Provinzialjurisprudenz." *ANRW* II.15 (1976), 288–362.

Liebs, D. "Privilegien und Ständezwang in den Gesetzen Konstantins." *RIDA*[3] 24 (1977), 297–351.
Liebs, D. "Juristen als Sekretäre des römischen Kaisers." *ZRG* 100 (1983), 485–509.
Liebs, D. "Promulgationslokale im spätantiken Rom." In *Satura Roberto Feenstra Oblata*, ed. J. A. Ankum, J. E. Spruit, and F. B. J. Wubbe (Freiburg, 1985), 215–28.
Liebs, D. "Unverhohlene Brutalität in den Gesetzen der ersten christlichen Kaiser." In *Römisches Recht in der europäischen Tradition. Symposion aus Anlass des 75. Geburtstags von Franz Wieacker* (Ebelsbach, 1985), 89–116.
Liebs, D. *Die Jurisprudenz im spätantiken Italien, 260–620 n. Chr.* Berlin, 1987.
Liebs, D. "Recht und Rechtsliteratur." In *Restauration und Erneuerung: Die lateinische Literatur von 284 bis 374*, ed. R. Herzog (Munich, 1989), 55–73.
Liebs, D. "Römische Jurisprudenz in Africa." *ZRG* 106 (1989), 210–47.
Liebs, D. "Die pseudopaulinischen Sentenzen II. Versuch einer neuen Palingenesie." *ZRG* 113 (1996), 132–242.
Liebs, D. *Römische Jurisprudenz in Africa mit Studien zu den pseudopaulinischen Sentenzen.* 2nd ed. Berlin, 2005.
Liebs, D. "Konstantin als Gesetzgeber." In *Konstantin der Große. Geschichte—Archäologie—Rezeption. Internationales Kolloquium vom 10.–15. Oktober 2005*, ed. A. Demandt and J. Engemann (Trier, 2006), 97–107.
Lim, R. *Public Disputation, Power, and Social Order in Late Antiquity.* Berkeley, 1995.
Litewski, W. "Die römische Appellation in Zivilsachen (IV)." *RIDA*[3] 15 (1968), 143–351.
Lo Cascio, E. "The Emperor and His Administration: General Developments." In *CAH* XII[2], ed. Bowman et al. (Cambridge, 2005),131–36.
Maas, M. *Die Darstellung des Kaisers in der lateinischen Panegyrik.* Stuttgart, 1994.
MacMullen, R. "Roman Bureaucratese." *Traditio* 18 (1962), 364–78. (= *Changes* [1990], 67–77.)
MacMullen, R. *Constantine.* New York, 1969.
MacMullen, R. "Judicial Savagery in the Roman Empire." *Chiron* 16 (1986), 147–66. (= *Changes* [1990], 204–17.)
MacMullen, R. "What Difference Did Christianity Make?" *Historia* 35 (1986), 322–43. (= *Changes* [1990], 142–55.)
MacMullen, R. *Corruption and the Decline of Rome.* New Haven, 1988.
MacMullen, R. *Changes in the Roman Empire: Essays in the Ordinary.* Princeton, 1990.
MacMullen, R. "The Historical Role of the Masses in Late Antiquity." In *Changes* (1990), 250–76.
Martin, D. B. *Inventing Superstition: From the Hippocratics to the Christians.* Cambridge, 2004.

Martini, R. "Sulla costituzione di Costantino in tema di parricidio (C. Th. 9, 15, 1)." *AARC* 2 (1976), 103–17.
Mathisen, R., ed. *Law, Society, and Authority in Late Antiquity.* Oxford, 2001.
Matino, G. "Innovazioni linguistiche nei testi giuridici tardoantichi." In *Le trasformazioni della cultura nella tarda antichità. Atti del convegno tenuto a Catania, Università degli studi, 27 Sett.–2 Ott. 1982* (Rome, 1985), 109–18.
Matthews, J. *Western Aristocracies and Imperial Court, A.D. 364–425.* Oxford, 1975.
Matthews, J. F. *Laying Down the Law: A Study of the Theodosian Code.* New Haven, 2000.
Mayer-Maly, T. "Vivicomburium." *RE* 9A.1 (1961), 497–98.
McGinn, T. A. J. "The Social Policy of Emperor Constantine in Codex Theodosianus 4, 6, 3." *TR* 67 (1999), 57–73.
Migl, J. *Die Ordnung der Ämter: Prätorianerpräfektur und Vikariat in der Regionalverwaltung des Römischen Reiches von Konstantin bis zur Valentinianischen Dynastie.* Frankfurt am Main, 1994.
Millar, F. "A New Approach to the Roman Jurists." *JRS* 76 (1986), 272–80.
Millar, F. "Italy and the Roman Empire: Augustus to Constantine." *Phoenix* 40 (1986), 295–318.
Millar, F. *The Emperor in the Roman World: 31 BC–AD 337.* 2nd ed. Ithaca, 1992.
Mitteis, L. *Reichsrecht und Volksrecht in den östlichen Provinzen des Römischen Kaiserreichs.* Leipzig, 1891.
Mommsen, T. "Observationes Epigraphicae XL. Ordo salutationis sportularumque sub Imp. Iuliano in provincia Numidia." *Ephemeris Epigraphica* 5 (1884), 629–46. (= *Gesammelte Schriften,* vol. 8, 474ff.)
Mommsen, T. *Römisches Strafrecht.* Leipzig, 1899.
Mommsen, T. "Das theodosische Gesetzbuch." *ZRG* 21 (1900), 149–90. (= *Juristische Schriften,* vol. 2, 371–407.)
Mommsen, T. *Codex Theodosianus, Volumen 1. Pars Prior: Prolegomena: Textus cum apparatu.* Berlin, 1905.
Morgenstern, F. "Die Kaisergesetze gegen die Donatisten in Nordafrika (Mitte 4. Jh. bis 429) im Zusammenhang mit dem antidonatischen Wirken des Augustinus von Hippo." *ZRG* 110 (1993), 103–23.
Neri, V. "L'Usurpatore come tiranno nel lessico politico della tarda antichità." In *Usurpation,* ed. Paschoud and Szidat (Stuttgart, 1997), 71–86.
Nixon, C. E. V. "Latin Panegyric in the Tetrarchic and Constantinian Period." In *History and Historiography in Late Antiquity,* ed. B. Croke and A. M. Emmett (Sydney, 1983), 88–99.
Nixon, C. E. V., and B. S. Rodgers. *In Praise of Later Emperors: The* Panegyrici Latini. *Introduction, Translation, and Historical Commentary.* Berkeley, 1994.
Nock, A. D. "The Emperor's Divine *Comes.*" *JRS* 37 (1947), 102–16.
Noethlichs, K. L. *Beamtentum und Dienstvergehen. Zur Staatsverwaltung in der Spätantike.* Wiesbaden, 1981.

Nörr, D. "Zu den geistigen und sozialen Grundlagen der spätantiken Kodifikationsbewegung (Anon., de rebus bellicis XXI)." *ZRG* 80 (1963), 109–40.

Nörr, D. "Zu einem fast vergessenen Konstitutionentyp: *De plano interloqui.*" In *St. Sanfilippo,* vol. 3 (Milan, 1983), 519–43.

Oliver, J. H. "On the Edict of Severus Alexander (P. Fayum 20)." *AJPh* 99 (1978), 474–85.

Orestano, R. *L'appello civile in diritto romano.* Genoa, 1952.

Padeletti, G. *Lehrbuch der römischen Rechtsgeschichte.* Ed. by F. von Holtzendorff. 1879.

Palme, B. "Die *Officia* der Statthalter in der Spätantike." *AntTard* 7 (1999), 85–133.

Paschoud, F., and J. Szidat, eds. *Usurpation in der Spätantike: Forschungsstand und Perspektiven. Akten des Kolloquiums "Staatsstreich und Staatlichkeit," 6.–10. März 1996, Solothurn/Bern.* Historia Einzelschriften, 111. Stuttgart, 1997.

Patlagean, E. "Byzance et le blason pénal du corps." In *Du châtiment dans la cité: Supplices corporels et peine de mort dans le monde antique. Table ronde organisée par l'École française de Rome avec le concours du Centre national de la recherche scientifique (Rome 9–11 novembre 1982)* (Rome, 1984), 405–26.

Peachin, M. "The Office of the Memory." In *Studien zur Geschichte der römischen Spätantike: Festgabe für Professor Johannes Straub* (Athens, 1989), 168–208.

Peachin, M. *Iudex vice Caesaris: Deputy Emperors and the Administration of Justice during the Principate.* Stuttgart, 1996.

Pergami, F. *L'appello nella legislazione del tardo impero.* Milan, 2000.

Pharr, C., trans. *The Theodosian Code.* Princeton, 1952.

Piganiol, A. *L'Empereur Constantin.* Paris, 1932.

Piganiol, A. *L'Empire Chrétien, 325–395.* 2nd ed. Ed. A. Chastagnol. Paris, 1972.

Porena, P. *Le origini della prefettura del pretorio tardoantica.* Rome, 2003.

Potter, D. S. *The Roman Empire at Bay, AD 180–395.* London, 2004.

Radin, M. "Oratio." *RE* 18.1 (1939), 869–73.

Remijsen, S., and W. Clarysse. "Incest or Adoption? Brother-Sister Marriage in Roman Egypt Revisited." *JRS* 98 (2008), 53–61.

Riccobono, S., J. Baviera, C. Ferrini, J. Furlani, and V. Arangio-Riuz, eds. *Fontes iuris Romani anteiustiniani.* 2nd ed. Florence, 1968–69.

Ries, G. *Prolog und Epilog in Gesetzen des Altertums.* Munich, 1983.

Rivière, Y. "Pouvoir impérial et vengeance. De *Mars Ultor* à la *divina vindicta* (Ier–IVe siècle ap. J.-C.)." In *La vengeance, 400–1200,* ed. D. Barthélemy, F. Bougard, and R. Le Jan (Rome, 2006), 7–42.

Roberts, M. *The Jeweled Style: Poetry and Poetics in Late Antiquity.* Ithaca, 1989.

Robinson, O. F. "Roman Criminal Law: Rhetoric and Reality. Some Forms of Rhetoric in the Theodosian Code." In *Au-delà des frontières. Mélanges de droit romain offerts à Witwold Wołodkiewicz,* ed. K. Pamiątkowe and M. Zabłocka, vol. 2 (Warsaw, 2000), 765–85.

Robinson, O. F. *Penal Practice and Penal Policy in Ancient Rome.* London, 2007.
Rodger, A. "Behind the Scenes of Roman Law." *Oxford Journal of Legal Studies* 3 (1983), 382–404.
Ronning, C. *Herrscherpanegyrik unter Trajan und Konstantin. Studien zur symbolischen Kommunikation in der römischen Kaiserzeit.* Tübingen, 2007.
Ronning, C. "Pontifex Maximus, charismatischer Herrscher, 'allen gemeinsamer Bischof' oder 'dreizehnter Apostel'? Das römische Herrschaftsverständnis und der christliche Kaiser." In *Konstantin der Große. Kaiser einer Epochenwende,* ed. F. Schuller and H. Wolff (Lindenberg 2007), 125–49.
Roueché, C. "Acclamations in the Later Roman Empire: New Evidence from Aphrodisias." *JRS* 74 (1984), 181–99.
Salama, P. "Anniversaires impériaux constantino-liciniens à Djémila." In *Institutions,* ed. Christol et al. (Rome, 1992), 137–59.
Sänger, P. "Die Eirenarchen im römischen und byzantinischen Ägypten." *Tyche* 20 (2005), 143–204.
Sargenti, M. *Il diritto privato nella legislazione di Costantino: Persone e famiglia.* Milan, 1938.
Sargenti, M. "Il diritto privato nella legislazione di Costantino. Problemi e prospettive nella letteratura dell'ultimo trentennio." *AARC* 1 (1975), 229–332.
Sargenti, M. "La compravendita nel tardo diritto romano. Indirizzi normativi e realtà sociale (Contributo all'interpretazione di Vat.Fr. 35)." In *St. Biscardi,* vol. 2 (Milan, 1982), 341–63.
Schallmayer, E., K. Eibl, and J. Ott. *Der römische Weihebezirk von Osterburken I.* Corpus der griechischen und lateinischen Beneficiarier-Inschriften des römischen Reiches. Stuttgart, 1990.
Schiller, A. "The Courts Are No More." In *St. Volterra,* vol. I (Milan, 1971), 469–502.
Schmidt-Hofner, S. *Reagieren und Gestalten. Der Regierungsstil des spätrömischen Kaisers am Beispiel der Gesetzgebung Valentinians I.* Munich, 2008.
Schulz, F. *Prinzipien des römischen Rechts.* Munich, 1934.
Schwind, F. von. *Zur Frage der Publikation im römischen Recht.* Munich, 1940.
Seeck, O. "Brevis." *RE* 3.1 (1897), 832.
Seeck, O. "Die Zeitfolge der Gesetze Constantins." *ZRG* 10 (1889), 1–44 and 177–251.
Seeck, O. *Regesten der Kaiser und Päpste für die Jahre 311 bis 476 n. Chr. Vorarbeit zu einer Prosopographie der christlichen Kaiserzeit.* Stuttgart, 1919.
Selb, W. "Episcopalis audientia von der Zeit Konstantins bis zu Novelle XXXV Valentinians III." ZRG 84 (1967), 162–217.
Sherwin-White, A. N. *The Letters of Pliny.* Oxford, 1966.
Silli, P. *Testi Constantiniani nelle fonti letterarie.* Materiali per una Palingenesia delle Costituzioni Tardo-Imperiali, 3. Milan, 1987.

Simon, D. "Marginalien zur Vulgarismusdiskussion." In *Festschrift für Franz Wieacker zum 70. Geburtstag*, ed. O. Behrends et al. (Göttingen 1978), 154–74.

Simon, D. V. *Konstantinisches Kaiserrecht. Studien anhand der Reskriptenpraxis und des Schenkungsrechts.* Frankfurt am Main, 1977.

Sirks, A. J. B. "Observations sur le Code Théodosien." *SGron* 2 (1985), 21–34.

Sirks, A. J. B. "From the Theodosian to the Justinian Code." *AARC* 6 (1986), 265–302.

Sirks, A. J. B. *Food for Rome: The Legal Structure of the Transportation and Processing of Supplies for the Imperial Distributions in Rome and Constantinople.* Amsterdam, 1991.

Sirks, A. J. B. "The Sources of the Code." In *Theodosian Code*, ed. Harries and Wood (London, 1993), 45–67.

Sirks, A. J. B. *The Theodosian Code: A Study.* Friedrichsdorf, 2007.

Slootjes, D. *The Governor and His Subjects in the Later Roman Empire.* Leiden, 2006.

Spagnuolo Vigorita, T. *Exsecranda pernicies. Delatori e fisco nell'età di Costantino.* Naples, 1984.

Spagnuolo Vigorita, T. "*Beneficium lenitatis nostrae.* Conflitto di interessi e munificenza imperiale in una costituzione di Costantino." In *Hommages à Gérard Boulvert, Index* 15 (1987), 357–65.

Stachura, M. "Kritik der superstitio und Affirmation der Orthodoxie in den Gesetzen des Codex Theodosianus." In *Studies on the Late Roman History*, ed. E. Dabrowa (Kraków, 2007), 33–62.

Stroheker, K. F. "Der spätrömische Kaiser und das Volk." In *Transformations et conflits au IVe siècle après J.-C.* (Bonn, 1978), 15–31.

Syme, R. "Fiction about Roman Jurists." *ZRG* 97 (1980), 78–104.

Szidat, J. *Historischer Kommentar zu Ammianus Marcellinus Buch XX–XXI. Teil III: Die Konfrontation.* Historia Einzelschriften, 89. Stuttgart, 1996.

Talbert, R. A. *The Senate of Imperial Rome.* Princeton, 1984.

Taubenschlag, R. *Das römische Privatrecht zur Zeit Diokletian's.* Kraków, 1923.

Tellegen-Couperus, O. E. *Testamentary Succession in the Constitutions of Diocletian.* Zutphen, 1982.

Thompson, E. A. *Romans and Barbarians: The Decline of the Western Empire.* Madison, 1982.

Torallas Tovar, S. "Violence in the Process of Arrest and Imprisonment in Late Antique Egypt." In *Violence in Late Antiquity: Perceptions and Practices*, ed. H. A. Drake (Aldershot, 2006), 103–12.

Turpin, W. "The Law Codes and Late Roman Law." *RIDA*^{3} 32 (1985), 339–53.

Turpin, W. "Adnotatio and Imperial Rescript in Roman Legal Procedure." *RIDA*^{3} 35 (1988), 285–307.

Van Dam, R. *Remembering Constantine at the Milvian Bridge.* Cambridge, 2011.

Van Dam, R. *The Roman Revolution of Constantine.* Cambridge, 2007.

Van der Wal, N. "*Edictum* und *lex generalis*. Form und Inhalt der Kaisergesetze im spätrömischen Reich." *RIDA*[3] 28 (1981), 277–313.
Varner, E. R. *Mutilation and Transformation: Damnatio memoriae and Roman Imperial Portraiture*. Leiden, 2004.
Vera, D. *Commento storico alle* relationes *di Quinto Aurelio Simmaco*. Pisa, 1981.
Vernay, E. "Note sur le changement de style dans les constitutions impériales de Dioclétien a Constantin." In *Études d'histoire juridique offertes a Paul Frédéric Girard*, vol. 2 (Paris, 1913), 263–74.
Vessey, M. "The Origin of the Collectio Sirmondiana: A New Look at the Evidence." In *Theodosian Code*, ed. Harries and Wood (London, 1993), 178–99.
Vidén, G. *The Roman Chancery Tradition: Studies in the Language of Codex Theodosianus and Cassiodorus' Variae*. Göteborg, 1984.
Vigneron, Roger. Review of *Recht und Rhetorik in den Kaisergesetzen der Spätantike*, by W. E. Voß. *ZRG* 102 (1985), 637–44.
Vogt, J. "Zur Frage des christlichen Einflusses auf die Gesetzgebung Konstantins des Grossen." In *Festschrift für Leopold Wenger*, vol. 2 (Munich, 1945), 118–48.
Vogt, J. *Constantin der Große und sein Jahrhundert*. 1st ed. Munich, 1949. 2nd ed. Munich, 1960.
Volterra, E. "Quelques remarques sur le style des constitutions de Constantin." In *Mélanges Lévy-Bruhl* (Paris, 1959), 325–34.
Volterra, E. "Il problema del testo delle costituzioni imperiali." In *La critica del testo*, vol. 2 (Florence, 1971), 821–1097.
Voß, W. E. *Recht und Rhetorik in den Kaisergesetzen der Spätantike*. Frankfurt am Main, 1982.
Voß, W. E. Review of *Die Zeitfolge der Gesetze Constantins*, by O. Seeck. *ZRG* 106 (1989), 632–45.
Wacke, A. "Die *potentiores* in den Rechtsquellen. Einfluß und Abwehr gesellschaftlicher Übermacht in der Rechtspflege der Römer." *ANRW* II.13 (1980), 562–607.
Wacke, A. "The *potentiores:* Some Relations between Power and Law in the Roman Administration of Justice." In *Estudios de derecho romano y moderno en cuatro idiomas* (Madrid, 1996), 69–86.
Waldstein, W. "Die Stellung der *episcopalis audientia* im spätrömischen Prozeß." In *Festschrift für Max Kaser zum 70. Geburtstag* (Munich, 1976), 533–56.
Waldstein, W. Review of *L'episcopalis audientia nelle costituzioni imperiali da Costantino a Giustiniano*, by M. R. Cimma. *Gnomon* 65 (1993), 745–47.
Watson, A. Review of *Tribonian*, by T. Honoré. *Law Quarterly Review* 94 (1978), 459.
Watson, A. Review of *Ulpian*, by T. Honoré. *Times Literary Supplement* (18 Feb. 1983), 164.
Watson, A. "An Open Letter to D. C." *Rechtshistorisches Journal* 3 (1984), 286–90.
Wenger, L. *Die Quellen des römischen Rechts*. Vienna, 1953.

Wieacker, F. *Textstufen klassischer Juristen.* Göttingen, 1960.

Wieacker, F. "Vulgarrecht und Vulgarismus. Alte und neue Probleme und Diskussionen." In *St. Biscardi,* vol. 1 (Milan, 1982), 33–51. (= Ausgewählte schriften, vol. 1 [Frankfurt am Main, 1983], 241–54.)

Wiemer, H.-V. "Akklamationen im spätromischen Reich." *Archiv für Kulturgeschichte* 86 (2004), 27–73.

Wienand, J. "Der Kaiser als Sieger. Untersuchungen zur militärischen Repräsentation Constantins I." PhD diss., Konstanz, 2010. (Forthcoming as *Der Kaiser als Sieger. Metamorphosen triumphaler Herrschaft unter Constantin I* [Berlin, 2012].)

Williams, W. "Formal and Historical Aspects of Two New Documents of Marcus Aurelius." *ZPE* 17 (1975), 37–78.

Wolff, H. J. "Das Vulgarrechtsproblem und die Papyri." *ZRG* 91 (1974), 54–105.

Woods, D. "Strategius and the 'Manicheans.'" *CQ* 51 (2001), 255–64.

Ziche, H. "Making Late Roman Taxpayers Pay: Imperial Government Strategies and Practice." In *Violence in Late Antiquity: Perceptions and Practices,* ed. H. A. Drake (Aldershot, 2006), 127–36.

Zilliacus, H. *Zur Abundanz der spätgriechischen Gebrauchssprache.* Helsinki, 1967.

Index Locorum

General Index